Sade

Sade

The Invention of the Libertine Body

Marcel Hénaff

Translated by Xavier Callahan

University of Minnesota Press
Minneapolis
London

The University of Minnesota Press gratefully acknowledges financial assistance provided by the French Ministry of Culture for the translation of this book.

Originally published as Sade, *l'invention du corps libertin,* copyright 1978, Presses Universitaires de France.

Published by the University of Minnesota Press
111 Third Avenue South, Suite 290
Minneapolis, MN 55401-2520
http://www.upress.umn.edu

Library of Congress Cataloging-in-Publication Data

Hénaff, Marcel.
   [Sade, l'invention du corps libertin. English]
   Sade, the invention of the libertine body / Marcel Hénaff ; translated by Xavier Callahan.
      p.   cm.
   Includes bibliographical references and index.
   ISBN 0-8166-2536-0. — ISBN 0-8166-2537-9 (pbk.)
   1. Sade, marquis de, 1740–1814 — Criticism and interpretation.
   2. Erotic literature, French — History and criticism.   3. Libertines
   in literature.   I. Title.   II. Title: Sade.
   PQ2063.S3H4413   1999
   843'.6 — dc21   99-15168

To the memory of Gilles Deleuze, who taught me philosophy, and to whose thought this book owes so much.

Contents

Translator's Note

If translation itself is a labor of love, the careful vetting of another's translation is a work of pure agape. I am deeply grateful to Jean-Louis Morhange, the soul of tact, for putting his phenomenal command of both French and English at the disposal of this volume and gently interrupting more than one lexical pratfall.

Mikkel and Charlotte Borch-Jacobsen's friendship and Rabelaisian zest were an unfailing source of strength and encouragement. Pamm Hanson offered material support during an early phase of the work and moral support throughout. Diane Thurlow's steady, unobtrusive presence was sometimes literally all that allowed the work to continue. The four of them, as well as my former Stanford colleagues Nathan MacBrien, who generously stepped in with bibliographical help at a critical moment, and Jan Spauschus Johnson, who was often and graciously there to lend an ear, have my warm and enduring thanks.

Thanks are also due to Douglas Brick, for being too busy himself to undertake this translation; to Biodun Iginla, who proposed that I take it on instead; and to William Murphy of the University of Minnesota Press, for his ingenuity and good humor. Also at Minnesota, I wish to thank Gretchen Asmussen and Laura Westlund, as well as this edition's copy editor, David Thorstad, and Daniel Leary, the book's production coordinator.

Most of all, I am grateful to the author, Marcel Hénaff, not just for writing this book but for being so thoroughly kind and patient through disruptions and delays that no one could have foreseen when the translation into English was begun.

For passages that the French edition cites from works originally published in French and other languages, every reasonable effort was made
to supply published English translations. No published translations exist in English for some of the French-language works, however, and for
others it was not always possible to track down the precise passages
that the French edition cites. Therefore, translations of passages from
any of the Marquis de Sade's works that are not included in the Grove
Press volumes *Juliette, The 120 Days of Sodom and Other Writings,* and
Justine, Philosophy in the Bedroom, and Other Writings are my own, as
are translations of passages from other works that were originally published in French or other languages but never in English, or for which
English translations could not, for one reason or another, be located.

Preface to the English Edition

It has now been some twenty years since this book first appeared in France. Unquestionably, for me, it belongs to that class of work called "juvenilia." Its tone, often bordering on temerity, has the energy of youth, and in its analyses there is an audacity that flirts at times with the arbitrary. I believe that it still has relevance despite these flaws; a fair number of colleagues or friends, having had occasion to read it and use it in their research, have reassured me on this score. I hope that its new readers, reached by this translation wherever English is read (which is to say, almost everywhere), will view it with equal favor. Here, taking advantage of the critical distance afforded by the long aftermath of this volume's first publication, I would simply like to make a few preliminary remarks — not to update this work (which would be to pile commentaries upon commentaries) but to clarify its predominating approach.

First of all, this is obviously not a historical study, although its title may create that expectation: to speak about the invention of a representation (in this case, the libertine body) usually means to attempt a reconstruction of the social and cultural conditions of its emergence. But I have made a different choice: to restrict my analysis to the realm of the Sadean text and show how, through its vocabulary, narratives, stagings, and characters, it came to constitute a hitherto unseen model of the body. I then show how this model reflects — without being reducible to — an original configuration of certain intellectual and historical particulars.

Hence the division of this work into two parts: a *poetics*, which brings out the philosophical dimensions and rhetorical components of this representation (the demystified body, the will to say everything, apathetic desire, a space of the masterly gaze, and a time made of repetitive sexual pleasure), and an *economics,* which brings to light the stakes of power found in the lexicon and the logic of production, waste, exchange, and seizure (even where the body's intimate functions are concerned). There is no question here of a reading that would take economics as its ultimate referent but rather of one that grasps the symbolic effects of economics through figures and narratives in which a new social order is manifested, the order that began to establish a technoeconomic reason whose project encompasses measurement, calculation, separation, investment, organization, and domination.

This is the order that is reflected, parodically, in representations of the Sadean libertine body, so different from representations belonging to the sixteenth and seventeenth centuries. Amorous desire now takes leave of the enchanted world of courtly love and gallantry, assuming and exploiting the promises of Cartesian mechanics and calculational reason. In other words, reason, which had seemed the antithesis of ancient rituals of seduction, opens the way to new games involving combinative operations and automata. Here, I believe, is where Sade's originality can be located. His work offers the paradox of a conflagration between the values of a world that was still perfectly aristocratic and representations of the body that took their schemata from a technoeconomic universe in the process of imposing itself, a universe containing the seeds of an extreme and as yet unknown violence. The Sadean text perceives the logic of this violence and shows, above all, the relationship of this violence to forms of desire. For this reason, the Sadean text is not only a major sign of its times but also, and perhaps more than anything else — through its frequently intolerable excesses — one of the most enigmatic and disquieting testimonies to the fate of our own civilization. This is what interests me about Sade, and this is how I propose that he be read.

Which is why — and this is the last of my remarks — it is utterly ludicrous to take Sade literally, to read his fictions as programs for crime and perversion. But this is what is still going on in some centers of thinking (or unthinking). A few critics have even recommended that Sade's name be crossed off the literary canon.[1] Are these critics unaware that Sade can be read only through a lens of derision? that he has to be read in the same way we read Rabelais (an author Sade was mad about)? If our era is once again judging Sade dangerous, this means that the danger is in our era itself. Sade's texts are a pitiless mirror. (You can elect to cover the mirror, of course.) If Sade does not make you laugh and make you think, then throw his books onto the fire; for them that would be a happier fate than being subjected to a moralistic or flatly realist reading.

At any rate, it is not my intention to plunge deeper into the tiresome debate over this new censorship, a censorship that informs us of little more than the new censors' private or collective distress. Besides, that would require us to update some recent discussions that, to me, seem to have been born obsolete; it is amazing how they repeat the commonplaces of right-thinking nineteenth-century criticism. Nor, from another standpoint, have I sought to engage with a number of excellent studies — of Sade himself, or of the body in the eighteenth century — that have appeared over the past few years. Several of these works' authors have cited this book, and so it would have been artificial, in discussing these newer studies, to pretend that this book, which actually preceded them, had been written after they were. Therefore, these studies have simply been included in an updated bibliography, as one way — too limited, I confess — of showing the esteem in which I hold them. In returning to the present text, I have confined myself to touching it up cosmetically here and there and giving additional clarification to some concepts that the original edition assumed, too hastily, were well understood.

To conclude this preface, I would like to pay tribute to the patient, subtle work of Xavier Callahan, this book's translator. With incomparable skill, she managed to render the book's nuances and tone. She was also very often able to take formulations that certainly needed clarification and make them more accessible and more precise in English. For all of this I thank her. I would also like to thank, as she herself has done, Jean-Louis Morhange for his excellent work in vetting the translation.

Finally, as will be noted, I have dedicated this edition to Gilles Deleuze. It is to him, my mentor and adviser while I was studying philosophy in Lyons, that I owe my interest in Sade. It was also he who opened up, to the ignorant young student I was at the time, the world of such authors as Klossowski, Bataille, and Blanchot, and it was he who steered me toward the seminars of Barthes, Foucault, and Lévi-Strauss, three more thinkers to whom this book owes a great debt.

M. H.
San Diego, California
June 1998

AFTERMATH I

Continuation As Incipit

On a Misunderstood Name

The name *Sade*: no one is prepared to be rid of it. We can whitewash the marquis himself all we like, and with good reason. He was brave enough, rebellious enough, brazen enough, frequently enough if unjustly harassed and incarcerated, and generous enough to deserve admiration and the fullest acquittal. With all due respect to his biographers, however, the question of his name is of an entirely different order. It scarcely even belongs to the body that it once designated, historically and individually; in the family circle, that is a job for the given name. May the shade of Donatien-Alphonse-François rest in peace. But the name *Sade*— still intolerable, still unredeemed—continues to be of interest. It will not be redeemed in these pages, but neither will it be condemned. It will be taken for what it is: the name of a body of writing that still arouses our fascination (delighted or disgusted, it's all the same) and is still misunderstood.

The fact is that, like it or not, Sade's name belongs not only to the presumably mature realm of reading but also, and perhaps first of all, to the realm of rumor, that is, the realm of scandal. Something of a tradition has grown up between these two realms, which is why we have not only the question of *how* to read Sade (as one might also intelligently ask in connection with Dante, Racine, Stendhal, or Joyce, for example) but also the question of *why* to read him. The full potency of his name looms precisely in that *why*. And what our century, all tricked out in

modernity, has understood better than any other is that there is nothing more violent than the name, no better time-traveler, no more effective producer of myth, seduction, error, and terror, and thus of adjec-
tives. In Sade's case, the historical figure once designated by this name,
the figure whose traces we still hope to discover, is released from his
own biography only to be born, monstrous and menacing, from a womb
of legend and fantasy.

The biographers can object all they like, denying that this was the real
Sade. They can offer proof that Sade the child was sensitive and affection-
ate, that Sade the adolescent was mischievous and witty, that Sade the
grand seigneur libertin[1] was an unrepentant atheist, a wild reveler, and
that, in the end, as the victim of his imperious, sanctimonious mother-
in-law, he was convicted of trifles that must have brought a smile to the
lips of the king whose lettre de cachet[2] put him behind bars for life. But
the fact remains that for us Sade is still a *name.* As such, he can be understood only from within the Law of the Father, the law of iron rule
and constraint — and not the constraint that requires one choice or another, but the constraint that leaves only one. Sade's name, understood
from within the rumors that surround it, ordains a single reading because his name is all that prompts us to read him in the first place. So
much for the question of why we read him. But reading and rereading
are also the very things that can dispel the rumors and separate them
from his name so that its body of writing can be restored to it. The point
of this separation is not to exorcise or minimize the violence of the writings. The point is to read this violence in another way, to see it somewhere other than in the nightmarish scenes of the writings, scenes that
our voyeuristic, disavowing desire imagines it can watch with impunity.
Then the question of *how* to read Sade can transmute the earlier misunderstanding represented by the question of *why* to read him, and we
will be drawn into that place of silence where rumor subsides, the place
for the metamorphosis of all the reasons why we were ever led astray.
There, beyond causality, beyond referents, the workings of the text can
show through. And then the question will no longer be whether Sade's
name is guilty or not guilty. The question will be, in any text designated
by his name, what is at work and what is not, what is revealed and what
is hidden, what seduces and what shocks, and — from the most odious
pronouncement to the most blatant contradiction — what exhibits and

what scrambles the codes of the established order. In other words, what is it, on the stage of the writing, that compels us to an extreme view, to see as obscene, intolerable, and outrageous what is perhaps our quite ordinary fate?

This, of course, is the whole question of literature. As for the word *Sade,* for us it will be simply the name of a writer, the only name he has — not the name of a monster, a victim, a criminal, an innocent, a dark prophet, or even a libertarian theoretician, but the name of a writer, of one who invents a machine for simulating, revealing, questioning, shaking things up, trying things out. What is this remarkable machine of Sade's? What are its inner workings? And when we venture inside, what can it do to us?

But *is* Sade a writer? Already the accredited stylists must be reaching for their red pencils. And perhaps they actually can prove, with examples ready to hand, that Sade's writings are often conventional, perfunctory, filled with stereotypes; that they really do not measure up to the subtle, inventive, complex writings of a Diderot, say, or of a Laclos (to mention only Sade's contemporaries). But is writing merely stylistic prowess? And is style itself merely felicitous form? If Sade disappoints the aesthete's reading, it is probably because he disappoints Lalittérature. This term, welding definite article to noun (as in Lacan's *lalangue*), exposing the absoluteness of a claim and the hegemony of a position, is the one we will use to speak of the ossified institution of belles lettres, that corpus of prescriptions, norms, and statements of the obvious hardened to the consistency of a field of knowledge. Sade, viewed from the solid headland of Lalittérature, is an illegal alien. But more than anyone else, precisely because of his position as an outsider and precisely because he disappoints and betrays, Sade can force us to notice Lalittérature's look of disapproval and, above all, to think in terms of literature — in terms, that is, of what the modern era calls the *text.*

As for the misunderstanding (or misreading) of Sade's texts, it may be the outcome, as we shall see, of a remarkable collision between two ways of reading. We can almost say that Sade does not *write* at all, for with him everything moves so quickly. There is no time for tidying up; the texts as such never try to seduce ("See how pretty I am"). We do not even see the writing, because it is so taut, denotative, and functional, in the grip of an illustrative mania that leaves it indifferent to its own effects. It never lets itself get caught in the act of pleasing. Form finds no reflection in it, as if for Sade there were never any question of pleasing but only of persuading, of advancing and refining the same arguments to the point of obsession: writing with a hammer, a pestle. At the same time, what he is saying baits a trap for our desire. All we see is the wording: unrelieved sin and orgy, sex and blood, as if the violence of the themes made the language of their enunciation more and more insubstantial, invisible, incorporeal, as if the form of the texts were being devoured by their object. And, to mention only the libertine texts, Sade clearly seems to have no concern of any kind for stylistic elegance (when we notice style at all, we see it in conspicuously hackneyed, conventional, hastily drawn stock figures), as if the urgency of speaking made the work of writing absurd. Surface erases medium; the image pervades the scene as a whole, with a light so dazzling, so prodigiously bright and sharp, that our overexposure to it almost allows us to claim that we have not read anything at all. The harshness of the censors is linked to this primary refusal. The censors, to punish their fascination with what is being said, intensify their concern for formal precision. Sound judgment is turned on its head; to say "Sade is no writer" is to say "I read but saw nothing."[3] The text vanishes. (Nodier,[4] for example, wrote in 1831, "I have no clear idea whatsoever of what he has written. Having glanced at the books and, rather than skim them, riffled through them backwards, from right to left, in order to see whether they were steeped in sin and murder, I retain of these monstrous depravities a vague impression of amazement and horror.")

But, like the gnome on horseback in Füssli's[5] The Nightmare who springs up from the body of the sleeping woman, some remainder slips out of these evanescent, all but evaporated texts, a consummate monster, the compressed residue of the censors' memory: obscenity. Here is where all the curses are called down and justified, all the imprecations and repressions that Sade's name has stirred up and brought together, so that his name becomes nothing less than the name of a scandal.

Or does it? Are we not actually talking about an *injury?* A scandal, by making theater of desire, almost always inspires an audience, overt or clandestine, which is why a scandal is so satisfying (or simply profitable). But an injury causes barren suffering. The blow that reopens the scar affords no forgiveness and receives none. Injury escalates to outrage.

And yet, what does Sade injure, especially where Lalittérature is concerned? The clinical file is a thick one; a few of its more noteworthy pages will serve our purposes here.

On the first and perhaps most incriminating page, we might read that what is intolerable about Sade's texts is mostly what involves their absolute shamelessness in depicting sex and blood — in other words, their total *demetaphorizing* of sex and blood. From the *Iliad* to the chansons de geste, of course, and from the Bible to classical tragedy, there has never been anything other than sex and blood. They are always there for some other reason, however, and under different names, as effects of or stakes in some cause (honor, justice, love, faith, the state) whose attainment "elevates" and "legitimates" them. But Sade — producing texts hallucinated by sex and blood, making sex and blood run gratuitously through the narrative, relating sex and blood to nothing outside themselves, and formulating this self-sufficiency as the blunt fact of sexual pleasure — disarms the metaphorical trick that upholds the entire rhetorical machinery of Lalittérature. This machinery shows an amazing capacity (or propensity) for domesticating the horrific, socializing the intolerable, expressing them euphemistically, and softening them in the inauthenticity of oblique vision, in the sort of provisional arrangement whereby mediocre neurosis mortifies its pleasures through denial. The Sadean obscene, then, is produced first of all from this shamelessness, from this short-circuiting of the metaphorical. (This does not mean that in the economy of the text of disruption, or in the points of disruption within any text, there is no place for a prodigious violence of the metaphorical, nor does it mean that the Sadean text unfolds in any kind of literal primitivism; rather, it means that the letter of the text is defined as the effect or limit of a process of extenuation or flattening of the metaphorical.) Even worse, this shamelessness has been brought to bear, not on some imaginary world, a utopian society remote in time or an exotic one remote in space, but on the practices of a society that is recognizably the author's own. And because Lalittérature believes in the referent, it keeps a lookout for unfaithful copies and punishes them with all due severity.

The second page of this file could be headed "Obstinate Irredeemability." In every narrative, as we know, the villain succumbs in the end, even if his downfall has to come at the price of the hero's death, the death of one of the hero's comrades, or some kind of suffering. Recent narratological studies have shown very clearly how this system of compensation works. The failure of the good is always temporary, and every loss of "earthly" advantage is repaid in the coin of the spiritual, with an exemplary metamorphosis, a reward of moral grandeur. Always, in however indirect or sublimated a way, we end up with the victory of the "equals" sign. The quality (or the compelling) of this redemption is directly proportional to the intensity of the excess that has been staged. There is always a rebalancing. Excess gets the narrative going, carries it along, and shapes the plot, but the narrative is not recognizable *as* narrative, not readable as such, until it finally reabsorbs and annuls this excess. Thus the narrative repeats the stratagem of the sacrifice (in its ritually encoded forms). Both narrative and sacrifice say that the world is homeostatic and that order must at all costs be restored. Sade himself did not hesitate to pay the price, if ironically, in the first editions of *Justine,* which were intended for a wide audience: he sent Juliette, crushed and repentant, off to the convent. But this was all over and done with in the libertine narratives that followed; he was through paying. Evil—murder, rape, theft, torture, betrayal—triumphed, definitively. And because the narrative contract imitates and confirms the social contract, what this signified was an irreparable loss for representation. The texts were burdened by an infinite debt. Is it any surprise, then, that the mob of reader-creditors rose to demand its due?

True, literature might already have promoted a few criminals or outlaws to the status of hero (the softhearted bandit, the rebel with a cause), but only under the ultimate sign of death or repentance. Never before had the odious, the cynical, and the murderous been given free rein, with full impunity, while the virtuous, the innocent, and the honest were declared the enemy. (The genre of "black humor" may have been an exception, but only when it declared itself *as* that genre and consistently produced that genre's signs, as Thomas De Quincey did, for example, in "On Murder Considered as One of the Fine Arts.") Before Sade, this kind of thing had never been seen, nor has it been seen since. Thus Blanchot is correct, if for different reasons, to see Sade's texts as a sort of absolute in literary history. The outrage is immeasurable, as great as the unredeemed evil.

Someone has to pay. And when the author does not want it to be his character, it has to be the author. This means that Sade's name is costly, all the more so because a time-honored clause of the literary pact makes the hero the author's spokesman, his textual lieutenant. When the character is thoroughly criminal, imagine what this means for the name signed to that character. Nero's thoughts — tiresome though it is to bring this up yet again — have never been imputed to Racine, nor Vautrin's to Balzac, but the words of Saint-Fond, Noirceuil, Juliette, and Blangis are regularly identified with Sade's philosophy. This is a strange and remarkably naive error, one that continues to lead even the finest pens astray as they too are taken in by the Sadean text's disconcerting break with the narrative contract and with the supposedly natural bond between author and hero.

A spiteful critic named Villeterque fell into this error after the publication of *Les Crimes de l'amour* (where this breach of contract is redeemed, though perhaps only at the last minute), and Sade sharply directed the following basic reminder to him:

> Loathsome ignoramus: have you not yet learned that every actor in any dramatic work must employ a language in keeping with his character, and that, when he does, 'tis the fictional personage who is speaking and not the author? and that, in such an instance, 'tis indeed common that the character, inspired by the role he is playing, says things completely contrary to what the author may say when he himself is speaking? . . . Ah, Monsieur Villeterque, what a fool you are![6]

Let us now pull a third page from the file containing the itemized record of injuries. This page might be headed "The Scrambling of the Codes" — that is, the brutal irruption of vulgar words into the scene of classical French, an irruption all the more violent for leaving the syntax of that language intact. The coexistence itself is what is rude and not to be borne, for this scrambling of the codes is read as a disruption of the class system. Indeed, if classical French was the self-styled language of an elite, at once the code of the court and the privilege of a nobiliary, bourgeois intelligentsia, then the presence within it of vulgar words, words of the *vulgus*, assumes the form of a provocation, of the welcoming of rabble into the manor house's drawing room. Here we have a new figure of obscenity, the most radical one of all for being inscribed within the form of articulation itself, and for being implicated in the most powerful and resistant element of any order: the signifier. We might view this disruption as nothing more than Sade's indulgence in a bit of exotic slumming, the noble's perverse and fascinated exploitation of the base and the crude. Even with this theory, however, the effect remains the same: Sade soils classical French, spatters it with the filth of the street, the filth of streetwalking;[7] he sullies the Mother. But he also makes an impossibility of community, for community is founded on the illusion of a language shared by all. Sade forces the admission that community can function only by bringing about pitiless social divisions. His writings produce a conflictive, antagonistic simultaneity of codes, exposing the repressed contradiction that sustains power, and revealing the brute fact of violence concealed by a contractual peace. (It is worth noting that this disruption of the class system repeats, more or less, the Marquis de Sade's own experience of class displacement as a noble enamored of his power and his rights, but also a country squire fraternizing with the help, even summoning them to his *réunions intimes;*[8] as a grand lord victimized by royal whim, but also lucky enough to have been freed by a popular revolution; as a militant republican and influential member of a revolutionary committee, but also a man made suspect and sentenced solely on account of his name and finally ruined, worn out by ordeals and expulsions, claiming only a single reason for being, a single title: "man of letters.")

If a Sadean violence does exist, it consists first of all (and perhaps only) in repeated injury to the symbolic body of the established order, in the rape of a language forced to take on horror stories and take in shameful words, in the provocation to tell of evil's triumph, in the unmetaphorical depiction of the forbidden. Because of this violence, the texts make identification utterly impossible, and they systematically destroy any chance of recognition; they deal in cruelty pure and simple. They stretch the logic of baroque expenditure — stretch it to the limit, perhaps, if we agree with Borges that the baroque is "that style which deliberately exhausts (or tries to exhaust) all its possibilities and borders on its own parody... the final stage [of any style] when that style only too obviously exhibits or overdoes its own tricks."[9]

We might suppose that the very effect of these texts' cruelty — in other words, the extreme nature of their humor — would be enough to separate the drivel from the rest of what is said about them. But there are also intelligent ways of missing Sade's point, and two deserve mention here. The first has its basis in poetics and unfolds in keeping with the following axiom: Sade is a text, nothing but a text, a signifying material whose workings can be demonstrated, and whose structures (narrative, rhetorical, thematic) can be exhibited. This labor of poetics is undertaken in the benevolent neutrality of knowledge, or in the graceful and sometimes humorous retreat that accompanies the meticulous deconstruction of a complex and interesting object. Sade's texts, methodologically speaking, find themselves proved innocent after all of being anything more than linguistic creatures with their own specific traits, internal constraints, laws of discursive organization, and original figures of speech. This style of analysis ascribes to itself a rigorously defined field of exactitude, and any issues that lie outside its scope seem to it irrelevant and trivial — issues, for example, like those produced by a reading based on ethics, which is the other and totally opposite way of missing Sade's point. The ethicist (if I may) accepts Sade's pronouncements in all their violence, without mediation, perceiving the shock of their provocation and sensing their power to incite. The ethicist could not care less about intratextual subtleties or the attractions of the signifying system; all the ethicist sees are contents and consequences, messages and responsibility for them, actions and effects. In other words, this is the philosopher's reading, which appears to find its justification in Sade's own intent to be recognized, if not as a thinker, then as a promoter of ideas. According to whether he arouses allegiance or condemnation, Sade is seen either as a pioneering materialist critic and liberator from prejudice (sexual, legalistic, religious) or as a dangerous perverter (of love, social bonds, responsibility to truth), even when it proves possible, *intelligence oblige,* to refrain from seeing him as a satanic master of torture and murder.

What is most remarkable is that these two readings, like some impossibly, incomprehensibly simultaneous view of obverse and inverse, can be produced only from mutually exclusive and mutually nullifying premises. Without negating the specific questions raised by either reading, I have attempted in these pages to blur their medullary division and overcome this hemiplegia by calling the two ways of reading a *poetics* and an *economics* of the text. As they meet in broadside collision, unreconcilable in their assumptions but united in denial, their conflictive unity may give them the look of a creature with two heads.

If the invention of the libertine body[10] is what will occupy us here, then what this means is that the body[11] — its treatment, its workings, and its fate, apart from its production as a boldly original trope — will be the major sign through which all other signs and their relationships are read. But why should this approach so privilege the body? It is because, as we need to recognize, we are dealing here with a concern that has shaped and permeated the whole of the modern era. From Freud to Husserl, and from Nietzsche to Foucault, the body has been named as the seat of everything that is at stake in the distribution of forces, power, and codes. The body is both the place where they intersect and the site of their concrete activity, both the converter of their multiplicity and the model for their extension, the point of concentration both for their implementation and for their crises. If the body tells a story, it also tells the shattering finale of that story. In fact, once we have begun to see the body, we see nothing else — not because of any fascination with the body as a theme, but because in the body we really do see *everything*.

In Sade's writings, the body is far from being comprehensible or readable only as a palimpsest underlying the words. Its omnipresence is striking, as if the body's true role of protagonist were a symptom of its acquired modern status as the obsessional object of power, knowledge, and desire.

The way the libertine body asserts itself — how it is put into play, put at risk, pleasured, circulated — speaks of several things at once. It speaks of a breach, contemporaneous with eighteenth-century materialism, in the reading of signs. It speaks of an investigation into the pleasures of knowledge, of a new organization in the perception of space and time. But it also speaks of a radical break with the modes of production and their techniques of domination. Finally, it speaks of the body's contradictory, wild, perverse resistance to everything that has designs on it or against it. The lingering, eternal paradox is that this libertine body attempts, on the basis of mastery and exclusion, and for the sake of pleasure, the impossible feat of encompassing in its revolt the very thing that it destroys. Libertinism, standing up to power, is still a passion of power. Is this an irritating limitation on Sade's part, or is it a contradiction exposed better by Sade than by anyone else? Is it Sade's blind spot, or is it fiction's responsibility to the extremes of provocation and cruelty?

This is the question that haunts these two ways of reading, the poetics and the economics of the text. Perhaps we can elucidate the question somewhat if we examine it on these two levels.

What does it mean, first, to speak of a "poetics"? In these pages we will not, strictly speaking, be working with any set of technical concepts so as to shape what could properly be called a "poetics" by today's standards, nor will we painstakingly summarize textual workings and narrative structures or construct models that might furnish a decisive reading of Sade's texts (all too often, such models serve as helpful guides only to themselves). We will leave this sort of patient work, with all the faith in science that it implies, to the textual engineers. The type of poetics to be sketched out here will assume that results like these have already been obtained (or that they can be obtained without undue difficulty). Our poetics, using a few of the Sadean text's oblique emphases to pinpoint a few obsessional formulas, proposes to bring about a kind of adjustment in the way this text is understood. More generally, our poetics also proposes to discover the threads of an organized disruption of the expressive body. This is the same body that, in keeping with classical theories of subjectivity, vouches for its own organic unity, configures itself in the giving of its word and the transitivity of its gaze, and assumes itself to be the medium for the manifestation or concealment of a depth. And this depth, in keeping with the values of secrecy, intimacy, and distinctive attributes, is where this body's truth is coiled up, the place where the substance of love ripens in memory and expectation. What we are witnessing in the horrific display of a desacralized, mechanized, divided-up, quantified body, a body grotesquely attached to an impassive head that "programs" its activities and monopolizes its sexual pleasure, is the wreck of this beautiful lyric unity. This reading constitutes a poetics, then, for it seems completely indifferent to ethical questions. It is content merely to record and give proof of this mutation, without wondering about who benefits and who is made to suffer, or about the forces and the history that have ordained this disruption in the body and this redistribution of its representation — without wondering, in other words, about where all of this has been negotiated. With whom? In whose interest?

These are exactly the questions that an economics would set out to explore. But what we need to understand by the term *economics* (as distinct from the term *economy*) is a textually based analysis that involves a specific process of symbolizing, a process that has its own way of re-producing and reallocating the forms of power and techniques of con-trol that are legible in the models of production and exchange, in the relations of greed and theft, and in the conflicts between wealth and misery that have helped to fashion the representations of the body that would be cataloged by a poetics. This way of posing the problem has nothing at all to do, as we might guess, with any problematic that re-gards the text merely as an effect or reflection of the social and economic contradictions belonging to the history at whose heart the text has been written. This sort of problematic functions, ultimately, on the prin-ciple of homology: a causal chain is established between the order of *reality* (a presumably knowable, scientifically definable order) and the order of *fiction* conceived as a mirror, a representational double in which the order of reality is inscribed, disguised or not (but especially when it *is* disguised, for then it serves the functions of obliteration and false con-gruence). The causal chain, once established, leaves the problematic rich in proofs for its own agenda. The first thing to be challenged in this sort of problematic is its instrumental positioning of language as a neutral medium: what an efficient little gadget we get when we wire historical materialism up to linguistic idealism! (This is why so-called ideological criticism is forever turning into a sociology of literature.)

An economics of the text, however, proposes to show that history's inscription within fiction is brought about by the specific signifying laws of language in general, and more particularly by those operations that the text performs on language. The relationship between history and fiction is not a causal one. Unlike the relationship between reality and image, the relationship between history and fiction assumes no pri-ority or anteriority. The text is always already history itself, which is to say that the text is the place where history is sensed, examined, and tested, in the staging and questioning of the codes that structure language and of the forces that animate or produce those codes. In this way, the codes — by being rewritten, unwritten, scrambled, highlighted, and filtered out — are exposed to view. Fiction serves as history's unconscious, and each text as its transcribed dream, which is why we find the same laws (dis-placement and condensation, the paradoxical coexistence of opposites) in both fiction and dreams. The text, read in this way, is a marvelous machine for playing out contradictions, though only when the analyst has an ear for them.

The whole of history, then, is to be found in the text, not as reference to the truth or as truth of the referent, but as that entity whose voice and body of symptoms the text *is,* as that entity's echo chamber: the place where its contradictions reverberate, are distorted, and come back to us all the louder for having become *other.* This may be asking a great deal of fiction; but, as Brecht has shown, if fiction cannot do this, it cannot do anything at all.

And one more point: If we call this reading an "economics" of the text, are we not yielding to the illusion that economics, as the guardian at the gates of the modern era, has the last word on the subject of "reality"? If this is what we believe, then we have merely switched theologies. What is being proposed here as an economics of the text is actually a *political* reading; and if politics truly is everywhere, as we are always being told, then it cannot be singled out as an object or isolated as a theme. Politics is deduced from all the relationships it touches, from all the forces composing it, economics chief among them — the sort of economics, that is, seen as holding the keys to power, as power's obsessional goal and universal condition, as the highest authority over the marking of bodies. What an economics of the text reads is the production of politics in the realm of fiction.

In this diptych of a book, relationships are not complementary, much less hierarchical. The second wing of the diptych does not enlarge on the truth of the first, nor are the two wings divided into structure and history, comedy and tragedy, surface and depth. It is even conceivable that somone contemplating the first wing, and the model of the body sketched out on it, might see there a few of the rhetorical figures of his or her own desire, enjoying them without necessarily going on to postulate the conditions of their operation within Sade's universe. All of this — artful combinations, a mania for variety, the fragmented sampling of bodies, a taste for new angles, the dividing up and branching out of time, as many "imaginables" as in Fourier, for example, and all of it lying outside any theory of cruelty, all of it, that is, within what we recognize as the domain of consent (here, surely, is the subversion of that domain) — all of this offers entry into an amatory utopia.

Where the political reading demands explanations and has suspicions about responsibility — in other words, where it asks *Why?* — the poetic reading welcomes differences and answers *Why not?*: the principle of utopia itself. Between these two sets of claims, I have chosen to risk a certain suspension, a pronounced gap, so as not to stifle the dissimilarity in their modes of questioning. I lighten the political reading's seriousness a bit, spoiling its appetite for Last Judgments by reminding it of fiction's levity and playfulness. But I also remind the poetic reading that the sexual pleasure of Sade's libertines comes, so to speak, at a price. Although I could have carried these two critiques out simultaneously, it seemed more to the point to differentiate them. Besides, that was what gave me pleasure.

Part I
A Poetics

CHAPTER ONE

The Overthrow of the Lyric Body

> Until now, no one has determined what the body can do.
> — SPINOZA, *The Ethics*

The Body, Literally

What is the amorous body in literature? It is a concert made up of innumerable voices, a moving mosaic made up of signs, signals, symptoms. The skin, the hands, the eyes, the face never cease to express, nor gestures to signify, clothes to symbolize, even silences to speak. All the states of the heart, all its agitations, all its transformations (doubt, jealousy, happiness, despair, tenderness), all its gradations—everything has to be marked on the body, exhibited on it, because the body is the necessary screen onto which everything is projected, the only possible meeting point, and point of articulation, through which the thread of the story or the metaphors of the poem can pass. It is their permanent medium and indispensable synthesizer. The counterpoint of the narrative is always the story of its proliferating languages. This body saturated with signs, this body that signals, proclaims, and—with all its modifications, movements, and expressions—conceals the figures of speech and the stresses with which the text stages the amorous state and amorous relationships: this is what we will call the *lyric body.*

The Sadean body, exiled from this lyric aura, shut out of this system of expression, neither hides nor flaunts itself. This body, as remote from hermeneutical coquetry as it is from hysterical bombast, is exhibited as bodies are in anatomical illustrations: coldly and precisely. Stripped of signs, symptomless, the Sadean body can do nothing other than put a stop to the classical mode of narrative, which itself is sustained only by the vast number of meanings that it conveys through characters' bodies. How could des Grieux persist in his love for Manon if her ingenue's eyes did not keep his illusions alive? ("Fortune and reputation are but slight sacrifices at such a shrine! I plainly foresee it; I can read my destiny in your bright eyes.")[1] How could Saint-Preux divine Julie's love without the gestures and looks that betray her agitation? ("At times our eyes meet; at the same time there escape from us a few sighs, a few furtive tears... O Julie! Were this harmony to have come from beyond... were heaven to have destined us one to the other...."; "Turn those eyes away from me, those eyes so sweet, fatal to me; rob my eyes of your features, your expressions, your arms, your hands, your blond hair, your gestures; elude the avid imprudence of my gaze.")[2] Amorous discourse is first of all an art of divination: an accurate decoding of the signs being broadcast by the beloved body, a decoding carried out for the purpose of knowing the intention that inhabits this body. Thus the symptom-laden body sets up the metaphorical order that establishes what we habitually consider to be literature. Why, then, should it come as a surprise that the archons decided there was no place in literature for Sade? Anyone who wishes to suffer the same anathema need only follow the Sadean recipe: Take a (human) body, strip it of all its symptoms, free this impassive matter of all expression, give a detailed description of its parts, just as you would of a machine's, and connect it to other bodies, for no grander purpose than sexual gratification. In this way, at one stroke, you will drain the metaphorical reservoir, eliminate the infinite network of causality that depends on it, destroy the material "proper" to narrative, and dash the very concept of literature. You will then be condemned to the production of a language based on nothing but its own repetitions, condemned to expose the fact that narrative reflects nothing but the narrator's own arbitrary nature. At the same time, you will liberate your readers from realist illusions and make them accomplices rather than victims. You will shatter the illusion of classical fiction by pointing out that the rules for its production are inherent in the material of which it is composed. In other words, you will be guilty of the crime of lese literature and will be pardoned only with difficulty, if indeed you are pardoned at all.

The Sadean body—defined by its plastic outlines, classified by its anatomical elements, treated as the simple object of an inventory—is *the body literally, to the letter.* But we should not understand this phrase as referring to some primordial simplicity, as being just an ordinary denotational term. Literality is not to be taken here as the primary meaning; it is what eludes metaphor, what resists the system of interpretation.

This body, precise and functional, purified of all lyric flamboyance, gets its nonsignifying flatness not from any claim to some precultural primitivity (to reverse the terms is to be forced into negation) but from the short-circuiting of two discourses: the discourse of literature with that of science. The body described by science is a material datum, a collection of organs, a system of functions—in other words, an anatomy and a physiology. Literature cannot take this body as its general object, much less as its exclusive one, without also having to give up making it into a "character"—an expressive and therefore narratable being—and without having to give up being literature. And yet this is the body on which Sade imposed literary existence, through a radical choice that continues to be seen as unacceptable. The logical consequence of this choice is that bodily relationships must be adapted to the level of bodily functions. This is a definite necessity to which any claim of meaning must yield. (One sees the questions coming: How to narrate this body that has no secrets, no mysteries? produce a quest with no amorous motive? articulate signs on an inexpressive body? And, even more generally, we may wonder how particular types of narrative might imply specific montages of bodily signs within the text, and vice versa.)

This, then, is *literally* a body, a body to the letter, in that it produces a writing. Nothing antedates the letter, and from it a writing arises: degree zero not as origin but as acknowledgment of material and process so that the letter is preserved only through not being allowed to dissolve in what it traces. At the end of the narrative, Juliette has not changed, and her body has no more memory than it had at the beginning: the letter can repeat itself indefinitely. Juliette, given the need for verisimilitude, has grown older, but that is all. She is no wiser and no more of a libertine, as she would have been in a coming-of-age novel. She has simply managed to approach the saturation point within the system of possibilities, and her body has accumulated the greatest number of the marks implied by its functions. Thus time in the narrative coincides with the time it takes to utter the statement that exhausts the great syntagma emblematized by her body, and her body expresses nothing more than that. It displays, in narratives, the tattoos of its sexual pleasure. It could all continue, or it could start all over again. The ending is as arbitrary as any other sequence. Thus the author/scribe, to conclude the narrative, decides to dedicate this body to silence, to disappearance — that is, to the retreat from any possibility of writing:

> The death of Madame de Lorsange [Juliette] caused her to disappear from the world's scene, just as it is customary that all brilliant things on earth finally fade away. Unique in her kind, that woman died without having left any record of the events which distinguished the latter part of her life, and so it is that no writer will be able to chronicle it for the public.[3]

Quartering

Don Juan was still a dreamer. He still wanted to seduce, to be loved for himself. He was still capable of swooning under the beloved's gaze. In spite of everything, he remained nostalgic for courtly love. He was still dragging the soul of a knight around in the new territory carved out and organized by technical, industrial reason. Though he already had a passion for great numbers, he did not see the change that was sweeping him along. In that respect, he lacked the means for realizing his desires. Sade was to give him the means. For the libertine, Sade would invent a body made to the measure of the fantasies poured forth by the new order of things. To achieve this goal, he would submit that body to a strict process of quartering, in quartering's double sense of geometrical operation and dismemberment. He would reduce it to a system of organs devoid of inner unity, to the gearwheel device of a piece of machinery, a set of denumerable quantities, a game of programmable variations and combinations. This was to be, all in all, a quadruple reduction in which the stage set of the text would clarify and confirm the philosophical master stroke prescribing the work of this reduction: namely, the peremptory elimination of the hypothesis of the soul. The body would find itself carried along by a tremendous movement of abstraction, a movement of dividing up, ordering, segmenting, and classifying, which would sweep away all the charms, gestures, and nuances (caresses, perfumes, games, signs, innuendos) that form the texture of the amorous body and the amorous relationship. From now on, always and everywhere, models would be chosen for their conformity to an original. There would now be an assessment of working parts, the repetition of gestures, and the imposition of selected patterns, all according to the unchanging assumption of an undisputed power ordaining such things — as if sex itself were not even the real object of these connections but were, by virtue of the energy it carries and the arrangements it requires, merely what permits the means or medium for a pure pleasure in combining, varying, and inventing a multiplicity of novel patterns; as if sex, in other words, were what permits both the production of a grammar of bodies and their constitution as a discourse (or, rather, a mathesis)[4] that submits their substance to the discourse maintained over them by reason, "to the point where, ultimately, this organization itself seems to be a more important element of erotic activity than the carnal matter that, in principle, is to be organized. This is equally true for all literature worthy of the name."[5]

Physiological/Surgical Reduction

Once the assumption of the soul is gone, what is left of the subject if not the body, the organism described by physiologists and dissected by surgeons? Here, Sade expressly imagines himself the heir of iatromechanics, the post-Cartesian medical tradition that imperturbably developed all the implications of a mechanical body. This model is where eighteenth-century agnosticism found ample materialist justification. In this model, moreover, Sade found reasons to use nature as the basis for a physics of the drives and a logic of destruction.

As its first effect, a physics of the drives invalidates everything that has been presented as the body's symptomatological functioning. Indeed, no symptomatology has been able to manage without the assumption of a psyche. Once that assumption is brushed aside, nothing remains but the muscular, nervous "machine" in the clutches of its functions, through which every passion is reduced to a condition of the glands and the nerves. Here, for example, is the explanation given for the criminal passions of the Duc de Blangis:

> He noticed that a violent commotion inflicted upon any kind of an adversary is answered by a vibrant thrill in our own nervous system; the effect of this vibration, arousing the animal spirits which flow within these nerves' concavities, obliges them to exert pressure on the erector nerves and to produce in accordance with this perturbation what is termed a lubricious sensation.[6]

What is pain? Noirceuil, quoting Nicole, replies:

> "Pain," logically defined, "is nothing other than a sentiment of hostility in the soul toward the body it animates, the which it signifies through certain movements that conflict with the body's physical organization."[7]

Sade calls for the overthrow of symptom by vibration, or by *secretion*. Thus the body is affirmed as the site of a certain number of materially discoverable, well-defined functions that never reflect anything more than physiological organization itself, and not as the site of any network of signs attributed to some secret authority whose mediating instrument the body must be. And yet the symptom of classical amorous psychology is surely a silent language of the body, which means that the body is inhabited by a "voice" (of truth, or awareness of feeling, or even nature). This unwanted tenant, this parasite, this killjoy, is what the libertine body evicts. The libertine body can admit of an Other inside the body only at the cost of losing control (and therefore sexual gratification), for it cannot serve two masters. The libertine's body can never contain any secret, any mystery, any *inside* to which external bodily changes might be attributed. The symptom cannot withstand confrontation with materialist assumptions about mechanics. But what undermines the symptom even more is its constitution as a silent language. Keeping still though wanting to speak is the distinctive feature of the victim, the hardship of virtue. To be a libertine is to identify language with discourse — that is, to exert control over the word as articulated in the two forms where it reaches its culmination in Western culture: story and concept, narration and definition (hence Sade's constant alternation between scene and dissertation). This is why libertinism is a question of the "head," a question of discourse (and thus of unfeelingness). As for the skin and the organs, they have nothing to say, only to do, and if they claim to speak, then surely they *do* nothing. To blush, to pale — in other words, to *express* — is to fall prey to the inner voice, to be in the grip of sensitivity. The symptom, falling within the province of Justine's complexes, indicates the axis of neurosis: denial. As the language of the victimized body, the symptom is correctly defined in Freudian terms as a substitution or compromise that announces, in the silent mode of displacement, the inhibited drive. And so the victimized body is doubly dominated: by the decoy of a voice that contradicts its desire, and by the discourse of another body, the libertine body, which, as a *fatal* return of the repressed, inflicts upon it the truth of its desire.

But the symptom is merely the cutting edge, the most spectacular element, of what makes up the ordinary system of the body as handed down by the metaphysical tradition: the system of *expression*, whose basic assumption is a referential structure of inside/outside and psyche/body. To express is to make the first of these paired terms pass through the second, to let the one be read through the other, and thus to set up an organic and signifying unity. From Husserl to Merleau-Ponty, phenomenology believed that this euphoric notion offered the opportunity to restore a bodily thinking opposed to intellectualism, never realizing that this notion brought with it all of idealism's most obdurate assumptions, and that it continued to stand for the dualism of the sign and the instrumentality of language. We are still hanging fire with an ethic of this-means-that[8] and an aesthetic of manifestation (hidden/revealed, buried/articulated, and so on), which themselves are leftovers from Kant and Hegel.

Dis-affected from any expressive relationship, reduced to its anatomical materiality, the Sadean body ultimately models itself on the flayed matter, the *écorché*, of the medical dissection lab. The Sadean body is by definition a body exhibited, divided up, and inventoried, which is why it is so lightly handed over to the torturer. The libertine who cuts the victim's body to pieces is simply carrying out, in the name of desire, what the surgeon lays claim to by authority of knowledge — but the libertine commits the outrage of admitting sexual pleasure in the act. Libertine torture pushes the logic of the body's anatomical/surgical reduction, as postulated by science, and takes it to the limit. In physiological knowledge and surgical practice there is a deferred aggression, mediated by an academic/humanitarian (knowing/caring) legitimacy, an aggression that the libertine appropriates and displays for what it is: the violent, cruel, primary movement of a drive. None of the types of knowledge or techniques that involve the body is constituted without foreclosure of the same sexual pleasure that constitutes their beginning and their end. The surgeon-libertine Rodin bluntly says so:

> All the sufferings that I produce in others, by means of surgery, or of whipping, or of vivisection, throw my spermatic organisms into such disharmony that there results a manifest pruritus and an involuntary

erection, which, without moving me in the slightest, brings me more or less quickly to ejaculation, as a function of the degree of suffering imprinted on the subject.[9]

Mechanical Reduction

Man a Machine, by La Mettrie[10] (whose works Sade read with enthusiasm), provides the ideal model for the system of well-arranged organs making up the soulless body. Turning the libertine body into a pleasure robot offers at least four advantages. The body conceived as a machine is no longer accountable to any transcendent authority (conscience, soul):

> We encounter the objection that materialism reduces the human being to a mere machine, that materialism is hence a dishonor to our kind; but is to honor this species to say that man acts at the behest of the secret impulses of a spirit or of a certain I don't know quite what which serves to animate him nobody knows quite how?[11]

By dispensing with the soul, the machine also does away with all the preconceptions of moral philosophy. In other words, impervious to pity or remorse, and inaccessible to any notion of guilt, it asserts that if the soul does not exist, everything is allowed.

A machine, moreover, is a device that, once set in motion, is no longer master of its own movements. These reflect nothing but the logic of their construction and the energy that propels them. Once begun, they can no longer be modified, and their effects are always inevitable and necessary. The mechanical body puts a kind of "destiny of the drives" into play. All claims to a responsible will are put out of bounds; what is essential is the fact of a material, blind order designated as "nature," to which one wisely submits with one's sense of humor intact. This is exactly what La Mettrie says:

> In no way do we determine what governs us; we are not at all in charge of our sensations; acknowledging their authority and our enslavement, we shall try to make them agreeable to us, persuaded that life's happiness lies in this.... Dependent on so many outer causes, and all the more on so many inner ones, how could we be spared from being what we are? How could we regulate forces of which we know nothing?... When I do good or evil—when, virtuous in the morning, I am given to vice at night—my blood is the reason, ["forces of which we know nothing" are] what thickens it, checks it, dissolves it, quickens it."[12]

Sade confirms this:

All these matters depend upon our constitutions, our organs, upon the manner whereby they are affected, and it is no more in our power to change our tastes in this connection than it is in our power to alter the form of our bodies.[13]

Relationships with others, as mechanized relationships, are themselves completely unburdened of psychology and especially of sentimentality. For the libertine, the other is primarily a system made of organs to be plugged in to his own system. What the libertine considers most important in the other's body will be those organs most likely to guarantee the best connection between the two systems. First the individual pieces will be assessed and described, and then a plan will be established for their operation. The language spoken here is the language of a technology of sexual pleasure; from this perspective, we can interpret "programs" like the one that follows (among many others):

Listen to me: Juliette is going to stretch out upon the couch, and you shall each in your turn savor with her the pleasure of your individual choosing. I, stationed directly opposite the scene, I shall take you one after the other as you've had done with her, and the lewd activities begun with Juliette will be brought to a conclusion with me. But I'll be in no hurry, my come[14] won't flow before I've had the five of you in my embrace.[15]

What could be less romantic? In the course of these arrangements, there is no opportunity at all for face-to-face lyric specularity. There are only pieces to be connected and the pleasure to be extracted from them.

Further, to arrange the group for an orgy in this way is to produce an effect of complete depersonalization. What is brought into being is an anonymous collection, the objectivity of a mechanism that, rather than being the sum of its individual parts, predates them and, as it were, produces them as such:

There was a moment when the entire Sodality united in a single immense group; not a member was inactive, and nothing could be heard but a deep murmur of voluptuous moans accented by the gasps and shrill cries heralding discharges.[16]

Identities are dissolved and names are erased in the plural operation of this pleasure machine; pronouns become impersonal ("they," "some," "all that"); verbs, participial or passive: an incandescent neuter in which the group body is being consumed.

> Over three hundred members had already arrived and there they were, all naked; some were encunting, some masturbating, some flagellating, some cunt-sucking, some sodomizing, some discharging, and all that most serenely and amidst perfect calm.[17]

> Everybody was in action. From all sides nothing could be heard but cries, whether of pleasure or of pain, and the whistling of thongs and the impact of leather on flesh. Everybody was naked; everybody illustrated lewdness in its most scandalous colors.[18]

We are moving, in other words, from automaton to atelier, from Vaucanson[19] to Jacquard,[20] with all the implications that this movement has for organization, productivity requirements, unremitting effort, and enthusiastic work, until at last we arrive at this bluntly humorous paradox: a Stakhanovism[21] of sexual gratification, a sheer energetic squandering—a "bachelor machine"[22] if ever there was one.

What the group-body finally brings perfectly into being is the libertine body (or the libertine corps, the body of libertines, just as we call the body of diplomats the diplomatic corps): a collection of individuals transformed into an institution through the exercise of a function. And now we understand why the mechanical functioning of certain individuals assigned to this constituted body is strictly a matter of their performing a service (the labor necessary for the luxury of sexual gratification) or, worse, of their being reduced to passivity. Thus we have furniture-bodies[23] like the ones to which the libertine ogre Minski helps himself:

> "The appointments you see here," said our host, "are alive; they move when the signal is given."
>
> Minski snaps his fingers and the table in the corner of the room scuttles into the middle of it; five chairs dispose themselves around the table, two chandeliers descend from the ceiling and hover above the table.
>
> "There is nothing mysterious about it," says the giant, having us examine the composition of the furniture from closer on. "You notice that this table, these chandeliers, those chairs are each made up of a group of girls cunningly arranged; my meal will served upon the backs of these creatures."[24]

In every victim, le meuble[25] (the inert, passive, instrumental, suffering body) threatens la machine (the active, productive, sexually pleasured body). No libertine is ever reduced to this function, which always connotes servitude, work, and annihilation (compare the way domestic servants are said, eloquently, to be "part of the movables" or to have been "sold with the furniture"). To be (a) movable is the underlying condition of the victimized body.

Arithmetical Reduction

The Sadean body—divided up, exhibited, mechanized—is also quantified. The quality of the organs that are being employed, the number of bodies that have been mobilized, and the importance of the orgy that has been brought off are always given in very precise figures. This practice yields four types of fundamental calculations—measuring the organs, assessing the number of bodies, adding up the acts, and drawing up accounts of the operations—in what can be called an arithmetical reduction.

Measuring. If no description of those bodily organs intended for sexual enjoyment ever goes unaccompanied by a numerical assessment of their qualities, it is because the statement of the designated object's dimensions is itself what establishes that object's value. So it is with the male sex organs (male potency revels in figures), as a few famous examples will show: Noirceuil ("A tool seven inches in circumference by eleven inches in length"); Saint-Fond ("His muscular member was perhaps seven inches in length by six inches in circumference"); Claude ("Over nine inches in circumference by thirteen inches in length"); Minski ("Eighteen inches long by sixteen around").

Perhaps Fourier alone also knew how to elevate this mania for numerical assessment to the level of a libidinal frenzy and make it the defining feature of a style. Sade uses statements of dimensions to make it perfectly clear that the desired body is nothing but a system made up of itemized parts from which a detailed sexual pleasure can be extracted. Variation or precision in these numbers is intended to introduce some specific novel detail, right at the point where the narrative itself offers only repetition. The requirement for details is set out explicitly in the text, whether by the male (or female) narrator who proposes to satisfy this requirement or by the audience that demands details of this kind. But we certainly cannot fail to notice that numbers, or at least measurable quantities, are always offered at precisely this point. Hence a surprising disparity: on the one hand, the general nature of descriptions of places, people, or actions; and, on the other, the highly precise numerical information about organs and acts of debauchery, as if this excessive precision had to compensate for what in other respects is a somewhat less than perfect plausibility. But this can be done only with great irony, for it would mean introducing ultrarealism into a domain where the literary code tolerates no direct expression of any kind. Thus the numerical assessment is strikingly incongruous with Sadean narrative methodology, in which emblematic scenery always gains the upper hand over realistic description. But this incongruity is particularly unseemly in its focus on a part of the body — the sex organs — that narrative normally permits itself to designate only through metaphorical tricks.

All in all, the Sadean pleasure in enumeration is a strictly libertine one, and explicitly so to begin with, in that it means taking measurements where measurements are simply not taken, at precisely the point where the code for the discourse of sexual pleasure calls for modesty and allusion — calls, in other words, for rhetorical detours. With Sade, we even approach a sheer sexual pleasure in numbers, as can be heard in this cry from Dolmancé at the moment of having himself buggered by Augustin, his valet:

> Dolmancé — Ah, by Christ! what a bludgeon! never have I received one of such amplitude . . . Eugénie, how many inches remain outside?
>
> Eugénie — Scarcely two.
>
> Dolmancé — Then I have eleven in my ass! What ecstasy![26]

At a more implicit level, the incredibly absurd work of taking these measurements, a task presupposed by all this precise numerical information (unless we assume, on the basis of his vast experience, that the libertine has a good eye), allows us to infer a sexual pleasure in enumeration. On the whole, realist texts use details in the service of a denotative system whose aim is to conceal the order of discourse under the order of the referent, but a totally different economy is at work here. Sadean details, as numerical details, lend verisimilitude only as a way of deriding and endlessly undermining the very idea of verisimilitude, by putting themselves at the service of what verisimilitude rules out: obscenity.

We may wonder whether this method of singling out body parts and appraising them has a precise correspondence in the operations of fetishism. Sadean desire is marked by disqualifications that admit of no exceptions, concerning not just the size of the penis but also the shape of the backside, the whiteness of the skin, the firmness of the breasts, and so on, to the point where the presentation of a character is often limited to the presentation and exalting of these elements, or of one among them. At first glance, this is fetishism itself—and yet, for Sade, nothing could be farther from libertine desire. The selective dividing up carried out by the eye on the desired body is marked not at all by a fetishistic emphasis, but rather by the precision of taxonomic reason. To privilege one element is only to choose the best way of connecting two bodies conceived as mechanical devices. This privileged element, always the same one, is inscribed in a series of other elements that carry out the same function. In other words, all these body parts, singled out as privileged objects of desire, constitute a class and recur by means of the individuals who populate the narrative. They are, as it were, the table of elements in a chemistry of desire, the elementary signs of its algebra. They are placed right from the start into the symbolic order. For precisely that reason, there is no question here of any fetishistic process, which characteristically takes a strictly individual object. The fetish has value only for the subject who chooses it; because it remains incommunicable and useless to others, the fetish object (a body part, an article of clothing) is absolutized, transformed into a focus for crystallizing all the energies of the drives. Thus fetishism radicalizes metonymic-metaphoric production by taking the part for the whole, to the point of blind fanaticism, reducing all libidinal sets to a single sign and elevating this sign to the rank of substitute (Freud's *Ersatz*) for the body itself. But this operation is unacceptable to Sade because for him the body is defined as what cannot be replaced, as what could never be delegated or represented. Scopic division singles out no *Ersatz*; rather, it upholds the stroke of the letter drawn by desire as the materiality of the designated organ.

Assessing. Quantity: this is what really fires the libertine imagination, and probably for several reasons. First of all, quantity connotes luxury, abundance, and therefore economic and political power. Moreover, it is a safeguard for desire: not only must the specter be put aside of any shortfall in the objects of sexual pleasure but, even after the most excessive expenditures (of energy, fuckers, virgins, victims), it is also necessary that the reserves appear scarcely to have been touched.

There are grounds for considering this requirement from the standpoint of an economics. For the moment, let us simply reprise the numerical information about the quantity of the bodies required or recruited for the orgies, noting that the orgies themselves are most often held in places where large numbers of people are already gathered (the convent at Panthemont, the monastery of the white friars in Paris, the convent at Bologna), or in places that can hold many people, such as castles, whose cellars are lively storerooms of "lust objects" (the manor of the Friends of Crime, or Saint-Fond's castle, or Minski's; the pope's palace, or the one that belongs to the King of Naples). Once again, precise accountancy is what maintains the inventory of available bodies:

> Among the facilities offered Sodality Members are two seraglios. . . . One is composed of three hundred boys ranging from seven to twenty-five years of age; the other of a like number of girls, from five to twenty-one.[27]

> I have two harems [says Minski]: the first contains two hundred girls from five to twenty years old. . . . Another tenscore women of from twenty to thirty are in the second. . . . Fifty servants of both sexes look after this considerable store of pleasure-objects; and for purposes of recruitment I have one hundred agents posted in all the large cities of the world.[28]

> I conversed with better than three thousand individuals in the one sex and the other in the course of that year [in Constantinople, according to Brisatesta].[29]

Relationships of quantity leave no opening for love relationships. Here, we find ourselves within the order of substitutability, the order of indifference in and toward the subject. It goes without saying that nothing resembling an encounter could ever make its appearance in the domain of this entertaining, unyielding accountancy.

Adding. If bodies are quantified, so are their acts, at least their acts of love, which moreover are reduced to sexual relations. Here again, the lyrical collapses under the arithmetical. Great sexual pleasure is not a sensation that follows on a long-awaited, well-prepared, finally consummated seduction or understanding; instead, it is the number of times one "discharges" in a given place, within a limited span of time.[30]

Right in the middle of her orgy with Clairwil, at the monastery of the white friars, Juliette is totaling up figures:

> Each eight-man platoon loosed two volleys, bringing first one of us, then the other, under fire, and the constituents of each changed posts; thus it was we each underwent eight such assaults, and when they were over we declared ourselves satisfied and at our hosts' disposal; they might do what they wished with either of us and to their hearts' content. So it was that Clairwil was fucked another fifteen times in the mouth, ten in the cunt, and thirty-nine in the ass; and I forty-six in the ass, eight in the mouth, and ten in the cunt. All told, another two hundred fuckings each.[31]

To top it all off, Sade adds the following priceless footnote:

In such sort that these two winning creatures, not counting oral incursions—for mouth-fucking produces upon the fucked too faint an impression to merit consideration here—had, at this stage, been fucked, Clairwil one hundred eighty-five times and Juliette one hundred and ninety-two, this both cuntwise and asswardly. We have deemed it necessary to provide this reckoning rather than have ladies interrupt their reading to establish a tally, as otherwise they would most assuredly be inclined to do.[32]

Even the quantity of sperm poured out is added up:

"The vigor of these men," the King [of Naples] went on, "at least equals their superiority of member; every one of them is the guarantee of fifteen or sixteen discharges, and not one yields less than twelve ounces of sperm per ejaculation: they are the elite in my realm."[33]

Drawing up accounts. It is well known that the passion for assessment is a defining feature of obsessional rituals, which are specifically described under the rubric *anality,* because assessment is less the measurement of whatever is designated by these calculations than the measurement of mastery itself. If the libertine keeps precise accounts, down to the unit, it is not because one stroke more or less would modify his sexual pleasure but because this very exactitude (however arbitrary), and its enunciation, are what engender his pleasure. He takes pleasure in counting up bodies and strokes on the spot; in the aftermath, however, drawing up an account of the proceedings gives him just as much pleasure. This account truly crowns his sexual pleasure by establishing it as definitive (the count is done), glorious (the count is enormous), and, above all, controlled (the count is known): at the convent of Bologna, "all the novices, a goodly number of nuns, fifty pensionnaires, one hundred twenty women all told, passed through our hands";[34] at the palace of the King of Naples, "all told, we immolated eleven hundred and seventy-six victims, which made one hundred sixty-eight apiece, among them six hundred girls and five hundred seventy-six boys."[35]

Balance sheets abound in Sade's texts, but the most amazing of them all, both for its meticulousness and for its expository turns of phrase lifted straight from accounting forms, is probably the one that concludes *The 120 Days of Sodom.* This exceptional document would merit quotation in full, but here we will cite only the finale:

Masters	4
Elders	4
Kitchen staff	6
Storytellers	4
Fuckers	8
Little boys	8
Wives	4
Little girls	8
Total	46

Whereof thirty were immolated and sixteen returned to Paris.

FINAL ASSESSMENT
Massacred prior to the 1st of March,
  in the course of the orgies   10
Massacred after the 1st of March   20
Survived and came back   16
    Total 46^{36}

Combinative Reduction

This type of reduction is, in a way, a condensation of the preceding types. Because the body is divided up, mechanized, and quantified, amorous relationships can mean nothing but combinations, which can be attained only through the construction of a system of variations meant to establish the greatest possible number of articulations among available bodies. And because sexual pleasure belongs to the order of quantity, the combinative operation provides the most logical solution to the search for optimal profitability of the corporal system that has been installed.

Any combinative operation (a game, for example) makes the assumption of at least two conditions — elements or units to be combined, and rules for combining them — that form an enclosure inside which the operation takes place and has validity. In the Sadean *réunion intime*, bodies and their organs constitute the elements; protocols of action and programs constitute the rules. What are the essential operations of combinative reduction? They can be stated as follows: *planning, execution, variation,* and *saturation.* We are already so familiar with the first two operations that we need not take them up again here. But what about the other two?

Variation. In general, the exposition of a program indicates the sequence of the variations that different bodies will be responsible for carrying out. In the course of executing its program, however, the group-body system, like an actual cybernetic machine, can modify or enrich the program so as to adjust it to any new members or to the fantasies that may occur to one or another of the libertines. As a matter of fact, almost every execution of any program oversteps its initial boundaries in this way, for the possibility of formulating the body's supposedly unlimited capacity for sexual pleasure resides precisely in the indefinite *addition* of combinations: "immediately we were all three plunged back into the wildest excesses of lubricity. We struck a thousand different poses"; "the situations were seven times varied, and seven times over my liberated come sprang in answer to divine cajolery."[37] But if this combinative work affords one outstanding advantage, it is the quality of *surprise* in the resulting figures, the quality of their being unpredictable, of their never having been seen before (which is the supreme libertine value) — the trigger of sexual pleasure not only because it produces the differentiating feature that symbolizes and condenses all differences but also because it constitutes the paradoxical success of creating an event from combinations:

> That libidinous drama was composed of three scenes: first of all, whilst with mouth, lips, and nibbling teeth I strove to rouse the deeply slumbering activity in Mondor, my six colleagues, grouped in pairs, were to strike the most suggestive sapphic poses for Mondor's contemplation; *no two of their attitudes were to be alike, they were all to keep in continual motion.* Gradually, the three couples merged and our six tribades, who had spent several days training for the occasion, *finally composed the most original* and the most libertine configuration you could hope to imagine.[38]

This way of using the technique of variation to pursue original figures dominates the whole narrative logic of *The 120 Days.* As we know, the narrative sets out to list and recount six hundred different "passions" — one hundred fifty per month. Of the many episodes that the storytellers relate, some differ only in small features. But one small feature is enough to make all the difference, to mark out an original passion. The slightest disparity, because it is a qualitative one, grounds the singularity of the resulting figure and, by establishing a new unit, permits an increase in the total. Hence the following paradox: the quantitative is what matters, but it is engendered by the qualitative. Libertine desire cannot get enough of variation; it yields only to numbers, but each variation must still possess its own irreducible singularity. This apparent double bind is one that the libertine sensibility nevertheless manages to negotiate by means of its capacity to perceive, in the slightest disparity, a *relevant difference*. The introduction to *The 120 Days* invites the reader to the same keen exercise of differentiation:

> As for the diversity, it is authentic, you may be sure of it; study closely that passion which to your first consideration seems perfectly to resemble another, and you will see that a difference does exist and that, however slight it may be, it possesses precisely that refinement, that touch which distinguishes and characterizes the kind of libertinage wherewith we are here involved.[39]

In other words, what we have here is the erotic equivalent of the Leibnizian *principle of indiscernibles* (or, to put it another way, the principle of discernibility):

> If one portion of matter is not distinguished by anything from any other part, equal in quantity and shape..., and if, moreover, the condition of a body at a given moment cannot be distinguished from the condition of the same body at another moment except by the transposition of portions of matter, equal in quantity and shape and similar in every respect, then it clearly follows from the perpetual substitution of indiscernible portions that there is no way of distinguishing the conditions of the corporal world in various moments.[40]

This is why it is necessary to assume that a qualitative difference grounds the singularity of each substance, and to state "*that there is never perfect similarity,* which is one of the most important axioms I have discovered";[41] or, again, "that it is not true that two substances entirely resemble one another and are different *solo numero.*"[42] Thus quality is the *inner* principle of change, but by itself it is not enough: "It is also necessary that, apart from the principle of change, there be a *detail of what changes,* which forms, so to speak, the specification and the variety of simple substances."[43]

Sade's question is obviously a very different one, but its logical solution is on the same order. For Sade, "the detail of what changes" is exactly what secures the specification of each passion (replace Leibniz's *substance* with *passion* and you have a text by Sade). In *The 120 Days,* or in *Juliette,* this need for the differentiating detail is constantly invoked; thus, in the appeal to order from the first narration at Silling:

> "Duclos," the Président interrupted at this point, "we have, I believe, advised you that your narrations must be decorated with *the most numerous and searching details*; the precise way and extent to which we may judge how the passion you describe relates to human manners and man's character is determined by your willingness to disguise no circumstance; and, what is more, *the least circumstance* is apt to have an immense influence upon the procuring of that kind of sensory irritation we expect from your stories."[44]

With respect to the genesis of the differentiating element that produces the variation, Sade asserts himself as a confirmed Leibnizian, if in a displaced and perverted way, but we see him take the opposite view of another principle necessary to the development of the combinative operation, a principle that can be called the *principle of greatest complexity.* For Leibniz, the "simple" constitutes true being — the monad — to the point where any complexity or multiplicity is merely phenomenal or accidental and ultimately must be reduced to the simple (see *Monadology*). For Sade, the compound is what suits libertine thought, given that the "simple" is on the side of the soul, and the compound is on the side of the body. In a Leibnizian problematics, the body is not a substance, strictly speaking, for its mode of organization is mechanics — that is, the means by which compounds *imitate* the inner harmony of simple substances. As we have seen, however, mechanics is precisely the mode of being that Sade claims for the body, with one difference: he attaches no soul to it. Leibniz's "simple" makes the soul the center of the human monad. For Sade, however, that can only entail the whole moral entourage of this metaphysics: the pure, the virtuous, the good, the just, the true, and so forth. And on the other side we would have the ugly, the vicious, the criminal, the treacherous — the values, in other words, of the reprobate body. The farther we move from the "simple," then, the more complicated things become, the more deeply we enter into the monstrous and the extraordinary, and the more unprecedented and exciting are the disparities we produce:

> Nature's disorder carries with it a kind of sting which operates upon the high-keyed sort with perhaps as much and even more force than do her

most regular beauties. . . . Furthermore, beauty belongs to the sphere of
the simple, the ordinary, whilst ugliness is something extraordinary, and
there is no question but that every ardent imagination prefers in
lubricity the extraordinary to the commonplace.[45]

Therefore, "the detail of what changes" is not, as in Leibniz, the specification of a quality aligned with the "simple"; instead, it is an incessantly more complex increase in combinable elements. On the whole,
the Leibnizian "detail" is the product of a metaphorical operation because
"every created monad represents the whole universe," and "compounds
use the simple to symbolize":[46] a logocentric system. With Sade, by contrast, the detail is on the order of metonymy in that it secures a kind of
complexifying that increases by accumulation, by a decentered and uncertain movement. The qualitative detail does not express any basic unity.
It increases the total, the quantitative; it feeds the combinative operation and thus favors the odds of desire.[47]

Finally, a third principle, one that governs the production of variations,
can be noted in addition to the principle of indiscernibles and the principle of greatest complexity. We will call this one the *principle of order*.
It is expressed at the beginning of every orgy: "Let us put some order
into our pleasures." Apart from this requirement's connotations of transgression and nonprofit exchange, which Barthes has already mentioned,[48]
a precisely logical necessity can be discovered in it, one imposed by combinative invention. There would be no fixed figures without the imposition of some order, only an informal swarming, and so there would
be no definable novelty, and no minimal disparity could be assessed.
Therefore, the principle of order underwrites "that refinement, that
touch" belonging to libertine judgment. It is the prime requirement for
the principle of discernibility as producer of relevant variations. What
is more, it grounds narrativity itself, since narrativity functions as an
exposition of the list of figures: if the orgy is a muddle, then everything
has already been said from the start, and the narrative ends with the
orgy. Order, by ensuring a precise, graduated unfolding of figures and
episodes, allows a variation to be specified by the slightest detail and legitimates the narrative that presents it.

Saturation. According to Hilbert,[49] saturation is a distinctive feature of
any combinative operation (such as an axiomatics). This is exactly where
Sade's combinative operation is headed, and necessarily so: the libertine
body, lacking any lyric depth, has nothing to offer representation or nar-

rative but discrete elements with no internal connection. At this level there can be no fullness through representation of an infinity, but only the fullest possible saturation of those elements that have been put into play. Saturation is to the libertine body what depth is to the lyric body.

The operation is accomplished on two levels: at one level, it has to do with saturating the body; at the other, with saturating the predicates of the body's action.

To saturate the body is first of all to occupy all its erogenous zones: "reluctant to see a single one of my orifices vacant"; "there was nothing I might not have done, no lewd act I could not have soiled myself with . . . my cunt, my ass, my breasts, my mouth were all used, befouled"; "when we go somewhere to be fucked, it is with the intention of having no part of ourselves left untouched."[50]

Next, saturating the body means connecting it to the greatest possible number of other bodies, and bringing the group-body into being. Sadean pleasure, because saturation is its keynote, cannot do without the group. Couples constitute an exception. They appear only in very specific situations — a first meeting, the making of an agreement, the sharing of a secret, the prelude to a torture — they appear, that is, whenever a decrement in sexual pleasure can be compensated for by some discursive or imaginative pleasure. It is always a question of some transitional situation; the true libertine holds the tête-à-tête in contempt because it signifies the specific attitude of virtuous love.

At the second level, where the predicates of the body's action are concerned, saturation is actually a question of sheer pleasure in language, of amassing different predicates on the same subject or causing permutation of the same predicate among different subjects.

The amassing of different predicates on the same subject is the pleasure of condensation or, as Barthes puts it, homonymy:[51]

"Excellent," says he contentedly once the whole complex operation is under way, "what more could I ask? My ass is being fucked, I'm fucking the ass of a virgin, I've got someone fucking my wife's. Indeed, unto my pleasure now nothing wants."[52]

Foul accursed unnatural son who all at one stroke was guilty of *parricide, incest, murder, sodomy, pimping, prostitution.* Oh Juliette, Juliette! never in my life had I been so happy![53]

This pleasure, as already mentioned, has its inverted counterpart: permutation of the same predicate among different subjects. Thus at Silling the four libertines conduct marriage ceremonies, marrying their daughters, their buggerers, and their little boys in turn and then forcing them to marry one another. And so the predicate "marriage" finds itself disrupted by this operation, as the predicate "sexual identity" does by another permutation:

> The quatrains that evening featured certain sexual changes: that is to say, all the girls were costumed as sailors, the little boys as tarts; the effect was ravishing, nothing quickens lust like this voluptuous little reversal; adorable to find in a little boy what causes him to resemble a girl, and the girl is far more interesting when for the sake of pleasing she borrows the sex one would like her to have.[54]

Perhaps nothing in this methodological technique of permutation can equal the nuptials planned by Noirceuil after his reunion with Juliette:

> It is a most extraordinary caprice I have been dwelling upon for a very long time, Juliette, and I have been awaiting your return with impatience, having in all the world nobody but you with whom I could satisfy it. I should like to marry... I should like to get married, not once, but twice, and upon the same day: at ten o'clock in the morning, I wish, dressed as a woman, to wed a man; at noon, wearing masculine attire, I wish to take a bardash for my wife. There is still more... I wish to have a woman do the same as I; and what other woman but you could participate in this fantasy? You, dressed as a man, must wed a tribade at the same ceremony at which I, guised as a woman, become the wife of a man; next, dressed as a woman, you will wed another tribade wearing masculine clothing, at the very moment I, having resumed my ordinary attire, go to the altar to become united in holy matrimony with a catamite disguised as a girl.[55]

Noirceuil, while acknowledging that he is only imitating an inspiration of Nero's, says that he is adding two novelties of his own invention: the double wedding on the same day and the whim of seeing himself imitated by Juliette, but especially his choice of brides and grooms: his grooms will be his two sons, and Juliette's brides will be her daughter and her pupil.

Everything is constructed so that no permutation will correspond to any norm. All the unions are *homosexual*; no heterosexual unions are proposed, not even under cover of transvestism. Noirceuil marries only men, and Juliette marries only women.

All the unions are also *incestuous*: in these nuptials, father is joined to son, and mother to daughter (Juliette's pupil clearly assumes for her the status of a daughter). As a result, when Noirceuil and Juliette regain their "normal" sex at the time of the second wedding ceremony, this normality vanishes in the union with a spouse in drag. The unstoppable effect of this system of permutations is necessarily a chiasmus in all the relationships, their automatic placement into a position of deregulation, of breakdown.

Saturation does not mean the attainment of every logically possible relationship but only of those that belong to the logic of transgression and involve some assault on institutionalized laws of exchange. Thus Juliette and Noirceuil must not marry each other, even in drag, for the liaison would still be encompassed by heterosexual normality. The limits of saturation, then, are defined by the need to stay within the domain of perversion. In other words, it is important to *saturate* perversion.

These nuptials of Noirceuil's take combinative reduction to a kind of logical perfection. Regardless of the game's appeal, however, we must understand its stakes. Its critical impact is considerable (not until Fourier will we again see its equivalent): by placing each "passion" (perversion, vice, whim) within the realm of the *list,* and by asserting each as legitimate and attainable, Sade destroys the paradigmatic limits and, along with them, the split values that prohibition allocates to the two sides of the binary terms *normal/abnormal, vice/virtue,* and *positive/negative.* The combinative operation demolishes this boundary and, with its modulations and metonymic outgrowths, endlessly enlarges the field of possibilities. If, like any other system, this operation has its formal limits, they belong not to the order of law (that is, to some external, imposed abutment) but to the order of saturation, the order of language and sexual pleasure, which comes to a stop when "everything has been said," and when sexual pleasure has been consummated.

In this de-normed, de-hierarchized realm, we no longer have perversion, strictly speaking, which is a concept necessarily derived from the *normal/abnormal* cleavage. What Sade is calling most profoundly into question is the notion that desire needs somehow to be taken in hand: all its forms, even the most extravagant, are legitimate and attainable. (What this comes down to, of course, is a preemptive dismissal of the analytical cure from which an obstinate orthopedism, even in its most liberal forms, takes its bearings. No matter how the analytical cure redefines the limits of normality, it can maintain them only if it denies the legitimacy of the cure itself. It is impossible, as we know, to be a psychoanalyst of any standing and still "stand" Sade — or Fourier, for that matter.)

But the consummate mischief worked by this recourse to mechanisms and combinative process is that those practices considered to be normal are not even rejected. To reject them would be to set them up in turn as prohibitions, and this would be merely a reversal of the terms, an exchange of negative for positive, and vice versa. To give an acknowledged practice, an accepted passion, the status of being just one term among others would be to push irony to the point where normality becomes a specific perversion. Thus the pitfall of a new cleavage is skirted, and because there are no more referential norms, the deviance itself is asserted as having come first—asserted as initial and not as innate, which is to say that in this system all entries are valid, all beginnings are possible, all terms are equal, for deviations are measured only against one another, not with reference to some center. This beginning, plural from the outset, is also the ruin of law. In its own way, the Sadean combinative signals the end of the binary era.

The Good-for-Nothing Subject

The indifference of psychoanalysis to Sade's texts, or its irritation with them (perceptible even on the part of Lacan in *Kant avec Sade*), probably results from the fact that these texts imply the absence of the principal justification and concern of psychoanalysis: the subject. Sade is suspected of unloading the subject rather too quickly. In Sade's writings the subject does not even have time to be split: with the elimination of the hypothesis of subjectivity, the subject is "disappeared" beforehand, conjured away right from the start, by the operation that reduces the individual to his mechanical status as a machine made for thinking and coming ("a head and balls," as Sade bluntly puts it), the head in no way a substitute for the cogito but simply the instrument, within the overall system, whose basic double function—speaking and imagining—allows the effects of nervous sensitivity to be amplified, refined, and multiplied.

This deficit of the subject is disturbing to us because the Sadean text stages the subject's sexual pleasure, and therefore its conflictive relationship to law. For us the subject is the exact site where the contradiction takes shape between desire, on the one hand, and sociohistorical and signifying activity, on the other. The subject is what inscribes the heterogeneity of the drive into the process of objectivity, and the drive always appears as the remainder of this process, its unintegrable fallout.

It is always the "missing person" of the product of signifying practices, and yet its relentless absence opens up meaning itself.

As soon as Sade perceives this contradiction, he seems to elude and resolve it by suppressing one of its poles. He makes the drives pass through the symbolic — on condition, naturally, of perverting the symbolic itself, shaking it up by imagining an *institutionalized* perversion, staging a countersociety with no laws other than those of libertine desire. If this law demands the overthrow of whole nations, of the world itself and even of nature, it is because heterogeneity can come only from the *outside,* can itself be produced only as a movement of objectivity — not as the sign of a contradiction marking the unascribable place of the subject but as the plan for a destruction that will be brought about in an outside that is modeled on desire.

This is why the frenzy of the drives must always appear to be socially systematized, institutionally encoded. In the most extravagant erotic and criminal orgies, this is always what the enunciation of programs and the declaration of rules are working toward, as if their function were to hold off the slide into uncontrolled delirium. The libertine knows no conflict, in the realm that he dominates, between desire and law. But this is precisely why he has had to establish himself as Master: *heterogeneity can be brought about only at his decree,* but at the price of another contradiction, the one between libertine and victim; the only way to escape from the first contradiction is to fall into the second. Libertine transgression, once it has formed the intention of becoming institutionalized, reproduces, if in a displaced way, the logic of power relationships (hierarchy, repression, exploitation). If we find Sade's approach outrageous and unacceptable, however, it is because since Sade's day we have discovered more flexible ways, not to mention more devious ones, of accounting for the heterogeneity in our codes. We can conceive of the articulation of sameness and otherness within the single field of the subject. We can stand the irruption of outside into inside without running the immediate risk of taking it as a sign of madness (taking it, that is, as the manifestation of an incommunicable, strictly individual code).

Things were not so simple for Sade. He had to work within the theoretical domain of the classical subject: the subject of the cogito, and the subject of law. Its rational consistency and its knowledge of itself as spiritual substance were directly structured on its juridical and social status, and they defined the threshold of normality, beyond which only animality or madness was possible. The division was radical, the line impassable, and Sade had to make do with an either/or proposition. He could stay in the domain of the classical subject, which he had inherited, like everyone else, and take the consequences (mainly moral and theological, such as immortality, virtue, kind sentiments, negation of the body, submission to society, and so on), or he could uncompromisingly do away with it at one blow, pit the primacy of matter against the subject, and oppose the subject to the body's sufficiency, its sexual pleasure, and its revolt — a mechanical soulless body, and happy to be one. Subjectivity was laid waste, utterly flattened, by the body's anatomical and physiological nakedness. Now sexual pleasure was a function of organic excitement and nothing more, with the multiplicity of its repetitions compensating for the overthrown emotive depth. This was quite a gamble, tantamount to taking a leap beyond the theoretical and social realm of reason. And Sade, without openly mentioning the stakes, had weighed them quite accurately: either this act of his would be thought mad or he would extricate himself from this slippery slope by reproducing the very conventions of normality, but turned inside out. There would be no lack of rigor in this discourse, which extolled what every other discourse wished to avoid. We see, then, that in order for heterogeneity (unthinkable within the order of the subject) to be granted recognizable status and articulated in the theoretical realm of classical reason, what was needed was nothing short of an outrageous countersociety (but a society nevertheless, with its own order, rules, and laws).

The subject of the cogito, intangible, solidly entrenched in its position, offered no hold that might allow its foundations to be shaken or its ramparts to be cracked. The only possible strategy was to go around it, pass it by, leave it behind, and thus bring into being — outside the subject, as the subject's "wrong side" — the very thing whose negation marks out and guarantees the subject's position. And so the countersociety is populated by good-for-nothing subjects, antisubjects: suffering and pleasured bodies for which the soul and its stakes are no more. These mechanical bodies go so far as to denounce and defy every human law, standing instead on the authority of animal reality and laying claim to unvarnished nature, with its innocence, cruelty, and irresponsibility, as the ultimate designation of subjectivity's dismissal.

We can say, then, that the radical nature of Sade's choice (*for* the mechanical body, *for* the whisking away of the subject) was imposed on him by the specific blocks that made up the domain of classical assumptions, blocks that had the look of a challenge if not of blackmail (either/ or else). Sade took up the challenge and attempted the all but impossible feat of thinking through the implications of the "wrong" side by exploiting the categories of the "right" side. Surely this is what accounts for an obvious dichotomy in Sade's writing, a new dualism that might be as disturbing as the old one were it not for the fact that the break is so clean — and here we see a tremendous change from the labored compromises of Sade's precursors (Diderot and Holbach, to say nothing of Voltaire), who were forever tacking between deism and atheism, between apologias for bourgeois virtue and denunciations of Christian morality.

Sade's narrative translation of this movement is the discrete presentation of each of the contradiction's two sides: as *Justine,* or the claim to still be a virtuous, guilty, obedient theological subject, and as *Juliette,* or the assertion of the body's freedom, its sexual pleasure, its animal selfishness, and its revolt. We really ought to write these two names as one, *J(ustine/uliette),* inscribing the contradiction right into the onomastic signifier and acknowledging its dichotomized, nondialectical resolution.

The two of them together would make one good subject (*Julienne?*)[56] — vice and virtue, cruelty and tenderness, cynicism and remorse — but that would bring us right back to the hysterical turnstile of perverse guilt and shameless virtue. It would mean the same old contradiction that creates tragic beauty. It would mean a tormented soul and a split subjectivity. In other words, it would be both Greek and Christian — a rich lode, this one, where the manufacturing plant of Romanticism would lose no time in setting up shop.

At least Sade, meanwhile, would have clarified the stakes, and if his dichotomism is troubling, it is first of all because it takes the conceptual familiarities around which our fantasies of the body have coalesced and rubs them the wrong way. Moreover, this "same old contradiction" is not unrelated to neurosis, which for Freud is precisely defined by the setting before desire of two irreconcilable objects, one of which necessarily nullifies the other; thus the recourse to denial, in order to have both: saying yes in no, and no in yes. This is what the libertine is spared from the start in that his choice is immediately fixed and definitive. His goal, his plan — "to say everything" — is also the requirement that the analyst establishes for treatment (Freud: *alles sagen*). But if the patient-analysand is just beginning to stammer out a few words, the libertine has already brought everything into discourse. This good-for-nothing subject has a lightweight unconscious. Freud assumes that the unconscious takes shape from an "original repression," through which a narrow gap (*Spaltung*) opens within the psychic system, marking out the zone of subjectivity and imposing upon speech a long birth within the narrow passes of the symbolic as it traverses the realm of the imaginary. If so, then we have to assume an "original *liberation*" for the libertine, which at once opens up the possibility of speaking, in an unqualified act of *saying everything* that participates in the violence of obscenity and is its paradoxical law: the gamble of deploying the forbidden throughout the network of discourse. Analysis interminable on the one hand, but immediately terminated on the other. The libertine's point of departure — symbolic mastery — is for the analysand the result of a long quest, of the patient and painful disentangling of his desire's confused, knotted-up threads. In other words, Sade assumes that the problem will be solved (and nothing prevents his solving it in the realm of fiction) on the simple condition of doing away with the realm of the imaginary and annulling time (or at least short-circuiting it). Just at the point where the neurotic's story ends, the good-for-nothing subject's activity begins. Born with and within discourse, he is not required to crawl. He has no memory and no past (the Sadean character never has a childhood). Everything moves quickly for him right from the start: he is born an adult, with no prejudices, no guilt, no Oedipus complex, and no superego. He seems flat and insubstantial to us, with our expectations of historical and psychological depth. But at least he forces us to confront the question of what presuppositions cause us even to *want* depth. How is it that depth was made a positive value? By whom? In whose interest?

The Body Beyond All Telling

Meaninglessness

If, as already suggested, an intrinsic relationship really does exist between the body's textual mode of being and the narrative system that produces it, then the body proper to novelistic narration (which is only one narrative mode among many others) is presumably the body as broadcaster of signs, the *expressive body*. Traditionally, the writer amasses collections of signs on the bodies of characters, but also on the bodies of things and places, and through these signs is able to arrange a network of clues laying out a mystery to entice the reader's desire, the desire to read now joined to the desire for knowledge in the pleasurable tension of coming closer and closer to solving that mystery.

This is why it is important both to scramble the signs — to make them ambiguous and indeterminate, whether through multiplication or overdetermination — and to put them in their places; and now the character's quest is doomed to become an exercise in interpretation. What novelistic narration produces first of all is a hermeneutics, and the degree of its complexity determines how fascinating the mystery will be. The excess of signs is as much decoy as clue. This ambivalence determines the ignorance of the characters, just as it determines the ignorance of the reader (and in the text, the ignorance of the characters represents the ignorance of the reader, just as the writer, who determines meaning and meaninglessness, occupies the place of the Master).

But the important thing to be noted here is how the narrated body is the medium par excellence of clues and signs. The semaphoring, broadcasting, interchanging, catalyzing body is the permanent, indispensable relay station of diegesis because it organizes novelistic space, the very possibility of novelistic space. The network of bodily signals making up the story's clues — for example, facial expressions (indifference, surprise, joy, embarrassment, disappointment, suspicion, complicity) or expressions of the hands (nervousness, mastery, impotence) — determines the order of the actions or reveals some aspect of the mystery. In other words, it defines situations and relationships among the characters and their reactions, and it confirms or nullifies other signs, words, and so on.

All novelistic writing begins in the fashioning of semaphoric language from narrated bodies and in the production of orderly transformations within this machinery of signs. Sade, throwing his lot in with the impassive, nonsignifying body, dispenses with the whole system of hermeneutical narrative; he dries it up at the source. The body, once presented, at the outset, as a rough sketch of general features, a sketch serving only to classify it into some known morphological and social category, is no longer a broadcaster of signs. According to its classification, it now acts (or is acted) and speaks (or is spoken) but expresses nothing. Right away, we know everything there is to know about it. (And if the narrator really does occupy the place of the Master, then it follows that Sade invites the reader to share in Mastery.)

The "program" determines the narrative. Programming is the opposite of interpreting. It means determining diegesis through a plan of action in which roles have already been assigned. No surprises: we have either victims or torturers, either the pious or the libertines. To the victims and the pious fall the misfortunes of virtue; to the torturers and the libertines, the prosperities of vice.

Everything is on the table: the result is known beforehand, set forth at the beginning, before there is any future. What counts is not discovery but renewal of the initial evidence, its indefinite repetition. If to be a libertine is always already to know, then to narrate is to make an inventory of the known world, to verify that it is exactly as one has defined it. The narrative's driving force, then, is not to be found in the ambivalence of the signs emitted by the body and giving shape to the mystery, but rather in the need to bring the body into contact with continents, societies, and locales where the thesis proposed at the beginning is seen to be confirmed. The function of the narrative is to detail the full justification of this thesis and stamp it with the seal and grain of the letter, in order finally to vouch, through this evidence of reality, for the truth of the knowledge that utters it.

To interpret, by contrast, is already to be a victim. Not only does it mean proving that one does not know and is out of the game, it also necessarily means misreading the signs, misperceiving their function as decoys, being unaware that they are, theoretically, conventional and hypocritical. They exist only to be ignored; they are empty. Their function is one of sheer vicariance: they are there only to "stand for"—morality, order, values.[57] Thus they separate the naïf, who believes in the signs and obeys them, from the sophisticate, who turns them to his own use and flouts them. And Justine, the very model of naïveté, takes the bait every time. She reads goodness, piety, honesty, or gratitude into faces and bodies, only to discover in the end that none of it has meant anything at all, that it has actually concealed just the opposite: cruelty, libertinism, trickery, selfishness—truly "upsetting," this overturning of the signs.

Thus we recognize the victim first of all as one who takes the decoy of social conventions for the language of truth, playing at hermeneutics and reading into bodies the signs of the soul and its values, whereas in fact there are only concealments of the body and its logic. The function of these signs, rather than being expressive (as any "proper" sign's function would be), is purely strategic. Instead of being appearances that translate realities, they constitute the perfunctory arrangement of a *veil* of appearances, the mocking tribute paid to the established order, because the structure of these signs is not one of reference but one of disjunction (naïveté versus sophistication, piety versus libertinism). This is more than a redirection of meaning. This is a breakdown of meaning, its disintegration.

Because she understands that heaven and signs are being emptied out in tandem, Justine clings to signs so as not to lose heaven. The greater the emptiness, and the clearer it is that nothing *means* anything, the more she sets her will to demanding explanations, using them to replenish the phantom signs and stanch this hemorrhage of meaning, wishing to know nothing about this explosion of meaninglessness, maintaining at all costs her unconsciousness of the continuous contradiction that this event imposes on her — a useful unconsciousness, one that sustains her neurotic consistency and feeds the pleasure she takes in denial. (And perhaps this pleasure, by nature a thwarted one — so close, in other words, to the pleasure that is normally our own — is what makes Justine's obstinate delight in being deluded seem more pathetic than pitiful, more moving than contemptible, the more so for being so unflappably maintained in all its awful logic.) Juliette, by contrast, gets it right the first time. She takes bodies literally, to the letter of their desire and their functions. She immediately classifies and arranges, organizing the action — the *réunion intime* — on the basis of the inventoried, chosen bodies. From them she extracts everything that can be physically extracted: not expressions or feelings, but caresses, semen, blows, secretions, cries — in a word, pleasure. The successful functioning of the bodies' mechanical systems is directly proportional to the elimination of the interplay of signs, and therefore directly proportional to the elimination of the principle of subjectivity that signs imply.

A novelistic narrative authority — confronted with this disaffected, nonsignifying body, no longer able to rely on it for conveying clues and expressions, and thus dispossessed of this shuttle for weaving the text — is forced into distortions and highly unorthodox restructurings, obliged to compose from models (fable, tale, myth, epic) that are not specifically novelistic. Surely this is the source of the discomfort that so many commentators have noted in connection with the Sadean novel, that hybrid irritant, which retains nothing of novelistic form except the novel's general framework, only to imbue it with modes of narrativity that apparently have nothing to do with any known or recognized form of the novel. One notable and serious deficiency of the Sadean novel (and now we understand why) is its psychological dimension, on whose quality, complexity, and "refinement" literary Last Judgments have been pronounced. It is not difficult to sense how this deficiency will impose a painful renunciation on the traditional reader, the relinquishing of what has been a customary payoff and essential benefit of reading: imaginary identification.

Nakedness

At the narrative level of the signified, the operation that most closely expresses the textual work of discrediting the order of signs is probably the undressing of bodies during an orgy. Thus Juliette, as early as her initiation into libertinism at the convent of Panthemont, hears herself greeted as follows by her instructress, the libertine abbess Madame Delbène:

> Do you blush, little angel? But I forbid you to blush! Modesty is an
> illusion — resulting from what? 'tis the result of nought but our cultural
> manners and our upbringing, it is what is known as a conventional
> habit. Nature having created man and woman naked, it is unthinkable
> that she could have implanted in them an aversion or a shame thus to
> appear.... But we'll chat about that later on. Let's speak of other matters
> for the nonce. Will you *join us in our undress?*[58]

The theoretical distinction is drawn from the very beginning: on the one hand, the expressive order of signs ("Do you blush ... ?"), identified with the Christian moral order (the virtue of modesty); on the other, the nonsignifying regime of the body (nakedness), proposed as the truth of nature. (For Sade, as we have seen, the concept of nature always has a strategic and polemical function, not a metaphysical one: it constitutes the evidentiary argument that leaves one's adversary speechless, with no way out. Therefore, within the conceptual limits of the era, it was first of all the best tool for the dissection of "prejudices.")

What should also be noted is that the undressing has to be *immediate*. In direct address, this need is indicated by the use of the imperative ("Strip!"), and in third-person narration by the transcription of an order that has been given. There are many examples; thus, in the underground passages of the convent of Panthemont, where Juliette is confronted by two clergymen: "*Therewith* Delbène *orders* Volmar to *undress* me."⁵⁹ Permanent nakedness even has its own article in the rules of the Sodality of the Friends of Crime:

> 12. During those hours devoted to corporative frolicking, all Members, male and female, are *naked*; they intermingle, in the melee partners are chosen indiscriminately, and there is no such thing as a valid refusal whereby one individual would deny his pleasure to another.⁶⁰

Here is how Juliette is greeted at the party given upon her acceptance into the Sodality:

> The Président bade me step up and stand on the dais opposite her; and there, a balustrade separating me from the very numerous company, *I was upon her instructions divested of all my raiments* by two servants who in *less time than it takes to tell* had off every stitch I was wearing.⁶¹

During her travels in Italy, Juliette constantly hears the order to nakedness (Minski, the ogre of the Apennines: "Strip naked!"). Let us note in passing that the first connotation of the imperative form, or of the indication of an order, is the inscription of desire into mastery. Even when bodies give their consent, the order remains peremptory, as if it were being used to ward off the age-old threat that spoils libertine desire: the opposition put up by the other, or the uncertainty in which the other allows his answer to linger (which leads to the need for pursuit, expectation, and subterfuge, with the risk of failure in spite of everything). The imperative marks the body's having become available of necessity, its obligation to remain permanently available, and its loss of access to defenses, to any possibility of retreat: it marks the naked body stripped bare.

The body stripped bare is no longer anything but what it offers to the eyes, nothing but that thing for which it is stripped bare: a system of sexualized functions at the disposal of sexual pleasure. The elimination of clothing says to the body, You are there only for my pleasure, and only in this respect do you exist. Consider the descriptions that usually follow a disrobing: the eye moves immediately to what interests it in a sexual sense, to what will functionally serve it. This libertine eye, rather in the manner of a skilled, hurried butcher, carves up the prime cuts, paying no attention to the offal, and the result is a kind of trunk-body, like the ruin of an ancient statue: head, chest, rump, sex organs. Nothing is said about the locomotor limbs, the arms, legs, feet, hands. Indeed, to invest any desire in them at all one would need those partic-ular fetishes (and the libertine, as we have seen, has no interest in the ersatz once he has unobstructed access to "the real thing"). A classic portrait:

> Alexandrine was of an extraordinary and eminently regular beauty; she could boast of a sublime bust, the prettiest details distinguished her form, her skin was glowing clear, her flesh firm, there was grace and ripeness in her limbs, heaven shone in her face.[62]

And another:

> Never, no, never had I seen forms so deliciously rounded, an ensemble so voluptuous, nor details so compelling; nothing so narrow as her sweet little cunt, nothing so chubby as her dear little ass, nothing so pert, so fresh, so winningly shaped as her breasts; and fully aware of what it is I am saying, and stating it as a cold fact, I do now assure you that Aglaia was the divinest creature with whom up until that time I had ever had anything carnal to do.[63]

Note the use of "never had I seen" and "nothing so" to indicate an extreme degree or quality (*"never had I seen*...an ensemble so volup-tuous," "*nothing so* narrow as her sweet little cunt," "*nothing so* chubby as her dear little ass"), as well as the highly abstract character of the de-scription ("forms so deliciously rounded," "grace and ripeness in her limbs"), against which background the only *named* parts of the body stand out: those that are quite obviously sexual ("skin," "bust," "cunt," "ass"). This is the way the desirable, available body is written.

In the *immediacy* of the undressing, moreover, is the collapse of some-thing essential to the traditional economy of the narrative, namely, the narrative motif that is valued above all others: *sex as a mystery*. Sex, as the goal of the quest—its inadmissible goal—can be indicated only obliquely. As long as this goal is blocked, as long as the path that leads to it is an obstacle course, what we have in narrative is a long subterfuge, a game of twists and turns, a work of cunning and deciphering. And when at long last the goal of sex is reached (or even if the goal is missed), its name is usually concealed by another word or another goal. The mys-tery of sex calls on narrative to fill and reduce the gap between desire and its goal—to tame, little by little, the dread of admitting this goal by weaving the textual fabric in which it will be set forth. And here, with the impossibility of naming the unnameable, it can be seen clearly enough how the whole question of castration comes into play: How name an object that can be experienced only through its loss?

What Sade gives himself the fairly intrepid luxury of abandoning is this peerless narrative argument: sex as a mystery. Sex is practically the only theme of his narratives, but it is sex in a wholly explicit mode. From the very beginning, the mystery—and, with it, metaphorical production—can only unravel, for to name sex literally is to be obscene. If the question is no longer the inaccessibility of sex (because sex is presented right away, and because the body is immediately stripped bare), how will narratives be constructed, and how will time be leveraged to the quest?

It is the very principle of the quest that is being turned on its head. What is sought is no longer the uniqueness of one body via the legitimacy of amorous feeling, but rather the multiplicity of bodies via the necessity of a drive. To be more precise, bodies are a given for the libertine master, and so the important thing is to multiply their variety, feel their differences, try them out as machines made of flesh. The principal verbs describing the libertine's activity are *vary, combine, remove,* and *resume.* What gives the story its authority can no longer be mystery, but rather the need to inventory. Right from the start, things happen after the fact; everything is already given, and so the task becomes verification. We already know the body's possibilities, which if multiple can still be listed (stripping, caressing, flagellating, erecting, penetrating, coming, molesting, mutilating, eating, defecating, and so on). *The 120 Days of Sodom* explicitly takes on the task of classifying and itemizing every imaginable variation on these basic "passions." Thus narrative time is no longer propelled by the amassing of signs and the gradual unveiling of the mystery, but rather by the necessity of carrying out the plan for "covering" bodies.[64] Ultimately, the narrative serves merely as an expedient for this exposition, as the simplest means for linearizing the classifications by setting them in motion within the lived plausibility of the story. We can say, then, not only that the stripped-down body (classified and functional) is emblematic of the mechanized, inexpressive body shaped by the work of the text but also that it is emblematic of the very form of Sadean narrative. This dexterous, immediate undressing—*Blitzentkleidung*—imitates, at the level of the signified body, the narrative principle that orders the novel. This is how Barthes analyzes it: "In Sade, no striptease. . . . Here, perhaps, is the reason. The striptease is a narrative: it develops in time the terms ('classemes') of a code which is that of the Enigma. . . . Now, in Sade there is no bodily secret to seek, but only a practice to achieve."[65]

The Sadean body: words cannot describe it.

Body/Text

> Suspect me neither of enthusiasm nor of metaphor.
>
> *— Juliette*

A hypothesis — that every mode of bodily presentation *in* a text determines a mode of "embodiment" *of* that text — has been envisaged here on the basis of Sadean narrative, not because it would have been impossible to establish the same hypothesis, and just as easily, on the basis of any number of other narratives, but because Sadean narrative, which functions as a *systematized reversal* of these other narratives, offers the advantage of forcing us to consider this very issue. If we say that the text — in its own structures, at the level of the signifier — imitates, at the level of the signified, what it proposes about the body, then we are assuming much more than a simple homological complicity. We are proposing that a signifying constraint exists between the two planes, a constraint articulated in the very operation of writing as anaphoric production. The represented body returns, in the form that represents it, as a displaced signifier. It metonymizes the text; the textual body *realizes* the signified body.

This proposition can be further confirmed by way of two more theses: first, that the symptomless body finds its correspondence in an underdetermined text; and, second, that the classified, divided-up body finds its correspondence in a discontinuous, broken-up narrative. The second of these two points will be elaborated later on, in connection with the question of time. For now, let us see where the first point takes us.

An Underdetermined Text

It is because the body has nothing to say that it is removed from the realm of expression, confined to the realm of action, its articulative function completely reduced to discursive statement. Here is the famous quasi-automatic alternation between scene and dissertation, which appears to be a result of oversimplified (if not utterly weak) narrativity but for which there is a logical need, given the body's impassivity. "Saying everything" is too important to be entrusted to epidermal reactions; hence the disjunctive relationship between speeches and skin. The more silent the skin is, the more the head controls its own statements. Nakedness connotes the silence of the body (the silence of nature, of animals). The more the body sheds, the more it renounces expression and invites the "head" to hold forth. Inversely, the more the body talks (as in the case of a victim), the less the head functions. Thus it is almost always in nakedness, in the middle of an orgy, that the libertines develop their grand disquisitions. The naked body is both testament to and practice of pure materiality, the theory of which is formulated by the head.

Is the head taking over here from the Cartesian cogito? Is this a sly embodiment of the Christian soul? Are we dealing with a simple displacement, a dressed-up dualism? At first glance, it is tempting to think so and to say that the Sadean "subject," like the "subject" of science, is removed from its own propositions. But that would underestimate the complexity of this operation, for the head also functions as a material instrument within the machine. It is at once filter and catalyzer, energy source and control center. To be a libertine body is a libertine theoretical possibility that is fulfilled only in the discourse that proposes it. This is why it falls to the head to purge, organize, set things in motion. The Sadean body, connected to an impassioned talking head, must remain mute and impassive. The skin's nonsignificance is proportional to the supersignificance of the head, and so all meaning must pass into discourse, all latency must be brought into manifestation — an inordinate, masterly ambition. In the realm of expression, latency — the product of original repression, closed off from the symbolic — returns in the body, in the form of the symptom, and displays its primary complicity with the workings of metaphor. This is the language of victimhood.

For Sade, by contrast, there can be no latency in the libertine body, because the body is theoretically caught up in an act of "saying everything," an act that liberates and exhibits the whole of desire. What this principle of exhibition requires is the provocative utterance of every fantasy, leaving no opening for retreat into the inexplicit. Everything can be named and denumerated because the infinity of desire is proposed as numerical infinity. If there is nothing that cannot be said, then there is no room for symptoms or, generally speaking, for substitution formations. The skin of the text, like the body's, does not tremble with emotion, commit Freudian slips, or contain hidden meanings. In other words, the underdetermined, unfeeling text of libertine (Sadean) narrative can be made to stand against the overdetermined, symptom-laden text of psychological narrative — but only, it must be noted, at the price of a massive foreclosure of subjectivity in the subject of sexual pleasure, a foreclosure seen in the disjunction between head and skin, or in the confrontation between torturer and victim. And this *is* the price, admittedly; but our question falls outside the gravitational pull of this reality and is simply this: What kind of text does this give us, and what displacements does it produce?

Indeed, it is as if the inexpressive model of the body were elaborating, as the articulated body of fiction, the very form of the writing that produces this model; as if the aim of wresting the body away from any kind of mystery, retreat, or prohibition were forcing the writing itself to operate without tricks or disguises, beyond any allusive or paraphrastic technique — in other words, beyond metaphor. The unfeelingness of Sade's writing is regulated by the inexpressiveness of the libertine body.

To be sure, the sparseness and cool blankness of this writing originated with the readability of the literary code then in force; the writing borrowed that code's refined elegance. With respect to sex, excrement, sexual pleasure, and crime, however — "things" for which this code had set up a whole recognized network of rhetorical figures forming a system of evasion — the writing lets the body be seen in a provocative nakedness to which the undressed skin is merely a pointer, for what dresses the skin is not so much articles of clothing as figures of discourse, or the parameters of codes. Obscenity, then, is what springs up from the suppression of the metaphorical.[66]

CHAPTER TWO

Saying Everything, or the Encyclopedia of Excess

Philosophy must never shrink from speaking out.
— *Juliette*

If we have not said everything, analyzed everything, tax us not with partiality, for you cannot expect us to have guessed what suits you best.
— *The 120 Days of Sodom*

Violence bears within itself this dishevelled denial, putting an end to any possibility of speech.
—GEORGES BATAILLE, *Death and Sensuality*

Everything and Too Much

"To say everything": this was the objective, apparently limitless and boldly announced, that Sadean discourse set for itself, and by which it intended to be defined. It is a disarmingly simple objective. And yet, if we look closely, we see that none could be more paradoxical. In fact, two contradictory connotations are wrapped up in this objective.

The first connotation is that of *totality*. To "say everything" means to undertake the encyclopedic project of surveying signifieds, collecting data, and accumulating arguments. From this standpoint, then, to "say everything" would be the exhausting, monumental task of literally saying *everything*, already an act of Hegelian ambition.

The second connotation is that of *excess*. Here, saying "everything" means the requirement to hide nothing, uncover everything, in the sense of the intention (or threat) to "tell all," or it means the kind of collusion observed between a Sadean character and his interlocutors when the character proposes to tell them the tale of his crimes: "I feel I can tell you everything." Here, the objective is breaking and entering, doing away with censorship, bringing the repressed to light. To "say everything" is the Freudian objective in its most literal sense: the fundamental principle of psychoanalysis as a technique for recognizing and acknowledging desire.

For Sade, then, to "say everything" was to call for totality and excess at the same time. And this is precisely the gauntlet that Sade threw down, for discourse has always been enjoined to choose between the two terms. Calling for both at once is perhaps what constitutes the basic logical impasse of *saying*, its fundamental aporia, inasmuch as the discourse of totality cannot take shape unless it shuts its eyes to the prohibition that makes closure possible and averts the possibility that anything will be left over. *Tout*, everything, is maintained only through the banishment of what is *trop*, too much. To confront and transgress this prohibition is the very impulse of excess, the impulse that topples dividing walls, blurs boundaries, and makes totality of any kind impossible, a joke.

Totality and excess: an either/or proposition. Normally, both claims cannot be honored at once without the risk of complete discursive paralysis, or at least of stammering. One cannot, in one and the same discourse, stand on both sides of the prohibition at the same time.

But this very aporia is just what Sadean discourse intended to sustain by bringing about what can be called an *encyclopedia of excesses*, combining the two contradictory connotations in a game of discrepancy, a constant shifting between theory and narrative, between dissertation and scene, foiling the logical constraint of *either/or*. This strategy — evading the form of treatise and narrative alike, using the one form to pervert the other, producing this strange theoretical-narrative hybrid — is one to which we will have reason to return.

The encyclopedic survey was a passion of the eighteenth century, which saw a proliferation of dictionaries — dictionaries of ideas, languages, civilizations, the arts, techniques. Nor were scholars and specialists the only ones who collaborated on these works: so did most of the well-known writers and philosophers of the age, among them Voltaire, Diderot, Holbach, Rousseau, and others.

To this list of dictionaries Sade added one more, a dictionary of the most deranged and reprehensible kind: a dictionary of "perversions." But this one made no claim to a dictionary's title or form, and it barely maintained even the dictionary's structure. This was a parodic dictionary, caught up in the fabric of narrative and carried away by a fiction that stripped it of any false "scientific" guarantees, all the better to point up what it did bring into play: not knowledge but desire, or desire within knowledge.

Of all Sade's works, of course, the one that best illustrates this undertaking is *The 120 Days of Sodom*. Sade himself states the two organizing principles of the text: the production of a list of the "passions," in which every reader can find those of his choice, and the integration of this list into a narrative that analyzes each term in the context of a situation, in the setting of a schema for a particular passion's realization. As far as the list is concerned, Sade tells the reader:

> Many of the extravagances you are about to see illustrated will doubtless displease you, yes, I am well aware of it, but there are amongst them a few which will warm you to the point of costing you some come, and that, reader, is all we ask of you; if we have not said everything, analyzed everything, tax us not with partiality, for you cannot expect us to have guessed what suits you best. Rather, it is up to you to take what you please and leave the rest alone, another reader will do the same, and little by little, everyone will find himself satisfied.[1]

As for the narrative:

> We have, moreover, blended these six hundred passions into the storytellers' narratives. That is one more thing whereof the reader were well to have foreknowledge; it would have been too monotonous to catalogue them one by one outside the body of the story. But as some reader not much learned in these matters might perhaps confuse the designated passions with the adventure or simple event in the narrator's life, each of these passions has been carefully distinguished by a marginal notation: a line, above which is the title that may be given the passion. This mark indicates the exact place where the account of the passions begins, and the end of the paragraph always indicates where it finishes.[2]

The pains taken to preserve the utility and skeletal structure of a dictionary underneath the "body" of the narrative go so far as to incorporate a fastidious didacticism, as well as instructions for how the work should be used:

But as numerous personages participate in a drama of this kind, notwithstanding the care we have taken in this introduction to describe and designate each one... we shall provide an index which will contain the name and age of every actor, together with a brief sketch of them all; so that should the reader, as he moves along, encounter what seems to him an unfamiliar figure, he will have merely to turn back to this index, and if this little aid to his memory suffice not, to the more thorough portraits given earlier.[3]

There follows a description of the characters, in the form of a data sheet listing their basic traits (age, social status, general physical type, sexual preferences, specific interests, and so on).

What is sought in this synoptic presentation — as in the meticulous typographical layout, with its marginal notations and use of indentation — is the flexibility of a dictionary. And because all the entries in a dictionary are reliable and self-contained, they can be read out of order. What matters most is always to know exactly where one is, and never to become confused about what means what. That is why it must always be possible to consult the "index." We know who is who, who is capable of what, who wants what, and so on. Everything is defined from the start, and nothing is so unimportant as to be left ambiguous.

But this unusual dictionary offers narratives instead of definitions, and, in place of an alphabetical method of classification, it proposes a logical one based on a gradation from the simple to the complex. This, then, is the simulacrum of a dictionary because all that remains of a dictionary is its blueprint, its formal design; the content is dispensed with.

The narrative is just as unusual, however ("a drama of this kind"), setting aside all suspense and laying its cards on the table from the beginning, confessing its own outline. And we certainly need to evaluate the paradox of a narrative that begins with an "introduction" to the characters and their goals and objectives. An introduction, after all, is a preamble more appropriate to an essay than to a narrative, for an introduction presents both the object and the methodology of a discourse. By contrast, the traditional stratagem of narrative has been to slip this kind of information between the lines, into the interstices of diegesis, or to graft it onto the narrative structure. This is basically what indices, informants, and descriptions are for. Information tends to be merged into and melded with the narrative element, until it is erased *as* information — that is, until it produces optimal "naturalization" of the narrative. Entry into the fictional world has to be immediate, and referential signs must be distributed so gradually along the narrative chain that their deployment becomes invisible. The "author" must withdraw from the narrative so as to give the "characters" all the benefit of reality.

These are a few elementary rules of the game that Sade flouts in *The 120 Days of Sodom*, replacing the artful relaying of implicit, oblique information with a didactic preamble that lays out the particulars all at once, or multiplying his direct remarks to the reader, pointing up the fictional nature of the text, and undermining any effect of illusionism:

> Thus, there resulted an arrangement which, for the reader's convenience, we shall recapitulate.[4]
>
> I leave to the reader to fancy...[5]
>
> ...do our best to portray one by one each of our four heroes...[6]

We know it all, all at once, and as readers we are taken in hand and invited to verify this information. It can be asked whether didactic authority (of the kind found in dictionaries, essays, and so on) might pose a threat of harm or even paralysis to narrative authority. But is it possible that Sade, paradoxically enough, inserted whole series of cryptic phrases (requests for the reader to wait, promises of future revelations) into the text of *The 120 Days* precisely because he was well aware of this danger? Such phrases, while allowing the preamble's overwhelming synchronism to be energetically diachronized, also permit the use of the time-honored hermeneutical ploy governing any suspense worthy of the name:

> But there is nothing to be gained by hurrying our story or by broaching subjects which can only receive adequate treatment in the sequel.[7]
>
> Durcet...was quietly perpetrating infamies the proper time has not come to disclose.[8]

This recourse to the hermeneutical theme of mystery is glaringly obvious, so much so that its handling is frankly indiscreet, quite removed from the deployment of the sign system that would be slipped subtly into diegesis in any conventionally well-made narrative montage. Here, the appeal to mystery is accompanied by the writer's striking projection of himself, in his use of the didactic "we" and his direct remarks to the reader. These requests for the reader to wait may derive less from narrative technique than from methodological imperative, and, far from having to come to the aid of a weak narrativity, they may belong wholly and clearly to the category of the treatise. The interpolated phrases distributed along the textual thread function less to bring about the revelation of some veiled mystery or truth than to scrupulously enforce the exposition's logical gradation as it has been arranged, and as it emerges from these other cryptic statements:

> We are in despair, for here we are once again forced by the design of our history to make a little detour: yes, we must for the time being omit describing those lubricious corrections, but our readers will not hold it against us; they appreciate our inability to give them complete satisfaction at the present moment; but they can be sure of it, their time will come.[9]

> We regret to say that the sequence we originally established for the treatment of our matter obliges us to postpone yet a little longer the pleasure the reader will doubtless take in learning the details of this religious ceremony; but the appropriate moment for disclosing them will surely arrive, and probably fairly soon.[10]

In fact, as the plan is being carried out — in keeping with the realm of exposition, which is a demonstrational realm, a realm of offering proofs — the information that was being withheld (rather than concealed) is disclosed: "The farther we advance, the more thoroughly we may inform the reader about certain facts we were obliged to no more than hint at in the earlier part of our story."[11] Dissertational authority and the dissertational model, like the tabular structure, persist strongly underneath this simulation of a cryptic code. This is both a dictionary and a narrative, and yet it is neither one nor the other: the "either/or" aporia is evaded in an alternating interplay between "both/and" and "neither/nor."

The dictionary, like the treatise, belongs to the realm of the serious, to the academic solemnity of science. A serious science of the "passions" can only be inscribed in the normative (in fact, moralizing) channel of metaphysical discourse. A list of perversions can only take the form of a toneless, pompous medical discourse. The dictionary in its classic form is clumsy, neutralizing, incapable of revealing the nuance that constitutes any one passion in all its specificity; it generalizes and defuses. But it has one advantage: it *names,* and since one of its functions is to list nouns and spell out their meanings, it has the unrestricted right to make inventories, even inventories of what can be classified as "indecent." It is completely acceptable to credit the compulsive, greedy appetite of science with perfect innocence: everything has to be explored and labeled. This is the dictionary's invaluable privilege, and this is what will be exploited.

Narrative, by contrast, particularizes "passion," giving it a very precise referent in which the marks of its specificity are staged. Traditionally, however, this staging does not *name*: it *suggests*. The more closely "passion" approaches the forbidden, the more metaphorical the narrative becomes. Hence the alternatives: the dictionary, with its right to name but its inability to particularize its object; or narrative, which does bring about this particularization, but at the price of being censored in the naming of its object.

Sade, by bringing dictionary and narrative simultaneously into play and short-circuiting their converse positions, gained the means to say everything. It should be noted, however, that his using the narrative form cannot be boiled down to his relieving the nomenclature's tedium by making it livelier. Rather, it answers a more essential requirement, inasmuch as there cannot really be a dictionary (or even a science, as Lacan says) of sexual pleasure. Sade needed a kind of *writing* through which the body could make its mark on language, and it makes that mark in step with the representation of a story where the constantly reiterated event of sexual pleasure is inscribed. What is at stake here is a bodily experience, one that, passionately caught up in an adventure, cuts across and obliterates all classifications (which is why the *journey*, for Sade, is a kind of prerequisite for the staging of desire).

And so we have both dictionary and narrative. This relationship, normally one of mutual exclusion (as is true in any paradigmatic structure), inevitably offers a temptation to libertine thought: that of subjecting this relationship to depraved permutations. To dress a dictionary up as a narrative, or to give the narrative a dictionary's orderly rigor, is to subvert the one with the other and force them to exchange places: the narrative can now call things by their names, and the dictionary can give them dramatic presentation. What we find here once again — in the blurring of established differences, in the amassing of contradictory predicates on the same subject — is the very approach that justifies incest. The Sadean text brings hybrid monsters into being: philosopher and adventurer, academy and brothel, science and debauchery, essay and orgy. Only in daring to say *too much* does it become truly possible to say *everything*. The *only* encyclopedia is the encyclopedia of excesses.

Journey and Exhaustivity: The Obsession with Residues

"Saying everything," considered as the ambition to "tell all," is normally the business of paranoia. How can it be managed by way of perversion? By replacing an undifferentiated, generalizing *synthesis* with a painstaking *tour* of knowledge and situations. It is both necessary and sufficient to cut up, subdivide, repeat. The succession of sequences, their variations, and the distribution and repetition of arguments all display the narrative body (just as the libertine eye divides up and parcels out the desired body), and listing is confounded with dismemberment, with an infinite unfolding.

The encyclopedic undertaking, in its pre-Hegelian sense, was in fact just this kind of methodical enumeration, the same work of classification and recapitulation—the equivalent, at the level of knowledge, of what the era's great maritime expeditions (such as those of Bougainville and La Pérouse) represented at the level of the planetary survey: a listing of the known world, and the appropriation of the new one. Everything either did or would end up patiently summarized in the pages of ledgers. The book was no longer fantasized to be a mysterious treasure chest concealing the secret of all knowledge (a myth analogous to the myth of the philosophers' stone). Now it was represented as writing's limitless *surface*, recording acquired knowledge and listing real objects—as a chart of knowledge, to be endlessly opened up and unfolded.

The surfaces of book, Earth, body: skins rich in folds and areas to be journeyed across, added to lists, saturated and modified. Discourse, voyage, and sexual pleasure all record, in different ledgers, the same gesture: the detailed, single-minded, maniacal survey, tacitly undertaken in the name of what appears to be the fundamental materialist assumption—namely, that the world is finite, and that a complete accounting of it can be rendered. No realms are off limits now, and there are no more prohibitions. To deny oneself any part of knowledge is to turn that part into a mystery, a taboo, to set up a god in this empty space of ignorance, degrading all other knowledge as a result. The stakes are all or nothing, and Sade is quite clear about it: "unless you acquaint yourself with everything, you'll know nothing."[12] What he means here is the desiring body in all its forms, and its particular relationship with the suffering body—in other words, the link between sex and blood, between sexual pleasure and crime: the twin major taboos on which any notion of community is founded, the things one cannot talk about without being ostracized, the black box of all other knowledge, the final terra incognita that inspires every journey and whose first bold explorer Sade intuits he will be. He has no doubt that everything truly will have been said after he has finished his summary, that the list will be complete.

But because this is a table of excesses, there can never be perfect certainty that the list is complete; some new excess can always be imagined. Here, the Sadean paradox consists in the attempt to give a systematic description of what can be defined only through its having escaped the system. And yet to fail at making an exhaustive list is to abdicate before the unsaid, to give up truly saying everything. This concern with missing some element, with leaving a blank, unleashes the whole repetition compulsion: a continuous resumption of the same scenes, the same essays, the same arguments. What we are witnessing is a virtual expiatory rite, obsessional in nature, with its compulsion to backtrack and its need to verify that nothing has been overlooked, nothing forgotten, to be in control of any traces that have been left behind, any groundwork that has been laid, any outcomes that have been arranged. The point, in other words, is to procure a list so complete that no residue remains and "too much" enters into the whole.

But doesn't this narrative relentlessness, this continuous dissertational scrutiny, betray Sade's great difficulty in mastering totality and completing the journey? Don't we find the same encyclopedic ambition reborn in the Romantic dream of absolute knowledge, from the unfinished attempt of Novalis to Hegel's monumental *Encyclopedia* (monumental not in the number of its volumes or the quantity of its assembled information but in its purely architectonic, all-encompassing logic)? Perhaps not, because for Hegel "saying everything" did not mean running through the whole list, or covering the immense territory of the known, or moving back and forth across the surface to which everything is added and on which one thing follows another and is lost and then found again. For Hegel, "saying everything" meant speaking the whole in each part, enunciating the development of the whole from the first moment to the last shape or form. In Hegel we see a journey without motion. It is a metamorphosis of substance-becoming-subject, through which each stage of its development sinks into memory: deep down, there is perfect retention of every moment, thanks to the constant work of the *negative*, which permits each overtaken form to be maintained as an internalized one — to be maintained, that is, as essence within the succeeding form. Thus the *Aufhebung*: an amazing machine for transformation with no remains, for accumulation with no residues, and for production with no surprises, because the final engulfment is already inscribed in the first moment, and every event is always already understood to be a necessity of discourse. We are no longer on a journey; we are now within a deductive methodology.

For Sade, by contrast, residues are not transformed but maintained in all their difference. The very impossibility of any negativity, and therefore of any dialectical assimilation (for in negativity there can be no contradiction), maintains the pure heterogeneity of moments, their succession without internal unity or logical integration, their artificial accumulation, their irreducible uniqueness. But what is affirmed and preserved in this way is the characteristic pleasure of travel — namely, *surprise*, prompt pleasure, successive and renewable for the duration of the journey. It is everything the libertine could ask for, the libertine who seeks no internal metamorphosis and acknowledges no subjectivity in himself. Thus substance can never become subject; it can only be immeasurably spread out, available for the journey. Bodies cannot be reduced; cultures remain heterogeneous (and it is possible for the oldest or most primitive ones to be more advanced or desirable than our own); desires are not transcended, time remains a succession of separate instants. The book, laid open, reveals no inside; we are always on the outside, on the surface. Infinity was only the illusion of immensity, and the inside was only an effect of surface density.

The Master of Discourse, His Accomplice, and His Other

> There is no Other of the Other.
>
> — JACQUES LACAN, *Écrits*

The tour has to be exhaustive, first of all because there can be no room for prohibition, but also, and especially, because no opportunity must be left open for contradiction of the type that could arise from a malevolent adversary — from something like the "bad genie" that Sade, not having been astute (or naive) enough to get rid of it at the outset through some technical trick, must now confront every step of the way. But who can this invisible, tormenting adversary be, if not the Master's Other? Isn't it his mirror image: the slave, the victim?

To "say everything" is the Master's exclusive claim, his essential privilege, his droit du seigneur over speech. If everything has been said, discourse is unanswerable, and speech is cut off from anyone who might offer contradiction. When everything has been said, there is nothing left to say. The Master, having offered his proofs, requires only agreement. This foreclosure of contradiction puts the adversary in the position of victim and thereby strips him of his very right to speech.[13] Not that the victim *could* contradict the Master; even *wanting* to contradict him means bringing the status of victim upon oneself and being unable, as a result, to say anything at all.

When everything has been said, the Master remains alone. His discourse has no residue, and he has no Other. All the victims have been sacrificed, and the narrative comes to an end. (Thus, in *Juliette*, the last and most recalcitrant victim is Justine, the one who has presumed to engage in discourse.) The only imaginable Other, then, must be the one to whom the story and its proofs are directed: the reader. But the whole apparatus of Sadean fiction functions precisely to turn the reader into an accomplice, one who thereby joins the Masters in their elite circle, the only setting for any possible reciprocity; in this way, all claims to any other discourse (which would be the discourse of the Other) are dismissed. The reader's complicity eliminates the last risk of contradiction; the conquest is complete. This is not self-evident, however; the reader's complicity is not obtained unless it becomes impossible for the reader to evade it—unless, that is, the reader's assent (like the assent to truth in Spinoza) necessarily follows when the tour of arguments and situations has been completed. In a way, then, over the course of the limitless demonstrational development conveyed by the story's great length, and as the bodies of the victims disappear, the body of the reader, of the Master-accomplice, is formed, engendered by the text.

This relationship to the reader is what imprints Sadean discourse with its constant alternation between *suspicion* and *seduction*. The suspicion (a formal, tactical one) is that the reader is not yet won over by the argument that has been put forward, so that the proof of this argument must be offered again: a doubting symbolized in the story by the interlocutor to whom this speech is addressed, and who has provoked this doubt by feigning ignorance about some point of doctrine, or uncertainty about its value or formulation. The seduction has to do with catching the reader in the movement of his own desire and making him acknowledge what his desire contributes to this discourse as a whole, and even to the whole of discourse itself. (Thus the relationship between scene and dissertation is not just an exchange-based interplay, a bit of sex for a bit of philosophy, but rather intratextual proof of the demonstration's libidinal impact.)

Direct address of the reader, it should be noted, was very common in eighteenth-century narratives, and they clearly acknowledged their fictional status in this way (not long afterward, however, the realist narrative, as a matter of course, would deny its own fictional status). Therefore, Sade seems merely to be following a very widespread tradition. Nevertheless, as we have seen, his use of this method is coupled with a thoroughly specific logical necessity: that of turning the reader into a Master so that the Sadean Master will have no Other. There is no room for an Other: the Sadean Master takes up all the room.

As for the victims, they pose no problem of otherness. Excluded from language, falling short of the symbolic order, they are not, strictly speaking, anything at all. For Sade there are no master-slave relationships of the Hegelian type (that is, relationships subject to dialectics), because for Sade the Master is formed not by a "struggle to the death" but by the circumstances of his birth, or by inherited or stolen fortune. There is never any face-to-face contact, never any confrontation, except with other Masters in positions of power, and these positions are obtained instead through assassination and betrayal. The Master is born into discourse, and there he stays. The victims can mount no opposition: having fallen short of discourse, they are without recourse or mediation, relegated to the silence of an anonymous mass incapable of revolt. The Master's limitless domination is set forth as a matter of fact, coextensive with the immensity of an unanswerable discourse. The only possible answer, the reader's, is precisely the one that the narrative form—and therefore, in other words, the narrative strategy—takes on the task of silencing.

Between writer and reader—between Master and Master—there is no contractual relationship; it is a relationship of *complicity*. To read is already to conspire. Thus "saying everything" defines a kind of power rather than a kind of wisdom, a power in which the reader, assumed and inferred to be a libertine and an accomplice, is invited to share. To read is already to be among the elect.

The Pleasure of Enunciation

> It is the force of speaking that realizes what is to be realized.
> —G. W. F. HEGEL, *Phenomenology of Mind*

> To speak while coming: no one can be held back from this experience, but to accept it is forbidden.
> —PHILIPPE SOLLERS, *Lettre de Sade*

> O Jesusfuck! . . . ah fuck! fuck! I'm discharging, you are slaying me with delight, enough! Enough, 'tis done . . . let's sit down now, let's talk a bit.
> —*Juliette*

If "saying everything" envisages the saturation of the Catalog as an encylopedic goal, then as a goal of excess "saying everything" means the very enunciation of sexual pleasure. The Sadean body, born of language and under its constant influence, remains a libertine body only by relating its acts to the discourse that calls them forth, programs them, defines them, and recites them. And this is not just because there is no sexual pleasure that is not joined to discourse; it is above all because there is no sexual pleasure that is not spoken, that is not itself engaged in holding forth. Expression, symptom, and gesture remain silent languages connoting the body of the victim. But the libertine body as such must speak incessantly of its own doings, echo its acts in their enunciation. Spoken discourse, the sign of mastery, becomes the very *element* of sexual pleasure. Libertine desire cannot be defined except through its passage into language. But it is also true that libertine desire cannot exist except through its origins in language. The Sadean realm is a place saturated with words, surrounded by them. The ear and the mouth are the libertine body's primary erotic organs. Here is how the introduction to *The 120 Days* presents the pleasure of hearing:

> It is commonly accepted amongst authentic libertines that the sensations communicated by the organs of hearing are the most flattering and those whose impressions are the liveliest; as a consequence, our four villains, who were of a mind to have voluptuousness implant itself in the very core of their beings as deeply and as overwhelmingly as ever it could penetrate, had, to this end, devised something quite clever indeed.

It was this: after having immured themselves within everything that was best able to satisfy the senses through lust, after having established this situation, the plan was to have described to them, in the greatest detail and in due order, every one of debauchery's extravagances, all its divagations, all its ramifications, all its contingencies, all of what is termed in libertine language its passions.[14]

This preeminence of hearing over the other senses is of course the preeminence of language itself. For Sade, the only sexual pleasure is the sexual pleasure of the head—that is, of representation. Libertinism, submitted to the law of language, penetrates the realm of reason, takes it over, and co-opts its structures and methods (such as order, classification, and systematization). The law of language is simply the Law. This is why desire, once in language, is in its proper place. And if Sade makes narration (and therefore the pleasure of hearing) a pleasure of the head, of knowledge, and finally of *imagination,* this is not because he is invoking the imaginary (that is, the realm of fantasy and ideal satisfaction of desire) but because he is invoking what we might call the *imaginable* (that is, the realm of those possibilities that can be classified within discourse).

It is here that Sade may be something of a Hegelian (but only up to a point: the question of language aside, nothing is more intolerable to Sadean thought than the logic of mediation). Hegel, in *Aesthetics,* notes that only two of our senses, sight and hearing, give rise to artistic production: "Artistic sensitivity has to do only with those of our senses that are intellecualized: sight and hearing, to the exclusion of the senses of smell, taste, and touch, which themselves have to do only with material elements and with those of their elements that can be immediately sensed."[15] The three latter senses are incapable of producing stable forms, which is to say that they are incapable of traversing and fixing time and space. Thus, the arts are exclusively visual (architecture, sculpture, painting) or aural (music, poetry). Of all the arts, however, poetry is the most accomplished, for it is produced within the element of language—produced, that is, from the only material element in which consciousness can achieve self-knowledge: language, in whose very form the presence of the universal, of the *concept,* is realized.

Hearing, language, concept: the trajectory runs from the organ to the essence thereby put into play. Sadean thought, like the rest of Enlightenment thought, more or less agrees with this formulation, without making it explicit. The pleasure of hearing is first of all the pleasure of understanding, so that this is less a question of pleasure in speaking than of pleasure in making speeches, in holding forth; even if there is a great flood of words, what counts is the theoretical form of the exposition. Language is the locus of desire, but what is desired is discourse.

This desire for discourse embodies a profoundly original principle, if we carefully consider the way in which tradition tends to articulate these two terms. Indeed, their relationship has always been set forth as a disjunctive one. On the one hand, we have knowledge, discourse, work, and tedium. On the other, we have sensual pleasure, nonchalance, relaxation, and celebration. And surrounding this paradigm, dividing the roles up into antagonistic pairs, are the figures of scientist and artist, scholar and bohemian, professor and dancer. In other words, the opposition between study and leisure is an unacknowledged cover-up of the opposition between the head and sexuality. Sade unceremoniously disposes of this age-old contradiction. What he is asserting is that theoretical exposition, or "dissertation," is not just an aphrodisiac but also the direct cause of "discharging" — but, obviously, only insofar as true libertinism is a question of methodology and understanding. Something has happened to blur the boundary between knowledge and desire: philosophy is taught in the bedroom, and exposition takes place in the midst of an orgy. But this is only the first, circumstantial, level of this blurring. If, at a deeper level, these incompatible realms begin to communicate with each other, it is because the object that is being dealt with has changed its nature, or at least its function. Desire will completely take words over, and the only one of their own effects that words will recognize will be sexual pleasure. Any kind of knowledge will be immediately concerned with the body, and it is the body as such that will be in question within any kind of knowledge. This is how the point of articulation between dissertation and scene has to be understood: as the point where each of these moments pins the other down and conditions its effects.

For Sade, the body as such has nothing to say, and it certainly does not "express"; what brings it into the realm of desire is what is *said about it*. Nakedness, always either proposed or actualized from the beginning, is still not really what excites the libertine; it connotes simply the creation of that state of immediate availability presupposed by mastery. The body, naked and silent, becomes a desiring and desirable body only when it is clothed in words: "I'm entirely naked. Make your dissertations upon me as much as you please."[16] On the whole, the work of the Bedroom Schoolmasters is primarily to name and classify. To enter into language, into knowledge, and into desire is a single operation. Eugénie's education, in *Philosophy in the Bedroom*, is her initiation into enjoyment of her body as a practice of language.

This is why the libertine never grows weary of speeches. An exposition, no matter how long or abstract, can never cause boredom or irritation, because it already *is* sexual pleasure, as well as the condition for the intensity of sexual pleasure. (Thus Juliette, despite her impatience to consummate her scene of debauchery with the pope, imposes the prerequisite of his giving a complete exposition on the need for murder.) Boredom with speeches is precisely what denotes and names the victim:

> "Feeble-minded creatures," [Noirceuil] murmured; "pleasure-machines, sufficient to our purposes, but, truly, their appalling insensibility depresses me."[17]

Thus we see even more clearly how knowledge and sexual pleasure hinge on each other. An exposition, no matter how theoretical, is always concerned with the imagination — concerned, that is, with thinking about transgressions, and with describing their potentialities. The imagination's intensity and development define the boundary between the logophobic body of the victim and the logophilic body of the libertine. To think is also to feel and imagine, and so theory has bodily effects and is necessarily concerned with sexual pleasure: "The person of superior wit and parts will always be found more apt to libertinage's pleasures."[18]

The time allotted to discourse does not diminish the time allotted to sexual pleasure, because discourse is part of sexual pleasure. Moreover, discourse constitutes a moment of energetic acceleration. Just as a meal break ensures the renewal of the body's energies, a "discourse break" ensures the renewal of the imagination's. This buildup of energy gives rise to an intense burning, connoted by lexicons of fire ("inflame," "warm," "kindle," "electrify") or intoxication ("inexpressible delight," "violent ecstasy"). Discourse, then, far from being foreign to sexual pleasure, affirms sexual pleasure as being only "of the head"; and discourse, by inscribing into the linguistic realm the physical debauchery imagined and programmed by sexual pleasure, allows this debauchery to become a genuine libertinism. Reciprocally, discourse has physical effects that are attributable to the same laws as those that govern the body's own physical effects: "Ah voluptuous creature, how you do stir up my come, how your statements and the uncommon temperature of your ass do excite it to discharge."[19] But what the relationship between speech and sexual pleasure produces, even more than this metonymic contamination, is similarity of operation. The Sadean paradox in general consists in presenting verbal utterance at precisely the point where words fall short or fail altogether: the point of violence, or the point of orgasm. Violence — the violence of crime, and particularly of torture — is silent, as Bataille has clearly demonstrated; this is why Sadean torturers are impossible as realistic figures. But this also means that Sadean crime, and likewise sexual pleasure, function only through language. To bring speech into a place marked for silence is not just to drive out the ineffable and to extend mastery; it is also to indicate that speech itself *is* what is coming. This is why speech is expended on exclamations: "Ah! I'm coming!" "Ah! I'm dying!" "Ah! Such delights!" "Jesusfuck! My ecstasy is complete!" When to speak is to come, we have a remarkable instance of the performative; the act is exhausted in its utterance, and the duration of the act coincides with the duration of its enunciation. This performative calls for a linguistic form that could be called the "first-person enunciative," and it requires the permanent irruption of dialogue into narrative. It also calls for glorification of the voice that *speaks out loud,* the voice of public utterance claiming space in a theatrical exhibition, with no holding back ("Saint-Fond's discharge was admirable, forceful, convulsive; it was accompanied by the most vigorous, the most impetuous blasphemies, pronounced in a very loud voice"):[20] the out-loud voice of sexual pleasure and obscenity versus the low voice of shame and secrets, the inner voice of conscience and virtue.

Inadmissibility, Obscenity, and Details

There is a Sadean encyclopedic project, but it is conceived as a *provocation* in that the domain assigned to the mastery of discourse is defined as what must *not* be spoken of — a strange sort of mastery, this one, applied to what normally is excluded from mastery. To say everything about what must be kept quiet is to step outside the law. What is at stake in this transgression, this crime of lese boundaries, is the destruction of the secret's last hideout, of the last possibility for prohibition. Everything must be said so that the ineffable will be left no toehold. Where excess is concerned, so long as what comes into play has not been said, *everything* has not yet been said; indeed, *nothing at all* has been said, in keeping with the principle that we'll know nothing unless we acquaint ourselves with everything: "At Cythera Venus had more than one temple, you know; come ope the most arcane, come bugger me, Delcour, make haste... for we must leave no delight untasted, no horror uncommitted."[21] This repletion of excess brings about a change in the nature of knowledge: no longer a simple knowledge of objects, but instead an experience of sexual pleasure that transforms the "normal" body into a libertine body. What is discovered in and through excess is not simply added to other kinds of knowledge. Instead, it radically overturns them by exposing the repressed elements of their operation: violence and desire. The most dangerous conceivable move, and the least tolerable act of aggression against any social order, may be to bring this exposure about and compel the admission of the inadmissible, if society is founded, as Freud says, on a collective crime of which we must know nothing.[22] Indeed, every emergence of a social order prevails through the repression of both anarchic violence and the particular drives of individuals or groups. The renunciation of this violence is achieved through sacrifice,[23] which imitates violence in order to master and exorcise it; in this way, evil is circumscribed, designated, and defeated. What is engendered by this renunciation is a symbolic order, a convention of exchange — in other words, a contractual system that makes possible something on the order of a community. (According to Marcel Mauss, there is perhaps no sacrifice that does not ultimately partake of the contractual.)[24] Any order of values, like any way of organizing knowledge, is founded on this compromise, which is also this order's founding prohibition. The point of the ferocious vigilance maintained by the order that stems from this prohibition is to keep the dozing monster asleep and contain at all costs the chaos threatening to spring up from the unleashing of the same forces that the sacrifice and the contract have managed to neutralize and remove from circulation and from discourse.

What is immediately indicated here is that all knowledge has a political genesis, and that knowledge gains recognition only by presenting its contractual credentials, by being a knowledge of *order* (which is why academicism and ossification are no accidents but rather signs of this structure's inevitable weakness; stupidity has no other history). What we ask of knowledge is that it *not know*; or, to be more precise, that it *know nothing about* the drives, to the extent that these bear within them desire and violence, sex and blood—the fornicating, murderous beast—the two interconnected, pivoting axes of chaos. Thus *sex* is incorporated into the system of differences and prohibitions constituting the family; *violence* (chiefly murder) is institutionalized and regulated within the structure of the state (for example, in the right to wage war, and in the death penalty), and the state makes violence the distinctive sign of state authority.

These were the stakes, and Sade, having perceived them quite clearly, could gauge the outrageous boldness of his breaking and entering into the "fundamental mystery." He could enunciate, with audacity and narrative, the boundaries of the speakable:

> And now, friend-reader, you must prepare your heart and your mind for the most impure tale that has ever been told since our world began, a book the likes of which are met with neither amongst the ancients nor amongst us moderns. Fancy, now, that all pleasure-taking either sanctioned by good manners or enjoined by that fool you speak of incessantly, of whom you know nothing and whom you call Nature; fancy, I say, that all these modes of taking pleasure will be expressly excluded from this anthology, or that whenever peradventure you do indeed encounter them here, they will always be accompanied by some crime or colored by some infamy.[25]

And yet to bring unspeakable horror to light was to bring it back into the contractual form of discourse. And here was the paradox, the all but impossible and specifically Sadean feat: to say, in masterly form, what mastery was created to oppose. This was not at all a question of challenging masterly form itself, and to do so would have been unthinkable: classical French, an object inherited as a natural given, left no alternative to enunciation. The point was not to reject classical French but to make it utter its own contradiction and repudiation, to inscribe on its body all the forbidden signifieds (sex, blood, excrement, crime, lies) that it had the function of repressing.

What Sade did not see is that language itself is the locus of prohibition, the absolute form of law. We have Saussure and Freud to thank for this insight, but eighteenth-century eyes looked right through language to nature, and nothing but the referent was heard in discourse. No aggression could be brought to bear on the signifier, which remained a blind spot. Classical French was an ether, an evidentiary medium for the spoken, a dense veil of transparency. Thus the only weapons that could be used against it were lexical ones, and the writing and rewriting of dictionaries was to become an enduring eighteenth-century strategy (the world could be remade with changed definitions and the imposition of new ones).

This is why words are what Sade tore into. To make their usages stray from respectability, to displace their conventional uses, to mix them with other, forbidden ("vulgar") words, was to mount an attack on meaning. Never for a moment was this a matter of calling the *structure* of language into question (because the structure of language went unseen). Acting against language meant overwhelming *the* language with all the statements it was designed to exclude. The effect of obscenity lay in the production of the gap introduced between traditional syntactical (or even rhetorical) form and the signified of vice, which presupposed a *society* (and therefore a political order, with its values and legal structures) that *ought not* to have been speaking the language of decent people and belles lettres.

It was this implication, this sort of collusion, that was felt to be intolerable and outrageous. Classical French's agenda of literary and political intimidation was intended to make collusion of this kind unthinkable; Sade's unforgivable (and unforgiven) provocation was to make its practice possible. This is why transgression, for Sade, took the form of "saying everything": proving, through writing, that received language really *could* say everything that it *ought not* to have been saying.

The risk had to be taken. Sade's assumption—his gamble—was that no such transgression, however perverse, was unspeakable. The barrier was perceived as existing in the imagination rather than in linguistic structure itself; the imagination was what had to be liberated, what needed to have its realm fully restored to it. This was why enunciation had to go all the way, scrupulously encompassing every nuance, capturing the tiniest difference, accounting for and thus absolutely liberating every signified—why, in other words, it had to move in the particular direction of *details*.

The need for details—the point where the real overtakes the imagination—is constant throughout the course of the narratives. In this sense, in this tour of debauchery where acts and situations are predictable on the whole, details are the mark of the unexpected, the feature that particularizes everything while enlarging the boundaries of the saturable.

In the cataloging of excess, details indicate desire's capacity for invention. And if details are where desire becomes inventive, if desire lays stress on the fringes, remnants, and fallout of discourse, it is because desire is excluded from the (official) scene of acknowledged generalities. Wherever these have slipped and are faulty, we find the gap that marks desire. This is why the enunciation of details always involves indecency and obscenity—always involves, that is, the inadmissibility of sexual pleasure ("you simply have no idea how those few details excite me").[26] Thus the enunciation of details is the specifically libertine test of the ambition to say everything, for it is just here that speech resists.

Freud was not unaware of this when he made saying everything—*alles sagen*—the fundamental rule for the analysand's enunciation, and attention to details the rule for the analyst's listening: "Now, these psychoanalytical matters are intelligible only if presented in *full and complete detail* just as an analysis gets going only when the patient distinguishes the minute details from the abstractions which are their surrogate."[27] This is where things happen. This is where the censorship brought about by secondary formations relaxes, and where the drives, in a proliferation of bungled acts and slips of the tongue, endlessly create symptoms, for this is where there is pleasure (as in wit), and where the unconscious speaks. As Freud explains in *Jokes and Their Relation to the Unconscious*, even small flashes (*kleine Züge*) of wit are enough to indicate that wit comes from the unconscious: "It is necessary in the work of analysis to go all the way, leaving nothing beyond articulation. An analysis is not terminated until *all* the obscurities of the case have been cleared up, *all* the gaps in the patient's memory have been filled in, and *all* the circumstances surrounding repression have been ferreted out."[28] Freud's opposing of "minute details" to "the abstractions which are their surrogate" is noteworthy in connection with the Sadean economy of saying everything. The term *surrogate abstractions* would adequately define the level of contractual exchange, the realm of the predictable, and general normality—that is, the ordinary level of behavior, the outcomes of which are neither excess nor expenditure. The term *minute details* would define the level of singularity, that is, the limits of exchange, the production of unique differences, the absence of equivalents—in other words, a new face of perversion, whose sudden appearance opens up the possibility of sexual pleasure as sheer expenditure (for it is stripped of all signs and substitutive structures).

In this connection, Freud does speak of a "localized savings" (*lokalisierte Ersparung*), but this is not saying nearly enough. What should be seen instead in the cathexis of details is the point where this kind of *Ersparung* fails, the way in which the economy of desire establishes itself as extravagant and even ruinous in its inability to recover anything at all, because it consists precisely in ridding itself of surrogate "abstractions" and general equivalents (any concept of money or system of exchange). As Luce Irigaray notes, the point is disruption: "The rule of *saying everything* puts inter-diction back into play: the unutterable articulation that passes from the interior of discourse to its exterior."[29]

The Secret Chamber, or How to Say the Unspeakable

> The crime is concealed, and what is most terrifying is what escapes us. We are obliged, in the night it offers our fear, to imagine the worst.
>
> —GEORGES BATAILLE, *Gilles de Rais*

> Hard by the public pleasure hall are located private cells whereunto one may repair solitarily to indulge in all the debaucheries of libertinage.
>
> —*Juliette*

> There is, after all, no equivalent to solitary crimes.
>
> —*Juliette*

In *The 120 Days of Sodom*, as in *Juliette*, everything takes place on the stage of the narrative; everything visible must be speakable. The realm of obscenity is defined by unreserved exposure, unbounded exposition. So radical is this endeavor that it is constantly brought to bear on its own limits. For this reason, Sade quite rightly senses that the locus of total exhibition cannot also be the locus of infinite excess. Every locus — that is, every marked space — defines an axiomatics, and therefore a combinative operation, a finite set of determinations, a saturable system. The orgy aims at repletion through a general requirement for order, permitting the exhaustion of sexual connections, a reduplication of pleasure in language, and a total view of the spectacle.

Torture is presented as a way to reopen the system. Tearing bodies to pieces disrupts the combinative operation and completely restructures the locus of sexual pleasure. A new and much more complex grouping begins to operate. Now pleasure is connected to suffering, and cries of pleasure are wrapped up with cries of pain. What is most important, however, is that the victims' bodies enter into a cycle of dreadful metamorphoses, a fall toward formlessness, toward an inorganic muddle. The formal variations on the victims' bodies — bodies whipped to the quick, flayed alive, slashed, burned, dismembered, mutilated — define new combinations, and thus new pleasures, at every stage of their destruction. A new realm, surrounded by screams and swimming in blood, offers distributions that are all the more radical for being more improbable and more chaotic. What was needed was that bodies be opened up, their forms torn to pieces, their skin broken, their organs and viscera put on display. Once exposed, however, the bodies and organs offer still more surfaces, obscenely exhibited — exhibited, that is, in an unmediated nakedness, a bottomless superficiality. There is nothing more under the skin than on its surface; the erotic surplus occurs right in the passage from above to below, which produces frenzied movements and unexpected figures in the body under assault. Thus torture reaches its goal: to produce novelty, set unprecedented cycles of possibility into motion, and offer entirely new pleasures to sight, hearing, touch, and imagination, the final pleasure coinciding, in orgasm, with the victim's last breath. Now the system is once again closed, and everything can begin anew. Torture pushes the limits by increasing the number of perverse combinations; every horror that can be named, short of an excess that would completely shatter the limits, is inscribed on the tortured body.

But how is such excess possible? Can the narration of an orgy, without itself being abolished *as* a narrative, glance over the sites and bodies forming its stage? A thousand kinds of madness and horror are possible, but only because they can be enumerated. If the Sadean narrative is extended, prolonged, tirelessly resumed, it is in order to come as close as possible to the final sum, the final number. That this final sum is finite is a fact known beforehand. The journey has its inevitably fixed end. The narrative must come to a close without the occurrence of any limitless transgression or any immeasurable act of insanity:

"I have conceived [said Durcet] of a thousand times more and better than I have done...."

"There are," said Curval, "but two or three crimes to perform in this world, and they, once done, there's no more to be said; all the rest is inferior, you cease any longer to feel. Ah, how many times, by God, have

I not longed to be able to assail the sun, snatch it out of the universe, make a general darkness, or use that star to burn the world! oh, that would be a crime, oh yes, and not a little misdemeanor such as are all the ones we perform who are limited in a whole year's time to metamorphosing a dozen creatures into lumps of clay."[30]

If an act of such madness were possible, it would have taken place at the outset, and there never would have been a narrative. The narrative begins only in desiring what could abolish it; it continues only because it fails to attain its desire, and it concludes by renouncing this desire. A voluptuous tour of a finite set, one known to be finite, would itself be narrative pleasure, for this finitude is vast and prodigiously rich in surprise, in the unexpected, in renewal: $(n) + 1$, indefinitely. New names (of characters, of places) are enough to launch new stories, even with old gestures, and even with thoughts that have already been spoken; it is enough to join the name with some detail, some variation, the $(n) + 1$ that permits a new combination. This is why it always becomes necessary for the narrative to be resumed: it is because the set of variations, if theoretically finite, is never exhausted.

Within the scene, then, a vanishing point must be found, an opening in its perspective, a point where the eye is no longer spoken of, and where gestures are no longer recounted — a means by which the incomprehensibility of the unspoken can leave imagination (and therefore desire) some possibility of infinite extension without threatening the pleasure of pursuing the narrative. This vanishing point is the *secret chamber*, a place where terrible things are not named:

So he and I, Bracciani, and Olympia removed into the secret sanctuary of the Princess' pleasures where further infamies were celebrated and, upon my honor, I blush at describing them to you.[31]

I have never been able to discover what went on in those infernal closets.[32]

And, together with Sophie and Michette, Durcet fled into his closet to discharge I don't know how, but none the less in a manner which must not have suited Sophie, for she uttered a piercing scream and emerged from the sanctuary as red as a cockscomb.[33]

This place of horror and secrets holds knowledge in abeyance. It is a place for *remains*—that is, a place where *everything else* goes on.[34] It is the beyond of the bedchamber, which itself is a place for narratives,

treatises, erotic practices, the visible — a place for the stage, which necessarily encompasses everything that can be said. This "offstage" chamber, if initially a sign of the Sadean narrative's failure to capture absolute
horror, actually constitutes a quite remarkable tactic of indicating horror. Absolute horror is inscribed in the blank spaces that remain after
the abdication of naming. We do not know what happens in the secret
chamber, only that something does happen, and so we are forced to imagine a reality more powerful than discourse, so violent that silence alone
can stand in for it.

The silence of the victims corresponds to this blank in the narrative.
Sadean victims in general do not have much to say for at least two reasons, as we know. First, only the libertine, as Master, is in possession of
language. Moreover, it is his linguistic privilege that, *in the text,* establishes him as a Master. And, second (but this is a corollary), only sexual
pleasure is enunciated, because it is an effect exclusive to the Master.
There is no way to speak of suffering, which belongs to the victim's side
of the equation. Suffering, in its role as stimulant of sexual pleasure, can
be indicated, pointed to; textually, however, by the rules of verisimilitude, it perpetually falls short because it is generally so insubstantial.

The libertine enters the secret chamber alone with his victim, for any
libertine who accompanied him might be able — and would even be
obliged by the logic of obscenity ("saying everything") — to bear witness
as a Master of language himself, and as the reader's representative on
this other stage. What a third party can witness, everyone can be told,
and so the boundary marking off what can be said becomes precisely the
boundary marking off the excluded third party. Reciprocally, this confirms the strange passivity of Sadean victims as an effect of their logical
nonexistence, their dispossession of the symbolic, an expropriation inflicted on them at the outset. And if the libertine is alone in the secret
chamber, it is because he can no longer be an object of narration; he
has been placed outside discourse — he has not merely fallen short of
it, like his victim, but is beyond it. With the destruction of this boundary
comes the beginning of inexpressible violence; definitive horror can only
remove itself from the familiar locus of language.

As readers, we are left standing at the door that, in the text, metaphorizes the boundary of obscenity — metaphorizes, that is, the impossibility of saying everything, the impossibility of adding new combinations to those that have already been used, the impossibility of adding

anything at all to the symbolic order that determines the specifically Sadean aggressive rage against the body, a rage whose purpose is to blow this closure open and break out of the prison house of signs.

Thus it comes as no surprise that the only thing to reach us from within the secret chamber is the *scream*, by way of its insertion into the narrative as a clue. The scream is the presymbolic use of the voice, the voice before it has been taken over by language, the voice that, like other secretions (sperm, shit, urine, farts, blood), escapes or is extorted from the body, the voice reduced to its pure material flow. The scream unites two constant Sadean necessities: *prediscursivity,* invoking the fantasy of a nature that antedates humans (an eternal, indifferent, innocent nature), and *transdiscursivity,* attained in the annihilated language of torture, in the flouted institution of orgy and crime (a violent, cruel nature that becomes accessible only through violence and cruelty). And the body unites these two registers upon itself. Led into the secret chamber, the body can no longer speak or be spoken of. The scream, not yet language, is at the same time an indication that language no longer has any place here, that it has been destroyed, that narrative must step aside, that, in the torturer's savage solitude, the extreme violence wrought upon the body has taken complete flight from any form of discursivity. The body is finally reduced to its "natural state" — to what is, in La Mettrie's system, its barest materiality: a mass of flesh, a network of nerves, an expanse of skin from which torture, for the sake of the libertine's sexual pleasure, extracts the last vital movements.

The scream changes nothing about the victims' silence, because it confirms and reinforces their exclusion from language. The scream is in no way speech but merely a sonorous eruption, a spurt of voice within a spurt of blood.

By contrast with what takes place in the other orgies, what happens in the secret chamber is never planned, because what can be planned coincides, obviously, with what can be narrated. Every "program" opens with the command "Let us put some order into our pleasures!" — that is, let us produce an axiomatics and a narrative, and, to boot, let us defy the law by bringing it into the forbidden. The secret chamber, on the contrary, is a place of disorder (the libertines emerge disheveled and delirious), a place outside narrative and therefore completely alogical, crazed, deranged: the chaos of the body in the gap left by an abdicated discourse. Here the limits (if not the failure) of Sadean trangression make themselves known. Obscenity, as aggression of and against language, has been formulated as an act of defiance, as "saying everything." But how is it possible to use language for what cannot be narrated unless language is interrupted, that is, unless the narrativity coextensive with language is eluded? Language holds up only within order or parodies of order. A delirium conceived as absolute excess cannot be spoken of; it can only be imagined at the boundary of words.

In the Sadean text, then, the secret chamber constitutes a strange and essential symptom—strange in that it functions as a prohibition, and essential in that it is a kind of empty (unnarrated) space around which saturated spaces revolve (those "speakable" realms where "programmable" orgies occur). It even creates these saturated spaces by presuming their incessant recurrence. Thus the secret chamber is perhaps the point where the narrative is revived and the stakes are raised. In order for us to be led into the secret chamber, there would have to be a *speech* capable of encompassing the inconceivable nature of the *deeds* presumed to be taking place there—but then we would find ourselves in a bedroom where, on the far wall, another secret chamber would offer its mysterious door, for as soon as discourse states an act, it moves that act into the order of the conceivable, into the combinative system of possibilities. Therefore, to define unspeakable horror is a wildly futile, fruitless endeavor. In fact, the relentlessness of Sadean narrative is brought up short by a paradox: namely, the fact that the body, even the disfigured, crushed, annihilated body, *resists*. The inaccessibility of the secret chamber now becomes a symbol of this resistance, but it is resistance to discourse rather than, as in Christian martyrdom, a claim for the soul's invulnerability. The secret chamber conjures up no world "behind" our own, no "beyond," but rather the quite positive existence of a back room where proof is given of the body's radical materiality: the skin and organs fallen away from language. The body's resistance may suspend speech, but it still invokes another mode of meaning. Indeed, there is something about this secret chamber that resembles the object in Zen practice, or in ancient Stoicism: it cannot be stated or described, but it can be *designated*. This is the *anaphoric* dimension, then, which inscribes the written work with the irreducibility of the body itself and with the irruption of the deed that marks out this blank space within the text, where the violence of the torturer is annulled in the silence of the victims.

Wittgenstein, in the *Tractatus Logico-philosophicus*, says that what can be shown cannot be said, and that what cannot be spoken of must be passed over in silence. And, as Bataille claims in *Death and Sensuality*, "Violence bears within itself this dishevelled denial, putting an end to any possibility of speech."[35] What more remains to be said?[36]

The Crime of Writing

> How can we have a writing that kills?
>
> —BERTOLT BRECHT

Within the order of the signified, the order of narrative statement, there is nothing more to be said. The discourse of excess has named everything that can be named, and the theater of crime has played out all its scenes. But here is the strategy, or the strength, of the writing: if the ultimate crime is unspeakable, then speech itself must be made an enduring crime. If language is the form of the law, if language is what allows society to be constituted, and if language is what society in turn produces and watches over so strictly, then any offense against language becomes itself the very possibility of crime, its general matrix, its pure model. This is the "moral murder... arrived at by means of... writings" that Juliette recommends to Clairwil, who has expressed the following wish:

> I would like... to find a crime which, even when I had left off doing it, would go on having perpetual effect, in such a way that so long as I lived, at every hour of the day and as I lay sleeping at night, I would be constantly the cause of a particular disorder, and that this disorder might broaden to the point where it brought about a corruption so universal or a disturbance so formal that even after my life was over I would survive in the everlasting continuation of my wickedness.[37]

This *crime of writing* is of course the one that Sade intends to commit by "saying everything." As an attempt to exhaustively name and stage the signifieds of debauchery, murder, and cruelty, "saying everything" produces the writing of obscenity, as a double betrayal of exclusionary rules: the exclusionary rules of communicative language, through the adoption of vulgar words that connote the common people, even (and especially) "the rabble"; and the exclusionary rules of literary language, through the radical rejection of metaphorical devices and the convention that upholds them. As a betrayal of class and culture within a generalized corruption of language, "saying everything" is, formally speaking, the crime that engenders all those it enunciates, the Sadean crime par excellence. There is no other, in any case.

CHAPTER THREE

Libertine Apathy, or the Pleasures of Methodology

> To become master of one's own inner chaos, to force one's own
> chaos to assume a shape, to act logically, simply, categorically,
> mathematically, to make a law of oneself: this is great ambition.
> — FRIEDRICH NIETZSCHE, *The Gay Science*

> 'Tis when we have achieved depravation, insensibility, that Nature
> begins to yield us the key to her secret workings, and ... it cannot be
> pried away from her save through outrages.
>
> — *Juliette*

The staging of the libertine body must confront a sort of paradox. On
the one hand, as a programmed and dissected body with no secrets and
no interiority, the libertine body is wholly turned over to the scalpel of
classifying reason. On the other hand, because this is a *libertine* body, it
is the desiring body, the seat of the passions. And the passions are precisely what reason finds it most difficult to conceive of. Descartes gives
exemplary proof of this difficulty. Having managed to set forth the cogito, and to take from it the certainty of God's existence and of mathematical truth, even without having assumed anything about the existence of the body and its feelings, Descartes needed a considerable labor
of logic (the whole second half of the *Meditations*) before he could reintegrate this body into the luminous scope of thought. As for feelings
(emotions, sentiments, passions), nothing less than divine intervention
was needed to account for their effects on the soul.

Without renouncing rationalistic ambition in the slightest (quite the contrary), libertine thought attempted to bring off what Cartesian philosophy had failed to do. Libertine thought hoped to discuss, within a rationalistic framework, what had appeared to be defined by an eluding of rationality. Reason, seeing in passion its own limits, had lacked audacity in the face of passion. It had persisted in regarding itself as a *substance* standing across from another, supposedly heterogeneous, substance. Then (thanks chiefly to Kant) reason discovered that it was a *form*, a universal form capable of imprinting and imposing itself on any substance — on the substance of passion, for example. If the substance of passion appeared to be unruly matter, an impetuous torrent, reason would now domesticate it and submit it to the precision of rational methods. It would make passion reasonable. To do so, reason would posit passion as the equivalent of a force, one whose impulses of contraction and explosion threatened to be dangerous, a force that it would suffice to break up, decompose, and thus regulate. This was a job for libertine apathy: to split the instinctual nucleus, refine it, and diversify it in this catalytic-cracking device. The passions would emerge purified, cleansed, allocated to precise objectives within the program of pleasures. They would become operational. But their passage through this rational fast-breeder reactor would not leave them intact, nor would their new way of functioning be without consequences: reason proposes no means without also imposing its own ends, and what would emerge from this passage through apathy was apparently a plan for unlimited mastery, mastery to the death.

Apathy/Passion: The Search for Constants

Apathy: this word belongs to the ascetic tradition, and the motifs of Stoic ethics are organized around it. Epicureanism also lays claim to this word, but only insofar as it attempts, betraying its initial position, to elevate the morality of its scandalous demand for pleasure by playing on the sophism that apathy, as a state of indifference to passion, and thus as an absence of suffering, constitutes the most evolved form of happiness. In other words, apathy is Epicurean only insofar as Epicureanism becomes Stoicism. In both cases, the intended result is the same: mastery of the instincts through the attainment of ascetic wisdom.

When Sade takes hold of this concept, he puts it through a fundamental mutation. Apathy is no longer targeted as a final *state* of passion's absence, or (in Freudian terms) as sublimation, but rather as a *technique* for exacerbating and increasing the passions. It is the condition for a superior eroticism, a mental eroticism: the eroticism of the true libertine. Apathy is the transformer that converts instinctual matter into "scenes" within the imagination so that the sex organs become wired up to the brain, desire takes possession of language, and the instinctual is inscribed into the symbolic. As a technique for bringing about a lapse (not a negativity, but a suspension) of consciousness, apathy isolates primary process from instinct and disconnects its socially normative object cathexes, in order to open it up to the endless polyvalence of desire's combinative operation. But how can passion, once driven out, be brought back in?

From the outset there is something surprising about Sade's opposing apathy to passion. Passion is always posited as the movement of nature within the individual, and thus as the basis of the need for sexual excess and criminal horrors. Nevertheless, whoever simply abandons himself to this movement is designated a victim or is at least excluded from the company of true libertines, offering himself up to the deadly risk of serving as the object of a scene — that is, as a particular "case" to be (mis)"treated." It would appear, then, that the issue should be expressed in terms of a *disjunctive* opposition between apathy and passion, with torturers and victims distributed along these two axes. But we see nothing of the kind: the libertine, no matter how impassive, is no less impassioned. How does he overcome this aporia?

It is precisely this question that serves as the topic of a dialogue between Juliette and Delcour, the executioner of Nantes. To Juliette, who declares herself persuaded that only by linking murder with orgasm, by being "mentally in a libertine furor," can an executioner find the sangfroid necessary to his task, Delcour replies:

> It is no longer contested, Madame, that libertinage leads logically to murder; and all the world knows that the pleasure-worn individual must regain his strength in this manner of committing what fools are disposed to denominate a crime: we subject some person or other to the maximum agitation, its repercussion upon our nerves is the most potent stimulant imaginable, and to us are restored all the energies we have previously spent in excess. Murder thus qualifies as the most delicious of libertinage's vehicles, and as the surest; but it is not true that in order to

commit murder, one has got to be mentally in a libertine furor. By way of proof I cite to you the extreme calm wherewith the majority of my colleagues dispatch their business; they experience emotion, yes, but it is quite as different from the passion animating the libertine as this latter is from the passion in him who murders out of ambition, or out of vengeance, or out of greed, or, again, out of sheer cruelty. Which is simply to indicate that there are several classes of murder, the libertine variety being but one.[1]

In this context, libertinism means passion par excellence, the type of passion defined as *sexual* desire. Juliette is asking that this type of passion be recognized as causing the type defined as *criminal* desire. Her thesis is that "libertinage leads logically to murder." What she means is that murder is in the service of libertinism, and so the whole appeal of murder would come down to the "discharge" that it brings about. Murder's position remains instrumental. Therefore, as a mediator of sexual pleasure, murder is not desired for its own sake, for its function is surmounted by a different one that is conceived as its goal. Thus Juliette shows herself to be a novice in "philosophy." She invokes causal hierarchy, which is why the executioner of Nantes will now give her a lesson in apathy, and he proceeds to do so, in two phases: first he makes every set of causes relative, and then he eliminates the very idea of causes. Juliette's thesis is not rejected but brought down to a particular case: one can commit murder in the grip of any number of passions other than libertinism (ambition, vengeance, greed), "which is simply to indicate that there are several classes of murder, the libertine variety being but one." Here we stand, then, before the table of possibilities — which nevertheless ceases immediately to be a realm of causes once apathy has entered into it (along with sangfroid, its practical equivalent), so that the very idea of any causal link is invalidated. Murder is no longer to be related to this or that passion; it is affirmed in and of itself, "out of sheer cruelty."

Juliette absorbs this lesson, but she maintains her demand for a necessary relationship between murder and libertinism (in the text itself, the term *libertinage* is often used synonymously with *lewdness* or *lust*). From this point on, however, libertinism is invoked not as a causal principle but as something else entirely, which may permit this aporia, this logical impasse of apathy versus passion, to be overcome.

Juliette acknowledges murder as an autonomous passion, but she still gets Delcour to concede that "libertinage" (lust, that is) is not just one passion among others: "Lust is to the passions what the nervous fluid is to life; it sustains them all,"[2] and so all the passions can grow from the passion of lust. Even though Juliette appears to be maintaining and even strengthening her position, however, she is no longer saying the same thing at all. She has comprehended Delcour's "methodology," which consists in modifying all the variables in the table of possibilities by a common factor, a constant — apathy — that disconnects them from one another, arranges them in autonomous sets, and renders them intransitive. Apathy acts as a solvent upon causality. It constitutes not one set among others but the element that circulates among them in order to detach them from one another and, as a result, flatten them out on the surface of the table of possibilities. Relativity invalidates relationship.

Apathy's special status as an extraserial element is what constitutes, for Juliette, a model that can be applied to the concept of libertinism. She preserves libertinism, but only by transforming it. She no longer asks that it be the sufficient cause of murder, that it be murder's justification. Now she asks that libertinism be, like apathy, a metaserial element, something by which all the other passions are transformed, invigorated, and glorified.

Thus we have a solvent (apathy) and an amplifier (libertinism), a principle of lucidity and a principle of exaltation. Apathy ensures the determination of the elements, their cohabitation, and their analytic precision; in other words, it establishes a topos. Libertinism causes the elements to circulate and takes them to their maximum intensity; in other words, it establishes an energetics.

Libertinism, then, is no longer one passion among others. It forms one of the axes (with apathy forming the other) on which the table of the other passions will be constructed. Each of the passions, whatever its particular nature, will be modified by these two factors. Thus we see how the aporia envisaged at the beginning — the logical impasse between apathy and passion — is resolved. Apathy, insofar as it renders desire indifferent — indifferent to motives, to the consequences of the delirium it acts out on the bodies of others, and, finally, to all the rules of normality — becomes the very condition of desire's power. Reciprocally, desire strengthens apathy by establishing an irreversible metonymic relationship between crime and orgasm, a relationship that leads to the practice of pure cruelty, that is, to the nullification of all causality.

Libertine Asceticism, or Practical Critical Methodology

For the libertine, apathy is methodology itself. It is a complete methodology, for it is every bit as practical as it is critical, and it simultaneously determines the activity of desire and the judgments of reason. Indeed, as Blanchot clearly sees, apathy as a practical matter is the indispensable means of mastering and concentrating the powers and energy available to the individual because it allows the individual to toss aside the inferior objects (inferior because illusory) over which vulgar debaucheries are scattered: "Sade insists that for passion to become energy it has to be compressed, it must function at one remove by passing through a necessary phase of insensibility; then its full potentiality will be realised."[3]

Instead of killing desire, apathy intensifies it by creating a vacuum of signs around it. At any rate, apathy is the quasi-mystical methodological secret that Juliette confides to her friend (and future victim) Madame de Donis:

Go a whole fortnight without lewd occupations, divert yourself, amuse yourself at other things; for the space of those two weeks rigorously bar every libertine thought from your mind. At the close of the final day retire alone to your bed, calmly and in silence; lying there, summon up all those images and ideas you banished during the fasting period just elapsed, and indolently, languidly, nonchalantly fall to performing that wanton little pollution by which nobody so cunningly arouses herself or others as you do. Next, unpent your fancy, let it freely dwell upon aberrations of different sorts and of ascending magnitude; linger over the details of each, pass them all one by one in review; assure yourself that you are absolute sovereign in a world groveling at your feet, that yours is the supreme and unchallengeable right to change, mutilate, destroy, annihilate any and all the living beings you like. Fear of reprisals, hindrances you have none: choose what pleases you, but leave nothing out, make no exceptions; show consideration to no one whomsoever, sever every hobbling tie, abolish every check, let nothing stand in your way; leave everything to your imagination, let it pursue its bent and content yourself to follow in its train, above all avoiding any precipitate gesture: let it be your head and not your temperament that commands your fingers. Without your noticing it, from among all the various scenes you visualize one will claim your attention more energetically than the others and will so forcefully rivet itself in your mind that you'll be unable to dislodge it or supplant it by another. The idea, acquired by the means I am outlining, will dominate you, captivate you; delirium will invade your senses, and thinking yourself actually at work, you will discharge like a Messalina. Once this is accomplished, light your bedside lamp and write out a full description of the abomination which has just inflamed you, omitting nothing that could serve to aggravate its details; and then go to sleep thinking about them. Reread your notes the next day and, as you recommence your operation, add everything your imagination, doubtless a bit weary by now of an idea which has already cost you some come, may suggest that could heighten its power to exacerbate. Now turn to the definitive shaping of this idea into a scheme and as you put the final touches on it, once again incorporate all fresh episodes, novelties, and ramifications that occur to you. After that, execute it, and you will find that this is the species of viciousness which suits you best and which you will carry out with the greatest delight. My formula, I am aware, has its wicked side but it is infallible, and I would not recommend it to you if I had not tested it successfully.[4]

One suspects, quite correctly, that something in this passage verges on a parody of mystical practices. It often reproduces, almost verbatim, the prescriptions given in Saint Ignatius of Loyola's *Spiritual Exercises.*[5] The libertine ascetic (if we may presume to combine these two words), like an Ignatian spiritual exercitant, forces himself, on the basis of three sets of conditions, to produce the optimal state of desire and sexual pleasure:

> *Conditions of place:* a darkened, secluded space inaccessible to external distractions and sensations
>
> *Conditions of time:* a period of preparation set at exactly two weeks, a precise demarcation that serves as a challenge, as a plan for triggering and compelling certain effects and signs, followed by a moment of meditation, with its work of remembering and rehearsal, followed in turn by a period of fulfillment
>
> *Conditions of discourse:* total suspension of speech by way of a retreat into silence, and recourse to writing as a way of fixing thoughts, rereading them, and comparing them (suspension of speech as a way of leaving oneself open to taking dictation from desire)

As in the Ignatian retreat, all three conditions aim at bringing about the sphere of exclusion mentioned by Barthes in *Sade, Fourier, Loyola.*[6]

But language is suspended only insofar as the authority of discourse is displaced, to be built on a foundation made of a different material, one more remote than speech: the one belonging to the attitudes and conditions of meditation, the one whose protocol takes the form of a sentence, which gives dramatic representation to an utterance that makes its appearance only when the pressure directed at signs has come to an end. The exercitant retreats from speech, but he does so in order to make signs speak, so that another voice can answer his call: for Ignatius, this is the voice of God; for Sade, the voice of desire.

What is noteworthy on the part of both Jesuit saint and libertine writer is that imagination is required to be the medium and instrument of this procedure. For Sade, this use of imagination would appear to go without saying. In the case of Ignatius, it is more surprising, since it presupposes a radical break with the previous Castilian and Rhenish mystical tradition, in which the ideal of a "vision of God" required the elimination of all contingent references, all material media. This negative thinking is now succeeded by the new realm of the sign, with its requisite classifying and listing of positivities. Ignatian imagination was already shaping the entry into this modernity; Sadean imagination establishes its peak. Ineffable vision is succeeded by views, images, and scenes. But although the two approaches mobilize the same faculty, they have profoundly divergent objects (as we would expect) and especially processes, even though in both cases, taken as a whole, we can discern the same formal objective: *investigation* and *fixation*. Ignatius, Barthes explains, treats the imagination as strictly voluntary and selective:

> As voluntary action, speech energy, production of a formal system of signs, the Ignatian imagination . . . can and must have an apotropaic function; it is first and foremost the power of repulsing foreign images. . . . This negative power is what must first be recognized in the fundamental act of meditation, which is concentration; to "contemplate," "fix," "see myself as through my imagination," "to see through the eyes of the imagination," "to place myself before the object," is first to eliminate, even to eliminate continuously, as though, contrary to appearances, mental fixation on an object could never be the basis of a positive emphasis, but only the permanent residue of a series of active, vigilant exclusions.[7]

And this selective vigilance is all the more strictly necessary in that imagination, no matter how indispensable to the concrete representation of Christlike acts and to the imaginary identification that these acts must ordain in the subject of the *oratio*, is still an ambiguous, error-prone faculty assailed by enticing images. This is why fixation merges with the exhausting task of elimination: a suitable image can be sustained only within the emptiness opened up around it. This is no longer even a problem for the libertine imagination, of course, which is completely hospitable to perverse enticements, and for which the issue is not to exclude but to indicate a preference, to invent a procedure permitting the choice of that image among the mass of images that can assert itself as the strongest, most voluptuous, and most suitable one for harnessing and marking the energy of desire.

Thus what is lost in the movement from Ignatian to Sadean prescriptions is the voluntarist position. The only decision required of the libertine "exercitant" is the decision to put himself actively into a state of passivity, to prepare himself to make an accurate reading of what is occurring inside him. Indeed, the process requires only a minimum number of steps, the first being the decision to enter into a libertine retreat. What is proposed for these two weeks of preparation is not a struggle but a simple suspension of desire, through the playful redirection of the attention to other objects — in other words, a quite hedonistic asceticism. The second step consists in secluding oneself and lying down alone "calmly and in silence," in order to become aroused and free one's imagination. (Couch, darkness, free association: the libertine exercitant is in the same situation as for Freudian analysis except for the absence of transference, but this is a great difference.) From this moment on, it is a third-person process, arising as if from outside the exercitant, who after having prepared a theater for it (this camera obscura) need do nothing more than be the voyeur of the spectacle he has set in motion, a spectacle surprisingly close to what, today, might be the projection of a filmstrip, with the possibilities of stopping, going in reverse, and adding elements from other filmstrips — in short, the whole labor of cutting that is filmmaking itself, for the activities of the third step (gradation, detailing, and reviewing) already constitute a work of this kind. These activities, the most imitatively Ignatian ones, are presented as the first serious attempt to organize the fantasy material. In other words, this step has to do with turning the fantasy material into a sentence (gradation), but also with giving it the texture of the real (detailing), by means of the most concrete possible representation. In fact, however, for Sade as for Ignatius, this imaginative concentration aims at nothing less than *hallucinating the referent*: one has to believe one is there. (Ignatius of Loyola: "During this meal, consider Christ our Lord as if you were watching Him break bread with His apostles—His way of drinking, looking, speaking—and endeavor to imitate Him.")[8] For Sade, this discursive work is an operation of filtration and selection. It has nothing to do with struggle or exclusion. In order for the best image, the most insistent (or resistant) one, to impose itself of its own accord (we might almost take this for a Gestalt experiment), it suffices to place this triple grid (gradation, detailing, and reviewing) onto the imaginative flux. The process is a specifically objective one. No longer does the subject have to fixate on the scene; the scene must fixate on the subject, take him over, and sweep him away: "Without your noticing it, from among all the various scenes you visualize one will claim your attention more energetically than the others and will so forcefully rivet itself in your mind that you'll be unable to dislodge it or supplant it by another." It is as if the libertine exercitant were creating the necessary conditions for being chosen, designated, by his own desire—as if he were establishing a mechanism for compelling the strongest, wildest desire to manifest and project itself onto the image into which the subject in turn has been drawn: iconophany becomes erophany. Through his artifact, the subject obliges what comes from within him to seize hold of him as if it came from somewhere else, and all he does is the work of recording the process running through him. The aim of his entry into retreat and meditation is to force signs to speak so that he can then let himself speak through them. Instinct must be given the face of destiny.

It is remarkable that this work of *recording* (as we will designate the fourth step) is identified with an operation of *writing*:

Once this is accomplished, light your bedside lamp and *write out a full description* of the abomination which has just inflamed you, omitting nothing that could serve to aggravate its details; and then go to sleep thinking about them. *Reread your notes the next day* and, as you recommence your operation, add everything your imagination, doubtless a bit weary by now of an idea which has already cost you some come, may suggest that could heighten its power to exacerbate. Now turn to the definitive shaping of this idea into a scheme and as you *put the final touches on it*, once again incorporate all fresh episodes, novelties, and ramifications that occur to you.[9]

Apart from the still obvious reference to Ignatius, what is most surprising about the introduction of writing into this mechanism is its similarity to the Hegelian "recipe" for the exhibition of the universal in sensation, as described in the first chapter of *Phenomenology of Mind*:

> To the question *What is the now?* we can reply, for example, *The now is the night*. A simple experience will be sufficient for us to feel the truth of this perceptible certainty. We note this truth down in writing; a truth loses nothing by being written down, and just as little by being preserved. But if at noon we look again at this written-down truth, we shall then have to say that it has gone flat.

From this experience, Hegel extracts the truth of mediation ("That which is now preserved is therefore not immediate but mediated") and, from it, concludes: "Therefore, the universal is the truthfulness of perceptible certainty. We also *utter* the perceptible as universal.... Language is what is most truthful: with it, we would even and immediately refute our own *opinion* [*Meinung*]." Without laying undue emphasis on a point-by-point comparison of these two texts, because they are by no means posing the same question or focusing on the same object, let us use their procedural likeness (writing/reading/rereading) to pinpoint their marked formal difference with respect to the act and function of writing.

If it is in fact appropriate to speak of a "recipe" where the Hegelian process is concerned, its use of writing remains completely inessential and is even explicitly minimized ("a truth loses nothing by being written down, and just as little by being preserved"). Here, writing is left with an instrumental status, an adjunct role: that of a neutral medium. It fixes something without changing it. Its function is purely one of recording. In itself, it possesses no energy of its own.

For Sade, however, the stakes are on a completely different scale. A truth, written down, finds itself essentially modified, and it gains enormously from being reread. This has nothing to do with any aleatory process but rather with a precisely willed choice of method. First of all, writing is not introduced merely to fix a sensation or an experience but instead to conserve its energy (the moment of renewal will be amplified by this energy reserve, and thus we will have an exponential accumulation). To write, moreover, is to make fantasy enter into a practice, submit it to reality's grasp ("turn to the definitive shaping of this idea"), and inscribe it into a sociality (that of language) and a regimen of objectivity (that of the symbolic). To write, in other words, is already to "execute" ("After that, execute it, and you will find that this is the species of viciousness which suits you best and which you will carry out with the greatest delight").

If, for Hegel, a piece of writing is the completely discrete, erased, and erasable instrument of a mediational operation, and if it is nothing more than the negligible medium of this operation, it is because what it preserves is not the moment itself, with its own texture and singular sensations, but that moment's nonbeing. The piece of writing, bearing witness against the moment, hails the truth of the universal; the passage through time invalidates the *content* of the writing. For Sade, by contrast, the piece of writing reaffirms, across time, the intact and even stronger return of this content. It is quite clear that, between the two processes, an irreconcilable conflict is being played out between two kinds of thought: for Sade, the thought dealing with the *repetition* of desire and its intensity; for Hegel, the thought dealing with the *mediation* of desire and its intensity, that is, with the sacrifice of desire and its intensity for the sake of the concept.

The Hegelian night, the night of nonbeing, brings about the death of sensation, the suppression of the immediate that announces the principle of desire's renunciation. By contrast, the Sadean night works to intensify desire and prepare its mortal, massacring return. The Hegelian night is where "Substance becomes subject," where negation of the moment is the prelude to the truth of day and the recognition of the Other. In the Sadean night, nothing is mediated; a sexual pleasure is rehearsed, and a mastery is exacerbated, that rules out any form of otherness ("assure yourself that you are absolute sovereign in a world groveling at your feet, that yours is the supreme and unchallengeable right to change, mutilate, destroy, annihilate any and all the living beings you like").

The Sadean mechanism remains strictly nontransferential; the Other does not even have the imaginary status conferred on it by Ignatius, the status of God's countenance, a countenance transmitting the signals occasioned, picked up, and interpreted by the appropriate device, the Exercise. The Sadean mechanism presupposes the complete immanence and radical intransitivity of desire, the transmitting source, which is why it is a mechanism less for reading than for practical selection. It is not so much a question of recognizing an uncertain voice as of arranging the logic of a categorical choice. In both cases, however, what remains remarkable is the construction of this mechanism, with its loci, its time, its gestural code, its treatment of the imagination, and especially its methodical production of a *void* (of bodies, signs, discourses) in order to make the element under investigation impose itself in all its imperious truth.

We see, then, that the practice of apathy as an *oratio libertina* is essentially the practice of a method, a diacritical method for clarifying judgment and disencumbering the libido, a method simultaneously affirmed as an art of intensifying orgasm: an alternating impulse of disinvestment and overinvestment. In this rarefied setting (more privative than negative), in the retreat's emptying out of the codes of everyday life, energy gathers itself, condenses itself, and finds itself compelled to produce an act of force, an act of judgment, and to execute the necessary choice.

In no way, then, is the product of the apathetic void the obliteration of passion; on the contrary, it is a refined technique for the aggravation of passion. This is why Blanchot is correct to see in apathy a means of developing the energy of passion. The issue is quite precisely one of *concentrating* passion, of providing it with a single focal point ("the species of viciousness which suits you best"). Fainting and methodical numbness then pave the way for the explosive, tumultuous condensations of sexual pleasure.

Nevertheless, when Blanchot writes, "Apathy is the spirit of denial applied to the man who has elected to be sovereign,"[10] he pulls Sade toward a problematics that seems not to suit him. Apathy is something quite different from negation. To the extent that negation is either an act of logical judgment or the dialectical operation of the *Aufhebung*, it does not account for apathy as an affective act, an operation of withdrawing libidinal energy from ordinary objects. There is no question of negation, but rather of simple disconnection; apathy does not eliminate signs, it empties them of all intensity; faced with the seriousness of negation, apathy maintains the suspension of humor. In other words, its action is that of distancing, understood here as an accomplished technique of dis-affection. It is a question of prizing affect away from the illusions on which it exhausts itself. To be more exact, the critical operation of apathy permits the dissociation of the instinctual (the energetic quantity) from the sentimental (the illusion that grafts itself onto the libido). Indeed, it is clear that for Sade the sentimental is the locus par excellence of the ideological, that is, of everything that was designated as a "prejudice" in the eighteenth century. We shall soon see why the sentimental lends itself so well to the manifestation of the ideological. For now, let us pose the problem of how to dispense with "prejudices" without also liquidating passion. To execute this division and bring this sorting operation about will be the precise function of apathy, for passion becomes truly libertine by detaching itself from the sentimental — that is, by emerging as a pure energetic element or, in other words, a principle of power, and therefore of pleasure. But it will now have to do with mental orgasm, an orgasm "of the head" — that is, an orgasm of discourse and, finally, of *representation*.

Enthusiasm, Causes, and Cruelty

> Causes, may be, are unnecessary to effects.
>
> — *Juliette*

There exists in Sade's writings the figure of the failed libertine. This figure is concerned with those who have not completed the critique of causes — those who, in spite of their crimes and all their debauchery and acts of violence, still give way to *enthusiasm* (as does Olympia, who in spite of her murderous exploits has not yet cured herself of this weakness and will finally be sacrificed by Juliette and Clairwil). Enthusiasm also takes the form of emphatic attachment to a particular passion. It is an incapacity for the detachment of apathy, or again it is the power of motivation, action "in the name of." To behave in this way is to revert to the victim's regimen of the symptom, to run the risk of being the effect and expression of a play of uncontrolled forces rather than the one who sustains discourse and masters all its logics, to inscribe oneself as a "case" within the scene and get oneself caught up and pinned down in it rather than being the one who constructs it.

Passion — trapped by enthusiasm within the network of causes, lacking the constant called apathy, and therefore lacking critical distance — causes the proliferation of illusory figures, such as the figures of amorous, religious, and humanitarian illusion. Libertine thought is employed toward the goal of their cruel, methodical overthrow.

What about love?

> I have never thought that from the junction of two bodies there need or indeed can result that of two hearts.[11]

Of all man's passions, love is the most dangerous and that against which
he should take the greatest care to defend himself. To judge whether love
be madness, is not the lover's distraction sufficient proof of it? or that
fatal illusion he entertains, which causes him to ascribe such charms to
the object he dotes upon and goes scampering about praising to the
skies?[12]

The libertine invokes a physics of sexual pleasure (as already discussed
in connection with the overthrow of the lyric body) in order to oppose
the metaphysics of feeling, but the first thing he combats in the heart's
ardent impulses is the invasion of a new morality, which the new bourgeoisie surreptitiously promotes on behalf of the "natural" virtues of
the people, as against aristocratic depravity.

What about religious faith? God is only a "mumbo jumbo" invented
for "enthusiasts, women, and simpletons."[13] Religion is a tissue of lies, a
vast enterprise of dupery and exploitation organized by priests and law-
makers. In his critique of religion, Sade, the disciple of Holbach, is always attempting to flush out the illusionists behind the illusion, to uncover the strategy behind the effects. Here is Holbach: "Religion is the
art of intoxicating men with enthusiasm in order to prevent them from
occupying themselves with the ills heaped upon them by those who govern them here below."[14] But, according to Sade, this trick works only
because it finds fertile soil in the sentimentality maintained by humanitarian preconceptions.

And what about brotherly love? about pity? This must be the last
refuge of the ultimate, most resistant, most universal illusion. One is
no less a man for having been taught a thing or two about love or dis-
abused of religious faith; that is, one is no less human, and so one is
still able to see oneself in one's fellows. Could this be the last bastion of
sensitivity, the one that the weapon of apathy must leave untouched?
Indeed, how can one move against it without being threatened oneself,
without breaking the social bond (not so much in its institutional forms
as in its very possibility) and thus exposing oneself to the terrorist relations of wartime, the infinite vengeance of all against all?

The libertine master does not hesitate. The destruction has to go
even this far. It has to go all the way to the negation of humanity, the
destruction of every form of recognition and reciprocity. This is an absolute break, the cutting edge. It is what is most chilling and most terri-
fying about apathy, what leads to cold-blooded murder, murder com-

mitted for no reason, or at least for no other reason than to confirm the severing of every bond, whereby the libertine becomes a lighthearted executioner, lighthearted because he is permanently empty, a crypt where a brain has been set up to orchestrate representations and displace orgasm onto discourse itself. Reason has now accomplished its conquest of the passions. It has imprinted its form on them and disciplined their substance: reason is what takes pleasure in the intensity that the passions transmit and in the objects that they invest.

How will this fearsome void, this violent eradication of all sensitivity, this polar icing of the heart, be brought about? Through a methodical attack on the feeling—pity—in which Rousseau found the alpha and omega of all humanity, its indisputable foundation:

> Men, in spite of all their morality, would never have been better than monsters, if nature had not given them pity to assist reason... from this quality alone flow all the social virtues.... Such is the pure impulse of nature, anterior to all manner of reflection; such is the force of natural pity, which the most dissolute manners have as yet found it so difficult to extinguish... a virtue so much the more universal, and withal useful to man, as it takes place in him before all manner of perfection.[15]

Rousseau's whole demonstration, in a subtle and paradoxical process of thought, will consist in showing that pity, through the mediation of imagination, originates in the very impulse of self-love. In pity, I represent myself in another. I recognize myself in him. I love him as my alter ego. Imagination cracks the isolating shell of self-love and, by opening up this possibility, is affirmed as the mark of humanity: it inaugurates language, thought, the social bond, and perfectibility, and all at once. But it also introduces the dangers of amorous passion and the selfish withdrawal that comes with it, a withdrawal intersecting with the other withdrawal that dominates the other axis of humanity: the realm of needs and reason ("it is reason that makes man shrink into himself"; "it is philosophy that destroys his connections with other men").[16] It will always be the province of pity to restore the first impulse of nature, in opposition to the perversion that is inscribed into history as injustice and decadence.

This complex, delicate genesis of pity in Rousseau is what Sade overturns, and rather lightly. With great exactitude, he rearranges the placement of the terms *nature* and *history* on the two series generated by self-love. The sequence *imagination-passion-pleasure-cruelty* is what Sade

assigns to the truth of nature; the *imagination-pity* relationship is where
he discerns the mark of history, that is, the mark of cultural relativity
and preconceptions:

> What do you call mercy? . . . That sentiment, chilling to the desires, can
> it find entry into a stern heart? And when a crime delights me, can I be
> stopped by mercifulness, the dullest, most stupid, most futile of all the
> soul's impulsions? . . . Are plants and animals acquainted with mercy, pity,
> social obligations, brotherly love? And in Nature do we detect any law
> other than self-interest, that is, self-preservation? The one great trouble
> is that human laws are the fruits of nothing but ignorance or prejudice.[17]

From the starting point of self-love, a point of departure identical
to Rousseau's, Sade's ironically opposite use of the concept of nature
(that unconditional reference of the early modern era) suffices to reverse Rousseau's demonstration. But whereas all Rousseau's concepts
are shaped by a duality that explains their paradoxical evolution, Sade's
concepts are ranged along both sides of a dividing line drawn by a presumably continuous and unlimited imperative of sexual pleasure. We
find no dialectic of division and surplus here, nor do we find any ambiguity. Here, theory has taken on the appearance of a coup. (But it must be
noted that the locus of articulation changes completely from Rousseau
to Sade: for Rousseau this locus is actual sociality; for Sade it is fiction.)

What the libertine critique seeks to knock down and finish off with
its denunciation of pity is the very possibility of the *social bond*. Pity,
by establishing the social bond in nature, simultaneously establishes law,
which is permitted to claim roots in universality; and now it is desire
that is made relative and forced to acknowledge its limits before the existence and liberty of the *socius*. Pity, in view of everything that is articulated within it or that develops from it, certainly seems to be the
last obstacle to libertine violence and mastery; its eradication throws
the doors of cruelty wide open, the cruelty of unmotivated, indifferent,
lightly committed murder detached from any reference or causality:

> The most enjoyable crimes are the motiveless ones. The victim must be
> completely innocent: if we have sustained some harm from him it
> legitimates the harm we do him, and lost to our iniquity is the keen
> pleasure of exerting itself gratuitously.[18]

One no longer kills to stimulate orgasm; killing is orgasm itself — or,
rather, crime and passion are indissociably fused in the cold incandes-

cence of apathy, in that union of cruelty and lust whose intensity offers itself as a *revelation* of the most exalted libertine thought, the thought in which Juliette instructs her overwhelmed listener:

> "Oh, Juliette," the Princess whispered, ... "the ideas you put in my head.... Ah, I was but a child, little did I know, less yet did I make of my opportunity—I realize it now.
>
> "Oh, my love," she said, and she was completely afire, "a thousand things astir inside me and are telling me how heavenly it must be to rob one of our fellow creatures of the treasure of his existence, the most precious in a human being's possession. To sever, to shatter the ties attaching that person to life, and this solely with a view to procuring oneself a little pleasant sensation, for the sole purpose of discharging a little more agreeably... oh yes! this shock delivered to the nervous system, resulting from the effect of pain undergone by others, oh yes, it makes perfect sense to me, Juliette, and I have no doubt at all the joy engendered by this concatenation of phenomena must culminate in the very ecstasy of the gods."[19]

The libertine law of pleasure is the law of absolute rejection of solidarity with humanity as a whole. It is in this sense first of all that the libertine law of pleasure deifies. Apathy brings about the marvel of producing infinite separation. The victory of the "head" is the victory of no longer having a body except as an occasion of pleasure for the mind. This is the "very ecstasy of the gods": the ecstasy of mastery over causes, of pure impassivity before the whole of existence. A strange gnosis: libertine apathy begets a mystical killer.

Mastery, Representation, Death

When its procedures and effects are reviewed, libertine apathy shows itself to be a method of surprising logic and precision. We can admire its flawless mechanism and functioning; we can be seduced by the perfectly regulated interactions that it establishes in the textual realm. But reading libertine apathy in this way, with the lightness of fiction, cannot prevent one from seeing something rather disquieting in it: the way it constitutes the symptom of a will to power, in which we see an ever more dominant reason clearing yet another rung of the ladder in its upward climb.

It is as if reason (claiming to be the realm of representations and order), coming face to face with nature (which would be the realm of the passions and the energies), were finding conquest blocked by the barrier of sensitivity; as if this sensitivity were the last hidden recess of the shadowy and the secret, pitting itself against the brilliant, all-consuming light of knowledge; as if this final desecration were needed to make mastery complete:

> 'Tis when we have achieved depravation, insensibility, that Nature begins to yield us the key to her secret workings, and . . . it cannot be pried away from her save through outrages.[20]

The job of apathy, in other words, is to make this barrier one that can be leaped over so that the form of reason can be imprinted on this nature, the passions can be categorized as representations, energy can be imbued with order, and, when all is said and done, every substance can pass into discourse and be submitted to classification, cataloging, and mathesis. Then the passions, purged and dis-affected by apathy, reduced to their pure quantum of energy, can be linked up to the table of representations. One sees the advantage for discourse in this colonization, which offers rational form to the passions, but only in order to appropriate their energy for itself. More than this, however, discourse wants to be what passion desires — it wants not just to dominate but to be loved for it, too. This is why it is important to discourse to inscribe every desire under the rubric of representation. It is here that libertine eroticism prides itself on being a mental eroticism, an eroticism "of the head," recognizing orgasm only as an orgasm of language (in the double sense of this genitive). Sadean mastery is generated within discourse. Its plan reaches successful completion only when it has managed to reduce orgasm itself to discourse. Sadean mastery requires that apathy carry out this arduous task, produce heat from cold, "fire up," "electrify," "inflame" the head with calculations, representations, and decisions of the coldest insensitivity and the most savage impassivity, with crimes of "sangfroid" — crimes committed in, precisely, cold blood.

The discourse of mathesis finds this enterprise of implacable disaffection necessary to the methodological constitution of its object through the removal of the subject from the playing field. With the decision to extend its procedures to passion and sensitivity, however, it becomes a merciless process, a structural and dogmatic exclusion of the Other who occasions desire, so that the only desire left will be the desire occasioned by representation. This is why the destruction of the Other must be signified indefinitely: the discourse of mastery, that insatiable Moloch, has a bottomless craving for corpses; it wants wilderness and depopulation (Saint-Fond dreams of exterminating almost the whole of France), and the only end it can imagine is the end of the world: "Ah, how many times, by God, have I not longed to be able to assail the sun, snatch it out of the universe, make a general darkness, or use that star to burn the world!"[21] For the master shaped by this lethal discourse, exempt from any kind of shared concern or reciprocity, there remains only the confrontation with "the Absolute Master" (as Hegel says): death, his own death. But the libertine's ultimate defiance, or subterfuge, will be to declare his death desirable, to crave it as the final orgasm: "there is pleasure in dying"; "death puts the thrill of lust in me"[22]—a paranoiac invocation that, logically speaking, brings closure to the project of libertine apathy.

CHAPTER FOUR

The Imaginable and the Space of the Tableau

Words cannot describe that divinely voluptuous scene; only an
engraver could have rendered it properly.

— *Juliette*

The relation of language to painting is an infinite relation. . . . It is in
vain that we say what we see; what we see never resides in what we
say. And it is in vain that we attempt to show, by the use of images,
metaphors, or similes, what we are saying; the space where they
achieve their splendour is not that deployed by our eyes but that
defined by the sequential elements of syntax.

— MICHEL FOUCAULT, *The Order of Things*

Sadean locales are varied indeed, and of a diversity in keeping with the
peregrinations on which the libertine, moved by a nomadic desire, finds
himself pulled along. It would be relatively easy to establish a typology
of these locales (fortresses, palaces, monasteries, salons, bedrooms, gardens, underground passages), but a labor like this would be useful only
if it managed to show what determines the very form of space in all
these locales — namely, the pictorial and the theatrical, which are no-
ticeably emphasized in the vocabulary: "That libidinous drama . . . com-
prised . . . three scenes"; "Very hot was the affray and very prolonged; . . .
I heard my performance praised when we had done."[1]

Whatever the locale, what matters is the development of a tableau,
in the sense of both *engraving* and *scene*. It is possible, however, on the
basis of the eighteenth-century *epistēmē*, to imagine that a third conno-

tation may not be altogether ruled out: that of the tableau, or table,² as a classifying *schema*, a catalog.

Tableau as Engraving, Scene, and Schema

The tableau as an engraving or scene generally can be thought of as indicating, first of all, the placement of bodies into the space of the gaze, the space of the initial cutting up that an elementally fetishistic desire carries out on those parts of the body that are to be enjoyed or mistreated. This initial act of cutting heralds the crueler, bloodier one realized in torture. But the purpose of this movement, the movement from visual cutting to actual rending of the victim's body to pieces during the orgy, would seem to be the resolution of an aporia articulated in the terms *scene* and *engraving*: the deadlock of animate and inanimate, motion and death.

To begin with, the body simply observed and described is the province of engraving, that is, of tableaux in general as the recording of features, the representational surface of values (erotic or aesthetic). The pose in which the body is offered maintains a distance, an inaccessibility connoting prohibition, the very prohibition connected with any form of representation. This is why elimination of distance is identified with an aggression that forces the engraving to move, features to come to life, organs to go into action (mouths, hands, genitals: words and cries, caresses and blows, ejaculations and sufferings). Engraving becomes scene; the pictorial evolves toward the theatrical, and motionless tableau toward *tableau vivant*: "At this point, Curval was moved to give the company a before-supper demonstration in fact of what Duclos had described in words."³ But this movement, which brings the tableau to life, comes to a halt at two points, one involving the victims and the other, the libertines.

In the case of the victims, scene reverts to engraving when the bodies, slaughtered and torn to pieces, fall back into the inanimate and into distance, both of which had characterized the visual act of cutting. Here, however, the cutting is irreversible, over and done, even overdone. Desire has withdrawn from its object. The body, disfigured, exhausted (as we might say of a fund or a lode), has nothing more to express; there is nothing left to do but get rid of it. The tableau demands its own elimination.

In the case of the libertines, the stopping point is provided by satisfaction itself. Orgasm brings motion to an end (hence Sade's whole strategy of retention, and the fantasies of loss, which should be understood as attempts to prolong the scenic phase, to keep the *tableau vivant* alive).

This is why the question leaps out here of the tableau's double emphasis on motion and motionlessness. The fulfillment of desire, by ending the scene, oppresses libertine mastery with the threat of death, a threat that libertine mastery otherwise attempts to deflect entirely onto the victim's body.

With ejaculation, in other words, everything moves too quickly. With death there is a race of sorts, and painters may know this better than anyone else: the painter wants to render motion but records only immobility. As in the Greek tradition, however, the fault is with the object: it becomes immobile even before the painter has had time to grasp it. The fulfillment of desire ends the scene, just as death does.

The paradox of libertine desire becomes the paradox of its representation:

> But words cannot describe that divinely voluptuous scene; only an engraver could have rendered it properly, and yet it is doubtful he would have had time to capture those many expressions, all those attitudes, for lust very quickly overwhelmed the actors and the drama was soon ended. (It is not easy for art, which lacks movement, to realize action wherein movement is the soul; and this is what makes engraving at once the most difficult and thankless art.)[4]

Although a movie camera could be assumed to satisfy this wish for instantaneity, that would not necessarily be true, for pleasure may reside in the (too) "lateness" recorded by the painter. Here, finally, is where the threat to the executioner looms, the threat that he will see his own status aligned with that of the victim. The threat is all the more inescapable for the fact that desire, all along, has been coiled up in representation. The body is still placed into a network of conventional values and references. In other words, it is still subjected to the assumptions and leverage of a cultural code ("a mouth made to be painted," "the beauty of Venus united with the charms of Minerva," "the waist of Apollo"). The Sadean act, radical though it may be, takes place within the encoded space of theater, and in mockery of theatrical scenery; hence the ambiguity of a transgression committed under the watchful eye of the theatrical. But perhaps this is also how transgression escapes the realist order of the referent and is able to play itself out in the ironic logic of the simulacrum. We will have reason to return to this point.

The tableau, or table, is also a catalog, a classifying schema—that is, a square-ruled surface for writing down all the relationships capable of filling in the field allotted to some characteristic (in this case, the characteristic of desire). In the eighteenth century (with Buffon, Linné, Adanson, Bonnet, and so on), this was how catalogs of natural beings (animal, vegetable, mineral) were established under the rubric of natural history, catalogs that, when all was said and done, were only lists of forms and their transformations, only their arrangement into tables or tableaux (systems of equivalence and difference), an arrangement whose typical expression, as Foucault observes, was the establishment of a botanical garden or a zoological collection:

> To the Renaissance, the strangeness of animals was a spectacle; it was featured in fairs, in tournaments, in fictitious or real combats, in reconstitutions of legends in which the bestiary displayed its ageless fables. The natural history room and the garden, as created in the Classical period, replace the circular procession of the "show" with the arrangement of things in a "table." What came surreptitiously into being between the age of the theatre and that of the catalogue was not the desire for knowledge, but a new way of connecting things both to the eye and to discourse. A new way of making history.[5]

In this work of classifying, of setting up tables and tableaux, the visible world was precisely what was valorized (to the exclusion of the tactile and the auditory) and therefore itemized: "Natural history is nothing more than the nomination of the visible," which "leaves sight with an almost exclusive privilege, being the sense by which we perceive extent and establish proof, and, in consequence, the means to an analysis *partes extra partes* acceptable to everyone."[6] In the observation-based sciences, knowledge found itself linked to (if not created by) the precision of *seeing*. This is why the *pictorial* or *scenic* tableau (already heir to a long process of education in the perception of forms, and to a perspectivist scholarly tradition) began to be seen as the semantic equivalent of the table or tableau as a *schema* or *catalog* that, under various types of signs and names, offered a totalizing view of the natural world. The equivalence was complete except for the fact that the table of the natural scientist was made of language. This is how the tabular model began to mold the very form of discourse.

Even more important, however, what is foreshadowed here is a break between signs and things. Before the classical age, signs *belonged to* things and were part of them; afterward, signs *represented* things: "Things touch against the banks of discourse because they appear at the hollow space of representation"; "the theory of natural history cannot be dissociated from that of language," and this implies "a fundamental arrangement of knowledge, which orders the knowledge of beings so as to make it possible to represent them in a system of names."[7]

The uncoupling of signs from things, indeed the break between them, brought about by tables of natural taxonomies, ushered in a new era: that of the autonomous potency of discourse. Everything now took place in and through discourse. The boundlessness of what could be represented by linguistic signs was to seduce Sade, leading him to risk complete disconnection between discourse and the norms that hemmed in and restricted what could be said.

Giving the shape of a taxonomic table to what desire could imagine meant metonymically conferring reality and gravity on the imaginable. It meant subjecting its baroque rhetoric as such, a theatrical and pictorial one, to the discipline of establishing a science, integrating varieties of depravity into the precision of a system of denumerable variations.

Engraving, scene, schema: all three are emphasized in the Sadean text and contribute to making it a space overdetermined—with the eye of the painter, the spectator, the scholar—by the multiform activity of *seeing*, which defines the scope of *saying*: the totality of the one is included in the totality of the other.

Saying Everything, Seeing Everything: The Erotic Panopticon

Saying everything, defined both as encyclopedic requirement and as obscene defiance, is not separate from the principle—indirectly but implicitly stated, and equally incontestable—of *seeing* everything. Discursive mastery implies visual mastery; pleasure in looking is still wrapped up in the pleasure of enunciation. What we have, in other words, is a double and identical mastery, a double and identical pleasure filling up the same field.

The master's voice lays down the law over the whole space carved out by his eye. Nothing can escape an eye like his, precisely because everything is assumed to have been brought into the tableau, which is coincident with the system, that is, with the totality of discourse. Everything that can be spoken must be visible, and everything visible must be spoken. This saturation leaves no remainder. The possibility of any uncontrolled remainder is averted by the assumption of a "secret chamber": the unseen can still be designated, placed at the edge of the imaginable, and therefore placed in reserve for some future statement.

The absence of any possible retreat from the tableau, the requirement for total exhibition: this is obscenity, the space of the all-seeing master. (And this formal requirement of discourse is echoed in the requirement for immediate nakedness in the signified of the scene.)

For the rest, it is because the master is an omnivoyeur that Sade makes no particular use of voyeurism. In the narratives of *Juliette*, or in the tableaux of *The 120 Days of Sodom*, voyeurism figures as a "passion" like any other, with no specific importance (at the very most, it is a narrative pretext for scenes that the storyteller has merely witnessed). With Sade, everything is visible on principle, and so voyeurism is not, properly speaking, a Sadean perversion. Everything must be offered to the eye without mediation, without resistance; like the body, the tableau must be uncovered at once. Among libertines, to see is immediately to be seen. What is obtained through this remainderless, shadowless crisscrossing of all the visual fasciae is a kind of total view and omnivisibility, with groupings so arranged that everyone can revel in the sight of everyone else's pleasures:

> "No more privacy, no more intimate conversation," said the King; "henceforth we must operate within full view of one another."[8]

> Owing to the studied placing of the glades there was not one table from which you could not see all the others; and the cynical spirit in which the whole thing had been framed was also evident in the fact that no lubricity here in the dining room would be any less visible to the observer's eye than had been that in the assembly hall.[9]

The arrangement that results is a sort of erotic Panopticon,[10] by means of which nothing about the bodies stays hidden and nothing about the space remains secret: exposure is total. ("And fucked, fucking, watching fuck,... the thrice-happy rascal hurls his thunderbolt"; "I... declared that I would like to have the entire world standing there, seeing me in this state of inordinate happiness.")[11]

What is brought into being, then, is a perfectly circular theater, one where differences are eliminated between stage and performance hall and between actors and spectators, and where there is constant permutation of places and roles: the flogger becomes the flogged, the sodomizer the sodomized, the masturbator the masturbated. We find the general principle of this permutation articulated in the course of every orgy: "Do unto me everything I have done unto you."[12] This language of permutation is anything but a language of exchange (nothing could be more remote from Sadean thought than contractual reciprocity). To permute is first of all to invert attributes: to separate what has been established as being connected, and to connect what has been established as being separate. Without leaving the field of classified terms behind, the combinative operation becomes perverse simply by establishing unforeseen or even excluded relationships among those terms (taken together, all these exclusions mark out the space of reason). Expansion of the catalog means unrestricted permutation of all its elements. Logic is not abandoned; it is unreservedly freed of all limits. The catalog is a theater for the unlimited exchange of roles and positions.

Most of all, however, where the pleasure of seeing is concerned, what the group of libertines gains by instigating these incessant permutations is the sum total of all possible points of view. At any one moment, of course, any one libertine has only one limited point of view, but by the end of the orgy his varied positions and roles will have allowed him to traverse the tableau from every angle, and in each of its configurations. What we have here is certainly nothing like Leibniz's God, the absolute center of vision, the perfect plane of all perspectives. Rather, the group itself constitutes a kind of single body with multiple eyes, hands, and genitals, a body totally saturated but without a subject (because sexual pleasure, for Sade, remains radically individual, not susceptible to exchange). There is no place in this group-body, this flesh-machine, for amorous looks or subjective emphasis. The circularity of the spectacle in no way implies any transitivity of the gaze, which is possible only within the expressive-lyric order of bodies—possible, that is, only through a reactivation that is ruled out for Sade because for him the unadulterated preservation of positive symbolic emphasis seems to be the very condition of the combinative operation's smooth functioning, and the imaginary is presented as the threat of its dissolution.

For Sade, then, bodies and their parts (including the eyes) are looked at, but looking itself is *not* looked at. To look at looking is to be placed in a situation of exchange, specular exchange, where what is expressed are the degrees, depth, and anxiety of amorous states. The lyrical gaze speaks of the "soul's" movements and silently articulates hidden feelings.

Libertine logic invalidates this hermeneutical relationship. Nothing is hidden in the space of obscenity; all desires amount to denumerable passions related to equally denumerable objects. Everything can be put on display, taken apart, and put back together.

And so the eyes have nothing to say. If they are mentioned at all, they are a taxonomic element in the rhetoric of the portrait, reduced to generic information ("blue," "black," "expressive," and so on). Whatever the singular difference for which the eyes may be the medium, within the tableau they are simply denumerated, and that is all. Even if they are said to be "expressive," we never see them express anything at all.

Looking Glass/Tableau: The Imaginary/The Imaginable

The emphasis on *tableau*-specific vocabulary needs to be set against the absence of *mirror*-specific vocabulary (which is not to say that mirrors are not mentioned here and there—for example, the mirrors in Dolmancé's bedroom are expressly noted and described, as are those in the libertine niches of the salon at the Château of Silling). But we never, or rarely, see them function *as* mirrors, either in erotic scenes or, more generally, in the narrative economy. The absence of mirrors is all the more remarkable in that the use (and sometimes overuse) of the mirror's effects of depth or ambiguity constitutes a trademark of the erotic literary tradition, as in the literature of the Baroque, for example, in whose chief representatives (Saint-Amant, Sponde, Tristan L'Hermite, T. de Viau, H. d'Urfé)[13] we can see a set of mirror-related phantasms at work, in connection with which Genette[14] speaks of a "Narcissus complex" interweaving themes of the double, escape, and reflection. The mirror (especially the *natural* mirror offered by water) becomes the privileged instrument for the metamorphosis of an unstable, evanescent subject uncertain of its identity and lost in its images. The reflecting surface baits a trap for depth:

> The most innocent aquatic surface lies over an abyss: transparent, the surface allows the abyss to be seen; opaque, it suggests an abyss all the more dangerous for being concealed. To be on the surface is to defy depth; to float is to court shipwreck.[15]

> In a pastoral, the sorcerer who is consulted for the truth about a love shows that truth in a mirror, the instrument of choice for magical knowledge. The aquatic mirror reveals invisible presences, hidden feelings, the secrets of souls.[16]

In the order of the Baroque, every surface is liquid and every reflection indicates an abyss. Like the well, the mirror in its bottomless darkness is the locus of truth; it gives voice to what is beyond it. If, finally, there is a baroque character that transects every figure, it is quite simply the *soul*—the psyche, that fantastic identity based on reflections and images, recognized in doubles, and concretized as a point and a form attributable to elusive specular depth. (Thus *psyche* or *soul* might even be a name for the phantasm, defined as what comes *to* the place, and *in* place, of a disavowed gap, in order to close it: the soul as the geometrical point and compendium of all denials.)

This delirious specularity is what Sade does away with, in a very *positive* way. But, far from renouncing the mirror, that classic accessory of debauchery, he keeps it and yet exorcises it, demystifies it, clears it of phantoms, instrumentalizes it, places it back into the series of available objects. Baroque fluidity is succeeded by the flat compactness of the tableau, the liquid mirror by the mechanical mirror, the surface of illusion by the surface of the tour and the catalog. Sade turns the mirror into a device for producing determined, denumerable erotic effects. In any case, what falls away like so much rubbish is what has constituted the baroque mirror's most important effect: the soul. On this subject, Barthes writes:

> The West has made the mirror, always spoken of in the singular, the very symbol of narcissism (of the Ego, refracted Unity, the Body reassembled). Mirrors (in the plural) are another theme altogether, whether two mirrors are set up to face each other (a Zen image), so that they never reflect anything but emptiness, or whether the multiplicity of juxtaposed mirrors surrounds the subject with a circular image whereby coming and going is eliminated. This is the case with Sadean mirrors.[17]

The Interplay of Mirrors, or the Tableau Machine

Madame de Saint-Ange, in the course of educating Eugénie and initiating her into the libertine philosophy of the bedroom, discusses the principle of the mirror, or rather the principle of mirror interplay:

Eugénie—Oh dear God! the delicious niche! But why all these mirrors?

Madame de Saint-Ange—By repeating our attitudes and postures in a thousand different ways, they infinitely multiply those same pleasures for the persons seated here upon this ottoman. Thus everything is visible, no part of the body can remain hidden: everything must be seen; these images are so many groups disposed around those enchained by love, so many delicious tableaux wherewith lewdness waxes drunk and which soon drive it to its climax.[18]

This is a principle of mirror *interplay* because mirrors (in the plural) are essential to Sadean thought. The point is not to meet one's own eyes in a narcissistic seduction, and still less to meet the eyes of the other in a lyrical, unfathomable one, but rather to set up a machine for increasing the number of tableaux *within* the tableau. This looking-glass machine, which rules out the psyche-as-mirror, operates only in the plural, thereby securing two essential functions: the proliferation of effects ("by *repeating* our attitudes and postures in *a thousand different* ways, they *infinitely multiply* those same pleasures"), and the comprehensiveness of what can be seen ("*for the persons* seated here [*aux yeux de ceux* qui les goûtent] upon this ottoman. Thus everything is visible, *no part of the body can remain hidden: everything must be seen*").

The goal of this mechanism, then, is to render space absolutely circular by way of omnivisibility, and to guarantee the scene's closure, as well as its mastery by the libertine eye. Not only does this mechanism serve the imagination's work of inventing tableaux, it also constitutes a sort of model for practical actualization of the imagination, an objective projection of imagination's internal structures. In fact, it is as if the function of the looking glass were not to mirror but only to manufacture tableaux, and to do so as a reflecting machine that, by following the movements of the eye, merely takes samples of the scene that the intertwined bodies compose. This is a machine in motion, flexible, with immediate effects: the means by which mimesis comes to be automated.

Therefore, looking-glass interplay must not at any cost become the tool of some illusion of reality—of some passive phantasmal projection, a waking dream, or anything else that might sanction a shift to the imaginary. This interplay must not absorb reality into dreams or dissolve bodies in the mist of its infinity. On the contrary, it reflects the whole of perceptible space back to the agents of the scene by dividing that space up into so many tableaux, which project every possible point of view onto the master's eye. This is saturated space, space with no remainder, space traversed through and through.

In the hands of debauchery, the Leibnizian monad would necessarily become Sadean. In other words, if there are no longer any unsettling depths, it is because depth has been brought back to the surface, where it is spread out in networks of relationships: the mirror has been purged of its shadows and mysteries, rebuilt according to Enlightenment thought — prized away, we might say, from any kind of metaphysics. Moreover, looking-glass interplay puts the finishing touches on the erotic Panopticon, the first version of which was an arrangement of gazes turned toward the variously arranged or connected bodies. With the interplay of mirrors, everything is reduced to the immanence of the libertine gaze. Mirrors secure the projection of a metavision into the setting of the stage. The duplicate offered by mirrors is in no way an unfathomable Other, but merely a replica of the other perspectives offered by the assembled bodies. This is why the mirror, far from expanding this system, secures its closure, its classifiable finiteness.

And so Sade speaks of mirrors. In addition to indicating their presence here and there, he even goes so far as to define their function explicitly, as we have just seen. But this definition plays a part only at the level of the scene's signified, and nowhere else. The mirror is never emphasized as a textual theme, and it never plays a role in narrative argument. This failure to make use of mirrors may seem surprising, not just because their manipulation constitutes a factor in the possible variations within perversion's combinatory operation but also because it seems that the mirror, as a multiplier of images, would necessarily fulfill the Sadean wish for saturated tableaux and for the exhaustive denumeration of their various components.

This would be precisely a matter of *images*, however, and nothing more: the body is materially absent from the scene played out in the mirror. The body in the mirror can know neither enjoyment nor suffering; immaterial, inaccessible, almost metamorphosed into a soul, it is a body betrayed and idealized, one that means, to the libertine, the exclusion of his desire. Therefore, mirrors have no place and no function apart from the libertine's involvement with the real bodies in the scene that the mirrors pick up and reflect. The specular image does not multiply the number of *bodies*, only the number of *points of view* brought to bear on them, and on the scene that these bodies compose. Multiplication of the number of bodies depends not on mirrors but on power, the kind that comes from wealth or tyranny and permits the inexhaustible stockpiling of victims. To form a tableau, a *tableau vivant*, the libertine does not need images of the body; he needs the bodies themselves.

The mirror, moreover, with its capacity to renew the process of primary identification, continues to enable phantasms of fusion (such as those connected with lyric illusions in encounters based on looking—lyric illusions being merged, for Sade, with religious illusions). The amorous look, like ecstasy, is silent: both come to a halt before the barrier of the symbolic, and the symbolic then becomes, of necessity, what obliterates them both. Justine calls on the inner voice as her only evidence against the detailed demonstrations of her torturers, and her body pays the price: it is dissolved, as it were, in the discourse of the libertines. As far as the libertines are concerned, then, the victim's body apparently stands in for the rejected mirror. At the level of primary process, the portion of instinctual violence that cannot be harnessed by specular fascination, and thereby find an outlet, is discharged onto that object which falls short of the symbolic order: the victim's body. As for this surplus of violence, this primary aggression that the symbolic has the function of controlling (through its contractual nature of reciprocal recognition and social structuring), Sade refuses to attach it to imagination. This refusal comes at the price of the perversion and corruption of the symbolic itself, however, for the symbolic can exist only through the Other's response. But the Other, for Sade, is not to respond; the master does that for him by appropriating the symbolic (such as language and institutions) in order to redirect it toward the ends of sexual pleasure. The Master is a pillaging conqueror, forever showing up afterward to seize upon results produced somewhere else, without him, and subjecting them to his law.

The symbolic, submitted to this act of force that establishes the Master as such, loses its contractual function, its value as a pact of reciprocal recognition, and baits a trap for libertine power. It ceases to act as a barrier to surplus violence. Instead, it welcomes this surplus violence into its own corrupted network and offers it, instead of a specular/imaginary fulfillment, a "real" object, one taken from the domain of the Other: a living body, which, through its having been selected, finds the status of victim inflicted on it. The body of the victim necessarily appears *at* the place, and *in* place, of the absent mirror.

On the stage of the narrative, any slippage of the libertine into the order of the imaginary must be avoided (or be paid for with the reality of his desire), just as it must be avoided in the formal relationship of reader to text. All works of fiction offer themselves for specular projection—offer themselves, that is, for a purely vicarious satisfaction in which the instincts are sublimated in the scenes that are being represented. The relationship between the text and its reader is radically transformed by this need to avoid the imaginary. The transference changes direction. Sade does not expect the reader to bury himself or lose himself in the text. That would be the classic ploy of fiction: suspending time for the reader by way of an illusory digression that allows the instincts to be discharged in imagination. Instead, the issue for Sade is how the text can affect and attack the reader's body and bring some change about in it. The mirror, barred as a specific object from the narrative, is also barred from any textual function.

In Sade's writings, this barring of any function for the mirror (in the singular) is directly proportional to the erasure of the *imaginary*. And, inversely, the model of the tableau reflects what can be called the *imaginable*, that is, something belonging both to the order of the Leibnizian virtual (the whole of simultaneously actualizable possibilities) and to the order of Kantian schematism (the order of the perceptible actualization of concepts). What this means is that the Sadean text rejects all the effects of identification but aspires to inscribe on the body—to "capture"—the possibilities of discourse. This principle of textual agency has been defined, very aptly, as the "Sade effect":[19] the tableau offers itself not as a surface for representation but as an instrument for acting on whoever lets his eye move over it, and the impact has to do with a not inauthentic possibility of actualizing desire, a possibility that Sade states as follows:

> Many of the extravagances you are about to see illustrated will doubtless displease you, yes, I am well aware of it, but there are amongst them a few which will warm you to the point of costing you some come, and that, reader, is all we ask of you.[20]

The impactive relationship of fictional text to reader's body in no way involves a concern for the effectiveness or organization of some code of conduct. What is at work here is not an ethic, not even an inside-out or perverted one, but rather a logic: the logic of the *imagination*, which is the organ of the *program*—the organ, that is, of what secures the shift from competence to performance, of what transforms phantasm into specific practice. The imaginable relationships belonging to the tableau as a taxonomic set are projected into such and such a tableau-scene, which actualizes an original figure capable of affecting such and such a particular reader, or involving such and such a "taste" in any reader at all. If the program of every libertine idea or criminal whim has to be stated before it can be carried out, it is of course because of the need for strategy (libertinism is too serious to be left to chance) and method (the method of progressively saturating the tableau of possible configurations by ensuring the novelty of any proposed configuration). More than anything else, however, this means subjecting the body to discourse, making the act the duplicate of its stated program, and modeling particular frenzies on the symbolic order, which is precisely the order required by the orgy as a condition of sexual pleasure.

This *imaginary*, then, forever being stalked by language and forever being transformed into the *imaginable*, occupies a strange position, to the point where "it might almost be said," as Barthes notes, "that *imagination* is the Sadean word for *language*."[21] As a result, expressivist subjectivity is eliminated, and a catatonic positivity affirmed, as if pliability of substance had to be exorcised by rigidity of structure. There is no middle course.

What is the advantage of a division like this one?

Probably this: the network already organized by reason is seized upon by the wildest frenzy, but only so that reason will be forced to take it in charge. To be more exact, frenzy, itself offered as a tableau — that is, as a *Characteristic*[22] of the "passions" — is thus presented as a rational order, a system of possibilities. In this way, reason is invited to find itself in frenzy and stretch to the limits of frenzy. Once all classifiable phantasms coincide with the Characteristic, there is no more imaginary: everything, even the forbidden, has been said. There is nothing beyond the tableau; what can be desired coincides with what can be thought.

This is also why Sade, by contrast with most of the other libertine writers of his century (Crébillon, Duclos, d'Argens, La Morlière, Baret), denies himself all recourse to the fantastic and to anything connected with it (the marvelous, the allegorical, the legendary). We do not even find a utopia in Sade, in any precise sense: "Fiction does not serve to distract man from his desire ... Sade's purpose is in no way utopian, and the imagination does not assume any dialectical function in this body of work, which is nevertheless fictional."[23] There is nothing fantastic, then, not even anything ambiguous or vague or disquietingly strange. Otherwise a symptomatology would be needed, which is to say that the characters' motives would have to be psychological, and psychology is precisely what Sade rules out. In Sadean narratives we do find cellars and undergrounds, as well as isolated, sinister châteaux, but only as agents and guarantors of the isolation and security able to establish the verisimilitude of the acts occurring in these places. The places themselves never assume the specific value of fright or anxiety developed in the same period by *romans noirs,* in which satanism, secrets, mysteries, and occultism are fetishized.

What matters to Sade is that desire, as unconditional, become a possible structure of the "real world"—that it be inscribed into societal forms as they have been handed down historically. Even in the wildest programs (such as those of the libertines of Silling, or those of Juliette's Neapolitan and Roman orgies) the boundaries of reason—that is, the boundaries of the referent—are not breached. The established order is not given the slip: it is made use of, redirected. The order of classifiable codes is never left behind, and into their networks is inscribed everything (characters, conditions, practical methods, instruments, articles of clothing) that has been imagined. The imaginary never surpasses the imaginable, which is to say, finally, that it never surpasses the speakable. All frenzies are still programmable, and this is how they are kept within the systemic confines. The oneiric would be nothing but a betrayal of desire, a slipping into the illusory, an imaginary compensation. Blanchot comments aptly on this refusal of Sade's: "Because his own erotic dream consists of projections onto characters who do not dream, but who act out in a real way the unreal movements of his sexual pleasures..., the more this eroticism is dreamed, the more it demands a fiction from which dreams are banned, and in which debauchery is actualized and lived out."[24] Deleuze interprets it this way: "What characterizes the Sadean use of phantasy is a violent projective force of the paranoiac type, by which phantasy becomes the instrument of an essential and abrupt change introduced into the objective world."[25] But this objective world is none the less the world whose scope the text defines, the world that the text produces as the referential filmstrip indispensable to the framing of the narrative.

Theatricality: Experimental Speech

The Sadean character is no more subject to a psychology than his locales and landscapes are products of individualizing descriptions. Space always assumes the form of an eighteenth-century theatrical tableau, which amounts to saying that places and landscapes appear in it only as *stage sets*—in other words, as series of painted backdrops ready to descend from the rafters and frame the narrative. Thus the narrator has at his disposal a moving background of interchangeable elements whose task is to signify the referent, at minimal expense; the referent figures only as that small amount of reality necessary and sufficient to the representation of the world in which the characters move about. Here, one's habits of reading are firmly thwarted because ever since the Balzacian novel there has been a demand for maximum referential density. We want the novelistic text to make us forget that it is a work of fiction, to claim that it is being offered as the chronicle of a historical truth (social or individual). Thus, as it naively attempts to amass indications of verisimilitude in order to reproduce, seamlessly, what it presupposes is "the real," it wears itself out erasing the artifact that sets it in motion. The Sadean story is still medieval in this respect. Like the medieval mystery plays, it operates through the staging of emblematic figures. This technique is one in which fiction does not hide that it is fiction, nor does it claim to be reproducing any particular "real," but only to be taking from it a certain number of meaningful fragments, for the purpose of showing how they work. Nevertheless, whereas medieval mystery has a connection to the infinity of Holy Writ and to dogmatic truth, Sadean emblems are offered as denumerable, combinable elements of a finite system, a system devoid of ultimate truth. What the stage set's backdrops are saying is this: There is no fundament; there are only backdrops; and narrative, like theater itself, does not *stand for* "reality" but is only a simulating machine, an experimental artifact in which something of the historical and social "real" is experienced, shown, and offered to the understanding of the reader/spectator in a way that enables him to avoid falling into the hypnotic trap of imaginary identification. What is asked of him instead is a reply, a practice implicating his own body (the "Sade effect").

Thus the Sadean typologies—whether they use landscapes (the French countryside, the Alps, the Apennines, the Roman countryside, Vesuvius, the Black Forest, Siberia), cities (Paris, Lyons, Turin, Florence, Venice, Rome, Naples, Moscow), or characters (kings, princes, dukes and other nobles, judges, financiers, prelates, prostitutes, madams, pimps, little boys, virgins)—operate within this system of emblematic staging and openly fictional fiction. As in the commedia dell'arte, all the elements are of fixed types; what changes is their particular combinations, and the variants are what create the novelty in each situation.

Scenographic invention, the precise regulation of programs, and the arrangement of stage sets all seem to produce in Sade's writings a space that depends only on its tableaux, and a time that is only the sum of its repetitions—a world, in short, that is seriously deficient in "realness," a world in the conditional. But this deficiency encompasses the collapse and dissolution of saturated commonsensical codes that posit their accumulated platitudes as the Real. Thus it becomes easy to see what is at stake in any text: that it be an experiment on the possibilities of language and on the limits of the speakable, which are also the limits of censorship. The line traced by the speakable is drawn as the walls of the City, as political power; which is to say that the issue of language is always political.

CHAPTER FIVE

Time Cut to Measure

Now, as from the desire to what the desire causes 'tis ever but a
single step with personages such as our heroes, they went
unswervingly toward satisfying themselves.

— The 120 Days of Sodom

All went at great speed.

— Juliette

An emphasis on three major themes cuts clearly across the many problematics of time contained within the European philosophical tradition.
These are the themes of *delay* (waiting, patience), *deviation* (mediation,
labor), and *interiority* (memory, depth). Working in counterpoint (and
often at cross-purposes) to the great systematic theses, manifest asser-
tions, and declared oppositions of the philosophical schools, these three
themes trace the oblique lines of the schools' shared assumptions and
undisputed evidence.

In Greco-Latin and Christian antiquity, for example, whether time is
regarded negatively (the fall from eternity) or positively (the preparation
for eternity), it can always be classified under the theme of *delay*. To live
in time means to live with waiting, whether we mean a return to the beginning of time or a prelude to the Second Coming. A metaphysical thesis is transformed into an ethic of patience, an ethic to which passion,
fundamentally impatient, is anathema. The ethic of patience becomes a

system for defusing desire because desire, wanting to put nothing off, demands pleasure this very minute, shutting out both beginning and end.

But it matters very little whether any particular problematic gives time
a negative value or a positive one. Temporality is posited as pure prohibition wherever waiting takes the form of a structure that transcends
it. Time is thought to block desire, and waiting is thought to extinguish
temptation. The law of time becomes the law in absolute form. All on-
tologies of time, then, disguise subtle systems for regulating libidinal
energy and discouraging desire. This is probably why the question of
time is stated so clearly in Sade's writings: the thesis of libertine desire
cannot avoid entering into open conflict with the theme of delay, and
all the more so because the theme of delay is restated and brought back
into play, but more profoundly (or more perversely) this time, as the
theme of deviation: the theme of time conceived as the negation of immediacy. Understood as leaving no trace, as being an absence of works,
immediacy is time that does not pass through time; hence the need, in
classical problematics, to suppose time itself as excising the immediacy
of the instant and thereby affirming nonimmediacy, or universality. No
one has surpassed Hegel in stating what the philosophical tradition requires of time, for Hegel, in the *Encyclopedia*, makes time the very form
of the negative, the self-movement of this separation, "the being who
in being is not, and who in not being, is."[1] Hence, for Hegel, the aptness
of the figure of Chronos: time devours its offspring, the instant. Time
in and of itself determines the negative ("posited thus for itself, negation
is time").[2] This is why time is what structures the dialectical operation
itself, which begins in restraint (*Hemmung*) and ends in release (*Aufhebung*). The moment of the negative prohibits desire from exhausting
itself in the consumption of its object, and it allows the object to be
preserved for mediating activity, the labor from which works are born.
As we know, accession to works by way of labor is, for Hegel, the truth
and revenge of the slave. The master, trapped by his own inactivity, allows the world to take shape outside him; little by little, as a result, he
loses control of it.

And so we find Sade's libertine, the master by definition, conceiving
and claiming this inactivity as the practical and indispensable condition
of his sexual pleasure. Thus, quite lucidly and by every means of power,
he sees to it that the slave is kept dependent because the master, for his

part, wants to know nothing about mediation or difficult access, and therefore nothing about renouncing immediate enjoyment of the object.

In this way, the Sadean text, breaking with the figure of Chronos, where instants are negated for the benefit of a transcendent, totalizing time, establishes a model of time conceived as a serial chain of sexual pleasure — that is, as a string of instants all related to single units (places, bodies, names, acts, sequences). In this patchwork construction, there can be no question of any ultimate synthesis or final unity; this kind of time is firmly resistant to any *Aufhebung*.

In fact, when it comes to time, what must be seen is that the postulate of unity always functions in tandem with the postulate of interiority (the third of our themes). In a famous analysis from the *Critique of Pure Reason*, Kant states this relationship as follows: "Time is nothing other than the form of inner meaning, that is, the form of our intuition of ourselves and of our inner state."[3] In these pages from *The Transcendental Aesthetic*, Kant is simply giving an extremely rational form to what Christian themes stated and proclaimed as depth and communion, whereby consciousness of the self was identified with memory of the self, and personal identity was vouched for by intimate perception of the temporal continuum that pulls successive subjective states together, in the single act of a subject. Time, then, is posited as the necessary operator of *I think*'s transcendental unity, by which the notions of time and interiority are permanently joined. Interiority never comes alone; all the values of "consciousness" and "the soul" are pulled along in its wake: individuality, profundity, intimacy, authenticity, and even those of the *belle âme*. These are the values on which the figures of idealist euphoria — the contemplative Christian, the lyric poet, the Rousseauian lover — are constructed. *To pray*, *to sing*, and *to love* are the infinitives of a practice governed by the same theory of time that governs the "intuition of ourselves and of our inner state." And now this form of time comes under attack by Sade, as in the system of libertine apathy (which, as we have seen, aims at the systematic disintegration of religious emotion, lyric effusion, and sentimental expressiveness). The libertine body, released from any kind of interiority, cannot be the underpinning of any sort of time other than a time that has no depth, internal continuity, or memory, a time sliced up on the chopping board of successive orgasms — in other words, a time cut to measure.

The Condition of Immediacy

No sooner said than done.

—Juliette

The whole Western literary tradition takes care to teach us that the game of love is a game of patience. What is required, in order to gain proximity to and possession of the desired body, is a long passage through the codes of gallantry, as well as the mastering of courtly rhetoric and the acquisition of conventional gestures. Even then, the outcome of this process is stated metaphorically, as the other's "ultimate favors" — a cynical enough admission of where the high point in lyric questing is to be found. Here, the metaphor exposes the very mask that it shapes and recognizes: these favors are the high point because there is nothing beyond them but another high point, the "ultimate outrage," whereby violence compensates, on behalf of desire, for the other's lack of consent. It may be that the amorous quest is merely the story of a long stratagem, a shrewd hypocrisy, a sophisticated feint, a patient deviation imposed by law. Sade the man must have known this better than anyone. His letters of seduction and his "mash notes" are fragments of a completely conventional amorous rhetoric, in which the cost of his pompous declarations ("I am madly in love with you," "I can no longer live without you," "Permit me . . . to throw myself at your feet") must be amortized by their speedy acceptance ("I shall expect your answer tomorrow").⁴ In the face of resistance from the woman in question, the suitor's impatience turns, as a last resort, to temporal pleading: "How cruel you are to *retard* thus the moment of my happiness! I live no more, I no longer exist! Let it be *today* at four o'clock! Such wickedness, this wishing to *delay*! Yes, you want me to die, how well I see it. You can still send me word, *today*, if you can."⁵

Epilogue: the suitor is dismissed.

The coded stratagems, the humiliating wait, the pangs of soft-focus love, the risk of rejection — Sade intends to release his characters from all that. Libertine gratification as a whole is mainly a system for reducing the temporal delay that separates desire from its realization. Urgent as it may be to come, not waiting to come is more urgent still, and only on condition of immediacy is there any coming at all. That is why it is important to secure the practical conditions of this urgency. Let us call this set of conditions the *system of availability* (or the system of what is *on hand*), essentially distinguishing three provisions of this system:

Stockpiling, for permanent access to many bodies

Nakedness, for immediate access to the whole body

Omnisexuality, for unrestricted access to all bodies (through incest, bisexuality, bestiality, and so forth)

Stockpiling. The worst misfortune that can befall libertine desire is to face scarcity and be sentenced to an uncertain quest, subjected to the codes of waiting and to the exhausting stratagems of seduction. Thus the first concern of libertine desire is to do away at all costs with any risk of a shortage of bodies, and to do so by two fundamental means: *violence* and *pacts.*

Careful reading shows that Sadean violence is not particularly sadistic. It is mostly functional; tyranny and force are required only as the simplest (if not the most expedient) means of securing access to the bodies that law keeps at a distance or makes inaccessible. If power fascinates, especially the power of money, it is because the power of money permits instantaneous removal of the distance set up between desire and its object:

Oh, my angel, we are going to be very rich! ... what delights await us! Nothing will restrict them but the laws of our desires. The *instantaneous* satisfaction of them all![6]

Above all, money permits the stockpiling of bodies, such as the reserves of the Sodality of the Friends of Crime or those of the great libertines (Minski's harems, Brisatesta's prisoners). In addition to these private reserves, there are the public ones — convents — which the established order unintentionally offers to libertinism. When the libertine is a prince or a prelate, however, all the subjects of his realm are virtually assumed to be at his sexual service, and because this kind of stockpile is theoretically inexhaustible, the libertine must either seize political power or be complicit with it. The capricious nature of despotism brings about the ideal relationship between desiring body and desired body because power, by laying aside all doubt as to the other's response, abolishes every temporal uncertainty and all waste of energy. Every desire, because it has the stringency of an order, must be carried out *as* an order; at the slightest sign from the libertine-despot, the desired bodies must be summoned and presented, ready to serve. The model is offered by this Neapolitan orgy:

> "Each shall, in his turn, select a victim from among the fifty representations surrounding him," Ferdinand announced; "he shall ring the bell corresponding to the object of his choice, his victim shall appear immediately in his loge."[7]

There exists, in parallel to this frankly cynical process, a more subversive solution, which would be the primary element of a libertine utopia: the libidinal pact. In *Juliette* we find it stated as follows:

> In what way does my proposal injure the creature whose path I've crossed? What harm will result from the proposal's acceptance? If about me there is nothing that catches his fancy, why then, material profit may readily substitute itself for pleasure, and for an indemnity agreed upon through parley, he without further delay accords me the enjoyment of his body; and I have the inalienable right to employ force and any coercive means called for if, in having satisfied him according to my possibilities — whether it be with my purse or with my body — he dares for one instant withhold from me what I am fairly entitled to extract from him.[8]

Attention must be paid to indications of time underneath the predominantly contractual language (which we will take up again in chapter 8, when we examine the question of noncontractual exchange): "an instant," "without delay," "immediately" — all of these mark this contract with a condition of immediacy. It is not enough to offer oneself; one must do so right away: the speed of the response must match the urgency of the desire. Nevertheless, the contractual domain must take account of the other's resistance, the limits of the other's own desire, and envisage the other's refusal. Therefore, the libertine stratagem will be to incorporate conditions of tyrannical power (money and violence) into the contract itself. Even in the utopia of the libidinal pact, force is still the surest guarantee of coming straightaway, the best recourse against the slow arbitrations of law.

Nakedness. The plethora of stockpiled bodies may ensure the speed necessary to the urgency of the demand, but the bodies being offered still need to give proof of their availability. Their nakedness is this proof. We have already seen what nakedness connotes in terms of a nonlyric eroticism (one reduced to its sexual function). We have also said that the almost constant use of the imperative (or indications of orders) to get bodies undressed articulates both the demand for immediacy and submission; the naked body is a body acknowledged to be sexual (nakedness thematizes desire) as well as a body without defenses (nakedness confirms mastery).

It is precisely here that Sade attacks, and with particular violence, something that moral tradition, with rare unanimity, sets forth as one of the primary feelings that can be classified as "natural," something that covers the body even more than clothing itself does, and which, more than any explicit prohibition, interferes with desire: *modesty.* Point for point, and quite directly, Sade takes aim against the theory (as put forth in *Émile*) of Rousseau, who analyzes modesty as a compensation within the cultural order for a virtue exercised *naturally* in animals, a virtue whereby the female rejects the male once desire has been satisfied: "What compensation will there be for this negative instinct in woman when you take away her modesty?"[9] But it is modesty that is the perversion, Sade replies, and nakedness and desire are natural; modesty, far from being a compensation, is nothing but a calculated surplus of feminine wiles for exacerbating and snaring men's desire:

> Modesty, far from being a virtue, was merely one of corruption's earliest consequences, one of the first devices of female guile.[10]

> Modesty is a ridiculous prejudice, absolutely unrecognized by, absolutely alien to, Nature.[11]

(Thus Rousseau and Sade both attempt to find the voice and truth of nature in woman's desire. If one of them hears the Virgin Mother speaking, and the other hears a libertine prostitute, it is because their hearing mechanisms are themselves constructed on the contradictions of masculine power and its phantasms; see chapter 9, which deals with the Sadean staging of the feminine role.)

Sade, identifying modesty with culture (and therefore with artifice), and immodesty with nature, is not satisfied with a mere ironic permutation of their places. He totally confounds them because the separation between them was brought about in the first place by the very prohibition that his permutation challenges. (Any reversal has the obvious weakness of being forced to maintain the terms it reverses—but then we must notice how the reversal *distorts* those terms.) We certainly need to see the logical objective of Sade's ferocious attack on the "prejudice" of modesty: the wrenching of nakedness from the domain of prohibition, and the demonstration that nothing should block constant, immediate access to others' bodies.

The condition of immediacy (which we have seen in adverbial expressions like "as soon as," "without further delay," "right away," "in less than three minutes," and so forth) must mark the victory of desire over time. Therefore, it must be intended to invalidate the antiquated negative definition of desire, as existing only in frustration and born only of its object's retreat into time. Within the Sadean perspective of bodily mechanics, desire is identified with instinct — affirmed, that is, as positive, indefinite energy. Sadean desire knows no negation, so long as we mean the master's desire, which, in theory, abolishes what contradicts it (the victim) and demands maximum power for banishing uncertainty and ambivalence, and thus for securing its own gratification every time, an unalloyed pleasure with no risk, no guilt, and no mystery.

Omnisexuality. Desire's urgency demands not just many bodies or the entire body but the *entirety of* crashing bodies. This condition is fundamental precisely because we are surrounded, in our social existence, by proximate bodies that are presented as inaccessible to us: the bodies of our blood relatives (parents, brothers, sisters, children), and the bodies of people of the same sex, to which must be added the bodies of animals (although the position they occupy in this system is not a symmetrical one). In other words, physically proximate bodies are removed from us by three very strict prohibitions — the ones against incest, homosexuality, and bestiality — which raise the issue, for Sade, of symbolic exchange (again, see chapter 8, "Noncontractual Exchange"). For the moment, however, only the temporal importance of these prohibitions will be of interest to us. The temporal importance of the prohibition against incest is measured exclusively by the effect of this prohibition: the imposition of exogamy on the clan or on the family. This imposed exogamy may be compensated with the assurance that one will be able to find, elsewhere, the body that is denied one under one's own roof ("The woman whom one does not take, and whom one may not take, is, for that very reason, offered up").[12] Nevertheless, according to Sadean logic, this arrangement still suffers from a major defect. It forces desire to delay gratification, and it claims to educate desire into patience and deviation — in short, into mediation. This defect induces an experience of time as negativity (Hegel) or renunciation (Freud). It means imposing the ordeal of negation onto desire, or assuming that desire has the structure of negation—a theory unacceptable to Sadean problematics, which then treats the supposed universality of the incest taboo just as it treats the universality attributed to modesty, by identifying desire with nature and demanding complete immediacy for it: "If one but reflects a little, one finds nothing odd in incest; Nature allows it, encourages it."[13] An entire short story from *Les Crimes de l'amour,* titled "Eugénie de Franval," is constructed on this thesis, which the incestuous father states as follows:

> You mean to say that a lovely girl cannot tempt me because I am guilty of having sired her? That what ought to bind me more intimately to her should become the very reason for my removal from her? . . . Ah, what sophistry! . . . How totally absurd![14]

Rejection of distancing: What better way to say that the practice of incest is first of all a *guarantee of availability,* and that incest ensures one's sexual proximity to and enjoyment of the body that is "naturally" closest—the body of one's blood relative?

An analogous requirement governs homosexual practices, if the term *homosexuality* can even be applied to Sadean thought. Indeed, all Sade's characters are indiscriminately hetero- or homosexual. The question does not even arise for them: they move in a kind of indifference to sexual difference, a difference annulled in sodomitic desire, with bodies made equal under the sign of anality. Even if it becomes blurred with a bisexual sodomy, Sadean homosexuality functions primarily to violate the prohibition that bars desire from same-sex bodies, and this infraction is essential to libertine desire's requirement of urgency. The closest body, regardless of its sex, is the body most appropriate to the gratification of this urgent desire: the first one offered is the best one *because* it is first. Thus Brisatesta, when he is in prison, quite happily secures his sexual pleasure with his fellow prisoners; once free, he procures women for himself, but he still keeps on hand Carle-Son, his faithful companion and homosexual plaything, to while away the time between coups de main or orgies. In the same way, Juliette supplies herself with men and women indiscriminately; meanwhile, her lady companions ensure her an uninterrupted sexual servicing. And so it would seem that the great advantage of homosexuality is that it turns friendship and complicity, which are accepted between people of the same sex, into permanent sexual availability. Thus libertine sexual pleasure ensures the elimination of "downtime."

As for bestiality, as it is called, this is not a routine practice of Sade's libertine, and for good reason: Sade's libertine, supposedly powerful and rich, has no need whatsoever to turn to a form of sexuality usually determined by a shortage of human bodies. If bestiality still makes an occasional appearance in the course of the orgies, it is a perverse extravagance whose sole function is to demonstrate that the domain of available bodies cannot be limited, not even to the human species, and that there can be no objection on principle to desire's impatience; every body necessarily falls prey to it:

> That accursed Borghese was prone to the most fantastic practices. A eunuch, a hermaphrodite, a dwarf, an eighty-year-old woman, a turkey, a small ape, a very big mastiff, a she-goat, and a little boy of four, the great-grandchild of the old woman, were the lust-objects presented us by the Princess' duenna.[15]

Within this procession of extremes and anomalies (old woman and child, eunuch and hermaphrodite), the mingling of animal body with human body is neither more nor less foreign but merely incongruent with the norm, simply because the animal body is not in its proper place. Therefore, it is the sign of a transgression that satisfies both the combinative imagination and the certitude of an unlimited mastery over all sexed bodies.

And so, through the system of availability's detailed procedures, the condition of immediacy is brought about as the assertion of an absolute rejection of waiting, and as an extreme attempt to disenculturate desire—that is, to release desire from the mediations and limits that every social system imposes on it. The resort to the concept of *nature*, then, appears to be a strategic operation by which the effects of a prohibition are made to contradict the prohibition itself (thus modesty becomes a perversion). The concept of nature is something of a screen, but a protective screen, because it confers an ideal provenance, and therefore legitimacy, on all the phantasms of transgression, allowing them to be symbolized as a speculum and a compendium. In a still naive way, the concept of nature plays the same role that, in a critical way, the concept of the unconscious assumes for Freud: as topos of the primary processes, with the demand for sexual pleasure initially asserted beyond the reality principle. Here, we should understand that "nature" according to Sade, like the unconscious according to Freud, knows nothing of time.

The Principle of Acceleration

It is important to do away with the waiting that would force desire to strategize, and thus be mediated and deferred. But it is also necessary, during the period of the orgy (a period that is already programmed, and therefore insulated from disagreeable surprises or contradictions), to be assured of an additional measure of control through maximum compression of time. Within the series of pleasures itself, in other words, it is also necessary to do away with waiting for the next pleasure. This is why the process of coming, once set in motion, has to go faster and faster. Sadean time, as we have seen, is composed of nothing but series of instants, and so the more instants, the more orgasms. In short, acceleration is to time what saturation is to space. Just as the group totally occupies both the space that it carves out and areas of the bodies that it enjoys, the group's actions saturate the time in which it operates. At the level of surface and quantity, the speed of the repetitions produces the ironic equivalent of abrogated continuity and fullness. No matter how quickly the chain moves, the dotted line is never transformed into a solid one. We still have the amassing of discrete quantities, the arbitrary movement of jumps and displacements.

One of the best accelerations is the one produced in the course of the famous orgy organized by the prince of Francavilla:

All the variations of this scene, what is more, were executed with astonishing address and celerity; never were we kept waiting for so much as a moment. Before our mouths, cunts and pricks and asses succeeded one another as swiftly as our desires; elsewhere, the engines we frigged had but to discharge and new ones materialized between our fingers; our clitoris-suckers rotated with the same speed, and our asses were never deserted; in less than three hours, during which we swam in unending delirium, we were ass-fucked one hundred times apiece, and polluted the whole time by the dildo constantly belaboring our cunt. I was nigh to slain by it all.[16]

On a similar note, here is a proceeding described in *The 120 Days:*

Fifteen girls arrive in teams of three: one whips him, one sucks him, the other shits; then she who shitted, whips; she who sucked, shits; she who whipped, sucks. And so he proceeds till he has had done with all fifteen; he sees nothing, heeds nothing, is wild with joy; a procuress is in charge of the game. He renews this party six times each week.

(This one is truly charming and has my infinite recommendation; the thing has got to move very briskly along.)[17]

In practice, this need to go fast is invoked and indicated for every orgy; thus the one programmed for the elderly libertine Mondor:

> True, all went at great speed: those slaps, that spittle, and the farts, perfectly orchestrated, rained down a very tempest upon the patient; passing strange it was, and most entertaining, to listen to the music wherewith the air resounded, a symphony of eructations, bass and tenor, the sharp percussive sounds of the blows, the flat notes of the expectorations.[18]

In these systems for acceleration, it is striking to notice how much the *speed of succession* has the effect of producing an equivalent of *simultaneity* ("Oh fuck! fuck! all of us, let's discharge together!").[19] This has to do, in other words, with the transferring of space's prerogatives to time (if it is true, as Kant has shown, that time is the order of succession, and space is the order of simultaneity). Time in the orgy must be pulled in and contracted to the point where, if it has not been nullified, at least it has the "compaction" of a snapshot. Likewise, in its movement of acceleration, the group-body reaches the apparent immobility of a rotary press running at maximum speed. (Indeed, Sade constantly situates this speed at the edge of the imaginable, and even beyond: "It cannot be imagined..."; "You cannot have any idea....")

At any rate, there is spatial simultaneity in those series that are determined by the erotic activities of each area of the body (hands, sex organs, anuses, mouths), but there is succession and rotation of the bodies or groups of bodies that cause those areas to experience sexual pleasure, and it is precisely this interval, the "downtime" made necessary by rotation, that must be nullified. Rotation guarantees pleasure by constantly infusing pleasure with difference, but the interruption necessitated by rotation would spoil this pleasure if the *speed* of the operation did not erase the interruption's effects. Speed reestablishes the spatial simultaneity threatened by temporal succession, and acceleration even manages to push time to the edge of condensation and coagulation. The series alternate so quickly that sexual pleasure manages to last, ensuring its own continuity without ceasing to be produced by the gaps that guarantee sexual pleasure. This is a stroboscopic machine, in other words, where speed diffracts, unifies, and immobilizes the series. Sade states its model explicitly:

> For the whole of one hour the lechers amused themselves with probing those four asses, passing them round with a swiftness that nigh to invoked the sails of a windmill. Such indeed— "the windmill" — is the name they gave to this arrangement, one with which we counsel every libertine to experiment.[20]

Paradoxically, then, at the edge of acceleration there is a phantasm of *immobility*, directly structured on the logic of mastery: a territory must be closed off in order to be controlled; no movement can be allowed unless it is internal, has a servile function, and is all but acknowledged as being no movement at all.

The libertine, in short, proposes to do nothing less than resolve a problem of ubiquity: how to be everywhere at once and enjoy everything at once (Juliette: "No sooner had I brought these marvels to light than I devoured them with caresses, and in my swift passage from one to the next, each time it seemed to me that I ought to have paused longer over what I had just relinquished for something equally wonderful").[21] What it comes down to is the inescapable requirement of libertine desire: everything, right away, and all at the same time; not merely to avoid waiting, and not merely to go faster and faster, but also to help oneself to everything at once. Sexual pleasure is a symphony, and the group-body is an orchestral body ("it was . . . most entertaining . . . to listen to the music wherewith the air resounded, a symphony of eructations, bass and tenor, the sharp percussive sounds of the blows, the flat notes of the expectorations").[22] If the merry-go-rounds of sexual pleasure (like the quadrilles and trios in the preceding citations) start off according to the art of the fugue ("*one whips him, one sucks him, the other shits; then she who shitted, whips; she who sucked, shits; she who whipped, sucks*"),[23] ultimately what is sought is the multiphony of a percussive system by which temporal series can attain, as nearly as possible, the form of spatial simultaneity: a coming-machine, a machine for integrating and diffracting meanings, a centrifuge of actions, a stroboscope of sensations, a musical top— motionless, fast, and single [célibataire].

There is, however, more than a formal enjoyment of simultaneity in this assembling of an acceleration system intended for the maximum concentration of time. In fact, what we see at work here is, strictly speaking, an economic model: the coming-machine demonstrates its power by its output, by the quantity of orgasmic units that it supplies. As Marx notes, productivity is defined essentially in terms of the factor of *time*.[24] Indeed, if determining an object's value comes down to determining its exchange value with respect to other objects—that is, if determining this object's value comes down to measuring the quantity of work that was invested in it—then this quantity itself is nothing but the time necessary for the object's production:

> We see then that that which determines the magnitude of the value of any article is the amount of labor socially necessary, or the labor-time socially necessary for its production.... The value of one commodity is to the value of any other, as the labor-time necessary for the production of the one is to that necessary for the production of the other.... The value of a commodity, therefore, varies directly as the quantity, and inversely as the productiveness, of the labor incorporated in it.[25]

As production time decreases, productivity increases and net costs fall. To begin with, the conquest of a market is a conquest over time. (There are many other conditions, of course, but this is the inaugural one.) The speed of an article's production determines the competitiveness of the article's pricing. Therefore, production needs to go faster and faster.

What we see percolating through the mechanical assembling of Sadean group-bodies, and being projected onto it as a fever of acceleration, is this nascent industrial-revolution model of productivity. Here, the compression of time exhibits a new economy of sexual pleasure, demonstrating its richness not by its uniqueness or profound duration but by the multiplicity of its results. In other words, we have moved from a metaphysical, artisanal temporality to a combinative, industrial one.

To introduce the measurement of time into a social activity is, in general, always to take a step toward abstraction—to take a step at the same time, that is, toward the "denaturalization" of this activity, toward its introduction into a system of conventions, regularities, and accounting, in a more or less complete split with its natural rhythms.

This disruption, projected onto and radicalized on the plane of sexual activity, is what shows up in the Sadean model of the libertine body, with its ordered, programmed, machinized, countable, quantified sexual pleasure. Here a new kind of happiness is defined, the happiness of apathy, of quantities: antilyric, repetitive, and abstract. It appears, on this basis, that there is possibly still another way of interpreting the program that governs erotic activity:

- The program is a way of minimizing the time necessary for the production of sexual pleasure, and thus it is also a way of extracting the maximum effect from the time that has been invested, first of all by completely eliminating "downtime" and allowing no spaces to slip into the pace of production. To program a system is to submit it to the stringency of restrictive regulation and remove all possibility of surprise. Most of all, however, to program a system is to make this system optimally profitable and to take it for what it is: a system of functions.

- The program also fulfills one of the fundamental laws of industrial productivity: the law of the division of labor. The Sadean programmer simply allocates tasks; to each his own action and his own function, and "everything" is then "executed" accordingly. This is a level of extreme abstraction, with each erotic act limited to and focused on some efficiency involving some segment of the body, or some segment in the series of acts, and then concatenated with other acts, in accord with the program. (Chapter 6 discusses this point more precisely, in the section titled "The Manufacture of Sexual Pleasure.")

Amnesiac Time

If the realm of memory is where poems grow and lyric celebration blooms, under the sign of Mnemosyne, then it would certainly have to be said that nothing is more impervious to poetry than Sadean narrative. We have already mentioned that what determines the narrative is not the hermeneutical principle of the *enigma* but the encyclopedic principle of the *list*. That being the case, the narrative is structured on confirmation rather than on surprise. The itinerary is simply one of unfolding the tables and opening them up, leafing through the volume of illustrative plates. Moreover, the only link between one sequence and another is the need to saturate the system with variations. Orderly succession is nothing but the imperative to spread all the pictures out over the time of reading and writing (and the pictures, properly speaking, remain contemporaneous). What results is maximum discontinuity, with a somewhat artificial infusion of legato, just enough to satisfy the rules of the genre. This is an odd successivity, one conceived as a palliative for an ideal simultaneity.

Sadean scenes are "shortcuts," as it were, in which everyone tacks on some feature relevant to the series. Like the parts of the body, however, the scenes are still *membra disjecta,* scattered segments resistant to any kind of organic integration; they are piecework quickly stitched together with coarse thread.

We see this coarse thread especially in the casual handling of transitions. Good transitions are exactly what constitute the test of a "good" storyteller. There is an art of using signs to prepare for a transition and make that transition first probable and then inevitable, so that the order of the narrative, through the working out of a necessity of discourse, completely erases its underlying conventions and successfully presents itself as a necessity of nature — that is, as a universal truth of objectivity (this is the familiar neurosis of mimesis, of saying "I am not an artifact but the *thing itself*"). One of the storyteller's major problems, then, would be knowing how, out of one situation (that is, one coherent organization of signs), to find another situation without erasing the first, knowing how to change without destroying, how to produce novelty without losing the benefit of what has been acquired, how to give the narrative an internal memory. Hence we have the whole mechanism of anticipatory and recurrent signs, which make the whole of the story itself a continual *transitio* and, ultimately, make the art of narrative an art of producing continuity, a layering of causes.

This is the art that Sade treats so cavalierly, not because he is incapable of mastering it (on the contrary, in such nonlibertine tales as *La Marquise de Gange* he shows himself to be an expert) but because narrativity, in the libertine text, is only a justification for the tableau, the instrument for the tableau's introduction, its seductive wrapping. This is clearly acknowledged in the introduction to *The 120 Days:*

> We have, moreover, blended these six hundred passions into the storytellers' narratives. That is one more thing whereof the reader were well to have foreknowledge: it would have been too monotonous to catalogue them one by one outside the body of the story.[26]

The "assembling" of *The 120 Days* may bluntly exhibit and justify the jerkiness of the narrative, the way it has been sawed up into layers of cuts (a succession of months and days, with the general presentation, the narratives of the storytellers, and the commentary of the libertines overlaid within them). Things are completely different in *Juliette,* however, a narrative of travel and adventure, and therefore a narrative with an obligation to represent continuity. In *Juliette,* every stopover or large city is presented as the topos of a series of acts and discourses, the place where a specific chapter of the Encyclopedia of Excess is written. The problem, then, is how to leave one topos, justify the exit, and, above all, get settled as quickly as possible into another. In general, the argumentum is "fleece the host, and flee." This transition, neither announced nor truly justified, but rather treated as an emergency, makes the writer's capriciousness perfectly obvious and freely acknowledges the narrative convention by which the transition has been produced (and by which the reader, like the innkeeper, is also fleeced).

Two examples, among others, serve well enough as illustrations: the flight from Minski's lair, and the departure from Rome. In the case of Minski, the ogre of the Apennines, Juliette and her companions feel threatened. In order to take their leave of the giant, they decide to give him a sleeping potion, and they rob him by securing the cooperation of the steward, who believes that his master has been poisoned: "Enchanted, the major-domo facilitated everything, concurred in everything, and for his cooperation was doubtless richly rewarded by the giant when upon awakening he learned of his losses and of our flight."[27] And here is the same swift ending, after the looting of the papal treasury in Rome:

> Braschi [Pius VI] never noticed the theft, or else deemed best to feign not to have noticed it. I did not see His Holiness again; he felt, I suspect, that my visits to the Vatican were a little more than he could afford. In view of these circumstances I saw no reason to remain on in Rome; indeed, it seemed wiser to leave.[28]

What is clearly disturbing about this speeded-up narrative is that there is no time for causality to take shape: chains of action and changes in behavior are so sudden that anything else might occur just as easily. In the face of such omnipotent capriciousness (the writer's privilege, and a libertine passion), the illusion of internal necessity dissolves, and the narrative is denaturalized. The dealer turns his cards over and says, "What's the difference? Let's play another hand."

Ultimately, what this evasion of transitions demonstrates is that the value of narrativity (the carrier of temporality) is merely instrumental. It is a means for laying out what cannot be presented all at once; the tabular model, the fixed system of variations, and the ideal of the dictionary persist fundamentally underneath this minimal chain of succession. This is the source of what is often a complete independence between and among sequences, to the point where one or another could be deleted without affecting the appearance of continuity: remove a link, and refasten the chain. (This explains the ease with which narratives can be interpolated, like Clément's into *Justine,* or Brisatesta's into *Juliette.*)

The characters are emblematic of this compartmentalization of sequences. Their appearance is always unexpected. Suddenly there they are, shining with all the brilliance of the most extreme debauchery or beauty, and then (except for major, active characters like Juliette herself, Clairwil, Noirceuil, Olympia, la Durand) they disappear (as do Delcour, Dorval, Mondor, Saint-Fond himself, Madame de Donis, Albani, Bernis, Pope Pius VI, the King of Naples, Cordelli), never to return. The characters are only as deep as their names — that is, only as deep as the types that they embody in the annals of perversion, and in the order of principles. A proper name is actually an elaborated theorem. It disappears down the QED hatch. This issue of the characters allows us to sneak up on the issue of narrative sequence, which structures the characters' fate at the level of the signified. A character, summoned by the writer to figure in the series, remains only long enough for the demonstration and then disappears (simply abandoned — thanked, but sometimes executed as well). As an *exemplary case,* the character attracts maximum narrative interest during the temporal segment useful for his examination, and then he loses all textual existence. This is because the purpose of the Sadean narrative is not to offer a copy of the historical world or be a faithful portrait of society, but only to demonstrate the relevance of a (libertine) praxis by making use of a certain number of types distributed across so many narrative sequences.

The realist narrative, by contrast, assumes an organic, interdependent world, a whole in permanent communication, with the characters' comings and goings as the sign of this whole's inner continuity, of its permanence within mutation and surprise — the sign, in other words, that history has value for individual consciousness and is pulled together by authority of the subject. That is why it is important, in this kind of story, for a character (and the author) to have a long memory; any forgetfulness, in the form of compartmentalized sequences, would be equivalent to the beginnings of dissolution. Everything has to accumulate through internalization; lost time would be a lost world. This is an exhausting task, work fit for a slave. Hegel was right: nothing is more difficult than holding it all together.

On that score, the libertine narrator has the innocence and uncon-sciousness of an amnesiac; for the sake of one new instant, he sacrifices the entire past. In fact, the formula for Sadean time is the *program*, which means that everything is a foregone conclusion, foreseen and under con-trol; nothing unknown will happen. Every libertine who programs a *réunion intime* is repeating the act of the writer who constructs the model of his narrative. (Sade's rough drafts testify to the meticulousness of his planned arrangements, and his remarks to himself, made in the second-person plural[29] — "Change this," "Verify that" — have the precision of orders to be carried out.) The program is the formula for Sadean time precisely because the narrative is not the staging or the revelatory arti-fice of a mystery but rather the unfurling of what is already known, as well as its projection into a chain of succession.

Dissertational explanation ought to suffice for this system of truths, but how is it possible to make this explanation heard without setting it forth in the all too human element of narrative method? Sade's pro-found suspicion of narrative method rests on its obvious complicity with the logic (or, rather, the ethics) of delay and deviation. By contrast, dissertational explanation says everything, and all at once, thereby en-suring sexual pleasure in the moment of its articulation and calling on the reader to act out his fantasies and confirm, in his body and in his practices, the force and truth of the principles that are being articulated (this is the "Sade effect"). Narration means striving to say the same thing, but with the patience appropriate to a chain of succession, and it means confirming the effects of these principles on the basis of a model that resides in the text. Therefore, in view of the genre's requirements, verisimilitude has to be contrived for progressions, clues have to be laid out, and the threads of relationships have to be coordinated. In other words, it is necessary to set out on a forced march of mediation and (what is most painful) to accept delayed gratification.

We constantly feel the Sadean text ready to break all these rules, but holding itself back from the edge of technical error. This is where it gets its shaky, tense rhythm, a rhythm between rigidity and black humor. And this is why the program arises within the thread of the text as a specific and strictly libertine source of happiness: now time will be determined, organized, cut up, and condensed, and the accelerated execution that fol-lows will offer the best revenge against the long deviations that narra-tive law has been imposing. This dream of speed is projected into a sort of *precipitate* narrative (in both the temporal and chemical senses), with the stroboscopic proceedings of the orgies (the "windmill," for example) as its emblem. Extremes of movement meet the fixed image of the tableau. The program aims first for this condensation. In addition, however, it confirms the way in which fragmented time accommodates the cut-up body, the machine-body. And, just as there can be no organic unity for the body, it follows that there can be no temporal continuum. Sexual pleasure, always divided up into small portions, is determined by overstimulation of one or another of the body's elements, or by a mechanical connection between them: to each part its specific sexual pleasure and temporal segment, so that time, here, is not what unifies but what separates. All the aims of sexual pleasure, by determining how the scene will be "cut," reactivate and reinforce this divisive character of time.

Sadean time (like Sadean space and the Sadean mirror) is totally flat and unresonant: absolutely nonlyric. The narrative has no memory of its sequences, events, or actors. This amnesia is the condition for the repetition of a sexual pleasure that exists only here and now; once it has been achieved, it has to begin all over again, for memory does not come. It is an event that leaves no traces because it has no (metaphysical) subject to recollect it and make it infinite. Time lost is lost indeed because no interiority is there to assume, deepen, and transcend. Thus there is no learning, that is, no change; there is nothing like an *Aufhebung*. We are at the pole opposite to the thoroughly Christian era of "relief" surfaces. There is nothing accumulating in the strata of an internalizing memory — *Erinnerung*. There is only a demonstration to be made, a system to be saturated, in which names and events are merely points of reference in this topological filling.

This is why the Sadean narrative (no matter what has been said about it) is not truly picaresque, not a coming-of-age novel. The libertine is uneducable — incorrigible, if you will. He is not the object of any future; he is the instrument of an indefatigably reiterated proof. He is not really confronted with cunning, malevolence, or trickery. He is not exposed to the risk of the Other. He moves within a secure destiny. His program is always already mapped out. His adversary has lost to him from the beginning — and, reciprocally, Justine is always shown, *beforehand,* losing to the libertine; she remains as immutable as he does. Everything must always begin all over again — a tremendous recalcitrance, in which the demand for narratives resides. The point is not to enrich memory but to mark bodies. Superficial effects, signposts: at the end of this journey, instead of memories, we have principles; instead of dreams, decisions; instead of regrets, an accounting (of goods accumulated and bodies encountered); instead of the vagueness of a mood-imbued memory, a body tattooed with multiple comings and a living catalog saturated with every imaginable excess. The invention of the libertine body is the list of all the marks inscribed on it by libertinism. Once everything has been enjoyed, it has all been said.

Part II
An Economics

CHAPTER SIX

The Libertine Mode of Nonproduction

The society had created a common fund, which each of its members took his turn administering for six months; the sums, allocated for nothing but expenses in the interests of pleasure, were vast. Their excessive wealth put the most unusual things within their reach, and the reader ought not be surprised to hear that two million were annually disbursed to obtain good cheer and lust's satisfaction.

— *The 120 Days of Sodom*

The gift would be senseless... if it did not take on the meaning of an acquisition. Hence giving must become acquiring a power,... which one acquires from the fact of *losing*.

—GEORGES BATAILLE, *The Accursed Share*

When we look closely, we find no Sadean model for society, only models for a countersociety or a parasociety. The libertine does not aspire to change the general structures of society but only to make use of them, which usually means redirecting them for his own benefit. Thus there is never any question of changing the conditions of production, but only of extracting the greatest possible profit from them. As always with Sade, causes matter very little; effects are what count. Nevertheless, bringing this redirection about while leaving the status quo alone does not mean leaving the system intact; quite the contrary, for it means confiscating, with unacceptable uses in mind, all the goal-directedness for which the status quo is working. But we should hasten to say that the status quo is working with a view toward its own reproduction, through the accumulation of a constantly reinvested surplus. The libertine's stratagem is to take possession of this process just before it becomes engaged in re-production, at the precise moment when wealth has been produced, and to claim this wealth for himself, spending it for the sole, sterile end of sexual pleasure. The libertine turns his body into a fantastic machine for consumption, for spending, with the absolute indifference to waste that this implies, as well as the systematic rejection of anything that might bear any relation to any kind of logic of production. Libertine sexual pleasure emerges at the tip of a pyramid of exploited labor, redirected wealth, and short-circuited profitability.

In Sade's writings, as a result, there is no model for a mode of produc-tion, but there is a strategy for redirecting production, a strategy that establishes a whole countersociety. This redirection has its own preci-sion and its own logic, and it could be called (in derision or complic-ity) the *libertine mode of nonproduction,* by which term it will also be recognized for what it is: a product of fiction, put into play not within a fantasy world but within the text, within a signifying practice where the logics of history have been invested and articulated. Thus it is not surprising to discover here, in this libertine mode of nonproduction, the outline for a mode of production that was under development in, and being imposed on, late-eighteenth-century Europe: the mode of pro-duction of burgeoning capitalist industry. We find, in fact, that this mode of production does not exist alone in Sade's writings but is overlaid by older forms of economic organization and exploitation, such as the feu-dal mode of production and the variant of it that was linked to the monastic establishment. And so the economic theory that governs Sadean libertinism — that is, the theory that the text stages and calls into ques-tion — is offered as a sort of genealogical foreshortening of the current and past history of desire's relationship to economic power, and to the conditions in which this power was exercised within established insti-tutional practices.

The Château, or the Feudalistic Model

The privileged setting for Sadean libertinism is the château: "In a nov-elistic universe where the picturesque holds no interest, the château is the only backdrop described in abundant detail. It is much more than decor; it is desire's setting itself."[1] The sign par excellence of nobility, the château also designates the libertines' favorite class, along with the

rights, privileges, and expectations of that class. Of the châteaux described, some, theaters for garden-variety *parties fines,* do have the charm
and openness of eighteenth-century buildings, but the château is usually a medieval fortress with thick layered walls, an impassable moat,
and a bare stone interior, blocked off with iron bars and fitted out with
a dungeon. Examples would be the châteaux of Rolland, Minski, and
Brisatesta, but especially their perfect model, as it were: the château at
Silling, situated in the heart of the Black Forest, protected by precipices
and high walls, and accessible only by foot, and then only with a guide.
As if all that were not enough, the bridge from the mountain is torn
down as soon as the four masters and their subjects are inside:

> But that was not all: having inspected the place, the Duc decided that,
> since all the provisions were within the fortress, and since therefore they
> had no need to leave it, it were necessary, in order to forestall external
> attack, which was little dreaded, and escapes from within, the possibil-
> ities of which were less unlikely, it were necessary, I say, to have walled
> shut all the gates, all the passages whereby the château might be pene-
> trated, and absolutely to enclose themselves inside their retreat as within
> a besieged citadel, without leaving the least entrance to an enemy, the
> least egress to a deserter. The recommendation was put into effect, they
> barricaded themselves to such an extent there was no longer any trace
> left of where the exits had been; and then they settled down comfortably
> inside.[2]

This simulated state of siege ("as within a besieged citadel") permits
all the signs of a feudal fortress to be summoned up at once, with all
their historical implications:

- The *military* signs are the system of defense, cloistering, and
  inaccessibility. This recourse to military signs is taken in spite of their
  futility (an actual attack is very unlikely, as acknowledged in the rather
  paradoxical formulation "in order to forestall external attack, which
  was little dreaded"), and this certainly shows that the intention here is
  to indicate feudalism to the extent that it originates in military power,
  from which, historically, it drew its legitimacy.

- The *political* signs make their appearance in the masters' whims. The
  state of siege is an *exceptional* state; the château, cut off from the
  outside world, knows no law but the law of its leader or leaders. The
  leaders of Silling go to extremes in exploiting their unlimited right to
  capriciousness. The citadel becomes a prison for the victims of
  "pleasure." Silling does reveal its resemblance to the Bastille, but this
  Bastille is infinitely worse than the original one, as we learn right at

the outset from the speech that the Duc de Blangis delivers to the residents:

> You are enclosed in an impregnable citadel; no one on earth knows you are here, you are beyond the reach of your friends, of your kin; insofar as the world is concerned, you are already dead, and if yet you breathe, 'tis by our pleasure, and for it only.[3]

- The *economic* signs contain two elements: autarky and luxury. The state of siege pushes the limits of the feudal domain's whole working model, whose goal is, on the one hand, to secure self-sufficiency of production and, on the other, to guarantee the masters lavish consumption of the goods produced by serfdom. Silling, doomed in its simulated state of siege to live on its reserves, consumes prodigious amounts of them — not just extravagant food and drink but also, as we shall see, speeches and bodies.

Sade's text, because it was contemporary with the French Revolution of 1789, was also contemporary with the whole process of the break that was taking place between the capitalist mode of production, which was then in rapid development, and those elements of the feudal mode of production that were still in existence, particularly those forms of the political establishment — such as the monarchy, nobiliary power, and ecclesiastical power — that were linked to it. From the regency of Philippe d'Orléans until the end of the eighteenth century, more and more signs pointed to the nobles' awareness of their irreversible decline and to their correspondingly obstinate, panicked attempt to maintain their threatened privileges at all costs and drain them down to the dregs. Against this backdrop — ultimate defiance, and the mortal agony of a system — Sade draws his libertine figures, giving them a degree of power and privilege that would have been unthinkable outside feudalism. Even if rich commoners do gain access to true libertinism (for money always leads to power), the authentic heirs of feudalism — the nobles — always have more of a gift for it, as far as Sade is concerned. And so it is at Silling: Durcet, the banker, who represents the rising power of capital, is the owner of the château, but the Duc de Blangis is the one who really feels at home there. He controls its defenses and becomes the undisputed leader; he is the one who gives the orders and the welcoming speeches. Sexually, he is the more vigorous and better endowed of the two. Among the four Friends' daughters, his alone will be saved, having proved herself a true libertine. This is class solidarity and privilege, and its logic is infallibly applied. If we recall, briefly, the forms taken by feudalism, we can understand the primary economic and political theory implied in the social workings of Sadean libertinism.

Domination and Exploitation

Research on the feudal period and its mode of production brings out three fundamental traits:

- Social relationships of production were essentially centered on *land* (the economy was primarily agricultural).
- Land ownership was reserved for a hierarchy of lords, with the people who worked the land enjoying only a right of use and occupation, in a relationship of dependence marked by the lord's right to impose levies on the products of their labor.
- Hierarchical relationships were conceived on a model of *personal* dependence (of serfs on lords, and of lords among themselves).

This image of feudalism is both the most highly developed one and the most general outline of it that we have. If we examine the origins of feudalism, an essential element appears: the military nature of its organization. The power of the lord was above all the power of arms. In an era of permanent warfare, the peasants, having been liberated by foreign conquerors, had no choice but to place themselves under the protection of these military leaders, who in return demanded an "eminent" (and, later on, actual) right to ownership of their dependents' lands: "Feudalism, from the perspective of the conquerors, had its origin in the military organization of the army during the period of the conquest itself; only after the conquest did military organization, under the influence of the productive forces found in the conquered lands, develop into feudalism properly so called."[4]

The medieval citadel, as a symbol of the lord's military power, is an ambiguous one because it is presented as the peasant community's refuge in the event of invasion or attack from outside, but it also carries the meaning of the lord's omnipotence over his dependents, as a result of which most of them lived in the semislavery that came to be called *serfdom.*

This symbol — this instrument — is precisely what interests Sade because it ensures and leads to relationships of domination. And it does ensure domination, if only a fictional one. (Serfdom had practically disappeared by the eighteenth century, but the medieval citadel persisted as a privileged sign of nobiliary power and its arrogance, and it was to

come under assault by the revolutionaries of 1793. Sade would experience the cruelty of this assault because his peasants, led by those among
them who were most well off, completely destroyed his medieval château
at Lacoste.) Thus, in *La Nouvelle Justine*, when the libertine Jérôme develops a plan to acquire a domain, he wants it strictly feudal:

> To my money-agent I revealed the desire I had of purchasing a lordly
> estate with the not inconsiderable funds in whose possession I found
> myself.
> "In this place," I said to that worthy, "feudalism is in full force, which
> is why it is here that I am fixed upon establishing myself: I wish both to
> command men and to cultivate the land, to rule equally over my fields
> and my vassals."
> "In that case," my interlocutor replied, "you can do no better than in
> Sicily; this is a land where lord wields over tenant the power of life and
> death."
> "That," I replied, "is what I require."[5]

Sade's intention, when he evokes the château as the locus of debauchery, is also to summon up the whole system of feudalism that it implies—
to summon up, that is, and first of all, its mode of production and the
nature of the relationships that stemmed from it. These relationships
were marked by the essentially local nature of political and juridical connections, which were not just local but above all personal: the connections of serfdom, like the connections between lord and suzerain, were
tied to the individual, in a personal relationship that, given the highly
elaborated capriciousness of feudal power, became rights over the serfs'
very bodies, with the famous droit du seigneur as a purely sexual extension of these rights. The *despotic* body lived, consumed, was pleasured, and died within the total physical control that it exercised over
the *enslaved* body, which was connected to the fief. Through a rigorously endogenous relationship—the relationship of head to limbs—
the land, the château, and the serfs went to make up the singular body of
the lord.

Unproductive Consumption

There exists among historians an entire polemic whose goal is to determine whether the French Revolution was or was not an antifeudal revolution—to determine, that is, whether feudalism did or did not per-

sist up to and including the eighteenth century. For certain Anglo-Saxon historians (Cobban, for example), feudalism was essentially a thirteenth-century phenomenon, one that, in any case, ceased with the Middle Ages; thus seigneurial structures in the centuries that followed were, strictly speaking, no longer feudal and need to be defined by other criteria. The "social historians" (such as Lefebvre, Bloch, Soboul, and others) counter that although feudalism in pure form had of course disappeared (at least in its juridical aspect, because serfdom had been officially abolished), it continued to be a reality, notably taking the form of the multiple levies that a lord could still impose on the peasants (levies on goods and services, or in the form of charges for the use of ovens, mills, and bridges, or charges for hunting rights, and so on), even if the peasants were themselves independent landowners. On the eve of the revolution, these various levies averaged nearly a third of nobiliary revenues—no small proportion. Historians such as Soboul propose that we refer to the prerevolutionary period as a period of "ancien régime feudalism," whose essential economic characteristic was "feudal levies."[6] Feudalism was modified by its having been superimposed on the new forms of merchant capitalism and on the centralized royal administration (which levied taxes of its own, making the peasants' condition even worse than it had been during the Middle Ages); up to the eighteenth century, however, the French peasantry did continue to experience feudalism in all its harshness.

What is paradoxical about feudalism's dogged survival well into the eighteenth century is its deeply irrational nature, in economic terms. It quite obviously provoked the peasant masses to the explosion of 1789, but it also provoked the rising bourgeoisie, which could no longer tolerate feudalism's character of sheer wastefulness, radical nonproductivity, and economic obstruction:

> In that economy, where landed capital constituted the principal source of savings, feudal rents, instead of being invested, were consumed by the privileged as extravagant goods and services; thus the economy was in service to the court, the nobility, and the haute bourgeoisie, . . . the sectors in which there was no productive activity, and which truly did live as parasites on the social body, that is, as parasites on the peasant world. . . . The products of agriculture were ultimately squandered on too many domestic servants, in conspicuous consumption, and in sterile expenditures.[7]

The question that Soboul does not ask, and the one that historians and economists are always dodging, is this: What were the reasons for the nobles' stubborn refusal to invest their rents? for their wasteful consumption? for their debauch of extravagant spending and conspicuous consumption? What was the inner necessity, the logical need, for behavior of this kind? for preferring the risk of suicide to a bit of wisdom and compromise? Any answer, it seems, would have to account for the part played by a noneconomic element that could be called the nobles' *obligations to the nobiliary code.* Indeed, we know that the code of nobility implied a whole series of duties that were linked to class recognition, and that anyone failing to observe them to the letter was seen as having lost his claim to aristocratic status. Thus the military service that every noble owed the king was imposed as the remainder and equivalent of the duty of military defense, a duty to which the old nobility, the only one considered authentic, traced its origins and its power. As a correlative of this military obligation, there was an absolute prohibition against working, whether the work involved artisanry or even industry or banking. The privileges of the sword left any wielding of tools radically out of bounds; to work was to become déclassé. Rich commoners (bankers and magistrates, for example) might become nobles, but one born to the nobility — unless he was willing to renounce, deliberately, the recognition of his peers — could not and must not devote himself to working, even if his survival depended on it. As for his fortune, all he could count on was the cultivation (or sale) of his lands. The extreme potency of these obligations to the nobiliary code may permit a clearer understanding to be developed about the nobility's blind obstinacy in maintaining its feudal privileges. The choice was between loss of status and economic survival, and obligations to the nobiliary code prevailed. It is easy to understand the difficulty that historians face in thinking about something as irrational as maintaining the duty of idleness to the point of courting utter ruin. But if historical theories fall short, we may find some theories among authors perceived to be on the fringe, such as Veblen (*The Theory of the Leisure Class*) and Bataille (*The Accursed Share*), whose analyses help us see how the phenomenon of suicidal squandering governs not just libertine excess but perhaps also every mode of production, whatever its apparently rational rigor. We will return to this idea (see "The Sumptuary Economy: Luxury and Consumption," later in this chapter).

The Monastery, or the Monastic Model

The medieval citadel furnishes the general framework of the libertine community, with everything that this implies about the safety of the group and the lordly status of its members. It must be noted, however, that the organization of life is strictly patterned on the monastic model. For the guests of Silling and the members of the Sodality of the Friends of Crime, the Regulations are the clearest sign of this pattern, defining rights and duties as well as attitudes.

Because we are dealing with Sade, mention inevitably will be made of the parodic and blasphemous way in which he uses monastic signs to organize the libertine community. This explanation is relevant, of course, but probably insufficient, as we will see. For now, we should at least record the importance of the monastic setting as such in the Sadean narrative and make the following observations:

- Juliette's account begins with the description of her libertine education in the convent at Panthemont, under the direction of Madame Delbène, the loose, ungodly abbess. All of Juliette's sojourns in monasteries or convents (the monastery of the white friars in Paris, or the convent of the nuns at Bologna) are marked by orgies, which arouse a very particular enthusiasm on her part.

- In the case of Justine, internment in the monastery of the libertine monks of Saint-Mary-in-the-Wood is what constitutes her central misfortune.

- In *The 120 Days*, la Durand's stories begin with her shameless exploits as a little girl with the monks in her neighborhood.

What is remarkable in all these monastic settings is that the acts of debauchery are quite strictly modeled on the rituals of religious life. All the signs and all the structures of the monastic system are scrupulously maintained, as if these signs and structures, far from thwarting the possibilities of libertinism, actually facilitated them.

If we acknowledge that the pursuit of a blasphemous irony is merely the most obvious aspect of the monastery's transformation into a place of debauchery, how do we explain Sade's infatuation with this way of life, which his quite violent atheism should have inclined him to denounce or despise? Where does this paradoxical indulgence come from? A possible answer is that the monastic structure, as much at the institutional level as at the level of relationships, furnishes the model that most closely approximates what the libertine community can be (as for the economic conditions of subsistence, they are more or less the economic conditions of feudal production).

The institutional level: the rule, the enclosure, and silence. Every monastic life is essentially defined by the adoption of a rule (in the strictly historical sense: the Benedictine Rule, the Augustinian Rule, the Dominican Rule, and so forth). This rule is a system for ritualizing and apportioning the hours of the day (the hours for rising, going to bed, taking meals, working), for imposing a certain bearing on the body (through clothing, gait, and silence), for making use of particular places (the garden, the cloister, the refectory, the cells, the chapel, and so on) at particular hours, and for using conventional formulas to offer greetings, ask for things, give thanks, and reinforce hierarchical relationships. In other words, what is literally fascinating about the monastic rule is its capacity to produce an order that does not depend on any external necessity, one that is equivalent to Order itself (theology, of course, would justify this order as a test of obedience, as abnegation of the will, as submission to God, and so forth). What is needed, then, is a rule for organizing time and space, actions and movements, as a discourse, a precise grammar, no matter how arbitrary the imperatives may be (the more arbitrary the imperatives, the more the order will be experienced as an autonomous requirement, as the unnecessary cause of indispensable effects). Continuous, empty Sadean time at last finds itself organized and apportioned, through the rule, into elements that can be combined and therefore manipulated by the whims of desire. (And here we have the interplay of two kinds of arbitrariness: the kind that pertains to apportioning through the rule, and the kind that pertains to the moods of desire; order is in the service of unpredictability.)

The second essential element of the monastic institution is the enclosure. The term *enclosure* designates the boundaries that the monk cannot cross without express permission from his superior. In general, it coincides with the precincts of the monastery, but it exerts a primarily symbolic constraint: because this constraint can be in effect where there is no appearance of any physical boundary, it puts the finishing touch, spatially speaking, on the rule's mode of constraint by determining an inside as opposed to an outside, sacred as opposed to profane territory, a secret as opposed to a public side. At an even more profound level, the closure marks the renunciation of life in the world and of the world's temptations; what Blangis offers the recluses of Silling is a virtual sermon on "taking the veil" ("insofar as the world is concerned, you are already dead").

We can imagine how this physical marking of boundaries serves Sade's quest for a coded, secret, protected place, since this is a place that facilitates combinative effects. Moreover, it has a particular historical advantage: namely, that the monastic precincts are a place from which secular power is banned, and everything occurring inside them depends exclusively on the special jurisdiction of the church. This, then, is the model for the society within a society that the association of libertines hopes to be. It is the paradox of a society that has the power to preserve its secrets, without being a secret society. What is more, it even manages to have itself respected and fawned over by civil power. Because Sade can imagine nothing better for his libertines, who lack the monks' phenomenal privileges, he turns the problem around and makes the monks libertines, too.

Finally, the imperative of silence is yet another important element. It is considered to be a condition for contemplation, study, and, ultimately, the orderliness of the monastery. Its greatest effect, however, may be to remove psychology from relationships and keep bodies at the distance created by ritualized acts and the abstraction of their emblems. This silence is not the absence of the spoken word. Rather, it is the art of making room for the only Word recognized as living and effective: the Word of God, proclaimed in public through the reading of the Bible or turned over and over in meditation.

In asking silence to assume the same function—as the art of order and attention, both of which are indispensable to pleasure—Sade finds it sufficient to replace the Word of God with libertine speeches. One article of the regulations governing Silling formally prohibits "the least display of mirth" during the orgies; what the regulations demand is undivided contemplation, as Juliette notes here:

> All these scenes of fuckery were preceded by a moment of suspense, of calm; as though the participants wished in stillness and contemplation to savor voluptuousness in its entirety, as though they feared lest, by talking, they might let some of it escape. I was requested to be attentive, alert in my pleasure-taking; for later I should be expected to report on the experience. I swam in a wordless ecstasy.[8]

The level of relationships: community, celibacy, and sexual segregation. Monastic life is, in the first place, a particular mode of community life.

The only thing that makes it possible is respect for the rule of the order, which is to say that monastic life exists only as the result of a code (and it is this that will probably interest Sade the most). Moreover, this community entails a solidarity that prefigures the complicity among the libertines; freely shared possessions foreshadow freely shared bodies.

Perhaps more than anything else in the monastic way of life, however, celibacy — that is, the purely moral choice of barrenness — anticipates libertine thought. Here again the monk, in his refusal to procreate or to reproduce the nuclear family, offers himself as a model. Male-female relationships have no connection with the monastery except in terms of disjunction: an all-male community, or an all-female community. A mixed-sex community is unthinkable because carnal temptation, in Christian terms, could only be heterosexual and would endanger the only paternity or maternity that is ultimately recognized: God's. In order to eliminate that danger, the monastic system exposes itself, paradoxically, to another kind of carnal temptation, one that is even more harshly condemned: homosexuality. Whether practiced or not, homosexuality is the only possible outlet for a sexual quest within the confines of the enclosure.

In other words, the entire mode of organization of the monastic life and all of that life's structures quite easily lend themselves to a reversal exhibiting this vector of perversity, as if the libertine, by bringing this perversity into being, were demonstrating that the monastic system as a whole is the painstaking if disavowed establishment of the conditions that libertinism hypothesizes. We see this especially in the overall effect of the whole monastic system, in the outcome and goal of all its structures: the organization and rationalization of the *otium*, which is neither idleness nor laziness but rather a kind of aristocratic repose, a glorification of uselessness, of not-working. The monk justifies this not-working as a necessity of prayer (that is, as celebration of the spoken word, the only advantage of which is to please God). The lord of the manor retains a well-defined function (to defend, to engage in armed combat); the monk reserves for himself the function of uselessness (contemplation, repetition of discourses). He is a proxy being: he prays for others, he intercedes.

The libertine certainly also secures this state of *otium* for himself, but with this slight difference: pleasure is substituted for prayer. The libertine comes in behalf of and in place of others, and in the luxury produced by their labor. This is a total parasitism, identical to that of the Tibetan monks, which Bataille analyzes, finding in it a solution to the question of surplus consumption: "Monasticism is a mode of expenditure of the excess that Tibet undoubtedly did not discover, but elsewhere it was given a place *alongside* other outlets. In Central Asia the extreme solution consisted in giving the monastery all the excess."[9]

The libertine: a pleasure-lama.

The Factory, or the Industrial Capitalist Model

At this point, inevitably, an issue arises: in the château and feudal power (even in redirected form), and in the monastery and religious order (even in parodic form), we already have two of the three figures belonging to the trifunctional system of the Indo-European cultural universe brought to light in a general way by Georges Dumézil, a system whose relevance to the Middle Ages has been demonstrated by Georges Duby.[10] This system, let us recall, comprises three orders: the order of those who command and make war (*bellatores*), the order of those who pray and control discourse (*oratores*), and, finally, the order of those who work and ensure the subsistence of all (*laboratores*). Is this third category also represented in the Sadean text? It is indeed, less by the mass of servants and peasants who secure the gains of the other two orders than by the great mass of men and women who serve the pleasures of the libertines.

Thus, following up our analysis of the château and monastery models, we might envisage this third category simply by remaining inside the hypothesis of the trifunctional system and, within this framework, analyzing only the sexual exploitation of the victims. A reading of this kind would be relevant up to a point—but only up to a point, for what constitutes Sade's profound originality is his having introduced a break into this third level, his having allowed the trifunctional world of tradition to be invaded by a completely new system of representations, one that imposes itself on the reader in a way both surprising and unimpeachable: the system of representations belonging to the capitalist factory. Sade does this by staging, first, the ever more pronounced power of high finance; second, the mechanical and factorylike character of the orgies' organization; and, third, the rationalized (that is, quasi-operational) exploitation of victims.

This is not, of course, a matter of plastering onto the Sadean text grids for reading that would be more relevant to the social novels of the nineteenth century. It is a matter of simply bringing to light, as boundary and presupposition of the Sadean orgy, the existence of new models for financial investment, for the production and administration of goods, and for the mobilizing and disciplining of bodies. By the second half of the eighteenth century, these models were much more developed than previously believed, not just in England but in France, Germany, and Italy as well.[11] It is also known that Sade, in this a typical Enlightenment thinker, had great enthusiasm for machines and was very interested in the development of manufacturing.[12]

It is the presence and insistence of these new models that will permit us to understand the true originality of the Sadean universe, an originality consisting in the irruption of financial power into the seigniorial world of the libertines, the incursion of machines and automata into the functioning of the desiring body, and the rational organization of individuals in the collective task that is the orgy.

Thus the model of the feudal fortress frames the setting for pleasure, and for the forms of power that are exercised in that setting. The model of the monastery primarily determines the attitudes and the organization of the libertine community. But the outline for the libertine community's operative economic plan is furnished by the model of the factory. This is a factory of a very special kind — a *pleasure factory* (that is, a factory for sheer expenditure, as we will see) — but, formally speaking, what we find highlighted here are the same features as in an industrial factory.

Outlays of capital. Silling and the manor house of the Sodality of the Friends of Crime are both enterprises "founded" at the initiative of very well-to-do members of the high nobility or the haute bourgeoisie. From the outset, then, the four libertines of *The 120 Days* are essentially defined and presented as redoubtable swindlers, holders of an immense amount of capital that they intend to "invest" in a fantastic four-month-long debauch in their château at Silling.[13] In addition to the fixed capital corresponding to this investment, variable capital and its management are explicitly specified:

> The society had created a common fund, which each of its members took his turn administering for six months; the sums, allocated for nothing but expenses in the interests of pleasure, were vast. Their excessive wealth put the most unusual things within their reach, and the reader ought not be surprised to hear that two million were annually disbursed to obtain good cheer and lust's satisfaction.[14]

The principals of this enterprise are selected on the basis of their capacity to make advances of capital, and failure to fulfill this condition constitutes grounds for elimination:

> Entry into the Sodality is barred to those unable to indicate a minimum yearly income of twenty-five thousand livres, dues of membership being ten thousand francs per annum.[15]

Raw materials. What is meant by this phrase in this context, of course, is the mass of bodies that will be used and "processed" in the operations of debauchery. Seraglios and harems constitute the permanent stock of the erotic factory.

Manpower. On the one hand, manpower is the throng of servants and other domestic workers (coachmen, valets, cooks) whose anonymous and almost unnoticed presence in the text ensures that the festivities run smoothly. On the other hand, manpower is the victims themselves, whose erotic function is often mockingly overlaid by a function of domestic service (thus, at Silling, the little girls and little boys have to wait naked at table).

Managerial staff. The managerial staff comprises, first, the countless pimps and recruiters who supply the raw materials, but it also comprises the torturers, storytellers, and go-betweens — in other words, all those intermediaries who do not belong to the inner circle of the libertines (members of the inner circle are selected for their capital) but also are not consigned to the doomed circle of the victims. Like any other managers, these are selected for their knowledge and experience, and so they already belong to the sphere of power, with all the impunity that goes with it. Thus Silling's four storytellers are assured that they will return to Paris alive, and the promise is kept. Cooks, too, in view of the exalted erotic function of meals, are promoted into the ranks of management and saved, but their assistants are sacrificed. We should note that the establishment of the "pleasure factory" contains the essential condition that determines, according to Marx, the movement from artisanal production to manufacturing-based production — namely, "the assemblage, in one workshop under the control of a single capitalist, of labourers belonging to various independent handicrafts."[16] Capital ordains this change, which becomes a change in the worker's technical and social status and is tied to a radical technological change — mechanization — that capital demands and depends on in equal part. And so the pleasure factory reproduces burgeoning industrialism's model of production by displacing it onto another setting: the setting of relationships of desire between bodies, a setting that offers something akin to a prism or, rather, a model of the conditions for the industrial model of production. But the pleasure factory does not so much reproduce this model as comprise one part of it or, rather, partake of the conditions for the reproduction of these new relationships of production.

The Masters of Capital and the Proletariat of Libertinism

If, theoretically, Sade's libertines must be or become very rich, it is because wealth is acknowledged as the privileged source of power. Therefore, wealth constitutes an indispensable prerequisite to the satisfaction of the libertine imagination's whims. Wealth is what secures unlimited access to the desired bodies, their stockpiling, and their manipulation, and wealth is what secures all the practical conditions (a safe house, comfort, rich food, idleness) for enjoying those bodies.

Here, Sade has invented nothing: he takes note of historical fact, of how relationships of desire are inscribed into relationships of power, and he takes the merciless logic of historical fact all the way to its dire consequences. Insofar as his intention is that his narrative meet the requirements of verisimilitude, he can only imagine libertine desire within the cruel actuality of existing relationships of force.

Where the age and tastes of the libertines are concerned, the requirement of verisimilitude entails its own chain of corollaries. The libertines are generally old or middle-aged (gerontocrats), for power and wealth come late in life, at an age when, given the weakening of sexual potency and the waning of ordinary sensation, extremes of perversion and violent sensation must be resorted to. Thus all this criminal excess occurs as the culmination of a logic whose first term is an economic one.

The possibility of libertine activity depends on another important link in this logical chain: the presumption of impunity. What we are dealing with here is a privilege whose beneficiaries are quite openly pleased with it, a privilege that proceeds from the collusion between wealth and political power. Wealth secures the complicity of political power; in the case of a sovereign, the two are blended. The arbitrary nature of impunity indicates that power still resides within the order of violence, and that the law is derisively honored in the breach, in its function of trapping the powerless into a reverence for power by presenting power as a real

mediation between individuals and sovereigns. Because the owners of
the state consider the law to be null and void, libertine excess would be
inconceivable if the self-interest of the masters of capital were not completely identical to the self-interest of the masters of political power.
What libidinal economy is exposing here is the repressed content of political economy.

Of course, this complete coinciding of self-interest began well before
the appearance of any kind of capitalist economy and likewise had been
preceded by manifestations of power in the domination of desired bodies. But the novel thing about this type of economy was the possibility
of envisaging relationships of domination that could follow the relationship model employed in the factory (the primordial setting of capitalist production), and according to the same conditions established
in the factory. The possibility of envisaging these kinds of relationships
is one that continues to be evaded, for it would completely expose the
cynical truth about the system. This admission might prove intolerable
and could lead to something quite like *The 120 Days.*

Indeed, Silling is the sign of something entirely new — namely, that
the specific nature of this place of pleasure is determined by the fact
that it exists only because of a *decision,* taken by a few masters of capital,
to concentrate a certain number of bodies within its closed, controlled
space, bodies from which a productive activity is expected within a limited time and to the limit of their capacities, a productive activity whose
surplus value will be the sexual satisfaction of the masters themselves.
The ascendancy that the masters exercise over these bodies (in terms of
order, submission, schedules, output, and instrumental status) is the exact replica of the ascendancy observed in the factory, that other realm
of concentration. Thus Silling probably would have been inconceivable
before the birth of industrial capitalism. Silling projects into relationships of desire the same principle of bodily exploitation that governs
the factory. Silling tells the dirty little secret about this mode of production: that masters of capital, through the factory system, become masters of bodies as well, and that the sexual exploitation of these bodies is
only the logical conclusion of their industrial exploitation. Only the suffering of these bodies can yield sexual satisfaction for the masters.

Thus there exists a whole proletariat of libertinism, and it is manifested on at least two levels. At one level, indirectly,[17] the primary issue
is the laboring masses who produce the wealth seized by the libertines.

This proletariat does not even enter into the text, because its reality was not even recognized by the economists of the time (it would take Marx to recognize labor as the source of all wealth). In the text, what marks this activity of proletarianized labor is the presence of a large domestic staff whose toil of service, caretaking, and attention is carried out in closest proximity to the master's body, or at any rate in his house, a staff that—from washing to cooking, from greeting to traveling—fully sustains the master's extravagant idleness with its obscure, constant labor, which is scarcely even registered in the text, because it blends in with an encoded "naturalness," and which, in the passive voice ("a magnificent meal was served") or in the cursory notations tacked onto the narrative fabric ("a servant receives us," "fifty valets of a most agreeable countenance"), scarcely even emerges.

At another level, and more immediately, this proletariat of libertinism is directly employed in the master's sexual satisfaction. It comprises the group of designated "lust objects": in other words, those who constitute the body of victims in sexual service to the libertine body—a proletarianized body that is manipulated, enjoyed, mauled, tortured, exhausted, and finally tossed aside after heavy use, when its erotic output becomes nil.

"Human material" (in Marx's phrase) costs the master nothing: capital readily procures it for him from among the impoverished classes; and, in the case of a sovereign, any subject is theoretically considered to be available sexual material. The brothels of Madame Duvergier are filled with penniless adolescents ready to sell themselves wherever capital is being offered, which is why Juliette finds herself there after the financial ruin of her parents, and it is in the face of this necessity that she launches her career in debauchery. Likewise, the seraglios of the various libertines (Saint-Fond, Noirceuil, Minski, the pope, Brisatesta, and so forth) are filled with boys and girls who have been sold or kidnapped with the guarantee of impunity conferred by wealth and power.

When Juliette and her companions arrive to visit the King of Naples, the whole population of the kingdom is put at the disposal of their libertinism. Sbrigani, their majordomo, immediately undertakes a very selective recruitment of manpower: "I have put twelve purveyors into the field and shall see to it that two dozen pretty lads between the ages of eighteen and twenty-five are regularly presented to you every morning."[18]

And when a guide has to be chosen for a tour of the countryside, the post is opened up to bids from the abundantly available manpower:

> They all agree to the bargain; we lower breeches, we excite, we frig; six are judged worthy of the honors of a spasm, and the biggest, that is to say, a funny fellow all in rags and tatters, whose leviathan stretched itself thirteen inches in length and filled out to nine in circumference, alone obtained, after having fucked us all three, the privilege of becoming our cicerone.[19]

In short, the workers' capacities are tested before the workers are hired. The margin of unemployment is sufficient to give the employer complete latitude in selecting the most productive workforce. Before a party at which several hundred victims will be on the program, the Queen of Naples articulates, with perfect clarity, the thinking that presides over this (sexual) domination and exploitation of the destitute masses:

> And of what account can the lives of all that trash be … when our pleasures are at stake? If we have the right to have their throats cut for our interests' sake, I see no reason why we cannot do the same for the sake of our delights.[20]

The energetic and corporal reserves of the dominated classes, taken for granted by the pleasure of the masters, are the same reserves exploited by capital in factory labor. Marx read the following notice in the report of a mid-nineteenth-century English factory inspector, but it could pass for an advertisement placed by a libertine recruiter: "Wanted, 12 to 20 young persons, not younger than what can pass for 13 years."[21] In that era, the labor of women and children was capital's radical attempt to appropriate all the energy that was available from "human material":

> In the notorious district of Bethnal Green, a public market is held every Monday and Tuesday morning, where children of both sexes from 9 years of age upwards, hire themselves out to the silk manufacturers. … The scene and language while this market is going on are quite disgraceful. It has also occurred in England, that women have taken "children from the workhouse and let any one have them out for 2s.6d. a week."[22]

What was new about this industrial exploitation of the workforce, as compared with the exploitation belonging to the previous phase, was the way it presupposed *direct aggression* against the worker's *body*, as well as indifference to the resulting loss of human life:

> We have aleady alluded to the physical deterioration ... of the children and young persons [and] of the women, whom machinery, first directly in the factories that shoot up on its basis, and then indirectly in all the remaining branches of industry, subjects to the exploitation of capital. In this place, therefore, we dwell only on one point, the enormous mortality, during the first few years of their life, of the children of the operatives.[23]

The cold, devouring monster of capital develops from the ruins of exploited bodies, from (among other things) "the converting [of] immature human beings into mere machines for the fabrication of surplus-value" and, in general, from the reduction of all workers to the state of "the human material that forms the principal object of capital's exploiting power," whose life force is drained by capital.[24] In order to describe the vampirizing technology of Silling, we would not need to add anything at all to this analysis. We would merely have to specify the way in which the general principle of exploiting energy and bodies becomes efficient only when it is applied within a whole network of institutions and techniques of coercion, such as those outlined by Foucault, for example, in *Discipline and Punish*.[25] Foucault locates these institutions (the school, the army, the factory, administration) and their techniques (regulations, systems of supervision, grades of punishment) earlier in time than the modern penal institution, where what he sees is bodily conditioning taken to an extreme. The industrial factory occupies a critical role within this configuration: it inherits all the previously developed traditions of constraint and discipline, harnesses them for its own profit, standardizes them as techniques for productivity, and invents new ones determined by the logic of its own needs.

Silling the "pleasure factory" is also, quite precisely, a penal environment. Here again we recognize the characteristics of the factory, with penal authority structuring its institutional framework according to a number of features.

Order and discipline. To make bodies yield the greatest amount of the energy that can be applied to production, it is necessary to secure permanent control over them with a whole system of measures that construct, little by little, an ordered, disciplined space.

CONTROL OF TIME. Strict allocation of time is a direct legacy of the monastic and military traditions. The first factories, turning to the same model, added yet another objective: that of "constituting a totally useful time";[26] for the employer, all paid time must be profitable. This effort has not been painless, as Marx notes: "Throughout the whole manufacturing period there runs the complaint of want of discipline among the workmen.... [B]etween the 16th century and the epoch of Modern Industry, capital failed to become the master of the whole disposable working-time of the manufacturing labourers."[27]

Austerity is the sign of time's profitability. Foucault offers this sample, from 1809, of a factory's regulations: "It is expressly forbidden during work to amuse one's companions by gestures or in any other way, to play at any game whatsoever, to eat, to sleep, to tell stories and comedies."[28] There is no joking about the duty of production, any more than there is at Silling about the service of libertinism:

> The least display of mirth, or the least evidence given of disrespect or lack of submission during the debauch activities, shall be esteemed one of the gravest of faults and shall be one of the most cruelly punished.[29]

As for the residents' time, it is planned with precision, and it is subject to strict scheduling ("punctually at six o'clock," "at precisely two o'clock"), with personal time so completely excluded that the exclusion extends even to the act of defecation (where a different logic enters in, as we shall see).

SPECIFICATION OF DETAILS. The demand for order could never be satisfied by general recommendations alone. The network of disciplinary measures must be so tightly woven that no energy is allowed to slip through and float free. This network must be constructed as a collection of minutely detailed obligations, leaving no action without a regulatory definition, and the need for order will turn into an economy of *details*:

> "Detail" had long been a category of theology and asceticism.... The meticulousness of the regulations, the fussiness of the inspections, the supervision of the smallest fragment of life and of the body will soon provide, in the context of the school, the barracks, the hospital or the workshop, a laicized content, an economic or technical rationality for this mystical calculus of the infinitesimal and the infinite.[30]

This is certainly what the masters of Silling have in mind when they promulgate regulations that program and impose the attitudes required in various situations, as in the following clause (among others):

> These little girls shall adopt the general custom of kneeling at all times whenever they see or meet a[ny of the four] friend[s], and they shall remain thus until told to stand.[31]

HIERARCHICAL ORGANIZATION. The "art of rank," as Foucault calls it,[32] in addition to the ancient practice of it in armies (starting with the Roman armies, where the model for it was already complete), became surprisingly widespread in Jesuit schools from the seventeenth century on, as part of a development culminating in the completely militarized Napoleonic academy:

> In organizing "cells," "places," and "ranks," the disciplines create complex spaces that are at once architectural, functional and hierarchical. It is spaces that provide fixed positions and permit circulation; they carve out individual segments and establish operational links; they mark places and indicate values; they guarantee the obedience of individuals, but also a better economy of time and gesture.[33]

These technologies of subordination were perfectly obvious in the factories of the early nineteenth century, as Marx points out; they "[gave] rise to a barrack discipline, which [was] elaborated into a complete system in the factory, and which fully develop[ed] the . . . labor of overlooking, thereby dividing the workpeople into operatives and overlookers, into private soldiers and sergeants of an industrial army."[34]

This hierarchical distribution is clearly noticeable at Silling. The grades of the hierarchy are as follows, in descending order: libertines, storytellers, fuckers, duennas, little boys, little girls, and wives (cooks have a status of their own, apart from direct sexual service). This hierarchy has its corresponding rights and privileges (to decide, to come, to punish, to destroy, and so forth).

Supervision and punishment. This ordered, disciplined space presumes a whole set of controlling activities: the group cannot be brought under control unless it is subjected to constant supervision, whose effects are felt in the system of sanctions. Here again, various means or techniques ensure the project's smooth functioning.

ENCLOSURE. The enclosure is an essential structure of monastic space, as we have seen, but it is one that belongs to every disciplinary institution from the factory to the prison, and from the school to the barracks. The cloister marks off a territory where entrances and exits are recorded, where a law other than common law holds sway: in other words, to cite Foucault once again, a "place heterogeneous to all others and closed in upon itself," and thus "the factory was explicitly compared with," for example, "the monastery, the fortress, a walled town."[35] This could be the very definition of Silling, which, like every other Sadean locale, is the object of a paranoiac closing off; the gates are even walled shut, to prevent "leaving the least entrance to an enemy, the least egress to a deserter."[36]

DISCIPLINARY OBSERVATION. Mastering bodies is a question of bringing to bear on them the certitude of a permanent and imperceptible control. To do this it is enough to structure the tight control of the group along architectural lines: assigning places, putting places off limits, linking places to particular kinds of clothing, and thus knowing at all times who is or is not supposed to be where. In *Justine,* the residents of the monastery of Saint-Mary-of-the-Wood are subjected to this kind of distinctive marking:

> As you observe, [we are] always in the uniform of our particular class; before the day is over you will be given the habit appropriate to the one you are entering; during the day we wear a light costume of the color which belongs to us; in the evening, we wear gowns of the same color and dress our hair with all possible elegance.[37]

A space like this one becomes "the diagram of a power that acts by means of general visibility."[38] It is both the economic operator of productivity and the irrefutable means of disciplinary control. The panoptic model of observation imagined by Bentham merely takes this supervisory control to its extreme limit. Silling, without having attained such perfectionism, is no less organized as a space of supervision: the supervision that the four libertines, always on the lookout to impose penalties, take upon themselves for its own sake; the supervision that falls to the duennas; and even the supervision that the residents are encouraged to exercise, going so far as to inform on one another.

PENALTIES. With the proliferation of regulations and prohibitions comes a resulting proliferation of opportunities to commit infractions. Thus there arises a new kind of penalty, this one determined not by offenses against the law but by offenses against the norms, and, from this point on, "the whole indefinite domain of the non-conforming is punishable."[39] Sade's perception of the perverse relationship between regulations and infractions, a relationship that cuts across all types of institutions, is quite explicit. Infractions exist only in proportion to the number of regulations that have been imposed, and, ultimately, the regulations are put in force only for the sake of providing and guaranteeing opportunities for infractions, thereby ensuring the citizens' guilt as an additional guarantee of their submission. The libertine does not fail to grasp this logic, in order to make extreme use of all its consequences, as Sade has one of the victims of Saint-Mary-of-the-Wood say with perfect clarity:

> Not that the libertines need all [these formalities] in order to vent their fury upon us, but they welcome excuses; the look of legitimacy that may be given to a piece of viciousness renders it more agreeable in their eyes, adds to its piquancy, its charm.[40]

This last remark, which belongs to the discourse of the victim, is immediately footnoted by the author: "It is not, in this case, justice that has charm; it is the theft that the libertine commits against the rights of justice."[41]

It is impossible to state more clearly than this that the establishment of the libertine masters took shape under the sign of parody, a parody that makes it possible to *see* the arbitrary nature of authority, as well as the paranoia of supervision and administrative control. Elsewhere, the same arbitrariness and paranoia operate under the indisputable sign of reality, masked simply by their acceptance as standards necessary to order and normality. In the pleasure factory, both Silling's "book of penalties" and the "table of punishments" of Saint-Mary-of-the-Wood (which even specifies how many blows of the whip or pricks of the pin are entailed in various offenses) echo the disciplinary models that run rampant in the industrial capitalist workplace, for the book of penalties and the table of punishments display the frenziedly arbitrary quality of those models. Thus, if it is at all accurate to say that there is a proletariat of libertinism, it owes its existence not just to everything that the sexual satisfaction of the masters of capital presupposes about confiscated wealth and slave labor but also to the way in which this enslavement is shaped by the new techniques of bodily conditioning, and by the methods of productivity that this new mode of production has developed or invented.

But the Sadean text reveals this dual exploitation of the body only by making this exploitation's repressed, perverse dimension explicit, even central: the technological and disciplinary control of bodies is tormented by a burning desire, but the very harshness of the principle of unlimited productivity is forever barring and removing this desire from any immediate possession or tyrannical enjoyment of those bodies. (In a good many of his metaphors, Marx lets this vampirish hypothesis show through — without, however, pointing to its implications.) The industrial capitalist master can enjoy only the *representation* of his power over the dominated and exploited bodies. His own logic dooms him to mediation, and he is obliged to marginalize his sexual pleasure. By contrast, the libertine master articulates the outer limit and aim of this desire by relating all the new techniques of domination to his body and his sexual pleasure. Libertine despotism tells the inadmissible truth about capitalist exploitation.

The Manufacture of Sexual Pleasure

In the Sadean text, as we have seen, the staging of the body ends in the complete disintegration of the organic model (that is, the model of an individual body structured on its own presence to itself). This disintegration entails the elimination of subjectivity by way of a quadruple reduction (anatomical, mechanical, arithmetical, and combinative) that constitutes a radical critique of the metaphysical tradition — or, specifically, of the metaphysical tradition insofar as it is Aristotelian. What Aristotle fundamentally theorizes as the organic body is the body of artisanal experience: the unitary functioning of the organs, both among themselves and in their relation to tools.

This model of the body lasted as long as artisanal experience did (artisanal experience being understood as the integration of manufacturing activity into the unity of the individual body), and it reached its highest point in the era of artisanal production's hegemony, the era of the medieval corporation. The word *corporation* says it all: the productive body extended and reproduced the model of the organic body.

But capitalism smashed them both to pieces. The disintegration took effect gradually, through the technology that the new mode of production required, promoted, and imposed. It will be interesting to see how this change in the model is echoed in Sade's fiction of the same era, and to examine how Sade's fiction exploits and represents this breaking up of the body, but to entirely different ends from those that were attached to it by the potency of capital.

Marx has shown that capital carried out the liquidation of the medieval corporation in three stages, in a sort of imperceptible progression that moved from manufacturing to the cooperative and to the factory. The cooperative left artisanal activity intact, but "the control of a single capitalist," which is what was eventually to destroy artisanal activity, had already been introduced. Capital would go on to assemble "in one workshop . . . labourers belonging to various independent handicrafts," thus establishing heterogeneous manufacturing. The watershed movement to serial manufacturing through specialization, and thus the movement to different types of labor, would be imposed as a necessity of rationalization: piecemeal virtuosity would reduce production time and increase productivity. The medieval corporation, already dead, dragged the model of the organic body into the grave with it. And this movement to the factory would introduce yet another break, of yet another order of magnitude: the disjointed body was to lose even its value as a force in production. Production was transferred to the machine, and the worker became nothing more than the machine's assistant. This was the stroke of genius that capital accomplished with the development of mechanization.[42] The individual body, as an organic body, no longer figured *as such* in the process of production. It was now only a system of diversified forces from which the process of production could pick and choose.

Marx's revolutionary discovery was that this development could not in any way be understood as an autonomous and necessary evolution of technology (notwithstanding the great naïveté of all the scientistic histories of science), but that it was instead the outcome of capital's methodical appropriation of the process of production. Capital determined and produced technological change and governed the forms that it would take: those forms that would allow it in every respect to control the process of production, reducing the worker to a divisible, quantifiable, abstract force. Starting from the protocapitalist stage of the cooperative, the formula was set in motion:

> The cooperative of wage-labourers is entirely brought about by the capital that employs them. Their union into one single productive body and the establishment of a connexion between their individual functions, are matters foreign and external to them, are not their own act,

but the act of the capital that brings and keeps them together. Hence the connexion existing between their various labours appears to them, ideally, in the shape of a preconceived plan of the capitalist, and practically in the shape of the authority of the same capitalist, in the shape of the powerful will of another, who subjects their reality to his aims. If, then, the control of the capitalist is in substance two-fold by reason of the two-fold nature of the process of production itself, — which, on the one hand, is a social process for producing use-values, on the other, a process for creating surplus-value—in form that control is despotic.[43]

The unity of "one single productive body" as an external "connexion," as "the powerful will of another," as "despotic" control: these are precisely the features defined by the conditions that exist at the pleasure factory known as Silling, and they ensure, more than metaphorically, the *manufacture of sexual pleasure*. Once the subject has been divested of it, sexual pleasure is merely a calculable, quantifiable result, the yield at the conclusion of a technical-economic process of production. This point deserves some elaboration.

It can be observed, first, that the Sadean "programmer" and the capitalist engineer have the same function. The appearance of this new figure, the engineer, signals the break introduced by capital between knowledge and practice, between the brain and the hand, a duality that within the medieval corporation had been integrated as ability or know-how. Henceforth someone with knowledge and control would be thinking about, planning, commanding, and unifying a manufacturing process that would be carried out through gradated, piecemeal gestures on an assembly line. The engineer represents the monopolization of knowledge by capital, as well as the cornering of the unifying function, because it is the engineer's task to conceive the synthesis of the chopped-up segments of production.

Thus we can understand the preeminent function of the *head,* so frequently extolled by Sade. The head conceives, plans, and brings order to what is executed. If the engineer of the orgy demands such precise order and such strict application of his program, it is because sound industrial logic says that the efficiency of the manufacturing process depends on cohesion and continuity, which then become the guarantees of obtaining what the orgy manufactures: sexual pleasure. And it surely must be noted that the libertine group is arranged in an assembly line, with tasks strictly allocated on the model of the division of labor, presupposing a virtuosity of action and detail (*"Fifteen girls arrive in teams of three: one whips him, one sucks him, the other shits"*).[44] In practical terms, all the descriptions of orgies are stagings of this specialized, parceled-out distribution of tasks. Among the most amazing of these is the description of the feast given by Francavilla; in connection with it, Barthes speaks of a "conveyor belt."[45] What can be seen here with even greater precision is the factory assembly line:

> Francavilla offered the world's most comely ass to our view; to two young children, stationed hard by that notable posterior, was entrusted the care of opening it, of wiping it, and of guiding toward the hole the monstrous members which, by the score, were shortly to fling into the sanctum sanctoris; twelve other children readied the pricks. I had never in all my days seen any service more nimbly accomplished. Thus prepared, those splendid members moved from hand to hand until they arrived in those of the children appointed to introduce them; they disappeared then into the ass of the patient: they came back out again, they were replaced by others; and all that with an effortlessness, a smoothness, a promptitude which compel wonder.[46]

Later on, in the course of the feast, this system becomes even more complex, through the addition of a machine tool — in other words, the transition from manufacturing to the factory. All that can be seen of the human agents plugged in to this "frigging"/sucking machine are the body parts (hand, penis, mouth, anus) supplying the appropriate action. Once this complex machine (with its springs, trapdoors, pulleys, hands, and sex organs) is set up and ready to go, the assembly line of sexual pleasure is set in motion and served by its maneuvers of lubrication, cunnilingus, "prick" arrangement, and perfuming. The libertine body, moving down the assembly line, is successively "processed" by all these specialized operations into a finished product: a body taking pleasure in its "discharge":

> Never were we kept waiting for so much as a moment. Before our mouths, cunts and pricks and asses succeeded one another as swiftly as our desires; elsewhere, the engines we frigged had but to discharge and new ones materialized between our fingers; our clitoris-suckers rotated with the same speed, and our asses were never deserted.[47]

What is also defined here is the principle of *productivity*, that is, the relationship between time and labor. In industry, thanks to the specialization of activities and the perfecting of tools and machines, time is saved, a time filled to capacity, a time from which nothing is lost, a time without pauses: a time appropriate to the speed required by the libertine assembly line. Because sexual pleasure is what is being manufactured, its value, like that of any other product, will be measured by the quantity of time that is "socially necessary for its production."[48] The manufacture of sexual pleasure has to move faster and faster, as in a factory, since "everything that shortens the necessary labour-time required for the reproduction of labour-power, extends the domain of surplus-labour."[49] Sexual pleasure, as a quantity and an accumulation rather than a state, is manufactured, and to say that it is manufactured is to say that sexual pleasure, like any other object of manufacture, can exist only as a "social product," as a consequence of what can be called the "collective pleasure-seeker," just as the industrial object is also a "social product" and consequence of the "collective worker." Thus we see that the Sadean orgy is the technical postulate of the pleasure factory: sexual pleasure entirely presumes the mechanical assembling of bodies whose underlying form is the completely objective and impersonal organism of the "huge automaton"[50] — that is, the neutral functioning of the impersonal group-body.

Thus it seems clear enough that for Sade the model of the industrial assembly line is what ordains the production of sexual pleasure, with all that this implies about socioeconomic conditions and the status of the body. But right away we must note that the importation of this model entails a whole series of paradoxes. The first of these has to do with using a model for maximum productivity in order to produce what labor rules out: sexual pleasure. This is certainly why the libertine master himself, by contrast with the master of capital, is operating on the assembly line, and with good reason: his own body is what is being offered for the transformation that the system must bring about. Nothing remains of the model but its form: all its functions have been redirected or falsified.

A second paradox has to do with the complete socialization of sexual pleasure, which can no longer be private, intimate, or singular, because it is worked out through multiple agents and becomes, like any other manufactured product, a standardized public object, a market good connected with a body that is itself on display, divided up, and portioned out.

Finally, the model is admittedly never pure and simple. According to circumstance, it may take the form of either serial or heterogeneous manufacturing, and sometimes we even see a partial return to the medieval corporation (for example, when the libertines, alone as a group, have no available manpower that has been assembled in one location by their capital and must limit themselves to being serviced by a few male or female companions). In general, then, we are dealing for the most part with an amalgam, a back-and-forth movement through forms that developed through history, forms that Sadean erotics plays at duplicating, condensing, and disfiguring. Sadean erotics was probably the first to take industrial capitalism's model for the body, and for relations of production, and run it so relentlessly and so radically off the rails. Thus, right at the moment when this text is being inscribed within a particular history, we see it being written in a radically different "elsewhere," through a displacement that both reverses and hijacks the facts of that history.

The Sumptuary Economy: Luxury and Consumption

> I shall give you a million to defray the cost of those suppers; but bear it well in mind that they are to be of unparalleled magnificence, the most exquisite meats, the rarest wines, the most extraordinary fowl and fruits will be served at them always, and immense quantity must be joined to the finest in quality: even if we were only two to dine, fifty courses would obviously be too few.
>
> —*Juliette*

Sadean libertinism, being founded on notions of *wealth* and *domination* (which is to say that it presupposes a vast exploitation of proletarianized labor, both anterior to and coterminous with itself), takes a comfortable pleasure in surplus value—it takes pleasure, that is, in squandering the surplus supplied by the mode of production in which Sadean libertinism functions, and of which it is an extreme symptom. In other words, the libertines constitute an exemplary case of what Veblen calls "the leisure class," and in their ostentatious orgies they consume what Bataille labels "the accursed share." It is not enough for them that their money and power can secure fantastic quantities of bodies, as well as the most complete impunity in manipulating them. All the signs of luxury and refinement must also be pressed into service, and, above all, the orgy must be accompanied by a choking waste of goods and energy. In short, the orgy has to be a *sacrifice*.

Nothing shows this better than the extravagant feast given in Naples
by the Prince of Francavilla:

> In all Italy, nothing equals Francavilla's magnificence and grand
> spending; there are sixty places set at his table every day, his guests are
> waited upon by two hundred domestics, all of the very fairest mien. The
> Prince, to receive us, had had a temple of Priapus raised in a grove in his
> garden. Mysterious pathways bordered by orange trees and myrtle led to
> this wondrously lighted sanctuary; columns wreathed with roses and
> lilacs were surmounted by a cupola beneath which stood an altar
> covered with soft grass, to the right; to the left, a table set for six; in
> the center, a great basket of flowers, whose shoots and festoons, laden
> with colored lampions, rose in garlands to the summit of the cupola.
> Different groups of practically naked youths, three hundred of them
> all told, were scattered about wherever there was space available, and
> atop the altar of grass appeared Francavilla, standing underneath
> the emblem of Priapus, deity in whose shrine we were forgathered;
> groups of children went forward by turns to bow down before the
> Prince.[51]

The dominating element within the religious and baroque framework
of this production is the sacrificial motif embodied in the celebration
of the love feast:

> The greatest supper ever seen by mortal eyes was therewith served by the
> Ganymedes, and the six places occupied by the King, the Queen, the
> Prince, my two sisters, and myself. There is no describing the delicacy
> and the magnificence of the fare: dishes and wines from all the countries
> of the world arrived in lavish profusion and uninterruptedly, and, mark
> of unheard-of luxury, nothing that was put on the table was taken off it:
> a viand or a wine was scarcely brought on when it was emptied into
> huge silver troughs, out of the bottom of which everything flowed away
> into the ground.
> "The wretched might profit from these leavings," said Olympia.
> "Wretched? Our existence upon earth denies that of our inferiors,"
> Francavilla explained; "I loathe the mere idea that what is of no use to us
> could afford relief to someone else."
> "His heart is as hard as his ass is generous," remarked Ferdinand.
> "I have nowhere encountered such prodigality," said Clairwil, "but I
> like it. That arrangement whereby scraps are saved for the scullery has
> chilling effects upon the imagination. Such orgies owe part of their
> success to the delicious realization that nothing and no one else matters
> on earth."

"Why, what do the underprivileged matter to me when I want for nothing," said the Prince; "their hardships add a further poignancy to my joys, I would not be so happy if I did not know there was suffering nearby, and 'tis from this advantageous comparison half the pleasure in life is born."[52]

What we have here is both the staging of waste, as analyzed by Bataille, and enjoyment of invidious comparison, as noted by Veblen.

Bataille, drawing his inspiration from Mauss,[53] sees the model for this squandering or nonproductive expenditure in the potlatch, a duel of feasting among certain indigenous North American tribes, in which enormous quantities of goods (animals, foodstuffs, jewels, cloth) are sacrificed so that the guest of honor (the chief of another tribe, for example) will be obliged to escalate the duel with an even more costly feast and an even more stunning degree of wastefulness.

In this sacrificial, extravagant orgy, what is radically invalidated is the rational (symmetrically contractual) form of exchange, on the one hand, and, on the other, the possibility of any capitalistic type of accumulation. An economy like this one is profoundly governed by the principle of nonproductive spending, of consumption — that is, by the decision to choose feasting and squandering over profit and thrift. There is a kind of reciprocity, of course, in the obligation to answer one potlatch with another. The ideal, as Mauss says, would be to give a potlatch and not have one given in return; and this is what often occurs, as was also true of the feasts underwritten by the wealthiest citizens of antiquity and the Middle Ages, feasts in which these citizens fulfilled a sort of duty to their status (a duty that can be understood as a subtle process of self-regulation, as a way for the group to limit accumulation), for if waste is absolute, if the gift is not matched, this is not to say that it has not produced an invaluable benefit: the acquisition of *rank*, prestige. As Bataille writes, "The gift would be senseless . . . if it did not take on the meaning of an acquisition. Hence giving must become acquiring a power, . . . which one acquires from the fact of *losing*"; the "subject who gives . . . enriches himself with a contempt for riches, and what he proves to be miserly of is in fact his generosity."[54]

The road to priceless fame and glory is the gift — that is, wastefulness — and this is exactly how wealth came to be granted both legitimacy (which normally had been conferred by valor) and the sacred character linked to consumption of "the accursed share." In the beginning, according to Veblen, valor was defined in terms of physical courage, as seen in the hunt or in war: the courage that enabled the capture of spoils and trophies, the plundering of enemies, and the taking of women and prisoners of war. With the movement to a sedentary way of life and to property, valor shifted to the acquisition of goods, and economic success became praiseworthy in and of itself: the ancient exploits of hunting and warfare were succeeded by exploits of finance, and yet "the propensity for achievement and the repugnance to futility remain[ed] the underlying economic motive."[55] The extravagant squandering of the potlatch is after-the-fact confirmation of the theory that situates prowess at the origins of wealth (effects return as causes), and the feast's blatant wastefulness gives it the aura of a ritual game of poker (Bataille), the fascination of risk and challenge. This is why extravagant wastefulness always determines what Veblen calls "invidious comparison," which finds its correspondence in the desire to astound that is essential to the potlatch and is cited by Bataille: "Once the resources are dissipated, there remains the prestige *acquired* by the one who wastes. The waste is an ostentatious squandering to this end, with a view to a superiority over others that he attributes to himself by this means."[56]

The resulting entitlement to *rank* establishes a hierarchy or, more precisely, a sacred order. Valor, wealth, and consumption: these were the same logical terms that governed nobiliary status in Europe until the triumph of the bourgeoisie, in the nineteenth century. It is impossible to understand the feudal mode of production, including its later forms, without recognizing the capital importance of obligations to the nobiliary code. These are what allow us to understand the *work taboo*, which, in being applied to the nobility, simultaneously imposed the duties of leisure and luxury: "During the predatory culture labor comes to be associated in men's habits of thought with weakness and subjection to a master. It is therefore a mark of inferiority, and therefore comes to be accounted unworthy of man in his best estate."[57] Already in Greek and Roman antiquity it was possible to see clear distinctions being established between the noble and the ignoble, the glorious and the base — distinctions between leisure and work, in other words, which were taken up again in the warring Middle Ages and revived by the new captains of industry:

> In itself and in its consequences the life of leisure is beautiful and
> ennobling in all civilized men's eyes.... Conspicuous abstention from

labor therefore becomes the conventional mark of superior pecuniary achievement....

As seen from the economic point of view, leisure, considered as an employment, is closely allied in kind with the life of exploit.... What it connotes is non-productive consumption of time. Time is consumed non-productively (1) from a sense of the unworthiness of productive work, and (2) as an evidence of pecuniary ability to afford a life of idleness.[58]

Hence the establishment of a whole series of signs (architectural and sartorial decorum, etiquette, language, "fine" manners, domesticity, the leisure assigned to wives) that stood as evidence of social and financial valor — the establishment, in other words, of everything that ultimately "testifies... to the fact that decorum is a product and an exponent of leisure-class life and thrives in full measure only under a regime of status."[59]

Indeed — and this is stating the case quite modestly. There is a deep logic permitting the leisure class (mainly at the stage of nobility) to consume surpluses, and to do so with a legitimacy drawn from the ideal of valor, and renewed in the risk of the loss exhibited in the wastefulness of feasting; nevertheless, it certainly cannot be denied that the resulting entitlement to rank, glory, and power has been perverted, historically, into arbitrary and cruel exploitation of servile labor. That was clearly the situation in France, at any rate, before 1789. And it is in precisely this double aspect that we must see the staging of the Sadean feast: as a glorious and luxuriant potlatch, but also as a redirection of the potlatch into the practice of class exploitation.

Thus the feast given by Francavilla, understood merely as a duel and a sacrifice, constitutes a fascinating debauch of goods and energy — a festival of consumption, a gallant show of sovereign destruction, an absolute disregard for thrift and accumulation. We could certainly interpret it this way and stand behind that interpretation. But then we would miss the Sadean demonstration's devastating irony, as well as the admission of cynicism about wealth and power that this potlatch assumes.

What we may notice first of all here, in fact, is that the feast no longer has anything at all of the public, popular character that Bataille imagines. It unfolds within a closed space to which (apart from the silent, mechanized domestic servants) only the privileged and powerful have access. The spectactular squandering that takes place here no longer has to ensure access to glory or recognition of rank; it merely confirms, among masters, the certainty of wealth and power already acquired. It does not *grant* status; it *indicates* status. The feast embodies the condensation of all the signs capable of configuring the privileges of the leisure class. It has become a strictly intransitive spectacle: it no longer entails any risk with respect to an audience, nor does it need to produce any events. It is valuable in and of itself, as the glamorous performance of obsolete practices, and it validates those practices while reaping their benefits. As a spectacle of make-believe, this feast is responsible for reenacting both the audacious birth of power and the magnanimous consumption linked to the logic of the gift. Even so, however, it loses none of its quite precise class function. Against bourgeois accountancy it exhibits its contempt for the useful and the thrifty, and against popular discontent among the working classes (the artisans and peasants) it exhibits its consumption of the surplus skimmed from their exploited labor.

And so the feast, because of its excesses, its sacrifice of victims, and its luxuriance, is first of all a feast of exclusion: the masters are happy because others are not there, because they themselves and they alone are the "we happy few" of enjoyment, an enjoyment that increases with the certainty of this knowledge. The more waste, idleness, and carelessness here, the more poverty, work, and submission elsewhere.

Hence this profound modification of the "invidious comparison" principle, which Veblen sees in older practices of conspicuous leisure: hostile duels and the open game of laying claim to rank become a cynical appraisal of the misery of those left out of the feast, a perverse enjoyment of inequality.

> If then 'tis the spectacle of the luckless who must necessarily complete our unhappiness by the comparison they furnish between themselves and us, one must take care not to relieve such downtrodden as exist; for by raising them, through this aid, from the class which provides elements for your comparisons, you deprive yourself of these comparisons, and hence of that which improves your pleasures.[60]

Sade, with the provocative irony of fiction, merely takes to extremes a theme that others, reputedly liberals, defend with all the seriousness of theory. Here is Voltaire:

It is impossible, on our unhappy Earth, for men living in society not to be divided into two classes: one consisting of the rich, who command, and the other consisting of the poor, who serve. . . . Mankind, such as it is, cannot survive without an infinite number of serviceable men who possess nothing at all.[61]

And here is Holbach:

Society, like nature, establishes among its members a necessary and legitimate inequality. This inequality is just, for the reason that it is founded upon the unchanging goal of society, I mean to say upon the preservation of its happiness.[62]

What Sade's text, through its excessiveness, shows about the quite common theme of "fair" inequality is this inequality's repressed erotic component, the knowledge that inequality causes enjoyment: enjoyment of power, privilege, idleness, and luxury.

In eighteenth-century philosophical circles, the debate over the principle of equality centered precisely on the question of luxury. The scandal of inequality, it was understood, was born of luxury—not because luxury caused inequality, but because luxury was spectacular evidence of it. Thus the issue was less to denounce the economic reasons for luxury than to reduce the provocative theatricality of luxury. Admittedly, the charge was led by the bourgeoisie, with liberal thinkers taking up the rear. But it was not so much the principle of luxury that they were protesting, because they were finally in the process of acceding to it, and because they also saw it as an essential spur to commerce. What they wanted was *reasonable* luxury and even, ultimately, at least in theory, luxury for all; what they condemned was the display of wealth, the senseless waste of it, the absence of economic rationality on the part of those who were carelessly enjoying themselves instead of reinvesting their wealth. In other words, two categories of squanderer were being condemned: great lords favored by power, and adventurers (the hucksters who had made rapid fortunes, the traffickers, the courtesans, and so on). These are exactly the two groups that, alone among all others, are privileged in the Sadean narrative—such figures as Saint-Fond, Noirceuil, and Francavilla, on the one hand, and, on the other, figures like Juliette, Clairwil, and Brisatesta—unrepentant heroes or heroines all, of unbridled and wasteful pleasure.

In the second half of the eighteenth century, Diderot played a considerable role in the debate. He defined his position for the first time in a reply to the famous chapter on ignorance that Helvétius, in *De l'Esprit*, had devoted to the question of luxury. He elaborated his argument in "Luxury," one of the longest articles in his *Encyclopedia*, and established what he considered to be the capital distinction between "ostentatious" and "decorous" luxury. Through Diderot and others, there took shape a whole literature of suspicion about the dangers of wealth and the sumptuary economy, with more and more panegyrics on moderation and peasant frugality (a convenient myth for the rising bourgeoisie, which allowed both condemnation of the nobles' decadence and the turning of a blind eye to the poverty of the countryside). All of this led to the promotion of a new concept of nonostentatious wealth — "affluence" — and was even extended to a generalized extolment of "happiness in mediocrity": "O felicitious mediocrity," cried the aptly named bourgeois writer Beausobre, "you it is who steer man between the Scylla of poverty and the Charybdis of wealth!"[63] The law of capital, it was understood, had left its mark. Surplus was being squandered, unproductively, by the sumptuary economy of the high-living nobles, and the greatest possible amount of that surplus had to be reinvested in production. At the same time, what had to be produced at every level was an ideology concerning thrift, moderation of desires, the seriousness of work, ascetic discipline, production, and, finally, money's respectability in and of itself. If the bar was lowered in the system of inequality, this system was no less savage than before, but it had learned discretion and modesty. What was most important was to put an end to spectacular, provocative signs of wealth, in order to make inequality tolerable. The era of excess was decreed to be at an end: enjoyment would have to learn silence and invisibility, or at least it would have to learn to take place somewhere else; and enjoyment would prove equal to the task.

This distancing and "normalization" are what Sade's texts so vehemently object to, grafting their protest onto the model of the sumptuary economy, with everything that this grafting implies in social terms. Given the historic constraints on what was conceivable and credible, we could say that there was scarcely any other choice, and we would probably be right. But whether there were other choices is not really the point; something of an entirely different order had come onto the stage of the text and passed through its logic. History, regardless of how heavily it persists or how much pressure its persistence exerts, is still, in the assembling of a fictional work, the object of a labor of displacement and representation. It remains to be seen what that labor has produced.

Mimesis, or the System of Nonproduction

If the economy of Sadean libertinism is ultimately an economy of consumption, then we have seen that it operates through the presentation of three different models, which are organized according to a layered structure: the military model of the feudal château, the religious model of the Christian monastery, and the industrial model of the capitalist factory.

In other words, we are dealing with the archaeological sediment of the various forms of production to which these models refer. Their specific effects' superimposition onto the text can be read symptomatically, particularly in the descriptions of sexual activity, through a semantic emphasis of three kinds: an emphasis on military language ("assault," "combat," "thrust," "victory"), an emphasis on religious language ("sacrifice," "incense," "altar," "cult," "sanctuary," "temple"), and an emphasis on technological language ("engine," "tool," "instrument," "operating," "positioning," "arranging"). If it is true that the libertine setting is structured along the lines of these three models, then it is even more true that the libertine setting is not identified with any single one of these models, precisely because it merely revives their signs and appropriates them by releasing them from any referential reality or causality. Silling functions *as* a fortress, *as* a monastery, *as* a factory; literally, however, it is only the libertine setting. This "as" is essential, though, since it shows that the model is being simulated only for the sake of capturing and redirecting its effects (whose causes, according to the Sadean principle of which we are so frequently reminded, are pointless). The result is a sort of ironic borrowing.

What is borrowed from the feudal château (other than its actual form) are the relationships of power (absolute and personal) that it presupposes, in addition to the preeminence of nobiliary names and especially the economic theory of exploited slave labor, which makes an extravagant idleness possible. At the same time, no defensive obligation or respect for the code of honor is imposed.

What is borrowed from the monastery is its communitarian organization: its order, its rule, its discipline, its homosexual structure, and its sacred idleness. At the same time, the obligation to asceticism (continence, abstinence, penitence) and to prayer is eliminated.

What is borrowed from the factory is the right that the capitalist claims to unlimited exploitation of energies and bodies (reduction of bodies to the status of instruments; submission and productivity). Nevertheless, the production of marketable goods is done away with.

The château is not under siege; the monastery is not at prayer; the factory is not producing any objects of manufacture. The three are merely being imitated, and they are needed in the shaping of the libertine system's space, which in this way is revealed as *theatrical space,* as a machine for simulation, an experimental assembly for the experiencing of effects that originate somewhere else, effects that, displaced onto and exploited in a setting incongruous with their aims, find their assumptions and structures laid bare. The theatrical artifact of the libertine setting functions as a machine for showing that social relationships as a whole, in their historical forms and with their contradictions, are implicit in and reproduced by sexual relationships and the fantasies to which sexual relationships give rise.

And this is how the Sadean text acknowledges what it is: a fictional text, which is to say that its function is not to convince, judge, preach, or legislate, but to *show.* What it shows is the underside of signs and codes, their repressed stakes, their function of illusion, their unacknowledged collusions. This is a labor of deconstruction, a blood sport, and if there is such a thing as Sadean cruelty, it is here that we must seek it out rather than at the representational level of the signified, where the naive imagination of the realist reading is convinced of having spotted it and caught it. Moreover, it is possible to read a fictional artifact not just in terms of the redirection of its models but also in terms of those models' contradictory superimposition on one another. Thus, although the extravagant waste of the feudal model is incompatible with the economic rationality of the industrial capitalist model, the two of them are mobilized *simultaneously.* What the logic of history can only separate, the logic of the text can assemble, cobble together, and condense. In this way, the logic of the text is analogous to the logic of the dream, as Freud described it. And the logic of the text can do these things because it perverts the models that it stages, by disconnecting them from any real function. Thus the techniques of enslaving the body, as we see them in connection with the model of the factory, actually become something quite different in the libertine setting—namely, processes for erotizing the body of the victim, since this body becomes desirable because of its passivity, dependence, and guilt. Regulations and penalties, inspired by existing institutions and apparently reproducing those institutions' aims, are needed only for the sake of imitation, to serve as elements of a perverse game, a game organized to produce pleasure in contradiction.

If desire, for Sade, is identified with power, it is not because power in itself is desirable but because the coherence and verisimilitude of the excess that has been imagined depend on power as a matter of necessity. Power, in fact, through a strange contradiction, is forever being questioned: although they are the masters of the state, these despotic pleasure-seekers engage in a continual subversive-anarchistic discourse about its destruction (a discourse against law, property, religion, procreation, and marriage, and in favor of crime, incest, adultery, theft, and the like). The text takes responsibility for this contradiction all the more easily because it continuously indexes its own excesses on those of its characters; hence, right at the heart of the verisimilitude that it assumes, the radical nonrealism through which it unfurls.

What Sade is talking about in this text hallucinated by sex is not a society but only pleasure. Characters, situations, places, models, and operations are the various predicates that are syntactically organized around a single subject: *the libertine body.* The enjoyment of bodies—diffracted through a multiplicity of names, episodes, and variations that serve to frame it, detail it, plan it, and give it narrative legitimacy—is the one and only event.

But sexual pleasure is not fabulous—that is, it does not constitute a narrative—until it is surrounded by the practical conditions for magnificence: wealth, power, and extravagance. Its glory requires luxurious settings (palaces, gardens), locales (famous cities and landscapes), ways of life (those of nobles, princes, prelates, bankers), bodies (in terms of quantity but also in terms of these bodies' names, when they are titled names), feasts (meals, scenery), and, finally, discourses (dissertations in the course of the orgies). Extreme sexual pleasure, because it is destruction and deadly consumption, evokes the presence of sacrificial frenzy.

The whole social, political, and economic staging of Sadean libertinism is built, at the end of the day, in the manner of a device whose purpose is to turn the *libertine body* into a fantastic machine for consumption, and for sexual pleasure in that consumption. But now it appears
that this system of nonproduction belongs to the *text* and is its principle
of expenditure and excess ("saying everything," saturating the imaginable, defying prohibitions on what can be said), its principle of intransitivity (everything takes place within language). And so this text, as precisely as it repeats the history at whose heart it is written, shows above
all that it is answering to history in the terms of another logic, the logic
of mimesis, a logic that displaces the forms of history, renders them indeterminate, parodies them, tricks them, even distorts them, and, in this
formal murder, displays the structures and codes of history, thereby producing itself as writing. Severo Sarduy defines the impulse of baroque
economy as "the impulse to squander language for purely pleasurable
ends (rather than for informational purposes, as in ordinary use) and
to attack the moralistic, 'natural' common sense that underlies the whole
ideology of consumption and accumulation."[64] Sade's text takes this impulse to the limit.

CHAPTER SEVEN

The Expenditures of the Body

Our men were warned against any intempestive discharging.
—*Juliette*

I've never eaten more delicious shit, I'd swear to that before any jury.
— *The 120 Days of Sodom*

Libertine sexual pleasure requires a staging of the social and economic conditions that make it possible. At the same time, it involves a model of the body that is structured on the system of those conditions, a model that symbolically replicates their operation—in miniature, as it were. It is as if the body, at the level of its energies or activities, were reproducing the logic of social expenditure from which it derives its status as a *libertine* body. It might be supposed that the general economic system according to which libertinism functions, and which is essentially oriented toward extravagant expenditure, would necessarily find its representation in the body at the moment of "discharge," as a "flood of come." But things are not so simple, and not just because "come," for the libertine (the "comers" are a different story), is not subject to unbridled squandering and, indeed, is even stored up. It is also because this "loss" is consistently (or almost consistently) indexed on the "loss" of excrement. Therefore, these two types of expenditure cannot be separated by any analysis of the economic model that organizes them, and any such analysis will have to show the *necessity* of their relationship, even at the cost of disappointing those who can see only a regrettable flaw in the intrusion of this anal, excremental dimension into the Sadean system of sexual pleasure.

The Discharge: Loss, Reserves, and Replenishment

The fundamental problem of Sadean narrative is probably that the only point of the narrative, as we have been saying, is the libertine body. Everything—journeys, discussions, meetings, expeditions—comes back to it. The narrative never attempts to reconstruct an era, describe a milieu, solve a mystery, or depict a political adventure. Its only goal is to stage the libertine body and, textually, amass the sum total of imaginable sexual pleasures on it. Situational variations (in terms of characters and settings) do nothing but multiply the instances of sexual pleasure, each time sketching out some notable singularity from among all the possibilities within the tableau of debauchery. In the end, all debauches resemble one another; only the use of a variable combinative operation makes it possible to distinguish any of these units from the repetitive sameness of the situations and acts.

Thus the position of the libertine body, as the sole point of the narrative, will pose a problem of narrative logic that can be formulated as follows: By what principle can situations be renewed for a subject to whom, theoretically, nothing can happen but the *same* thing, indefinitely? But this question encompasses another, which is more decisive and has to do with a symbolic economy: By what means will this libertine body, whose only possible adventure is sexual pleasure, conserve its strength in order to remain capable of continuing as the subject of this single repetitious adventure? Because every instance of sexual pleasure is also defined by intense waste and fatal destruction, will the libertine body have a sufficient store of energy available for the new expenditures? The rigor of the narrative logic (its systematic coherence, as well as the degree of its verisimilitude), which is itself easy enough to read, will depend, in a formal and more profound sense, on how the text stages the symbolic workings of the economy by which the body's strength is distributed, invested, spent, and renewed.

The body, always drawn to and drawn on by sexual pleasure, must confront the threat of entropy, of energetic exhaustion, which would then be projected into narrative collapse. Thus the body must resist so that the narrative can take place, continue, and begin anew. But this need for the body to resist is not admitted as such. It emerges symptomatically, in a series of persistent formulas. From these it is possible to re-construct the set of assumptions reflected by this need, and through which the body seems to be identified, symbolically, with an economic unit within which issues involving loss, reserves, and replenishment might be raised, on the model of other issues better known by the names *capital, expenditure,* and *reproduction.*

The Phantasm of Loss and Inhibition

It is remarkable that Sade, to express the concept of "discharge," almost always chooses verbs of loss or cost (of semen); verbs of pouring forth or spilling over are comparatively rare. This semantic consistency is anything but disconnected from the workings of the Sadean libidinal economy; it exhibits this economy's paradoxical nature. In fact, the lib-ertine, having turned all his efforts toward establishing the system of sex-ual pleasure, might seem to be applying himself with equal rigor—and precisely at the point where all the elements required for the realiza-tion of his desire have been assembled—to the delaying of his desire's fulfillment.

This is strange behavior, in view of the requirement for immediacy that governs all the libertine's relationships with the objects of his desire. At first it is necessary to play for time against the Other's resistance; hence the phrases ("I want you this instant," "Get undressed") that order the slave's nakedness and submission. Once the Other's resistance has been worn down, however, it is necessary to play for time against death.

Indeed, the libertine body, faced with its own death, remains alone, without a counterpart—that is, without mediation. The elimination of the Other is simultaneously the elimination of law and prohibition, of all societal resistance, but the only threat prior to any kind of insti-tution—the biological end—still has the libertine body in its sights, no matter how masterly and victorious that body may be. Death is there, all the more threatening because the elimination of the Other has released death from any dialectical stratagem. It is presented as pure, inevitable, unimpeachable "nature." Here again we have the radical confrontation, risk of collision, and vertigo that are peculiar to Sadean goings-on, and which are evaded not through any symbolic contract but through the contract's simulacrum or redirection.

In fact, surprisingly, the libertine body is trapped by its own mastery. The irony is complete, since the Other's reduction to the status of a purely nonsymbolic instrument will enable unfettered sexual enjoyment, entailing a wasting of strength and a fatal exhaustion of the body, which recognition of the Other (and of the Other's resistance) would prevent, in the "normal" order of things, through the obligation of containment and delay. The challenge for the libertine, then, is to maintain immediacy, unilateral control, and the head-on threat of death without himself being swept away by the process of destruction. (The equation of the sex act with destruction and even death is an ancient phantasm running through all folklores and literatures; Freud, as we know, discerns a form of the castration complex in this phantasm.)

Sade frequently interchanges the verbs *lose* and *cost,* and this is one of the usages most symptomatic of the loss of semen as a loss of value. At the same time, this usage signifies that semen, before it is lost, is fantasized as a reserve or, more precisely, as banking capital. The whole libertine economy of the body is modeled on the economy of libertine society: just as wealth is stored up merely for the pleasure of squandering it, semen is stored up with an eye to its being lost in orgasm. The feast, with its proliferation of scenery, servants, food, clothing, objects of debauchery, and victims, is a social orgasm, and the orgy that follows or accompanies the feast is the body's extravagant expenditure. The two expenditures are not simply homologous; they are one and the same economy, in which sexual expenditure can be imagined only as reflecting social expenditure, and vice versa.

If sexual pleasure is identified with loss itself, then a sort of unbridled squandering would be expected on the part of the libertine, a continual rushing toward the instant of discharge, because the Sadean strategy as a whole aims at the radical elimination of anything that might block desire or merely delay it or oblige it to be put off. Indeed, the libertine system as a whole tends to make bodies and their nakedness as immediately available as possible, and so it may seem rather surprising that the libertine, once the orgy has begun, should apply all his artfulness to delaying the gratification he so craves. There may not be a single orgy scene in all of Sade's writings that does not include this condition of withholding:

Chigi, a miser with his come, did not discharge.[1]

But no sign of come; it was becoming rare, they had failed to exercise any restraint at the outset of the holiday, and as they realized the extreme need of seed they would have toward the end, Messieurs were growing more frugal.[2]

The Président, made desperate by his loss of come, . . .[3]

These unclean stunts over and done with, and the doing having cost only one discharge, . . .[4]

We could be talking here about a virtual pleasure in inhibition, a pleasure inordinately overdetermined because it functions on a number of levels at once. In the first place, this inhibition brings back into the realm of transgression the time-honored prohibition that obliges desire to be deferred. The renewal of this prohibition is completely parodic because it operates from within the certainty of sexual pleasure and introduces a playful hesitation into this certainty. It is, after all, an entirely cerebral operation, which arises from imaginative strategies whose whole point is to bring about the awareness of these delays. Blangis, in *The 120 Days*, clearly formulates the principle of this operation:

> But one must behave oneself . . . ; in having thus to wait a little while for our pleasures, we make them far more delicious.[5]

> It is not in desire's consummation happiness consists, but in the desire itself.[6]

What is perhaps more essential, however, is that this withholding encompasses the libertines' boastful enjoyment of avarice, an enjoyment found time and again in the sight of gold:

> My friend, let us not forget the treasures I am to examine. You must have gold, your greed is legendary; I share that vice and would fain plunge my hands into heaps of those gleaming, fresh-minted coins that are so agreeable to the touch and to the eye.[7]

Gold and semen are permeated with the same process of withholding, as if their representational functions, at the symbolic level, were identical or at least had interchangeable properties — as if gold, in being the condensation of power, had come to be the pure representation of every imaginable good, and as if withheld semen had come to be the pure representation of every possible pleasure. In both cases, their very *scarcity* is what gives them their role as substitute or general equivalent: they stand for everything else, and they determine the same representational enjoyment:

Sade, through the *form* of the universal substitute for value, is not enjoying this or that particular good. He is enjoying the general possibility of enjoyment, a polyvalent power. He is enjoying the virtual omnipotence conferred by the general equivalent.[8]

It is impossible, then, to interpret this withholding as a concern for reciprocity or efficiency, or as a seeking of intensity (such as it would be in Tantric practice). It is to be interpreted quite directly as the expression of a process of economic symbolization, a process that governs, through accumulation and withholding, the anal enjoyment of value in and of itself, and which increases this enjoyment under the sign of scarcity, the sign of pleasure taken in privilege and exclusion.

The Representation of the Meal

> Only by eating well can one hope to discharge copiously.
>
> — *Juliette*

Barthes, writing about the Sadean meal, notes that "Sadean food is functional, systematic. This is not enough to make it novelistic. Sade adds to it a supplementary utterance: the invention of detail, the naming of dishes."[9] We should perhaps specify that this kind of "supplementary utterance" is rather rare, but that generic notations — "they then went to dine," "they seated themselves at table" — are inevitably made in connection with every orgy. This sort of notation has little narrative efficiency or usefulness. The characters can be assumed to eat, and this is what the reader does assume at the referential level. There are many, many narratives in which the "biological necessities" (eating, sleeping, defecating, and so forth) are not (or need not be) narrated, not even to sustain the function of verisimilitude, and so the reader would be willing to grant that the libertines are not starving to death — quite the opposite, in view of their income. Therefore, if Sade goes out of his way to tell us that the libertines are eating — in other words, if there is some textual need to take note of this fact — his doing so has nothing to do with any ordinary concern for realism, but it does have a great deal to do with the economic functioning of the libertine body. Indeed, the meal has to restore the strength that was lost in the orgy, and so talking about this restoration becomes just as essential as talking about the scene of sexual pleasure. The moment of the meal is not a secondary, decorative narrative element: on the contrary, it is a powerful narrative moment insofar as the libertine body is the narrative's only subject. To talk about the meal, to represent it, is to talk about one of this body's fundamental modes of representation and to ensure the textual preservation of this body because any history that this body could have is wholly the repetition of its sexual pleasure through the renewal of its strength. The representation of the meal, by saving the body, saves the narrative itself.

There is, then, a *formal* (textual, narrative) need to represent the meal, but it is at the same time an *economic* need: the meal restores the reserves as soon as they have been spent. *Juliette* expresses this principle perfectly: "A delicious collation, which we took entirely naked, soon restored to us the strength necessary to begin afresh."[10]

Sexual Pleasure and Destruction

There is an enjoyment of inhibition, but loss *is* enjoyment itself. This loss is a fatal one because it exhausts the body at the moment of overwhelming it. If "nature" (such is her monstrous cruelty) offers this trap, then nature must be answered with a stratagem of delay and permanent recourse to dietary restoration. It is even more necessary, however, to control death, or at least to foil it, by giving it something to fasten onto: the victim. What is at stake in this deplacement?

For Sade, as we have seen, there can be no mediation of desire — that is, desire must not be made to relinquish its own movement and its own drive through investment in some intermediate object. Why this inhibition, then, since inhibition (*Hemmung*), according to Hegel, is precisely the condition for mediation, saving the object by blocking the destructive movement of desire? Pure strength, transformed by a *Mitte* (an intermediary, a means), whether through nomination, procreation, or production, constitutes the word, the child, or the tool — or, more generally, the system of language, society, or objects. Libertine desire, short-circuiting every *Mitte*, is itself threatened by death, just as it threatens its own object. Thus libertine inhibition, the momentary delay that libertine desire permits itself, allows all aggression to be focused on the object: the victim. During this delay, destructive violence becomes inflamed. This is the moment when tortures are determined and their forms are planned. Inhibition provides the *time* for displacing the whole fatal burden of desire onto the victim, and it enables the mastery of apathy, thanks to which the threat of death, which hovers over the subject of desire, is evaded by means of this subject's exemption from the humiliating passage through mediation. Mediation's initial phase, simulated at first, is soon totally redirected. The torture of the victim pays ample tribute to death, a perfect death in that it leaves no traces behind. Consumption is total; other victims will be sacrificed to new desires, and there can be no mediation, for the victim—the *servus*—is not saved. Nothing is left but desire itself, the energy of the libertine body. Restored by the meal, the libertine body is now ready to resume the same murderous pleasure.

This is why Sade's writings contain, in addition to the stratagem of order that prepares, organizes, and controls this pleasure, a whole staging of *disorder* (although this has received little comment). Disorder is tied to the explosive expenditure indicated and brought about by sexual pleasure—"Thereupon, in the most anarchical fashion, we fling ourselves at the nearest object to hand: we fuck, have fucked, are fucked"[11]—and it may end in the spectacle of chaos: "Gorged on murder and impudicity, we at last fall asleep amidst cadavers and a deluge of wines, spirits, shit, come, and bits of human flesh."[12] With this disintegration of the group (ordinarily under strict control and held to its program), we seem to be quite far from the mastery of apathy, supposedly indispensable to true libertinism, as if Sade, carried away by the need to brand sexual pleasure with excess, could no longer follow the principles to which he subjected sexual pleasure at the outset—unless the order that was required in the first place, the sangfroid that is consistently required, and the painstaking arrangement of postures and actions all had the precise function of producing a balance doomed to the *disruption* that ensures sexual pleasure. Libertinism creates order for the sole purpose of destroying it. The rules that libertinism imposes on disorder are made to be broken in the great excess indicated by orgasm, orgasm as equated with an energetic potlatch, as a moment of explosion, unleashing, and total wastefulness whose logic of destruction ineluctably includes murder:

> The human being reaches the final paroxysm of delight only through an access of rage; he thunders, he swears, he loses all sense of proportion, all self-control, at this crucial moment he manifests all the symptoms of brutality; another step, and he is barbaric; yet another, and he has killed.[13]

Not the least of Sadean narrativity's paradoxes is that orgasm, the most frequent event and almost the most ordinary of libertine actions, is at the same time fantasized as an exceptional state. This paradox cannot be understood apart from its connection to the economic logic that controls it, namely, the logic which says that the only enjoyment is the enjoyment of loss. In other words, loss *is* enjoyment: a debauch, in both its economic connotation and its erotic connotation. Thus organization, method, inhibition, and mastery, so striking in Sade's writings (and freely noted by all commentators), are established only to be wasted. And once this wasting — brief, intense, and immediate — has been carried out, the cycle (discourses, programs, control, and so forth) begins all over again, but it will still end in waste.

Therefore, it is not so difficult to understand why the paroxysmic staging of orgasm summons up images — of ecstasy, madness, monstrosity, animality, catastrophe, drunkenness, frenzy, rage, violence, volcanic eruption, flood — that belong to the register of abnormality. Nor is it surprising that, at this moment of frenzy, cataclysm, and destruction, the most remarkable sign of order's collapse should be the complete loss of discursive language: in orgasm, exposition is supplanted by the *cry* ("a ringing bell announces his ecstasy, he utters wild blasphemies").[14] The cry, we should note, is normally the only speech allowed to victims; the victims are the ones who observe silence when the libertines expound. The victims' cries occur at the end of their silence, as the period, the full stop, of their linguistic sterility, and as the coup de grâce that finishes off their insensible bodies. The cry of pain belongs to the economy of nondiscursive exhaustion. The economy of the cry of sexual pleasure, however, is a completely different one. It comes in at the end of libertine discourse (whether this is the theoretical discourse of the dissertation or the practical discourse of erotic postures) as an exclamation point, as what finishes discourse off by consuming it, demolishing the system of discourse. If the victim's cry indicates the impossibility of speaking, the libertine's cry is an extravagant squandering of the reserves of language. Sexual pleasure, converted into a cry, becomes nonsymbolic, but this blankness of signification and this disruption of order are a luxury: the frenzied expenditure to which discursive mastery helps itself.

The Excremental Cycle

Neither the ritual expenditure of "come," for all its refinement, nor the economic plan (inhibition, loss, restoration) regulating the production of that expenditure, for all this plan's specificity, is sufficient to form a strictly libertine operation. What gives Sadean libidinal expenditure its scandalous, unclassifiable character is the way it necessarily and consistently links pleasure in sex, properly speaking, to pleasure in excrement. Sadean libidinal expenditure assumes not just simultaneity but also a complete correlation between the two kinds of pleasure. Within the *same operation*, it brings into play the noble, valued body of the reproductive and nervous systems and the vile, devalued body of digestion and defecation. This means mixing what has been posited as a vital and creative element with what has been rejected as a dead element, or as waste (just as it means, at the level of the writing, intertwining classical French with vulgar words). It means, in other words, articulating the phallic body and the anal body within the same field, and thus it means overthrowing the standard of value itself, bringing about a completely different distribution of the energies whose release gives rise to the libertine body's specific sexual pleasure.

It is worth noting that readers whose admiration of Sade is as militant as it is unconditional are nevertheless fond of demonstrating their critical position by displaying their strong reservations about his saturating the tableau of perversions with scatological practices, for which they denounce his all but unforgivable lapse of taste. Gilbert Lély, the most lyrical of these readers, writes of *The 120 Days* that "one *persistent error... in many places* reduce[s] the didactic value of his work — namely, the monstrously exaggerated place which he [gives] to the coprolagneic aberration carried to the extreme of excess" and goes on to say that, in addition to "*the monotony which results from such an abuse*," in *The 120 Days* "verisimilitude is very often diminished by the *quite unnecessary imposition of the ugliest of departures from normality, in place of which many other essentially erotic variations might equally well have stood.*"[15] Apart from the touching naïveté of judging a text from the normative standpoint (Sade should have written in some other way, or he should have written something else), and apart from the naïveté of gauging a perversion's acceptability by its prevalence ("coprophagy... must be classed as one of the less widespread sexual aberrations"),[16] the most amusing thing about Lély's comment is his horrified, sententious recoiling from precisely what constitutes Sade's most vigorous and most rigorous audacity. Daring to open language up to the horror of the vile and the low — in other words, to the horror of the excremental — means toying with a taboo that is stronger than the taboos against sex and blood, both of which never cease to invoke the eloquence of desirability and sublimity. Moreover, civilizations have more or less always acknowledged their own relationship to sexual or sanguinary violence in the form of sacred orgies, ritual or legalized prostitution, human sacrifices, wars, pogroms, torture, public corporal punishment, and so on. This repressed content remains remarkably manifest, sketching out the eminently dialecticizable field of negativity: in carnivals, feasts, public executions, in all these organized transgressions, terms change seamlessly into their opposites. Sex and blood receive continual social recognition, and horror of sex and blood is continually raised to the grandeur of a poetics, or of a tragic theater.

But bodily wastes remain truly irredeemable, unspeakable. No poetics could take them up without itself being destroyed, because their inaugural rejection is what makes any kind of poetics possible. Nor would a teratology be of any real use, for bodily wastes do not possess even the fascination of monstrosity. They evoke dull, ordinary horror of what is vile, worthless, and contemptible — a pile of shit, in the vulgar phrase that indicates an act of foreclosure. Of all the foreclosures on which culture is founded, this one is the most violent, and therefore the most necessary. It must leave behind no traces and no memory. It is outside history, dissolved in utter amnesia. It does not belong even to the order of negativity, for it has no opposite. Rather, it is the "disjunctive underside"[17] of culture. And yet here, at the edge of this dark pit of degradation, is where the sublimated face of culture is most usefully revealed.

The Excremental Prohibition

The emergence of culture cannot be separated from the establishment of a certain number of prohibitions, which have been well documented by ethnologists — the prohibitions against incest and cannibalism, among others, and the obligation to bury the dead — and whose strictness and enforcement vary according to the social group. These are combined with other, more specific prohibitions (dietary, territorial, hygienic, and so forth). There is one prohibition that should have been the object of special attention from anthropologists, given that its enforcement is as universal as it is rigorous — namely, the excremental prohibition. Curiously, however, it has been, if not completely passed over in silence, then at least very poorly noted and analyzed.

It is as if knowledge of this prohibition were itself prohibited — as if even to talk about this prohibition were to violate it, and as if the possibility of discourse were based on the categorical repression of both this prohibition's object and the words capable of designating it. The scholar who takes this prohibition up feels threatened in his own discourse, to the point where he renounces knowing anything about the prohibition, the better to safeguard what he has to say about everything else. This fact merely highlights the merit of Freud's attempt at his own theoretical approach (especially in chapter 4 of *Civilization and Its Discontents*). Admittedly, he makes this attempt in a note — that is, in a part of the text that is not closely scrutinized, and where additions and audacity are permitted. Freud remarks in this note that the human being's acquisition of the ability to stand upright made the genitals visible and gave rise to the phenomenon of modesty, a substitute for the physical protection that had been ensured by a hunched posture. Freud then offers the hypothesis that the sense of sight, now that the head was no longer oriented toward the ground, evolved at the expense of the sense of smell, which had been linked to crouching. It was precisely this predominance of the visual over the olfactory that would play a role in the establishment of the excremental prohibition:

> The incitement to cleanliness originates in an urge to get rid of the excreta, which have become disagreeable to the sense perceptions. We know that in the nursery things are different. The excreta arouse no disgust in children. They seem valuable to them as being a part of their own body which has come away from it. Here upbringing insists with special energy on hastening the course of development which lies ahead, and which should make the excreta worthless, disgusting, abhorrent and abominable.... Anal erotism, therefore, succumbs in the first instance to the "organic repression" which paved the way to civilization.... Thus a person who is not clean — who does not hide his excreta — is offending other people; he is showing no consideration for them. And this is confirmed by our strongest and commonest terms of abuse.[18]

Melanie Klein makes the profound comment that the unconscious recognizes no differences among bodily substances, probably for the same reasons that, according to Freud, it knows neither time nor negation.[19] For a time, this lack of discrimination causes the unconscious to predominate in the child, before language and the social milieu have taken him fully in hand and socialized him. Thus he is, as Freud puts it, a "polymorphously perverse" being, and his polymorphous perversity can be seen primarily in his total lack of shame about his excreta. Instead, he conceives of them as a magical product of his body and makes a "gift" of them to his family circle, or he offers this gift to one person in particular.[20]

Thus the child experiences, quite painfully, the requirement to be clean as a harassment against which he endlessly rebels through his compulsive insistence on soiling himself (Fourier, remarkably, also understood this). Cleanliness is just an attitude, then, one that not only comes late but is also compensatory, as Freud says: "Cleanliness, orderliness, and reliability give exactly the impression of a reaction-formation against an interest in things that are unclean and intrusive and ought not to be on the body. ('Dirt is matter in the wrong place.')"[21] What is unusually interesting about these analyses is how clearly they indicate that the archprohibition, or at any rate the most archaic one, may be the excremental prohibition, on which "civilized" order is so firmly founded that the knowledge of this prohibition is itself repressed, as if it were unacceptable to remember, even by way of a disclaimer, what excrementality and animality point to (that is, the intact reality of the biological necessities), and as if it were at all costs necessary for culture, in its position of sublimity (cleanliness, clarity, odorlessness, spirituality), neither to betray those things of which it has cleansed itself (dirt, stink, matter) nor to admit that culture is defined only by their exclusion.

There can be no knowledge, no order, or no determination of any object without this operation of exclusion. Whatever is known, affirmed, and promoted is known, affirmed, and promoted only at the price of a rejection that establishes and designates what is *not* to be accepted and *not* to be recognized. Order exists only through the positing of its opposite. Obscenity is only an effect of this split. Waste exists only because it has been discarded. Beauty, sublimity, and the like cannot live without what they deny: ugliness, vileness, contemptibility, nonentity — *shit*.

Thus the question of excrement is central to the ancient distribution of values (high versus low, heaven versus earth, sight versus smell, distinguished versus common, grand versus shabby, human versus animal) from which we continue to operate (we live more than ever in an antiseptic civilization). Because the terms used by this ancient distribution of values designate only the denial by which this distribution is produced, it is not as simple as it seems.

Language is precisely where the problem lies when the issue is excrement — and, more generally, waste and filth — because the excremental prohibition is first of all a prohibition of language. Within the very realm of language, a division is operating between what can and what cannot be articulated, between what can and what must not be said, and, ultimately, between the beautiful and the vulgar. Therefore, excrement is in no way unspeakable; on the contrary, it is what lends itself to a naming that circumscribes the discarded portion of language. But *how* was that portion discarded? After all, the fact of its being discarded is not something that has simply befallen it, like an illness. A pariah-language presupposes a master who is excluding it and who, by means of this domination, is establishing himself in all his difference. The recognized identity of the *ob*ject is affirmed in the denial of identity to the *ab*ject. This distribution of discourse is indexed on class distribution.

Excrementality, like sexuality, is the object of both a metaphorical and a medical terminology. Metaphorical terminology evades the excremental through displacement of images. Medical terminology disinfects the excremental through the positivity of clinical knowledge. If clinical knowledge can speak of this object without compromising its own "dignity," this is no doubt because what is disgusting is not the thing itself but rather the *word*. What constitutes the "vulgarity" of a term is nothing other than the use of "vulgar" words, words of the *vulgus*: the common people, the plebeians. The degradation of a word is a class indicator. To the master, what is in fact obscene is the slave as such, the slave who, at the moment when the master assigns him the place of a dead man, suddenly appears before him as the heterogeneous element of contradiction. Sensed as such — as a corpse — the slave stinks, and he inspires fear. He is hideous, this dead man who moves about and raises such a stink. He is supposed to be silent (the common people either have nothing to say or have spokespersons) but here he is, speaking *otherwise*.[22] With respect to received and imposed linguistic norms — that is, those of the dominant class — the form and the economy of the slave's language present an unbridgeable gap. The heterogeneity carried and manifested by his language is the heterogeneity of a threatening, denied force, which may come to be the force of rebellion. Thus the excremental becomes disgusting only when it is expressed in the words of the people. What we have, then, is an extraordinary sort of turnstile involving the excremental prohibition, revolutionary heterogeneity, and obscene language. Thus there is a profound logic in the fact that, for the common people, an assertive rejection, saying *no*, is the equivalent of saying *shit*. The point of invalidating the slave's language is quite simply to bar him from language altogether, to keep him either silent or ashamed of what he is saying, as if his impotence of speech could guarantee his impotence of action. For the one who is privileged — the one who has power, language, and knowledge — a popular insurrection is (as Bataille says) obscene, like the overflow of a cesspool.

And so the introduction of scatology into the Sadean narrative can be seen as a paradoxical questioning of the libertines' supposed power, such as that power has been represented, because scatology comprises what threatens and denies libertine power. What is remarkable, at any rate, is that Sade, in the face of a solid foreclosure of the excremental and all its connotations of vileness, dirt, and contemptibility, dares to put shit right in the middle of the text, so to speak. He never uses such rhetorically acceptable or medically authorized terms as *posterior, excrement, feces, flatulence, defecation,* or *urination,* but only *ass, shit, farts, piss,* and the like — filthy language that is perceived as filthy only because it cannot be *represented* within the language that rejects it. The effect of crassness is only the sudden appearance of this unacceptable otherness.

Sade's betrayal of aristocratic language may look like a surprising defiance. But it would be a mistake to see it merely as a provocative degradation, or only as the convenient production of a subversive deviance, for what it shows most profoundly is that sexual pleasure comes upon the body only through a provocative breaching of the class codes that fence the body in, and through the smashing to pieces of the language that defines and shapes the body. (Given Sade's revolutionary involvement, the historical stakes of the intrusion of obscene words into classical French should also be noted. At the level of the symbolizing process, it signified a plebeian irruption into the aristocratic realm. Sade, as the Marquis Sans-Culottes,[23] stands for obscenity in two ways because he "showed his ass" twice: once as a libertine, and again as a revolutionary. He desublimated his class position, styling himself Citizen Louis Desade, just as, inversely, Isidore Ducasse sublimated his own class position, styling himself the Count of Lautréamont. Thus one action on Sade's part has two logical articulations: not denying obscenity in language, and recognizing in heterogeneity a popular force on the march.)

It is because of this stake in the symbolic that Sade stages—with grating humor, and primarily in *The 120 Days*—what could perhaps be called a ravenous scatological instinct. His practice is first of all one of transgression ("great pleasures are only born from surmounted repugnances"),[24] but it is also one of reminiscence (he comments as follows on the coprophagic games of Blangis and Durcet: "they had been friends, as I have said, from childhood, and since then had never ceased reminding one another of their schoolboy pleasures").[25]

This pleasure is taken to paroxysmic extremes at Silling because the "subjects" are all but forbidden to wipe themselves or, without explicit permission, defecate anywhere else but in the mouths of the four Friends: "You know damned well that we are prepared to receive shit at any hour of the day or night."[26] Having an "ass" that is "beshat" (as Juliette learns abruptly from Saint-Fond, who is examining hers) becomes a badge of libertinism:

"Did Noirceuil neglect to tell you in what state asses are to be when presented to me?"
"No, my Lord, of this Noirceuil told me nothing."
"I like them unwiped, beshat. . . . I like them perfectly foul—but this one is scrubbed, fresh as new-driven snow."[27]

Repugnance, Sade insists, is not connected with any "natural" impulse but is an effect of educational "prejudices" (which, in sum, is also Freud's theme). Sade carries out his demonstration by transferring properties from diet to excrement, sketching out a kind of gastronomy of the inedible: "No habit is more easily acquired than mard-savoring; eat one, delicious, eat another, no two taste exactly alike, but all are subtle and the effect is somewhat that of an olive."[28] (What is savory here is the unexpected, completely meridional detail that gives this phantasm its grain of truth.) "Eating shit," then, permits an accumulation of pleasures: the pleasure of tasting a flavorful dish, as well as the pleasure of eating what is not to be eaten, the waste products of food—the pleasure of paradox, which is specifically a libertine pleasure:

In each of five white porcelain bowls reposed two or three mards, exquisite in form and exceedingly fresh.

"I always take them after dinner," the ogre told us, "nothing is more helpful to the digestion and at the same time nothing so pleases my palate. These turds come from the best asses in my harem, and you can eat them safely."[29]

The consumption of excrement is the high point of the erotic banquet, and, to complete the identification, it calls for the language of rich food and easy digestion: "I've never eaten more delicious shit, I'd swear to that before any jury."[30]

The reversal is accomplished: the vile becomes noble; the disgusting, delicious; the contemptible, worthy of adoration; the low, high. At Silling, the sign of this reversal is that the "wardrobe" (the toilets) is set up in the chapel. The locus of divine glory, the spiritual heart of the building, the space of divine office comes to be the chosen site of defecative ritual, and, through a consummate show of derision, the right to relieve oneself there is called "permission to go to the chapel." Once shit has become divine, the distribution of values is turned completely on its head: properties begin to circulate freely, merging substances with subjects, and something breaks apart within language itself because its system of naming cannot be sustained without this distribution of values.

The Anal Interdict

Obviously, the anal and excremental prohibitions should not be confused, because one involves an object and the other an organ. It would be wise in this analysis to distinguish what is at stake in each of these prohibitions, even if the stakes should turn out to intersect.

What can be said about the anal prohibition as such? Here again, the primary sources — Freud's texts, especially the one on infantile sexuality in his *Three Essays*,[31] and the one from 1908 called "Character and Anal Erotism"[32] — must be consulted.

In opposition to a whole entrenched tradition of denial, Freud essentially asserts that the anal region is first of all an erogenous zone, and even that "the erotogenic significance of this part of the body is very great from the first" and "retains a considerable amount of susceptibility to genital stimulation throughout life."[33] Freud then establishes that anal sensitivity immediately comes to be the object of severe repression on the part of educators, especially parents, as if this avenue of sexual enjoyment should be avoided at all costs or should not even exist. He appreciatively acknowledges Lou Andreas-Salomé's clear perception of this, as well as her demonstration that

> the history of the first prohibition which a child comes across—
> the prohibition against getting pleasure from anal activity and its
> products—has a decisive effect on his whole development. This must
> be the first occasion on which the infant has a glimpse of an environment
> hostile to his instinctual impulses, on which he learns to separate
> his own entity from this alien one and on which he carries out the first
> "repression" of his possibilities for pleasure. From that time on, what is
> "anal" remains the symbol of everything that is to be repudiated and
> excluded from life.[34]

This censuring of the anal region is all the more remarkable in that the same kind of censure is never brought to bear on the region of the mouth, whose pleasures of sucking, kissing, eating, and smoking are subject only to quite relative constraints.

As for the oedipal prohibition, which is a purely cultural stratagem, a finely tuned structural mechanism, it contains and programs its own resolution by means of the separation that it carries out between law and the underside of law. It compensates for what it excludes (polymorphous perversity) by overvaluing what it offers and imposes: the appropriate genital object. Only the anal remains strictly repressed, with no possible substitute and no authorized external investment, not even by way of displacement. Nothing is left to the anal but autoerotic satisfaction, that is, a narcissistic object choice:

> Children who are making use of the susceptibility to erotogenic
> stimulation of the anal zone betray themselves by holding back their
> stool till its accumulation brings about violent muscular contractions
> and, as it passes through the anus, is able to produce powerful
> stimulation of the mucous membrane. . . . Educators are once more right
> when they describe children who keep the process back as "naughty."[35]

We can say, then, that intestinal withholding seems first of all to be a protest against parental aggression, which surreptitiously but relentlessly aims at de-eroticizing the anal region.

Here we must take care to be very precise: What is meant by the term *anality*? Is it the reaction formation known as retention? Or is it the anal drive, with its own erotic charge? If by the term *anality* we mean both aspects at once (as is often the case in the psychoanalytic literature), then this means that we are using the same concept to designate two contradictory possibilities; hence the great confusion characterizing the debate. Freud, however, clearly establishes a distinction between anal *character* and anal *erotism*. The first term, which has to do with fecal retention as a reaction formation, has three principal components: orderliness, parsimony, and obstinacy. The second term refers to the primary process of a sexual drive that remains poorly analyzed precisely because it is totally repressed and all but extinguished in adults: "We must conclude that the anal zone has lost its erotogenic significance in the course of [adult] development, and that the constant appearance of this triad of peculiarities [orderliness, parsimony, and obstinacy] in [adult] character may be brought into relation with the disappearance of... anal erotism."[36] By contrast, "one may expect to find but little of the 'anal character' in persons who have retained the erotogenic quality of the anal zone into adult life, as for example certain homosexuals."[37] In other words, where there is less repression of anal erotism, there is less manifestation of anal character.

Before we consider anality in the context of Sadean libertinism, we should note that Freud, although he brings the erogenous nature of the anal region to light, does not clearly wonder *why* it is the object of such merciless banishment. Why is it so frightening to allow the development of anal erotism? The answer seems self-evident: what is frightening is the degenitalization of sexuality. For the social group, anal sexual pleasure equals the threat of sterility, the danger of biological extinction.

Freud does sketch this explanation out implicitly, however, in the *Three Essays*, when he links the question of anal sexual pleasure to the question raised by masturbation. This is a deep insight, for from the group's standpoint these two forms of sexual pleasure are linked to each other by the same reproach. It is important in both cases to do away with autoerotic satisfaction, which could devalue the object choice and evince no interest in reproductive genitality. We find the same logic and the same concern in the exclusive valorization of heterosexuality, and in the strict condemnation of sodomitic practices (even within a heterosexual couple). It is a question of warding off the abomination of a sexuality that is playful or perverse, unconcerned about reproduction, and indifferent to the biological survival of the group. The anathema pronounced against the practice of sodomy (even between spouses) is intended to eliminate the redoubtable competition that the anus poses to the vagina, and therefore to the womb, for, in addition to the sterility ensured by this rejection of procreation, there is the blasphemy of uniting "the fluid of life" with "dead matter" (in the old ecclesiastical terminology). Sperm mixed with excrement is a monstrous union of life and waste, a victory for waste, the sterilization and degradation of what has been established as a creative process.

This threat is the operative keynote of what could be called a symbolic compromise between the anal and the phallic: give up the first to enjoy the second (or, in practical terms, disown the turd to save the penis); identify the one with vileness, and thus ensure that the other will be identified with glory; in exchange for leaving indeterminacy, chaos, and cloaca behind, gain order, system, and identity.

The body's standing upright, like the phallus's erection, is a conquest won at the expense of the animal body's or defecating body's contemptible squatting, at the expense of excrement understood as what drops and is squashed. This dual erection establishes at one stroke both culture and masculine control. Thus it appears that woman — excluded like the body, and having lost all claim to phallic erection — has no other choice but to phallicize her whole body as the object of seduction or to be identified with waste. Through this rejection, however, she becomes precisely the means by which the initiation into anality is carried out (as President Schreber learns and tells us).[38]

What is perhaps more fundamental, however, is that the phallus gets its position of authority (as we have known quite well since, and in spite of, Lacan) from being the foundation of the symbolic order (if only as a missing signifier in its place) — from being the foundation, that is, of the system of recognition and contracts. This system is not without its own "disjunctive underside":[39] namely, the anal, the waste product of the symbolic. Floating and reviled on the fringes of the symbolic, incapable of entering into — and, a fortiori, of establishing — a dialectic of recognition, the anal remains as the lost, nonsignifying element, worthless to anyone but the one who possesses it, like a nondescript, disconnected, irrelevant object, a purely unexchangeable element. In other words, it is *private*. (Thus, at the same time, it lends itself to being fetishized as unique, particular, and unknown: the object of phallic contempt boomerangs into an object of adoration.) This is the point where the anal prohibition and the excremental prohibition intersect. The anus designates the site of the body's vileness. It is condemned as the mouth of waste, the "shithole" (Artaud), the shameful underside of the glorious body, the glorious body's emblem of death, powerlessness, and sterility. The anus is what gives every underside its connotation of vileness and its aspect of degradation. This is why the Father's — the Ruler's — great fear is of betraying the anal decadence beneath his phallic sublimity. The King could never have an ass or an anus: his scepter guarantees it.

The Anal Master, the Retainer

The libertine, whose power is established by discursive mastery, is also — and this is not the least of Sadean thought's paradoxes — the one who dares, without shame and without risking his own degradation, to confront anal vileness and, with it, the plebeian element that is barred from language. Although this element may not short-circuit the phallic order of the symbolic, it does at least create some noticeable interference.

The libertine pulls off the bold feat of making the anus public, yanking it out of the privacy in which it has been locked up. If it is necessary to say everything, then the anus, more than anything else, must be articulated because it is what has been most repressed within discourse. Once the anus — the last word in the private and the particular, the least exposed organ — has been put on display, nothing more can escape the repertoire of articulation; there is no place left to hide, and the barrier between the public zone of the phallic and the private zone of the anal comes down.

The surplus of power that falls to the libertine comes to him precisely because he dares to flaunt his anal pleasure, thus escaping from the trap of denial. Once there is nothing left to hide (especially not his ass), everything has been uttered, even waste. The libertine boldly takes the symbolic from behind, from the wrong side. What is more, he calls wrong side right — that is, he asks discourse to take on the very thing that, in order to establish itself, it had rejected. At the same time, excrement and the anus, loosed from their confinement in the ghetto of fetishism, open up the realm of the combinative operation.

This is a surplus of power for the libertine because, by joyfully taking upon himself what is disgusting, what has been discarded, and taking it to the point of obscenity, he ensures that nothing can be turned on him. He is the absolute rear echelon, and the unassailable position of strength is his. He plays wrong side against right, attempting to absorb his own contradictions. This, at least, is his stratagem.

Denial of pleasure, by contrast, and denial of anal pleasure in particular, is what constitutes the victim (Justine, for example, the perfect victim). Thus the victim defines the average state of common neurosis; the victim is both its product and its symptom. Victims call down upon themselves the vengeance of what they condemn. They call down upon themselves the libertine executioner, who takes the law that they revere and inflicts it on them as violence, and who takes the anality that they impugn and turns it on them as aggravated mastery and fatal suppression. (For Sade, there is not and cannot be any educating of the victims, because there are no persuasive arguments against *ortho-doxy*; there is only merciless elimination, and contradiction disappears in the liquidation of the one who contradicts.) The libertine, capturing the symbolic order for the benefit of his sexual pleasure, and taking on its repressed excrementality and anality, affirms himself simultaneously as both someone who speaks and someone who holds back. Reciprocally, victims are recognized by their being forbidden to speak and defecate. Because they do not want to know anything about the anus, because they cannot know anything at all, their mouths are condemned and they cannot play with the law, for the law is what defines them. To know and manipulate the law is to demystify it by way of its derisive wrong side, its anal underside.

The retentive master, by making decisions with respect to the victim's defecation, asserts his hold over the most privatized locus of the body, the point where the individual has felt, from the beginning, the group's repressive control over him, and the point where his protest has taken the form of a symptom: intestinal retention, the last hope of revolt in the silent language of the body when speech is unavailable. The anal master extends his potency to this extreme point: the victim is a perfect victim when even the holding back of his feces is in someone else's power. In other words—in Freudian terms—the libertine claims the traits of the *anal character* (orderliness, parsimony, obstinacy) and subjects the victims to these traits in order to redirect onto his own body all the *anal pleasure* from which the victims have excluded themselves. Anal mastery of the victim's body is practiced at Silling according to a precise method that is dominated by the following three procedures:

1. *Control over the rhythm of defecation* (the demand for retention):

> The subjects were expressly forbidden to go to the toilet or in any other place to move their bowels without individual and particular permission, this in order that there be held in reserve matters which could, as the occasion arose, be doled out to those who desired them. The visit [to the children's quarters] served to determine whether anyone had neglected to comply with this order; the officer of the month carefully inspected all the chamber pots and other receptacles, and if he found any that were not empty, the subject concerned was immediately inscribed in the punishment register.[40]

2. *Control over the nature of the excrement* (the form of nutrition):

> That morning, after having made some observations upon the shit the subjects were producing for lubricious purposes, the friends decided that the society ought to try something Duclos had spoken of in her narrations: I am referring to the suppression of bread and soup from all the tables save Messieurs'. These two articles were withdrawn, and replaced by twice the former quantity of fowl and game. They hoped to remark some improvement, and in less than a week an essential difference in the community's excrements was indeed perceived: they were more mellow, softer, dissolved more readily, [and] had an infinitely subtler flavor.[41]

This unfailing regimen, imposed on Madame Duclos by her lover d'Aucourt, is presented as follows by the storyteller of the twelfth day:

> I was expected, indeed condemned, to eat four meals whence were excluded a great number of things I should have adored having: I had to go without fish, oysters, salted meat, eggs, and every kind of dairy product; . . . The basis of an ordinary repast consisted of an immense quantity of breast of chicken, of boned fowl prepared and presented in every imaginable fashion, little beef or other red meat, nothing that contained grease, very little bread or fruit. . . . The result of this diet, as my lover had calculated, was two bowel movements per day, and the stools were very soft, very sweet, . . . of an exquisite taste which could not be obtained by ordinary nourishment.[42]

3. *Control over lapses in retention*: anal mastery extends to the indulging of whims over how often the victim defecates — extends, that is, to the provocation of supplementary and unexpected stools through a subtle technique that makes use of indigestion:

> At the orgies, Duclos having overheard the friends discussing
> the new diet we alluded to earlier, whose purpose was to render
> shit more abundant and more delicate, at the orgies, I say,
> Duclos noted that she was truly astonished to find connoisseurs
> like themselves unaware of the true secret whereby turds are
> made both very abundant and very tasty. Questioned about the
> measures which ought to be adopted, she said that there was but
> one: the subject should be given a mild indigestion; there was
> no need to make him eat what he did not like or what was
> unwholesome, but, by obliging him to eat hurriedly and
> between meals, the desired results could be obtained at once....
> From that time on not a day passed but they'd gently upset
> those pretty youngsters' digestions in one way or another, and
> the results were simply beyond anything you could imagine.[43]

In short, the victim's body is merely an adjunct system of the libertine body, a passive annex, a body whose will is centered outside itself and inside another. The victim's body, plugged in to the libertine body, finds all the servile functions assigned to itself, in an arrangement that permits the libertine body an effortless enjoyment of pure sexual pleasure. The victim's body is a laborer's body working to anticipate and satisfy an idle body. Ultimately, it is nothing but a subservient system, a machine for manufacturing an erotic substance. It is adjusted and readjusted according to its user's whims and submitted to a technological knowledge that guarantees the outcomes expected of such a machine (in terms of quantity, quality, and productivity). Above all, this technological knowledge ensures the mastery over time that is so essential to libertine desire: the technique of indigestion procures the *immediate availability* of the desired product. There is presumed to be, at the boundary of the libertine body, a class of bodies dedicated to the labor of producing the economic surplus that permits the libertine body to be an idle, sexually pleasured body. Within this idleness itself, however, it is also necessary to have a class of bodies laboring for sexual pleasure as such and existing only for its sake (these bodies are not subject to the servile tasks of household or kitchen; they are subject at most to service at table, which is transformed into an erotic ritual).

The libertine body appears at the end of a chain of exemptions from every kind of work, including the minimal work required for sexual pleasure. The victim's body accumulates the properties of servility and dependence, to the point of no longer having even its organic functions at its disposal and being robbed of all privacy—completely expropriated.

In contrast with the Hegelian slave, the Sadean victim has no chance of turning the process to his advantage by means of his labor, for this labor is not the kind on which the economic system is based, the kind that produces a surplus of goods. This labor is only the kind that takes place as service to the master in the stage of consumption, the kind that produces a surplus of sexual pleasure—that is, something unavailable for any kind of mediation and therefore useless, over the long term, for any reversal of power. The victim is done for, annulled in the expenditure of the sexual pleasure that he serves. The dialectic can do nothing for him. His ruination is silent, total, and irremediable.

The Intestinal Circuit, or the Bowels of Silling

We are often underground with Sade. Every grand setting of debauchery has its cellars, dungeons, and tunnels. What is most horrible and most exciting—torture and execution—is created here, in the "bowels of the earth," to use the torturer's pet phrase. The bodies that have borne the brunt of sexual pleasure and become its waste products are thrown into the oubliette. What occurs between the dungeon's entrance and this pit seems to resemble what goes on between mouth and anus. There is an intestinal circuit in the Sadean château, just as in the body itself, and what takes place within it brings the extreme excesses of debauchery into play. The signs and properties of the terms *château* and *body* are interchangeable. The bowels are clearly one of the great Sadean phantasms, but a phantasm that follows a logic and an economics that are quite distinct.

The oral-anal axis. At Silling, between the mouth and the anus and vice versa, there is a strange cycle of nourishment that implies a model of the body totally out of keeping with the commonly accepted one. The latter model is based on a series of such noble elements as bone, muscle, arteries, and nerves (which govern sublimating metaphors of an architectural, technological, military, or political kind) and, dominating them all, the arborescent, imperial, columnar image of the vertebrae, the spine holding the body upright and keeping it erect, firm, and spiritualized: "The body's blood flows upward and downward in equal measure, but everything that rises is preferred, and human life is regarded, erroneously, as an elevation."[44] Conspicuously absent from this classical model is the oral-anal axis, the digestive and intestinal tract. This is the hidden, rumbling, disgusting body of the bowels (the "offal" body), masked and unrecognized beneath an impeccable anatomical plasticity. It is this body that Silling glorifies and erotizes.

The first step is to plug the anus directly in to the mouth, placing them end to end in continuous circulation — that is, the unidirectional, linear trajectory of nourishment is turned into a circular one, an alternating current. Food, having become excrement, passes through the mouth once again and retraces the trajectory. Naturally, this arrangement implies the interplay of multiple orifices, of the plural body as a group-body.

In this way, the function of the mouth is denatured. The mouth, created for speaking and eating, has now become an anus in reverse, swallowing what the anus spews out. As a result, food is likewise perverted, assimilated only for the sake of producing excrement and forced to share with excrement the organs for ingesting food. The body from mouth to anus is now nothing but a column of shit, an excremental axis saturating the digestive tract and the stomach, looping back to the intestines, and calling the privileged status of the spine into question. The oral-anal axis is beyond redemption, against nature, a libertine artifact that blends high with low.

But what is even more serious is that this model of the body totally annuls sexual difference. The oral-anal axis is equally masculine and feminine. This is a neuter — or bisexual — body of sexual pleasure, a body of undifferentiated male or female orifices into which natural or artificial organs (penises, dildos, hands, tongues, turds) are indiscriminately plugged. The order of differences and trajectories is disrupted precisely because the anal, exempt from symbolic precision and its structural compartmentalizations, permits all conjunctions and all combinations. This is not the undifferentiation of Deleuze and Guattari's "body without organs";[45] rather, it is a perversion of the organic, a perversion controlled through the pluralization and permutation of organic functions.

Overabundance: reserves and expenditures. "Come" is costly, as we have seen. It is also lost. It belongs to the system of scarcity. Its production is limited, varying with individuals and diminishing with age. Therefore, it must not be lost unless one is sure of the quality of both the moment and the cause. Because it will be wasted eventually, it is held back at first, for the sake of being *well* wasted. Its scarcity demands the strictest strategy of masterly apathy.

Shit, by contrast, is available in great quantity. Its flow remains constant and can even be increased by overfeeding and indigestion. Identified with overabundance, it fulfills the libertine wish for luxury and immediate availability: the supply of shit will never run out. Because of its abundance, then, it offers a kind of revenge against the scarcity of "come." But its abundance is accompanied by a paradox, which makes it more enjoyable: shit, because it is already lost, could normally never be an object of loss. As the rejected element of the nutritive cycle, it no longer has any nutritional value. Eliminated from the body, just as it has been eliminated from the codes of culture, it is always already in the domain of death, sterility, and worthlessness: the degree zero of matter. As matter transformed by the body, however, it is already erotized. Its very nullity and nonproductivity are what unerringly make it precious and desirable to libertinism. It is libertinism's most accomplished stratagem: what is null but abundant is overvalued without ceasing to be abundant. The winnings are total, almost magical. This is the elderly libertines' perverse revenge against the limits of nature.

It is a guarantee of endless sexual pleasure as well, for this overabundance is also a reserve. The colony of subjected bodies constitutes a vast bank of excrement, a bank where the libertine exercises the permanent and unlimited right of withdrawal. To be more exact, this group of bodies presents itself as both a system of production and a place for storing reserves, like a beehive—a body-machine/body-coffer producing and stockpiling the wealth of Silling.

Thus we can say that the withholding of sperm and the consumption of excrement are a remarkable symbolization of capitalism's two principal phases of development. There is, on the one hand, the primitive phase of accumulation, marked by the need for savings, harsh calculations of productivity, and strict refusal to make any sumptuary expenditure. On the other, there is the phase of elaborated consumption, when possibilities for production become secondary to the multiplicity of markets, and when it becomes necessary not just to produce goods, along with a desire to consume them, but also and even more radically to create a desire for the very form of capital's circulation. As Marx says, it becomes necessary to create a desire for exchange value, as if it were use value—a desire for money itself as fetishized in gold and in the symbols of luxury. In other words, this is a question of creating a desire for general equivalents, for the *signs* of value, in a sort of idolatry of the signs of exchange—the final effect of capital's logic, and a return to the practices of Roman decadence, such as the practice (cited by Marx) of eating pearls in salad, a practice on which Goux comments as follows:

> The desire to consume pearls comes about because of the *concept* of pearls (as a general form of wealth), not because of their material being, and because of their aspect of universality, not because of their limited quantitative exchange value or their narrow qualitative use value. The desire to consume pearls is a desire to consume them as the abstract power of *every* enjoyment.... In capitalism, general exchange value or liquidity, not limited and particular use values, must become the fetish object, the imaginary cause of satisfaction. The reason is very clear and very well known: from the standpoint of production, use value is not what interests the capitalist (to paraphrase Marx's polished language, the capitalist could not care less about the shit he produces); all that matters to him is exchange value.[46]

And this is, for Sade, precisely the status and function of shit (or gold, or any other precious substance in which value has been fetishized), the meaning of its accumulation and consumption. From the standpoint of capital, the shit-eating libertines are repeating the act of the pearl-eating Roman decadents. Sumptuary squandering and sterile consumption find their perfect symbol in the extreme act of consuming excrement. Far from pointing to an earlier mode of production (namely, feudalism), sumptuary squandering and sterile consumption constitute a quite accurate staging of capital's ultimate profile.

This reading is certainly relevant, but it misses the disruptions and multiple overdeterminations produced by the text, and through which models are interchanged, overlapped, annulled, and left open to penetration and disfigurement by instances completely foreign to them. Any unilateralist interpretation becomes unilaterally deficient, exposing itself to endless refutation by the irreducible polylogy of contradictory determinations.

This is why the famous equivalence that Freud establishes between excrement and money takes a much more complex form at Silling, for at Silling this equivalence revolves not just around the *product* but also around the productive *process*. The genesis of the capitalist factory is duplicated, in miniature and in symbolic form, by the excremental circuit in the system made up of the libertine's and the victim's bodies. The master of capital is identified with the anal master. But the effects of this system are wholly related to luxurious consumption of the feudal type in that the capitalist machine is directly connected to the despotic machine. The relationship between master and producers is still a personal one, even in terms of physical dependence: the victim's body is grafted directly onto the libertine's body, and the system tends toward a completely autarkic functioning. During those one hundred twenty days, nothing comes into Silling and nothing goes out. Incest, endogamy, endophagy: the circles of sameness tighten concentrically around one another, and the excremental cycle closes the ring. Little by little, everything that comes out of the bodies goes back in. Reserves and expenditures are merged on the same segment of a vast circuit that passes through bodies from mouth to anus, and from anus to mouth. The high-low (oral-anal) axis is delinearized into a movement of circularity, with the superimposition and blending of elements that were never intended to meet or return. This process no longer corresponds to any model at all. Terms are constantly permuted and superimposed. Causalities and equivalences go through mutations that make them indeterminate: to defecate is simultaneously to produce, to lose, and to stockpile. Models that have been discerned come to be unrecognizable. Mastery of capital turns out to be scatological vampirism.

Sterile Coupling

For Sade, the body is, as it were, a phenomenal erotic transformer. If excrement has come to be a substance whose sexual overdetermination is much greater than that of food, and if excrement is affirmed as infinitely desirable (to the point where seeing it or eating it is enough to provoke orgasm), then this is because excrement appears to be a pure product of the body itself (of the body as an *erotic* body). Food, no matter how essential as the condition for the restoration of sexual energy, retains a basically functional value. It is glorified by its passage through the body and its transformation into waste, which belongs with sexual pleasure because it belongs with the nonfunctional—with sheer expen-

diture, overabundance, and luxury. Above all, however, waste is sur-
feited and marked by the transgressive value of the prohibition imposed
on it, both because it is an obscene object (see "The Excremental Prohibition," earlier in this chapter) and because it is exuded by a shameful orifice (see "The Anal Interdict," earlier in this chapter). Where law
has been implacable and prohibition strict, sexual pleasure is extreme.
The body is the erotizer of the substances that it manufactures, a magical transformer and a machine for glorifying waste, but only insofar as
it is a mass marked by forbidden (and therefore sacred) places: what
comes out of it comes to be all the more desirable for being the more
repulsive.

Thus it would take all the flatness of an aestheticizing, moralizing interpretation (see the cries of indignation cited in the opening pages of
this book) for one to remain blind to the reality of a text like *The 120
Days* (blind, that is, to its work of staging a process of symbolization),
exhausting oneself calling for quarter in the face of such a shitty exhibition, and not seeing that all the fuss is about the logic of desire. This
logic is pushed to its most extreme consequences when it is offered within
a deranged representation of value, and its most disreputable effects are
exhibited in a radical way. It is possible to notice, of course, as Barthes
does, that shit in written form does not smell, and thus call attention to
the division between the realm of the referent and the realm of fiction.
But it is still necessary to see (as we have tried to do here) that shit in
written form can only constitute part of a discourse and be the object
of an economically determined signifying game, one to be interpreted
in terms of "come" and "shit" as an operation of coupling within a single
system.

An expenditure limited to the term *come*, no matter how extravagant, would fall within the register of the recognized body and normative sexuality, the normality of organs and heterosexual bipolarity (man/
woman, penis/vagina), with reproductive legitimacy as its frame. But
when this expenditure is linked in a necessary and consistent way to
anal sexual pleasure, and when excrement is made an object of desire,
the force of intransitivity is introduced into the schema of sexual pleasure. To make the excitement occasioned by excrement the cause of "discharging" means to link nobility with disgrace and fecundity with sterility. It means short-circuiting phallic organization with anal asymbolism.

It means demonstrating that the libertine body remains radically re-
fractory to all kinds of sublimation, and that the system it brings into
being remains, stubbornly, a system of nonproductivity, a "bachelor
machine"[47] in a state of accomplished dysfunction with respect to production and the codes of reproduction (family, culture, power, and the
like). Libertine sexual pleasures are full-bodied expenditures of the body.

CHAPTER EIGHT

Noncontractual Exchange

Oh, those of you who have the temerity to govern men, beware, I say,
put no bonds upon any living creature! Leave him free to shift for
himself, leave to him alone the task of seeking out that which suits
him best, do that and you shall speedily observe the state of affairs
ameliorated, for it can only improve.

— *Juliette*

All of Sadean derision is brought to bear on the theory of the contract.

—GILLES DELEUZE, *Présentation de Sacher-Masoch*

The libertine economy staged by the Sadean text—an economy of luxury, a system of consumption whose logic extended all the way to the
functioning of bodily organs and the designing of their enjoyment—is
at the same time a continual harassment and undermining of what it
recognizes both as its opposite and as a threat to itself: the merchant
economy governed by contractual exchange.

From Locke to Rousseau, from Hobbes to Hume, and from Kant to
Hegel, eighteenth-century political thought formulated its debates and
choices around the whole issue of the contract. In fact, however, when
we look closely at its history, the use of the concept of the contract in
political theory is rather surprising and even paradoxical. Indeed, this
is, in the first place, a concept derived not from public law but from
private law. As defined in ancient Roman law, and then taken up again
in the Justinian code (the sixth-century *Codex Justinianus*) and maintained throughout the Middle Ages, up to the time of the jurisconsults

of the seventeenth century, the contract was a form of obligation that followed on a commitment between partners and was applied to the transfer of goods, to loans, and to partnerships. In the beginning, at Rome, it was a solemn commitment made in the presence of a witness; the necessities of exchange then simplified and diversified its forms. But nowhere do we find, in either classical or medieval law, relationships of citizens between themselves, or of citizens to a sovereign authority (whether this authority was an individual, such as a prince, or a political body, such as a senate), that could take the form of the specific covenant between individuals that is the contract. This formula was never envisaged in the theories of ancient Greek or Roman political philosophy, any more than in the political philosophy of the Middle Ages, because that sovereignty was conceivable only as transcending the individuals composing the collectivity.

It has been established that contractual theories appeared only after certain convergent phenomena had attained sufficient development. One such phenomenon belongs to the political order, properly speaking, in connection with the new investigations into the origins and foundations of sovereignty. Bold questions, these, given that the answers, as far as traditional—and official—Christian thought was concerned, were not supposed to be in doubt and were contained within Paul's adage "All power comes from God" (*Omnis potestas a Deo*). From the beginnings of the Renaissance on, these new questions were posed in nonscholastic centers of thought before coming to more forceful expression in the vision of the Reformers. But this strictly political investigation probably would have been impossible without a cultural transformation that took place in society as a whole, and which involved a more pointed affirmation of individual rights and individualist practices. Now it was no longer a matter of discovering, first of all, how the individual was situated in society but rather of discovering how society was possible, starting from individuals. As soon as the question of society's origins was posed in these terms, the question of sovereignty was formulated in a different way. The question now became one of discovering how it came about that individuals who had agreed to live together were led to place themselves under a sovereign authority. The notion of sovereignty was no longer a postulate but a conclusion. And it was on the basis of this position that contractual theories, long a fixture of private law, were called to the rescue and transposed to public law.

It is also well to note that among the many juridical forms of the contract, one in particular inspired the seventeenth-century jurisconsults. Indeed, in the golden age of Roman law's reformulation, the time of Justinian, three broad categories of contract were distinguished: (1) *solemn contracts*, which operated on the basis of questions and answers, following ancient rituals; (2) *real contracts* (where "real" meant simply what had to do with things and goods in kind), which did not give rise to interest but merely implied agreements about returns (the *mutuum*, for example, or the deposit); and, finally, (3) *consensual contracts*, by far the most common and the most recent kind, which had to do with the sale, rental, or delegation of power or proxies. This third category is where we find a very particular type of contract called the *society* or *partnership contract* (*contractus societatis*), and this is what will interest us here, for its formulation obviously inspired the political theoreticians—a fact that has been insufficiently noted. One modern commentator describes this type of contract as follows: "The *society contract* assumes that two or several persons agree to place something in common, with an eye to reaching a legitimate goal from which mutual benefit will be derived."[1] This kind of contract involved several persons simultaneously, the principle being that although their contributions might vary in material terms (services, goods, money), the contributions had to be equal in value; profits and losses were the same for everyone, in the absence of an agreement to the contrary—such as, for example, when one of the partners, with the agreement of the others, made a larger contribution, in which case profits, and losses, would be proportional (but if the group agreed to more advantageous terms for one or another of its members, this would then be called a *lion's-share* or *one-sided contract*). This kind of contract is certainly economic in nature, but it has the peculiarity of being an agreement among several partners simultaneously rather than between only two. Each member of this *societas* becomes the partner of each other member by virtue of having made himself, in the beginning, the partner of them all. Each partner does this by adding his signature to the text that describes the group and that proclaims its statutes and goals. This is a *societas* that exists only as an effect of mutual recognition brought about by formal means.

In fact, all these formal ingredients are precisely the ones that were to enter into the contract's being defined as the foundation of political society. This genealogy seems not to have occurred to historians of political thought. All the same, it is obvious. The importance that this model assumed from the Renaissance on, and especially during the seventeenth century, cannot surprise us when we observe the extent to which the affirmation of individualist theory was developing at that time. This model's importance grows even greater when *interest* comes to be considered as an essential legitimizing factor of social and political organization,[2] as if society's existence were the effect of a decision made by individuals taking the initiative in forming a partnership under conditions that would be profitable to them all. Clearly, the ancient Roman partnership contract is what became the model for a contractualist foundation of human society.

Indeed, the same model is found in Hobbes, Locke, Pufendorf, Burlamaqui, and, finally, Rousseau, despite the considerable differences among these authors. Thus Rousseau radically disagrees with Hobbes, but, like Hobbes and all the other contractualists, he can develop his position only because he has already accepted two fundamental assumptions: first, that what is meant by "nature" or "man's natural state" is the independent individual, free and equal to others; and, second, that society exists only as a voluntary association of individuals so defined.[3] Contractualist thought puts forth as a fact of nature (that is, as a primordial given) a figure that is actually the fruit of a long history: the modern autonomous individual. This point has been widely made by classical sociology (in the work of Weber, Simel, Durkheim, and, more recently, Dumont), notably through an awareness of how much the development of this figure owes, in the West, to urban bourgeoisies, and more particularly to artisanal and commercial partnerships. The contractualist theory of society's origins certainly receives its warmest welcome among these social strata. But it is precisely against such a conception of the origins of society, and of the political order, that Sade directs his attacks, explicitly or implicitly. Why? It would be tempting to answer that Sade's rejection is essentially an aristocratic one. But that would be to overlook the fact that a large portion of the aristocracy did subscribe to contractualist theory, at least as formulated by Hobbes or Pufendorf. Sade's position is much more complex and is developed at two levels.

At the first level, there is his cut-and-dried conviction (in the manner of Plato's Callicles) that power is defined by *strength* alone, and that all strength establishes domination. Strength alone is real; everything else is manipulation for the sake of strength's being recognized. Thus, if the partnership contract is not a means for the weak to capture the strength of the powerful by submitting it to the control of the majority, then it is conducive to the one-sided contract, which causes the majority to accept the control of those who are more powerful by making strength pass for the result of everyone's agreement. In either case, the contract is a sham. The libertine position, then, is to affirm naked, undisguised strength or to recognize it wherever it is obliged to operate in disguise.

But there is another level to this rejection. It stems from the Sadean conception of exchange. According to Sade, every exchange is agonistic; every exchange is—has to be—a challenge. Reciprocity is not an amiable agreement between contracting parties who measure their mutual contributions fairly and exactly. It is not the "sweet commerce" of business celebrated by the Enlightenment thinkers. It is combative exchange, the reciprocity of partners engaged in a duel. It is the logic of gift and countergift in its extreme form: the form of the potlatch, or of revenge.

From this standpoint, the contractual relationship is an abdication or domestication of strength. The libertine can only oppose it with the most extreme energy. This is the first condition for the possibility of games and pleasure. And this is also why the only form of partnership envisaged by Sade is the form whose goal is not the universal union of men but the rejection and derision of such a union. This kind of partnership must allow its members to unite so that they can assert their strength and their pleasure against others. This is a partnership of criminals, a partnership established by the libertine pact as absolute derision of the so-called social contract. As we shall see, this kind of contract is opposed in Sade's writings by the conspiracy of the Masters (which, point by point, negates the whole logic of the contractual bond).

There remains, finally, another aspect of the Sadean rejection of the contract. This aspect has to do with the contract's regulatory character, its capacity for blocking action, for barring the unpredictable. Indeed, the contractual bond is the strangest form of voluntary mutual submission. Is shared freedom its aim? Or is its aim not, in fact, to inaugurate a totally constraining mutual dependence? The goal is to have every single remaining activity or behavior defined and programmed by some article of law, and therefore established as a reciprocal balance of rights and duties.

This system of constraints, insofar as it was modeled on mercantile relationships, would become an enduring target of Sade's criticism.[4] It was a system of constraints because the new law (which was still being sketched out and developed) tended to mediate every conceivable relationship, leaving nothing undefined and blocking every field of improvisation, as well as all efforts toward individual solutions. It demanded virtue, not in the sense of *virtus* (courage, decisiveness, and innovation), but rather in the sense of conformity to a profusion of rules. What is remarkable, however, is that this extension of the juridical-disciplinary network occurred in the form of a precise, programmed exchange, with nothing left over, an exchange in which a new universe took shape: a universe of savings, accumulation, profit, and unlimited investment, and therefore a universe of scarcity and pettiness. Festive spending was precisely what was condemned — senseless luxury, but also the unpredictability of desire.

But even if Sade did borrow some elements from the nobiliary code of honor, hospitality, magnanimity, courage, and strength, he did not simply revalorize this code in opposition to the system of contractual exchange. What his criticism outlined, in fact, was an attempt to return to the roots of a world presumed to antedate all laws and codifications, a jungle where the law of conquest had known no bounds, where no holds were barred, and where everyone made his own laws and tested his own mettle — except that those who were hurling themselves into the world of this jungle were already assured of power in the world exactly as it already was. Hence the peculiar anarchism of the libertine masters: no God and no People; neither honorable relationships nor contractual ones; war against all forms of rule; the quest for domination over others and for unlimited exploitation of their bodies, with sexual exploitation as the final emblem of that quest. It is as if these invaders from within, these cynical barbarians, had the function of unmasking the truth about violence and sexual pleasure, which, underneath the appearance of its founding alibis, is the truth about any kind of power.

Theft and Embezzlement

> I accord no importance whatever to gifts, only what I take counts in my eyes.
>
> — *Juliette*

Theft is an everyday affair, of all the whims to be found in man not
one is more natural.

—*Juliette*

It would be rather simplistic to credit the Western bourgeoisie with the
invention of contractual mercantile trade. This mode of exchange is
probably as old as mercantile relationships themselves. But what the
bourgeoisie did invent is the extension—or, rather, the generalization—
of this relationship model to the whole field of economic practice, as
well as to the field of the symbolic relationships articulated with economic practice. What we see at work here is not just the reduction of
every product to its exchange value, which hides both productive labor
and the forces of production, but also the reduction of the whole order
of signs and symbolic goods to their function of exchangeability, to their
capacity for remainderless signifying, with their equivalence measured
against the universal standard, the abstract stand-in for every kind of
value: money.[5] To say, by the way, that the bourgeoisie invented this trade-
derived model for reducing the relationships of production may be to
misstate the case. Rather, the bourgeoisie *was invented by* this model
and is one of its effects. In France, the end of the eighteenth century
marked the moment when this effect became hegemonic and when, as
a result, the bourgeoisie *knew* that it truly had power, and that it had to
produce and control the institutional forms of this power.

Sade perceives the rise of the bourgeoisie without expressly theorizing
about it, and what we see him reject with such violence, in the thought
sketched out by his fiction's figures and logic, is the change in symbolic
relationships that was implied by the rise of the bourgeoisie. But Sade's
rejection is not formulated prospectively, as a revolutionary liberation
of the forces of production. Instead, it is formulated regressively and
anachronistically, as the intensified affirmation of an archaic, purely
predatory, bellicose style of relationship that antedates any kind of exchange and does away at the start with any form of reciprocity or mercantile law. Nevertheless, his questioning is not entirely without rigor.
It replies methodically to the dual gesture of mercantile trade—which
can be defined as giving-and-receiving, or selling-and-buying, and which
is governed by the transitivity of equivalence, compromise, and formal
equality—with another dual gesture that is purely intransitive, indeterminate, arbitrary, and excessive: stealing-and-squandering.

Stealing is the acquisition of goods by theft, abduction, extortion, em-
bezzlement, and betrayal-acquisition, that is, generally by means of
violence and contempt for the rule of law and for recognition of ownership. To squander is to give without recompense, to give as magnanimity and lordly extravagance. It is festive display, expenditure at a loss.
Squandering defines the use of all libertine wealth.

What stealing-and-squandering so vehemently invalidates is the dual
gesture of working-and-saving insofar as the economy of this gesture is
governed by mercantile trade. The contractual form of mercantile trade
presumes the equivalence and linear positioning of those who are doing
the trading: to give is immediately to receive, and the terms are presumed to be reversible. We find ourselves here in the realm of equivalence, where no one is presumed susceptible to either injury or gratification. Exchange postulates perfect equilibrium, at least formally. Its
emblem is the scale.

The libertine gesture shatters this linearity and reversibility: the one
who gives receives nothing in return, and the one who receives simply
consumes. This movement is completely intransitive and asymmetrical,
immune to all legality and convention. It is unpredictable, senseless.

We have seen how this extravagant squandering derives from nobiliary values and takes its design from the model of feudalism. But this
model's presumed activity of theft and predation pushes the regression
of squandering back toward an even more archaic domain: the domain
of *hunting*, the domain of the undefeated and unmarked, where everything is allowed because nothing has been codified, and where the only
laws are those of strength and trickery. For a libertine, to steal is to affirm that the world is a jungle where nothing can be safeguarded, no
rule of law has been established, no reciprocity is owed. It is to declare
that all the signs of law are laughable. It is to say that war has resumed,
and "might makes right." To steal is to reintroduce an artifact of "nature" into the heart of "policed society." The libertine Dorval offers the
following proof:

> Kind friends, by a single feature alone were men distinguished from one
> another when, long ago, society was in its infancy: the essential point
> was brute strength. Nature gave them all space wherein to dwell, and it
> was upon this physical force, distributed to them with less impartiality,
> that was to depend the manner in which they were to share the world.
> Was this sharing to be equal, could it possibly be, what with the fact that

naked force was to decide the matter? In the beginning, then, was theft; theft, I say, was the basis, the starting point; for the inequality of this sharing necessarily supposes a wrong done the weak by the strong, and there at once we have this wrong, that is to say, theft, established, authorized by Nature since she gives man that which must necessarily lead him thereto.[6]

The purpose of the argument from nature, invoked in this way, is merely to call for a degree zero of legality. The values of *risk* and *deeds* are revived along with the fact of strength; hence the Sadean fascination with adventurers and adventuresses, with the thieves, brigands, courtesans, great nomads, and great predators who plunder princes, devastate families, and deride custom and law. Opposing the sedentary values of work, trade, and power, they valorize the archaic nobility of acquiring goods through *capture* and *seizure*. As Veblen notes, "Property set out with being booty held as trophies of the successful raid," but "possessions... [came] to be valued... as evidence of the prepotence of the possessor of these goods over other individuals."[7] This is certainly also why Sadean theft is never on the order of financial speculation or a long-term operation. It is always on the order of a surprise attack. Calculation, delay, and mediation belong specifically to the realm of procedural patience and bourgeois trade.

Thus is it is always necessary to interpret the Sadean critique of property, a critique that continually skirts praise of theft, as a valorization of both adventure and predatory expeditions. Sedentary power, legalistic apportionment, and acquisition through trade are sanctioned by property. Theft, on the contrary, restores the values of liberty, initiative, and even true justice:

> If we glance at the history of ancient times, we will see theft permitted, nay, recompensed in all the Greek republics; Sparta and Lacedaemon openly favored it; several other peoples regarded it as a virtue in a warrior; it is certain that stealing nourishes courage, strength, skill, tact, in a word, all the virtues useful to a republican system and consequently to our own. Lay partiality aside, and answer me: is theft, whose effect is to distribute wealth more evenly, to be branded as a wrong in our day under our government which aims at equality? Plainly, the answer is no.[8]

This possibility of primitive justice is precisely contrasted with contractual injustice, the injustice of the "absurd" oath to respect property, an oath that had just been called for by the National Convention of 1792–95 and that "order[ed] the man who has nothing to respect another who has everything."[9] Bourgeois law, as a perfect swindle, must be answered with derision: "punish the man neglectful enough to let himself be robbed; but proclaim no kind of penalty against robbery."[10] This line of argument from *Yet Another Effort, Frenchmen, If You Would Become Republicans* (like the arguments concerning murder, incest, calumny, and so forth) attempts the all but impossible feat of legitimating, in the eyes of the law, what any law is intent on eradicating. The specific paradox of this text is that it takes libertine requirements, defined by nothing if not by their evasion of the social, and makes them *principles* of the social.

But the derision does not stop there. It grows even more intense in that libertine theft, rejecting all utilitarian intentions, does not have the function of establishing wealth — in other words, it is practiced *for nothing*. If someone gets rich from libertine theft, that is a bonus but not its purpose. Libertine theft is an act of sheer mimesis. It contains its end within itself, as the sign of the overthrow of the mercantile and institutional order. It aims neither to hoard nor to establish a negotiable, investible stock. It stands for itself as the sign of adventure, liberty, strength, and invalidation of law. This is why it can cultivate the paradoxes of gratuitousness: it is good to steal from the rich, but it is better to steal from the poor; it goes without saying that you steal when you have to, but it is sublime to steal when you are rolling in wealth:

> Nothing amuses me like stealing others' property; and although I have better than one hundred thousand *livres* a year, not a single day of my life goes by but I steal for enjoyment's sake.[11]

This superfluity is the hallmark of libertine necessity. The whole saga of Juliette can be read as a methodical apprenticeship in unmotivated theft, as if this practice, even more than crime and sex, were the distinguishing feature of libertinism. Indeed, the very first of Juliette's concerns is always to size up the fortune of her host, lover, or admirer and systematically organize its plundering — wherever she goes, but especially in the course of her journey through Italy, where the number of her victims grows to include the King of Piedmont, the Florentine lords, the Roman cardinals, the pope, and the King of Naples. In the case of the latter four, the organization of the theft becomes a narrative theme as important as the theme of staging the orgies, and the pleasure procured by theft is presented as even more urgent because the greater of two libertines is the one who steals from the other.

Pleasure in theft is so great that it equals or even determines sexual pleasure: "When I steal I experience the sensation an ordinary woman feels when she is frigged."[12] Theft, divorced from all causality, is the act par excellence of detached apathy: "I declare to you, that had I an income of two million a year, you would still see me a thief out of libertinage."[13] Theft, as sheer pleasure in transgression, is an intellectual pleasure. Its intensity is in its condensation: theft ties together, represents, and implies a great number of transgressions (or, rather, their very possibility) as it holds mercantile trade in check, unbalancing and overthrowing the whole ethic derived from mercantile trade, an ethic exalted by the bourgeoisie and articulated in the values of honesty, equality, and reciprocity (we know how Kant presents the duty to repay a trust as the prime example of practical reason's categorical imperative of reciprocity). This is why theft is perhaps the initiatory offense of libertinism, as well as the offense that continually ensures the stimulation of libertinism and measures its progress. The more gratuitious the act of theft, the more purely it functions as an emblem of transgression. It needs no cause; it is self-sufficient as an effect. The less utilitarian it is, the more it *points to* rank, condition, and choice. The *as if* of its realization has the magical power of simultaneously carrying out and representing the invalidation of the whole system of economic and symbolic exchange. This operation is exacerbated by another practice of libertinism: lying.

The Word Betrayed

> No blood attachment is sacred in the view of people like ourselves.
>
> — *The 120 Days of Sodom*

A troublesome point for liberal thought of the eighteenth century (for the century's bourgeoisie, that is) was this: If authority no longer had a transcendent basis, and if the time had passed for monarchies that laid claim to "divine right" — if, in other words, there was no longer a God — then truth would no longer have an ultimate foundation. Therefore, no one's word would be sacred any longer. It could no longer be assumed that promises would be kept, and there would no longer be any decency or fairness in trade. Even without God, however — even without recourse to the Absolute — one's word still had to be kept, commitments had to be respected, positions had to be assigned in keeping with the new postfeudal hierarchy, and an order (a reconstituted order) that could stand the test of time had to be imposed. In other words, a social bond had to be both conceivable and legitimated. If no Divine Judge, no Judge of laws and retribution, would be there any longer to decree that lies and betrayal were sins, then some other principle would have to be found for holding them in check and, above all, preventing them.

This is why, as God withdrew, the bourgeoisie invented conscience. But God was not allowed to efface himself too quickly: in his role as Supreme Being, he was still able to furnish a good number of services, and so from Voltaire to Napoleon, by way of the Jacobins, it was incumbent upon the God/Menace to carry out the duties of his office. If moral conscience henceforth upheld him, it was in an entirely different register: moral conscience was no longer the internalization of a divine commandment, but rather an introjection of the law issuing from the consensus of political power. Henceforth it would be assumed that a contract, freely entered into, tied every citizen to all the others. A neutral, arbitrating third party—the expression of the general will, the state— would oversee the honoring of this contract. Personal, vertical, feudal relationships based on word of honor, which had presumed religious faith and a sacred order, would be succeeded by abstract, secular, calculable relationships based on contractual commitments.

What could be discerned in this enormous change was the liberal capitalist bourgeoisie's entrance onto the scene, as well as its coming into its own. It was chiefly Rousseau who gave political coherence to the statement of this theme, but it was probably Kant who most systematically articulated its moral necessity and its legitimacy. He did this by linking, for all ethical norms, the formal duty to oneself (each one being the representative of universal reason) and the formal duty to others (as members of the rational community, or of society established on the basis of law). The contract was the embodiment of reason. It represented the regulated exchange of rational subjects. From now on, acts of abomination would be understood less as freaks of nature than as misbehavior on the part of individuals who had placed themselves beyond the pale of the only relationships by which they could be recognized as creatures of reason: relationships with a basis in law. The contractual order, with all its imperatives, and equated with the domain of reason, would be efficiently substituted for the failing order of faith.

But law, having become perfectly immanent, was no less constraining. As we see in Kant, law no longer acknowledged the special cases (the whole point of casuistry) whereby theologians had recognized the right to dispensations in view of particular circumstances. God's infinity could tolerate leeway and accommodations and still emerge unscathed; contractual logic could never exercise this kind of tolerance without the risk of coming completely undone.

We see the proof in Kant, with the famous example from *Metaphysics of Morals* in which the rigor of this logic seems to verge on absurdity, when Kant maintains the necessity of telling the truth to a murderer who has asked where his intended victim is hiding. Kant's example brought a rejoinder from Benjamin Constant, who pointed out that the truth is owed only to those who deserve it, and that it is therefore perfectly legitimate to tell a murderer a lie. Kant challenged this argument, pointing out that truth as such is not a question of rights, that truth is not derived strictly from the domain of the will, and that the real issue is everyone's duty to be truthful, as the foundation of a *right to truthfulness*.[14] (And here we see both sides of Kantian reason, with its essence exhibited in the subject and its reality within the socius; in this way, the principle of ethics, or of formal duty to oneself, ends up as the principle of the rule of law, or of formal duty to others.) Therefore, "truthfulness in statements that cannot be avoided is the formal duty of man to everyone, however great the disadvantage that may arise therefrom for him or for any other."[15] Having resorted to the all-or-nothing argument of "formal duty," Kant should now have nothing more to add, which is why it is so remarkable that he reinforces his point with an argument grounded in the *contract*. An untruth, he writes, "bring[s] it about" that "statements...in general find no credence, and hence also that all rights based on contracts become void and lose their force, and this is a wrong done to mankind in general."[16] If this is true where rights are concerned, it is also true with respect to duties:

> Whoever tells a lie, regardless of how good his intentions may be, must answer for the consequences resulting therefrom even before a civil tribunal and must pay the penalty for them, regardless of how unforeseen those consequences may be. This is because truthfulness is a duty that must be regarded as the basis of all duties founded on contract, and the laws of such duties would be rendered uncertain and useless if even the slightest exception to them were admitted.[17]

Thus Kant presents the invalidation of contractual relationships as the most serious consequence of lying. If we follow his reasoning closely, however, it seems that this "consequence" is in fact posited as a *premise*, which could be restated as follows: lying is strictly and absolutely unacceptable because the contract (the new foundation of the social bond and political power) must be preserved at all costs. Here we have the fallacious argument of contractual reason, a fallacy that goes unnoticed by the strict logician of "pure reason," for it is no less remarkable that the violence of power ("a civil tribunal") is immediately invoked against offenders (whatever their good intentions). The principle of morality is assumed to establish the rule of law, and the rule of law is assumed to establish power. In fact, however, power was always already there to quell all breaches of the principle of morality. The punishment hanging over the subject's head "helps" him think of himself as a reasonable subject defined by his "formal duty" to himself and to others. Bleeding through all the impeccable logic is a realpolitik with an altogether different pedigree.

The unleashing of Sadean irony — with its cynical advocacy of lies, hypocrisy, calumny, perjury, ingratitude, and betrayal — should be seen in light of these radical theories about the truthful (just, sincere, loyal) word, under authority of the contract. Sade's irony is quite sure of its target: all these marks of "deviance" take aim at the theory of reasonable reciprocity, the order of contractually regulated exchange. Thus Sade immediately strikes a nerve in the new and developing social tissue, wounding its brand-new claims. For Sade, the point is not a simple, unimaginative replacement of virtue by vice. The point is to challenge, in a radical way, the relationship to the *socius* presumed by the notion of virtue, and to mercilessly disabuse the reader of all belief in a just, shared power, a belief perpetuated by the contract:

> There is no governing human beings unless you deceive them. To deceive them, you must be false.[18]

> Employ hypocrisy, it is indispensable in this world.[19]

> Let us hence very carefully avoid any declarations prejudicial to calumny.[20]

> One ought normally to desire the death of the benefactor from whom one is not yet discharged of obligation, and I am never surprised to hear of accounts being settled by a murder.[21]

In this escalation of intransitivity, which moves from the debunking of the "word of honor" to the deriding of "just" action, what is called into question is reciprocity as a duty, and therefore as a *virtue*. Truth and justice are merely validating and ideal authorities of the order of egalitarian exchange (gift/countergift, lending/returning), and so the libertine master denounces the order of egalitarian exchange as a fraud, the machinery of illusion. Underneath it all the reality of power remains intact, for how could power ever flow from reasonable understandings and freely entered agreements? Power is always a relationship based on strength. Pacts do not end wars; pacts manage them, and cynically. As far as Sade is concerned, it was clearly Hobbes who had it right.

If the contract is illusory, then everything is permitted, which is to say that nothing — not truth, recognition, or sworn faith — is *owed* any longer. The outcome is the failure of liberal thought as a whole, for the contract is where liberal thought had found its religious principle — that is, its binding principle, its replacement for the sacred.[22] But underneath the law, which liberal thought posits and celebrates as an expression of the general will, what Sade finds intact is the diktat of the mightiest. The contract merely brings about the submission of everyone to everyone else, under the implacable control of the appointed sovereign. The libertine, declaring that the war never ended, resumes his right to conquer and forces the admission that the world is still divided up between lords and vassals, masters and victims.

The upshot is that one's word, like one's wealth, is not negotiable. It is taken and not returned — except in the form of sumptuary spending, for we should note that exchange is by no means completely absent from the libertine universe. In this universe, as a matter of fact, exchange takes place quite often. It is not determined by *debt*, however — that is, by quantifiable egalitarian relationships that leave no remainder — but by *revenge*. And so exchange of this sort partakes of the order of the *duel*, the order of glorious, sacrificial squandering, which finds its realization, for Bataille, in the potlatch. (Thus the phrase that so frequently recurs in the course of the orgies — "Do unto me that which I have done unto you"[23] — comes under this kind of agonistic riposte and extravagant one-upmanship, which throw the partners into a dizzying expenditure of energies and erotic figures.)

It must be clearly understood, moreover, that what defies expectations for any kind of contractual relationship and even rules them out altogether is the designation of this dueling exchange as a whim, an amusing game. The principal implication is that the form taken by this game can never be understood in terms of any external authority, and that the parties to this kind of exchange make up the rules as they go along, determining the duration of the exchange and the details of its implementation: not only is it unvouched for, it is also indeterminate. This state of affairs is a dual abomination from the standpoint of the contract, which entails the following characteristics, among others:

1. The ability to constrain, and thus the recognition, by the contracting parties, of a *third party*'s authority, a party to whom the other two have transferred the exercise of force, and whose unmitigating supervision of their contractual agreements has been requested

2. A methodical distribution of time, annulling any empirical hesitation that might slip in between a promise and the signatures of the two contracting parties (thus the contract, by assuming an ideal simultaneity of agreement, eliminates the threat of hesitation and completes, at the institutional level, the binding of time that the category of "formal duty" had ensured at the level of conscience)

The contractual system, against the great danger of capriciousness, is presented as the last word in ensuring reciprocity. And it is, except that one must still *believe in* duty, which is another way of saying that one still has to desire reason as the order of reciprocity, and desire oneself as a subject of this order. In other words, this is a convention, which in constituting law suffices to constitute truth and reality. And because Sade perceives this convention in all its obvious relativity, he plays in his fiction at breaking it down: a few lies, some perjury, calumny, and betrayal, and the whole construction is undermined, the whole order collapses.

The slick trick of contractual reason was to have located its legitimacy in the transcendent authority of truth, whereas truth in turn could resist only by appealing to the sacredness of the contract. From this turnstile a whole ethic was engendered. Honesty, truthfulness, gratitude, sincerity: each of these terms was shaped by the demand for trustworthiness, which was itself presupposed by the mercantile relationship within the act of exchange. In this relationship, truth was something that was owed, and one's word had to be an unadulterated commodity. In the war on lies, the first thing to be denounced was the counterfeit nature of lying, its being false coin. What showed through underneath these sublime principles was the pettiness of calculations, the clear-minded management of interests. Sade articulates this with a clarity that proclaims all his contempt for contractual reciprocity:

> And in my view the value of the virtuous sentiment further deteriorates when I remember not only that it is not a primary natural impulse, but that, by definition, it is a low, base impulse, that it stinks of commerce: *I give unto you in order that I may obtain from you in exchange.*[24]

Intransitive Sex

Among relationships subject to contracts, sexual relationships are privileged. As Kant, in all his priceless precision, says in *Metaphysics of Morals,* the marriage contract is a necessity arising from the law of humanity, and if a man and a woman wish to take mutual enjoyment in each other, they have to marry, marriage being a necessity according to the legal principles of pure reason.[25] For sexual relationships to be extricated from the temptation of uncontrolled spending, for the dynamism of sexual relationships to be deflected in the direction of the interests of political power, for control over sexual relationships to be ensured, and for sexual relationships to be restored to individuals only as an earned privilege—in other words, for sexual relationships to be thoroughly enculturated—they must be made to enter into the coded system of exchange by being made both a *stake in* and a *means of* coded exchange. Contractual relationships reclaim sexual relationships, with nothing left over, but at the price of surrounding sexual relationships with a strict chain of prohibitions (against incest, sodomy, masturbation). Sadean textual logic works methodically to remove these prohibitions, countering them not with practices devoid of all exchange but with sterile, wasteful, intransitive exchanges.

Incest: Unmediated Exchange

> If one but reflects a little, one finds nothing odd in incest.
> —*Juliette*

In the Sadean text, the staging of incest constitutes a topic for passionate dissertations about this obsessional desire shared by the great libertines. Saint-Fond, Noirceuil, and the four Friends at Silling all secure their sexual enjoyment of their daughters, as Clairwil secures her sexual enjoyment of her brother. Juliette seduces her father. Several short stories in *Les Crimes de l'amour* ("Florville et Courval," for example, and "Eugénie de Franval") have incest as their only theme. But this surprising emphasis is more than a theme. There is a rigorous proof at work here, and its logical framework can be matched point for point with the one that Lévi-Strauss develops in *The Elementary Structures of Kinship*. As Lévi-Strauss explains, kinship structures can be grasped and understood only on the basis of the general organization of the exchange system itself, which in "primitive" societies depends entirely on the issue of prohibiting incest. (Thus all biologically or psychologically based attempts to explain the ban on incest are eliminated at the start.) What is important about this prohibition, according to Lévi-Strauss, is its paradoxical character of belonging to two mutually exclusive orders of reality at once: the order of nature (the prohibition of incest is a universal fact) and the order of culture (this prohibition is a social rule). Therefore, it is the stuff of scandal — or rather, as Benoist says, the stuff of enigma:

> This prohibition is an enigma in the sense that it is never revealed at the level of an empirically determined surface structure. Instead, it is an *operator*, the operator that puts culture-as-communication in motion, the operator of the generalized exchange whose invariant consists of the very movement that carries this generalized exchange along: the movement of connecting the disconnected, disconnecting the connected, disconnecting the disconnected. It is an operator and a system of rules that will help in transgressing the habitual relationships between nature and culture, between life and inert matter.[26]

Where alliances between men and women are concerned, nature prescribes sexual union but stops short of indicating who should mate with whom. The ban on incest takes care of establishing the rules for permissible and impermissible alliances. Thus a newly erected, irreducible order makes its appearance: the human order as such. In other words, before the ban on incest, "culture was not yet a given; with this prohibition, nature ceased to exist for man as a sovereign influence. The ban on incest was the process by which nature was left behind."[27] What the ban on incest marks, then, is the very emergence of culture through the imposition of rules onto elements from the natural order. This prohibition, without identifying with either of these two orders, connects one with the other; the function of the prohibition is the *movement* from one to the other.

And now the question must become more precise: not "What does the ban on incest mean?" but rather "What purpose does it serve?" Why does this prohibition rule out certain kinds of alliances while permitting others? Lévi-Strauss's answer is that it makes social life possible for the group:

> Like exogamy, which is its widened social application, the prohibition of incest is a rule of reciprocity. The woman whom one does not take, and whom one may not take, is, for that very reason, offered up. . . . The content of the prohibition is not exhausted by the fact of the prohibition: the latter is instituted only in order to guarantee and establish, directly or indirectly, immediately or mediately, an exchange.[28]

At this level, another question emerges: Why is the principle of exchange *in general* articulated through the exchange of *women*? Lévi-Strauss answers as follows:

> On the one hand [it is] because women are the most precious possession, . . . but above all because women are not primarily a sign of social value, but a natural stimulant; and the stimulant of the only instinct the satisfaction of which can be deferred, and consequently the only one for which, in the act of exchange, and through the awareness of reciprocity, the transformation from the stimulant to the sign can take place, and, defining by this fundamental process the transformation from nature to culture, assume the character of an institution.[29]

As a result, then, the ban on incest establishes and articulates both the symbolic order and the social order. Moreover, it works in such a way as to permit the inference of other mental structures, which are, like the prohibition of incest, universal in nature:

> It seems there are three: the exigency of the rule as a rule; the notion of reciprocity regarded as the most immediate form of integrating the opposition between self and others; and, finally, the synthetic nature of the gift, i.e., that the agreed transfer of a valuable from one individual to another makes these individuals into partners, and adds a new quality to the valuable transferred.[30]

These, briefly, are the principal conclusions of Lévi-Strauss's ethnology, and this short review of them will be of considerable interest here, for it is precisely this set of structures that is linked to the ban on incest under attack by Sade. Removing and denouncing this prohibition also means deconstructing and disrupting the whole system that depends on it.

The attack turns first to an analysis of the nature/culture dichotomy — that is, the universe of necessity versus the universe of rules; or, again, the neutral universality of matter versus the comic relativity of institutions. One issue of radical importance to Sade, and always at the heart of his demonstrations, is that no rule is compulsory, because any system of rules is necessarily arbitrary, irrational, and trivial; "nature" in neutral, amoral, cruel, innocent motion is still the only relevant term. Against the movement of culture's emergence — culture equated with the system of rules — Sade proposes a movement of immersion in nature through the practice of everything that culture finds objectionable (murder, theft, lying, incest, and so on). For Sade, nature as a concept becomes another name for the removal of prohibitions.

Sade also recognizes that the emergence of culture — and therefore the emergence of "rules for the sake of rules" — is intrinsically tied to the actuality of the ban on incest, and to this prohibition's implied principles of reciprocity, exchange, and even exogamy. For the libertine, all agreements made under the influence of rules are annulled by the primacy and urgency of sexual pleasure. Therefore, sexual pleasure permits no reciprocity, and any substitution for its requirements would be unthinkable. Sexual pleasure kills exchange. What, Sade asks, are all the earth's creatures, compared to a single one of the libertines' desires? Our duty to others vanishes the moment we find the strength to renounce what we expect of them. How did incest become the founding principle of this selfishness? It all comes down to saying "We do not exchange. We do not give. We *take* it all, everything that seems desirable, especially the very thing, our daughters and sisters, that we are asked to give up in order to institute exchange."

Thus, for Sade, the first aspect of the challenge represented by endogamy is radical rejection of the system of reciprocity, the nonrevertibility of the gift. Moreover, Sade's rejection constitutes a practical objection to (and can be understood on the basis of) Lévi-Strauss's remark that the founding of the symbolic order along with the order of exchange depended on "the only instinct the satisfaction of which can be deferred," that is, the sex drive. Hence this specific prohibition, different from any other, since it defines the "transformation" of the sex drive from "stimulant" to "sign" and, "defining by this fundamental process the transformation from nature to culture, assume[s] the character of an institution." For Sade, what this means is that institution and culture — language — come at the price of sexual prohibition. But the price is exorbitant, and one should refuse to pay it. The libertine, then, will be the one who does not defer his desire and does not accept its inscription into the exchange system and therefore into the system of relay and redirection. In concrete terms, what incest signifies for Sade is "I am taking the woman closest to me because she is the one I can get to most quickly."

The requirement for exogamy, by contrast, which is tied to respect for the ban on incest, distances woman in space and time, obliging man to pursue, entreat, and wait. It humiliates, controls, and exacerbates desire, driving it to despair. Exogamy, in other words, is desire mediated, enculturated, policed: an abomination. Incest, however, is unmediated sexual pleasure—but it is also, as a result, the destruction of what the prohibition has established: the system of those differentiations that constitute culture. Incest blurs established differentiations, producing differentiations that cannot be exchanged, "monsters," *impossibilia* as opposed to *compossibilia*. It annuls generational hierarchy and amalgamates terms that ought to have been kept separate. In short, it realizes the utopia of a world without rules, which, invoked as a natural state, is actually only the production of an "unruly," deranged world as the a priori condition of all "unruliness" and derangement.

Indeed, the challenge represented by endogamy, while wreaking havoc with the exchange system, also opens up, to the practitioners of endogamy, a space of initiatory mysteries: the mysteries of the incestuous elect. Incest becomes the rite of entry into the exclusive circle of the libertines, those who, having committed this transgression, will no longer retreat from any other crime, because what has now been shattered is the universe of rules itself. This elect makes up the nobiliary class of evil, which also tends to coincide with the nobiliary proper (to which Sade belonged), the class that the bourgeois, trade-based mercantile class was in the process of supplanting, and whose last resort was an exacerbated endogamy that marked off a space of luxury, spending, excess, and exclusion.

Sodomy: Sterile Exchange

As a practice, incest has the aim of confounding the order of socially recognized alliances, but in its very excessiveness it still confirms the normality of heterosexual relationships. This is why another practice—sodomy—has the task of advancing the challenge to contractual legality by exaggerating the intransitivity of sexual relationships.

We have already seen that there is no homosexuality in Sade, properly speaking — none, at any rate, in today's sense, the sense of an emotional investment that denies the amorous canonicity of heterosexual relationships. Sodomy in Sade should be understood first of all for its demonstrational and polemical value, as a methodical practice of deposing the reproductive imperative. Invariably, praise of sodomy is followed by a diatribe against "propagation." Sodomy is the choice of the sterile anus over the reproductive vagina, the choice of wasteful, goal-free, norm-free ejaculation over any inscription into the religious/familial/conjugal order. For Sade, then, the polemic against "population" and the celebration of the sodomitic virtues are one and the same — "There is not one corner of the earth where the alleged crime of sodomy has not had shrines and votaries"; "In all the world there is no mode of pleasure-taking preferable to this; I worship it in either sex"[31] — a point on which civilization and desire seem to agree. Therefore, "propagation is in no wise the objective of Nature; she merely tolerates it; . . . Eugénie, be the implacable enemy of this wearisome child-getting."[32] From time to time, sodomy in Sade may privilege homosexual relationships, but in principle it is perfectly bisexual. Male/female differences are annulled in anal equivalence. Although sodomitic relationships between men may seem more indicative of the characteristically sterile nature of this kind of exchange, it is in fact the female anus that more than completes the demonstration because it can never be offered without also deposing the reproductive womb. Enjoyment of the female anus is enjoyment of the unmediated negation of its compulsory alternative. If a woman, insofar as she is proposed to be the instrument and sign of normative exchange, refuses her function in the name of her desire, her refusal can all the more securely be labeled "natural." Hence the need for dildos: women must sodomize one another, if only artificially, to give absolute proof of the primacy of the anus. As a bonus of perversion, the vagina itself partakes of anal indifferentiation and can be offered to the neuter, sterile prosthesis without arousing suspicion. The contractual purpose governing the relationship between the sexes is finally obliterated under the sign of the intransitive anus. (It should immediately be added, however, that this incorporation of female sexuality under the sign of the anus must be understood as the male libertine's will to power, his will to recognize a woman only as an accessory to his own desire, and thus to make her forced renunciation of her difference the condition of her initiation into libertinism and its privileges, as well as of her access to the sodomitic conspiracy of the fathers and sons; see chapter 9, "Woman, Prostitution, Narrative.")

Masturbation: Exchange Denied

Masturbation, in the Sadean context, may seem a paradoxical practice because traditionally it has been conceived of as a substitutive practice, a palliative for the scarcity of bodies. But an abundance of bodies is, as we know, an unvarying given of libertinism; no one is a libertine without also being a master and having all the objects of his desire available to him. Sadean masturbation is rarely a solitary practice, however. It is simply one among many figures in the erotic combinative operation. It is nevertheless the object of very particular attention. At Silling, the four Friends personally take charge of instructing the "subjects" in masturbation. As for the libertines who appear in Duclos's narratives, they all "discharge" almost exclusively in this way. But they also do so only in keeping with the principle of *representation*: they are stimulated by having their fantasies presented in tableaux and set in motion. Thus masturbation stands out as the most perverse and intransitive form of sexuality, the form indexed on mental eroticism; the mere prospect of a crime, for example, may be enough to provoke it (Juliette: "I frigged myself deliciously at this idea"). At this level of self-reliance, sexual pleasure, removed from any kind of sociality or hypothetical control, is the fulfillment of the subject's specular confinement within his own fantasies.

Reviewing the system as a whole, and revisiting what anthropologists have marked out and defined as the three levels of exchange — exchange of goods, messages, and women — we can say that the first kind of exchange is undermined by theft, the second by lying, and the third by incest. Point for point, and at each of these points, Sade methodically constructs a perverse reply.

Torture and Debt

At least when crimes are committed, they should be committed with pleasure: there is nothing else good about them; and, apart from pleasure, there is not even the slightest justification for them.
— STENDHAL, *The Red and the Black*

Mercantile relationships, by postulating both the need for equivalence and strict isonomy in social relationships, also establish the possibility of *debt*. Reciprocally, every debt reaffirms the authority of the contractual relationship in its extension to violence itself and its guarantee of the legal use of violence. The rediscovery, in Sade's staging of torture, of this logic and of its reversal may permit it to be interpreted in a completely different way, under the fascinating rubric of horror.

Habeas Corpus

Any kind of torture is authorized only by law; as such, it is veiled by an ethics. This means that torture is possible only through its inscription into the pattern of those goals and intentions that refer to transcendent terms of justification. At least two can be assumed in this case: *truth,* which authorizes torture as a means of obtaining a confession (the Inquisition, the police); and *justice,* which authorizes torture in terms of the need for punishment or reparations.

Torture, thus inscribed into the general framework of law, seems removed from the arbitrary and enters into the great circuit of duly coded and cataloged functions. Torture is where law meets violence, and where law exhibits its capacity for domesticating surplus violence — that is, for diverting violence to the ends of law, and especially for turning it against any kind of unexpected, exogenous violence.

In the normality of the order of law, an unavowable consequence, a surplus value of the code, is precisely what is repressed by this dual *Aufhebung* of torture: *sexual pleasure,* a consequence that necessarily involves violence itself inasmuch as truth and justice are merely fronts for violence. It is as if a different scenario, inadmissible and obscene, were taking shape through the prerogatives of law, a scenario continuously censored and repressed but nevertheless real: the reciprocal genesis of violence and sexual pleasure. Sade expressly says so: that man in every age has taken pleasure in spilling the blood of his fellows, veiling this passion at times under the cloak of justice, at times under that of religion, but always and everywhere on the basis, and with the goal, of sexual pleasure. This reciprocal genesis is unacceptable, however, because truth and justice are the only two principles acknowledged as authorizing violence, for beneath these two masks it all comes down to the principle of political authority itself. The admission that sexual pleasure is operating in the background, and that violence is connected to desire, brings a pained expression to the face of law. But law can stand to wear any number of pained expressions if this is the price of belief in its authority, for what law finds absolutely necessary, strategically speaking, is to prevent the manifestation of sexual pleasure as such, as well as any explicit expression of violence. In other words, sexual pleasure and violence, in their constitutive relationship, must be prevented from constituting a discourse — prevented, that is, from taking over the symbolic order through which the very form of sociality is constituted and articulated.

Sade's extreme defiance, his intolerable radicalism, is that he establishes the discourse of the cycle of violence and sexual pleasure and relates all possible discourse to that very cycle. Thus discourse accords to madness the status of reason, and to perverse desire the place of law, whereby the obscene element of the repressed is established as a perverse normality, a general structure of objectivity. Removing cruelty from any kind of transcendental causality, and thus from any kind of legitimation, and relating it exclusively to sexual pleasure means shattering the order of law itself and, worse, proposing a simulacrum of the order of law, one that is literally imperceptible, because this is not an operation of negation but rather one of corruption. The cruelty of torture, related exclusively to sexual pleasure, is removed from the contractual economy and aligned with the gratuitousness of the spectacular; it ceases to be exemplary and normative. Unmasked as sheer violence and arbitrariness, it falls under the law of the repetition of pleasure, the ruin of any sort of purposefulness.

What the contract takes on to begin with — and, when all is said and done, what it protects — is the body itself as ultimate property. Habeas corpus is the last resort of the accused, and the last challenge of law to the arbitrariness of the despot, for it is the last warrant of the symbolic identity of the subject of rights. Classical thought naively admits this, by authority of Descartes: "Not without some reason did I believe that this body (which through *a certain private right* I called my own) belonged more *properly* and more strictly to myself than to any other."[33]

This remark by Descartes encompasses the well-known *jus fruendi,* the right of use linked to private property as such. The submission of use to the order of rights, which also ensures the body's status as private property, is precisely what Sade's text, through the logic of torture, makes apparent in all its laughableness. The point is to show what this disavowal has repressed, by using the violence inflicted on the body to demonstrate how a sheer, groundless sexual pleasure, without rights and engendered by violence alone, looms underneath the so-called right of use.

Torture merely completes the victim's dispossession of his body, which began with his being put into play purely as a mechanism and with his exclusion from any form of subjectivity. It is of no critical advantage, however, to eliminate the notion of the soul if the attributes that define it are surreptitiously grafted back onto the body itself, under cover of such terms as *own, mine, secret,* or *intimate.* It is this ultimate fallback, this last recourse, that the Sadean critique flushes out with its aggression against the body. Every form of interiority must be made to disappear, even the completely physical interiority of the internal organs and secretions. Everything has to come out and be put on display, spread out, brought to light, cataloged, named; depth must rise to the surface and unfold *partes extra partes* so that no mystery remains, everything is said and known, and nothing resists. This, the farthest outpost of a dominating reason, the hallucinatory rigor of libertine logic, leads to torture as the conclusion of an implacable, impeccable syllogism that, beyond deposing the notion of the soul, attempts to confront and violate a deeper, even more tenacious prohibition, one connected with the sacredness of life itself: the prohibition against blood, a prohibition that protects life (just as the prohibition against incest protects the family). The body holds more tightly to blood, the loss of which is fatal, than it does to "come." But law watches more vigilantly over blood than nature does.

It is this last obstacle, this last fallback of the "inside," this last resistance put up by the notion of the self, that the libertine's right to murder means to destroy. It is not murder that causes pleasure; rather, it is the way murder is affirmed as the ultimate victory over the body's withdrawal, its claim to secrecy, its demand for selfhood as the body belonging to the subject of rights. Murder means that there is no possible immunity for the Other nor any conceivable recourse to any kind of habeas corpus. By annulling recognition, it becomes the fulfillment of knowledge.

The Creditor-Executioner

To take up the other side of this question, why are Sade's libertines necessarily executioners? Why, for Sade, is sexual pleasure inseparable from cruelty exercised against others? In an even more global sense, we have to wonder what makes the master an executioner, and the slave a victim. This last question (on which the first one depends) is the same one that Nietzsche poses in *The Genealogy of Morals*.[34]

Nietzsche wonders how it was possible to turn man into an animal capable of making and keeping a promise (and therefore a contract). His answer is that it was possible through the association of promises with violent markings of the body, and through corporal mistreatment as punishment for broken promises, punishment that might go so far as to encompass mutilation. The creditor, as compensation for goods that have not been repaid, has the right to carry out this punishment against the debtor, as if the pain inflicted were equivalent to the goods that have been lost. Nietzsche then asks:

> To the question how did that ancient, deep-rooted, still firmly established notion of an equivalency between damage and pain arise, the answer is, briefly: it arose in the contractual relation between creditor and debtor, which is as old as the notion of "legal subjects" itself and which in its turn points back to the basic notions of purchase, sale, barter, and trade.[35]

To vouch for the seriousness of his promise and oblige himself to keep it, the debtor, Nietzsche explains, does not hesitate to wager, above and beyond his goods, the greatest of his possessions — his family, his freedom, and, finally, his ultimate property: his body. It then becomes possible, in keeping with the codes, for the creditor to mutilate this or that part of the debtor's body in proportion to the importance of the unsettled debt. But what does such a practice mean?

> Let us try to understand the logic of this entire method of compensations; it is strange enough. An equivalence is provided by the creditor's receiving, in place of material compensation such as money, land, or other possessions, a kind of pleasure. That pleasure is induced by his being able to exercise his power freely upon one who is powerless, by the pleasure of *faire le mal pour le plaisir de le faire*, the pleasure of rape. That pleasure will be increased in proportion to the lowliness of the creditor's own station; it will appear to him as a delicious morsel, a foretaste of a higher rank. In "punishing" the debtor, the creditor shares a seignorial right. For once he is given a chance to bask in the glorious feeling of treating another human being as lower than himself — or, in case the actual punitive power has passed on to a legal "authority," of seeing him despised and mistreated. Thus compensation consists in a legal warrant entitling one man to exercise his cruelty on another.[36]

In this analysis of Nietzsche's, the following dual origination appears: on the one hand,

creditor → executioner → master

and, on the other,

debtor → victim → slave

From the beginning, then, there is *debt*, and it is what establishes not only the right to cruelty but also hierarchical superiority.

Can we find an analogous process in Sade? Does a preexisting debt establish the libertine in his function of executioner? Apparently not, which is why the process is completely inverted in Sade, and why debt does not make its appearance until the end, as a consequence of mastery—a simulacrum of debt that justifies, by recurrence, the right to be an executioner. Indeed, Sade's libertine does not need to become a master: hypothetically, as a libertine, he *is* a master. His mastery is granted from the start by his initial choice of evil and violence—a choice made in absolute contempt for the lives of others, and in a break with any kind of contractual reciprocity—whereby he places himself above the law and so asserts his hierarchical superiority over all those who submit to it and respect it.

The libertine becomes an executioner by virtue of his mastery: the torture inflicted on the victim serves first of all to verify hierarchical difference, to confirm it, and this confirmation is what procures sexual pleasure. It is not the victim's suffering in itself that is delectable (as the popular notion of sadism would have it), but rather the positing of the victim *as* a victim by the very fact of the libertine/master's initial rejection of the law, a rejection through which he acquires the right to be an executioner.

The right to be an executioner is normally established and controlled by law, under the transcendental authority of truth and justice. The libertine grants himself this right, under the immanent authority of sexual pleasure and the arbitrary. As a result, the very possibility of law is threatened, for this means doing away with causes in favor of (repressed) effects, and even putting effects in the place of causes.

Thus the libertine usurps and diverts the right to torture: he debases and invalidates the general relationship to law. Even more perverse, however, is his debasement and invalidation of the relationship to the contract, in particular through his setting himself up as the creditor in a simulated debt.

Indeed, that the master should be an executioner is, in a way, a condition within the subject. By law, however, the executioner is normally the creditor or his deputy (the creditor can be the lending individual as well as the social group constituted through consensus or contract). The libertine master/executioner's establishing himself as a creditor is therefore a surplus outcome, a bonus, of the terms *master* and *executioner*: by declaring all his potential victims to be in general debt, he justifies by recurrence, through the prerogatives of (parodic) law, his right to cruelty. This is how he gains absolute ascendancy over others, and especially over the victim's ultimate property: his body.

Thus we have the following dual origination:

1. master → executioner → creditor ⎫
                                    ⎬ simulated "debt"
2. slave → victim → debtor   ⎭

Here, then, debt becomes an effect, and no longer a cause. It is a simulacrum of debt obtained through a mockery of causality, whose formula is contained in the famous Sadean adage "Causes, may be, are unnecessary to effects,"[37] which also defines the term *simulacrum* itself. (To be even more precise, what should be seen here is that the simulacrum is the product of a *deviation* brought about through the trick of the metonymic syllogism *master → executioner → creditor, and therefore debt*.) To be an executioner, the libertine need not be a creditor; because he necessarily *is* an executioner, however, he can don the mask of the creditor *in addition*, to draw on the pleasurable outcomes that are linked to it, granting himself the pleasure of *apparently* acting within the law even while acting outside and against it.

Thus we have two orders of origination for the executioner/creditor: the order of *causality* (as analyzed by Nietzsche), and the order of the *simulacrum* (as staged by Sade). The starting point for the order of causality is an actual origin, a socially and juridically established fact: we are in the midst of a firm continuity, a warranted normality, which is why the effect of surplus value itself remains controllable and limited. In the order of the simulacrum, there is nothing at the beginning but a break with the law — the violent activity of difference, that is, which is repeated at each moment of this origination because each of its moments remains within the illegality from which it proceeds, so that "debt" itself, *simulated* debt, remains outside causality and in the position of a derisive surplus.

In the first case, because debt is an actual cause, mastery is the sum of a foreseeable series of legally linked effects, and so this is a minor mastery through simple projective participation (as Nietzsche writes, quite precisely, "the creditor shares a seignorial right"). In the second case, mastery is actual, previously acquired through an act of power, through violence, and each of its effects echoes this act, this leap. This is why the debt is not deduced from antecedents but is decreed to exist and is justified after the fact, through the prerogatives of metonymic trickery.

The trajectory of this logic prescribes its conclusion: what gives the libertine master pleasure is not the victim's suffering as such but crime itself as the disintegration of law, and cruelty as a crime within crime. Crime causes pleasure only because it presupposes mastery (given the important condition of impunity) and confirms it. Mastery itself is sanctioned by the "pleasure of comparison," which guarantees a hierarchy, a sheer power that does not ask to be recognized, is not negotiated or exchanged, but is seized. For the libertine, going all the way to crime and torture means going to extremes of intransitivity, to the point where any kind of mutual recognition not only is actually abolished but also becomes inconceivable. Only in this way is the contractual relationship of giving and receiving overthrown, and the sumptuary law of plunder and waste imposed. If nothing is owed, everything is there for the taking, and that includes the last, unappropriable enclave: the Other's body. And it is appropriated not by right, not legitimately, but through sheer arbitrariness, as the final indication of power's limitless nature, and as the inadmissible truth about all power. The other is not excluded so that he can be crushed; he is crushed so that he can be excluded, for only from this exclusion can mastery be established.

The executioner's interest is not fixed on the victim *as such*. This paradoxical disinterest (proof of how unsadistic Sade really is) can be read explicitly in the writings about torture. What is described are either the *means* of its implementation (dungeons, machines, instruments) or its *moments*, whose concatenation must form a grammar, as in an erotic figure; or, again, the *effects* on the libertine are described: the effects of sexual pleasure, which is also to say the effects of discourse. Everything unfolds in total accord with the ritual prescribed by the Catalog. From the standpoint of the criteria for realist description, nothing could be more abstract. The horror of the settings and the terror of the victims are erased by the insubstantiality of the stereotypes. We are told nothing about the victims' distorted faces, nothing about their trembling or moaning, nothing about rent flesh, shades of suffering, the flow of blood. We are scarcely even told that the victims have cried out. Ultimately, in other words, it is as if the victims' bodies did not exist. This textual ellipsis tells the whole story of Sadean torture's specific character and its status as a purely demonstrational element. Never for an instant do we find ourselves inside the personal, subjective, psychological relationship of executioner and victim, a relationship that realist description demands, and on which the concept of sadism depends. Sade is not a realist. The protagonists have no expressions with which to challenge one another. The victim, irremediably mute, is only the guinea pig in an experiment, the argument in a demonstration. The cruelty exercised against the victims is not directed at them as *subjects*, for they are not even that, and so they are also not the *objects* of any intention to degrade or humiliate. Their neutral, affectless deaths are read between the lines. Blood written is blood that does not flow, but it flows even less for not having been written at all. The symbolic elimination of the victim is confirmed in the rhetorical exclusion of horror. Torture is contrived only with an eye to the effect of sexual pleasure, which it secures; and torture is desired only because, formally speaking, it offers the most intense outcome: that of the greatest transgression, and of definitive excess in which everything, "come" and victim alike, is lost, the "come" lost because the victim is, too. Thus torture is not an outcome of debt or of what is owed; rather, it is proof of this excess. It is the point of no return, where mediation of any kind is no longer feasible. The marking of bodies does not arise from any intention to educate or condition, as in the cultural behavior analyzed by Nietzsche. Wounds, blood, and death constitute neither memory nor positivity and redeem nothing, or nothing that could be assumed by an *Aufhebung*. There is no cause to be defended, no goal to be attained. What there is, in abundance, is excess of loss and exorbitance of sexual pleasure, a vast abyss in the face of death. All the victims are engulfed by it, all for nothing; and the master's ultimate trick, his mastery's last act of defiance, is to desire his own death, also wasted and also not exchangeable:

Not only do we cease to behold death with alarm and repugnance, but it becomes easy to prove that death is in reality nothing more nor less than a voluptuous pleasure.... Every one of life's necessities is pleasure-producing. Therefore, I reason, there is pleasure in dying."[38]

To make death itself the supreme pleasure is to say that no future is worth any kind of work whatsoever, and that libertine mastery does not aim to reign over anything that has a place in civilization or history, anything that leaves a trace or makes a profit. Mastery revels in *opposing* the prerogatives of inscription; it revels in the sheer luxury of losing everything, even itself. In its own death, everything is consumed.

The Libidinal Pact, Inclusion of the Outsider, and Libertine Utopia

> Pray avail me of that part of your body which is capable of giving me a moment's satisfaction, and, if you are so inclined, amuse yourself with whatever part of mine may be agreeable to you.
>
> —*Juliette*

> Sexual needs are not capable of uniting men.
>
> —FREUD, *Totem and Taboo*

Against the evidence of a Sade who firmly resists contractual agreements, we could raise the objection that some of his texts do seem, on the contrary, to be calling for contractual agreements and proposing precise formulations for them, as if libertine power, weary of its own violence, were agreeing to establish pockets of peace, renouncing brutalities and the right of conquest, attempting to obtain through persuasion what ordinarily it prides itself on wresting away by force, under the hypothesis of an unlimited domination. Is this a simple fit of moderation? an outburst of fair play? a trick? a contradiction? a parody? Listen as Clairwil speaks:

> Oh, Juliette, as it is always to the disgust, to the restlessness, to the despair at not ever having found either a mutual understanding or mutual pleasure with the object to which we are conventionally bound that are owing all of wedlock's miseries, to remedy this hideous situation, to counteract the hideous social practices whereby mismatched individuals are imprisoned all their lives in nightmarish unions, it would be necessary that all men and all women federate into ... clubs. A hundred husbands, a hundred fathers, corporatively with their wives or daughters, are availed thereby of all they lack. When I cede my husband to Climène, she obtains everything her own husband cannot give her and from the

one she abandons to me, I derive all the delights mine is incapable of
providing me. These exchanges multiply and thus, you see, in a single
evening every woman enjoys a hundred men, each man as many
women; in the course of these forgatherings characters develop; one
has an opportunity to study oneself; the most entire freedom of taste
or fancy holds sway there: the man who dislikes women amuses
himself with his fellows, the woman who is fond of persons of her own
sex simply follows the dictates of her penchants also; no constraint, no
hindrances, no modesty, the mere desire to increase one's pleasures
ensures that each will offer all his resources. Thereupon the general
interest maintains the pact, and particular interest coincides straitly
with the general, which renders indissoluble the ties forming the society:
ours has been fifteen years in existence, and all that time I have never
witnessed a single squabble, no, not one instance of ill-humor. Such
arrangements annihilate jealousy, forever destroy the fear of cuckoldry,
two of life's most pernicious poisons, and for that reason alone merit
preference over those monotonous partnerships in which husband
and wife, pining their lives away one in the presence of the other, are
doomed either to everlasting boredom and displeasure, or to grief at
being unable to dissolve their marriage save at the price of dishonor for
them both. May our example persuade mankind to do as we.[39]

This is already an amazingly Fourierist text, where we find all the
elements and all the dreams of the "harmonian society": endless combinations and exchanges ("These exchanges multiply and thus, you see,
in a single evening every woman enjoys a hundred men, each man as
many women"); mutual education ("in the course of these forgatherings
characters develop; one has an opportunity to study oneself"); freedom for perversion (incest, homosexuality); the development of limited
communities ("clubs," Sade calls them); sharing of goods ("the mere
desire to increase one's pleasures ensures that each will offer all his resources"); the group's libidinal founding on the basis of passionate attraction ("When I cede my husband to Climène, she obtains everything
her own husband cannot give her and from the one she abandons to
me, I derive all the delights mine is incapable of providing me"); the
complete absence of relationships based in aggression ("I have never witnessed a single squabble, no, not one instance of ill-humor").

This play of exchanges has the very precise form of a pact, but the pact
is conceived strictly as a reply and alternative to the contractual relationship, and it is a pact made in order to "counteract the hideous social practices whereby mismatched individuals are imprisoned all their

lives in nightmarish unions." The combinative, omnivalent quality of a pact open to outsiders is presented as the remedy for the bilateral, constrictingly binary, closed quality of a contract that can be used to exclude outsiders. Clearly, the opposition between the pact and the contract is linked to the opposition (so well analyzed by Deleuze) between institution and law. The pact is a space for invention of body-to-body relationships; everyone, on the basis of his or her desire, regenerates the whole network of bonds. And, because there are as many bonds as subjects, instants, and whims, there is neither the compromise of the contract nor the abstract generality of the law; instead, there is for everyone, every time, the microgenesis of his or her relationships with others, within a recognition that is always being re-created. The compromise of a contract (like Rousseau's) is that a bit of one's freedom is exchanged for recognition from everyone else; hence, of necessity, the abstract mediation of law. The reply of Sade's libidinal pact is that one's total freedom resides in everyone else's desire, and everyone else desires one's own total freedom to desire. (In other words, this pact would be drawn up along the lines of the unconscious, for, like the unconscious, it knows nothing of negation, and because desire within the pact is merely an instinct, it takes the place of law; a utopia is indeed a society of dreamers.)

It seems that this multiple game of bodies, these myriad knots tied and untied and tied again, this free exchange of sexes and fantasies, is what is also proposed in *Yet Another Effort, Frenchmen, If You Would Become Republicans*:

> Various stations, cheerful, sanitary, spacious, properly furnished and in every respect safe, will be erected in divers points in each city; in them, all sexes, all ages, all creatures possible will be offered to the caprices of the libertines who shall come to divert themselves, and the most absolute subordination will be the rule of the individuals participating; the slightest refusal or recalcitrance will be instantly and arbitrarily punished by the injured party.[40]

And what is good for the gander is good for the goose:

> I want laws permitting [women] to give themselves to as many men as they see fit; I would have them accorded the enjoyment of all sexes and, as in the case of men, the enjoyment of all parts of the body; and under the special clause prescribing their gender to all who desire them, there must be subjoined another guaranteeing them a similar freedom to enjoy all they deem worthy of satisfying them.[41]

This is apparently the same proposition, but something in the tone has changed. What is present in the first text but absent from the second is precisely the condition of *violence,* so dear to libertine power ("and the most absolute subordination will be the rule"; "the slightest refusal or recalcitrance will be instantly and arbitrarily punished"). What has happened? It could be answered that, between the first text and the second, the type of society has changed. In the first text, we have a private community, a club; in the second, we have political society organized according to the form of the state. An attempt to graft the structures of the Sadean club onto the state leaves one caught in an insurmountable contradiction. The political domain, acknowledged exclusively in terms of state order, inevitably leads to contracts and constraints — that is, to violence. A genuine libertine utopia leaves off where the classical political domain begins. Sade could not have thought the whole matter through, but he lets his contradictions reveal, very clearly, the radical split between the two perspectives.

It is not difficult to conceive of a libidinal origin for consensus within the libertine community — the club — because entry into the group presupposes total agreement on freedom of desires, and so the miraculous correspondence observed here between general and particular interests becomes almost redundant. This is the peace of the oasis, the closed-circuit utopia; where actual conditions are concerned, however, this peace comes at the price of two blind spots. First, problems in the area of *needs* are presumed to have been resolved. The communism practiced here is a perfectly aesthetic one: wealth is shared, but only because it has been produced elsewhere, by others, to be luxuriously consumed here. The libertine utopia, of course, can only turn a blind eye to the antagonism posed by this initial, inescapable question of inequality. The second blind spot is connected to the first and involves the form of political power exercised in the society on whose margins the club has been organized. If the libidinal pact gives rise to no authority or hierarchy, it is because all power has already been handed out at another place and time, and because the reality of power is maintained intact outside the closed circle of the club. The club adjusts its exceptionality to the status quo.

As a second possibility, freedom in relationships of desire could be extended to an entire society politically organized in the form of the state. Here, we are no longer dealing with a select group but with the abstract universality of the citizenry as a whole. There is no longer any prior agreement that guarantees the availability offered to the club, nor is there a limit marking off the privileged space of libidinal consensus. Therefore, inevitably, the limit has to pass through everyone, and because it cannot be a choice, it must become a duty. A limit of this kind has a name — law — and what reappears along with it, inevitably and necessarily, is control in the form of reciprocity, that is, in the form of the contract. Because Sade has not challenged the structure of the state, he cannot escape it. What results is a strange paradox: the use of constraint to bring about total freedom in relationships of desire. Thus Sade, envisaging women who through faithfulness or modesty might shirk their duty of availability, makes Le Chevalier say, "It cannot be denied that we have the right to decree laws that compel woman to yield to the flames of him who would have her; violence itself being one of that right's effects, we can employ it lawfully."[42] We are now some distance from free, passionate attraction. In the movement from the club to the state, however, we also move from libidinal consensus to the contract of prostitution. The state necessarily entails law and legalized reciprocity, but also the violence that keeps watch over their enforcement. The libertine's trick is to get the state to acknowledge that it is nothing but violence, and to propose that the state administer a program of erotic despotism — a proposal and a program inconceivable except in terms of outrageous humor or extreme lack of awareness, for of course this would mean asking the state to work toward its own demise.

There remains an unbridgeable gap between the two forms of utopia. This breakdown is one way of saying that desire cannot be *politically* socialized, which is already to say that Freud is right: sexual need *is* insufficient to unite men — unless, of course, sex itself is made the object of union within a privileged group that is protected from need (as is Sade's "club"). But this in no way affects the established political order, for wanting to extend this erotic utopia to the state does not mean transforming the state into an amorous club. It means bringing eros under state control, letting it be absorbed and crushed by relationships of legality and control: a dual lack of fulfillment, and a double bind.

For the libertine utopia there remains another way, the way most commonly practiced, a way that is not intermediate but displaced and lateral. It consists in taking a bit of consensus and a bit of violence and weaving together some persuasion (which is desirable) with some violence (which will be used as needed). What is proposed is a sort of hit-

and-run pact, which introduces a bit of utopia into the existing social order and opens a zone of power to the libertine, a zone whose provisional lawmaker he becomes. Here is how Madame Delbène lays it out:

> Come, come! what wrong do I commit, what injury do I do when, encountering some attractive creature, I say: "Pray avail me of that part of your body which is capable of giving me a moment's satisfaction, and, if you are so inclined, amuse yourself with whatever part of mine may be agreeable to you." In what way does my proposal injure the creature whose path I've crossed? What harm will result from the proposal's acceptance? If about me there is nothing that catches his fancy, why then, material profit may readily substitute itself for pleasure, and for an indemnity agreed upon through parley, he without further delay accords me the enjoyment of his body; and I have the inalienable right to employ force and any coercive means called for if, in having satisfied him according to my possibilities—whether it be with my purse or with my body—he dares for one instant to withhold from me what I am fairly entitled to extract from him.[43]

The reasoning that founds a utopia invariably ends up in the violence that established it. The confict between contract and desire remains intact unless the contract is turned into a parody, and desire into an implacable instinct legislating the nonexistence of the Other.

Conspiracy: The Masters' Deadly Game

To the contractual society that it defies, Sade's fiction responds with the conspiratorial society. This means that there is no Sadean plan for society; his plans are always counterplans. The club is a secret society, and conspiracy signifies that the libertine program will necessarily be clandestine, subversive, defensive, and selective. This is what clearly stands out in the statutes of the Sodality of the Friends of Crime:

> The Sodality therefore stands protectively behind all its Members, guaranteeing all of them aid, shelter, refuge, allies, funds, counsel, everything needed to counter the maneuvers of the law; all Members who violate it are safeguarded and championed automatically by the Sodality.[44]

What it requires of its members in return is the utmost concealment with respect to the order that has been instituted, and it imposes the rule of nonintervention:

> Under no circumstances does the Sodality intrude or interfere in government affairs, nor may any Member. Political speeches are expressly forbidden. The Sodality respects the regime in power.[45]

It places itself above the law and flouts all the principles of morality, but only within the inviolable secrecy of its enclosure:

> The disorders of its Members, transpiring privately, ought never to scandalize either the governed or their governors.[46]

Perhaps it could be said, then, that if Sade defies every kind of ordinary contract, he does so for the sake of promoting the only kind he recognizes, the one on whose power the inessentiality of the others depends: the contract that binds libertine masters to one another. But, to be more precise, this alliance takes the form of anything but a contract (unless we understand this concept in a vaguely analogical sense), for the alliance accepts neither the contract's form of commitment nor its system of warrants. Contractual commitment focuses on external terms, in the name of an abstract convention that constitutes their symbolic system; conspiracy, by contrast, reconstitutes the archaic solidarity of the clan or the family:

> The members of the Sodality, united through it into one great family, share all their hardships as they do their joys.[47]

The forms of address within a conspiracy are the consanguineous (and therefore familial and familiar) "brother" and "sister," and external hierarchies are erased:

> No distinction is drawn among the individuals who comprise the Sodality.[48]

Trust takes the place of the formal commitment warranted by a third party:

> Where disbursements have exceeded revenue, a tax is levied and the deficit made up to the Treasurer, whose word in these matters is always accepted without question.[49]

As for libertine agreements in general, just as signatures uniting the parties to an exchange used to be written in drops of blood, they are now signed in "come." When Juliette makes Clairwil swear to admit her to the club, the oath is sealed with "fresh outpourings of come,"[50] and when the two of them reach an agreement to have an orgy with the white friars, it is signed in the same ink: "All subscribed to the bargain, all signed it in sperm."[51]

Such is the libertine mode of exchange, the "roué's probity" of which Eugénie speaks.[52] Even then, however, it has no value outside the club or any other place of pleasure that presupposes collaboration among desires. Outside such a place, there is no guarantee of solidarity even among libertine masters. There is mutual recognition only to the extent that the other is judged to be at least as perverse and criminal as oneself, and it is always the business of discourse to give proof of perversity and criminality, as if the libertine masters' mutual survival came only at the price of a permanent discursive challenge, of one-upmanship in the articulation of libertine thought: a deadly potlatch and a theoretical maximalism; at the first show of weakness, the accomplice turns into a victim. Let the game of purging begin: Juliette is condemned by Saint-Fond for shuddering at the unveiling of a plan to poison half of France (but of course the narrative, by its very existence, saves her). Saint-Fond himself, whose thought is a black theology, is eliminated by the more radically materialistic Noirceuil. Juliette and Clairwil end up executing their favorite accomplice, Olympia, who is guilty of enthusiasm. And Clairwil, the most radically ungodly and unrepentant of all, is eliminated by the stronger Durand, who convinces Juliette to execute her.

The libertine accepts this pitiless logic of elimination; even more than that, he desires it: it is inherent in his radical rejection of all bonds ("No blood attachment is sacred in the view of people like ourselves"). Every libertine enters into the conspiracy already a traitor. Conspiracy contains the principle of its unilateral revocation. Contrary to the aims of the contract, conspiracy offers no guarantees about the other's actions and thoughts. It does create a kind of intimacy or solidarity among conspirators, and one is constantly required to live up to it; but conspiracy expressly forbids any reciprocity. Every libertine admires in the other what he cultivates in himself, and what defines him: absolute selfishness. Therefore, conspiracy includes suspicion, threats, and unpredictability. Several times in the course of the orgies, Juliette sees herself destined for death, and her very pleasure is constituted by this risk, for the libertine insists on affirming and safeguarding the idea, no matter how high its price, that all relationships are power relationships, that every encounter is a challenge, that nothing can be ensured or marked out or secured, and that the field of adventure, which is the very field of desire, is still infinitely open and available.

But, by staging this conspiracy as strictly a conspiracy of the rich and powerful, Sade reveals that the contract is a sham, what one most hates once one has come to power, and that, even if one accedes to power under contractual guarantees, it is by conspiring that one stays in power and enjoys power. Hidden behind the mechanisms of law and the contract, which ensure peaceful production and exchange, guaranteeing order and safety to those who submit, the masters who pull the strings invite one another to a strange game of poker: the game of the supreme pleasure, the risk of death. Not a struggle to the death over power, for their power is taken for granted, but a game played with death for the sake of pleasure, a game that is the mark of a strictly *libertine* mastery and is the ultimate affirmation of luxury, a risk that establishes the absolute privilege of exposing oneself, helpless, to sheer strength, forsaking all guarantees. What is at stake here is discourse: maximum intensity in the enunciation of crime and horror. In a way, this very intensity is what determines life or death for the players, as if—in the midst of the spheres of codified, legalized, organized activity, and concentrated inside the sphere of conspiracy as the site where all other spheres are annulled, as the geometrical plan and negative of their functions—the libertine masters were affirming the absolute sovereignty of those through whom the unlimited freedom of desire survives only in the permanent risk of the death to which these masters have elected to expose themselves. Conspiracy offers the ultimate luxury of the deadliest spending.

CHAPTER NINE

Woman, Prostitution, Narrative

> The three storytellers, magnificently dressed as upper-class Parisian courtesans, were seated below the throne upon a couch, and Madame Duclos, the month's narrator, in very scanty and very elegant attire, well rouged and heavily bejeweled, having taken her place on the stage, thus began the story of what had occurred in her life.
>
> — SADE, *The 120 Days of Sodom*

Economics, although it appears in the narrative and frames its logic, is there only to reflect the staging of the narrative economy's origins. To say so means to assume that the text contains some figure or element functioning as the emblem and generator of this economy, some element or figure that, in any one statement, signifies the structuring conditions of its enunciation. Where Sade's texts are concerned, once this issue has been raised, an issue that involves the form of *narrative* economy that can be discerned in *narrated* economy, we see the outlines of the following hypothesis: *women* sustain and uphold the narrative and are its necessary social, economic, and therefore logical figure; and, at the same time, a strange relationship is woven between the writer and the despised figure of the Mother. It is as if the Mother, in spite of being She-Who-Is-Excluded-from-the-Text, still holds the revolted, fascinated, "incestuous" and "criminal" son in thrall, if not to her breast, a son who writes only to desire her through her profanation, and only to seduce her through her submission.

Thus it would be irresponsible to take at face value (that is, as the author's opinions) the thoroughly misogynistic statements of this or that Sadean libertine, and to see Sade as a fanatical woman hater. If we were to assume that he was one, we might be right, but for all the wrong reasons. Such an interpretation neither sees what the text is doing nor hears what it is saying. One thing, at least, ought to give this kind of reader (and, more generally, this kind of critic) pause: not only are the two main Sadean characters women (we find no male hero of the same caliber as Justine and Juliette) but only women are accorded the privileged function of the narrative *I*, a privilege so marked for Sade that this function is identified exclusively with the figure called the *historienne*, or storyteller. The storyteller figure is never a man, and even if a man does by chance happen to tell his story, the name *historien* is never bestowed on him.

This difference in status is not unimportant. It proceeds from the most rigorous logic, a logic engendered by the economic/symbolic stakes that, historically, have determined women's social role and women's relationship of dependence on men, who, whether in marriage or in prostitution, establish women as objects and signs of social exchange. These economic/symbolic stakes are what the Sadean text, through a somewhat paradoxical displacement, problematizes not merely as one theme among others but as an element that calls into question the very form of narrative and its economy.

Sade and the Women Novelists of the Classical Era

> For some time now, the best of our French novels have been written by girls or women.
>
> — BAYLE, "Virgil," *Dictionnaire historique et critique*

It is impossible to understand the exceptional narrative privilege conferred upon women by Sade without locating the stakes of this privilege in a famous debate, one in which criticism was embroiled throughout the seventeenth and eighteenth centuries, and which had to do with determining whether the novel as a genre was or was not "by its nature" a genre for which women (by contrast with men) had a unique predilection.[1] Little by little, two main theses were sketched out through this debate, and they can be summarized as follows:

Because the novel was a minor genre, women, as equally minor beings, turned to it and were brilliantly successful.

Because the novel dealt with amorous passion, women, who threw themselves into amorous passion more intensely than men did, could also talk about it more fully and more delicately.

People chose up sides around this collection of effects raised to the rank of causes. On one team were the enemies of the novel, for whom it was one and the same thing to denounce the dangers of amorous passion, the seductions of women, and the novel as a genre. On the other were the friends of the novel, for whom it was one and the same thing to defend them.

This debate will seem strange if we do not also know that the novel as a genre managed only with great difficulty to assert itself over the course of the eighteenth century. There was a virtual barrage of fire from the official critics — writers and pundits. Their mission was to thwart a genre whose growing success seriously threatened the hegemony of such canonically recognized genres as tragedy or lyric and epic poetry. The many attacks on the novel were condensed into two arguments, the first an aesthetic one: that the reading of novels degraded taste, and that novels, in their abundance and in their composition, were altering the other literary genres. The *Encyclopedia* itself was harsh (see the article titled "Roman"), and Voltaire, in 1733, reached the following conclusion: "If some few new novels continue to appear, and if for a time they constitute an entertainment for frivolous youth, true people of letters hold them in contempt."[2] To this criticism was added the moral argument: the reading of novels was hazardous to moral standards. The Jesuit Porée, in a famous harangue of 1736, loudly denounced this danger and tried hard to prove that "novels cause dual harm to morals, by inspiring the taste for vice and by smothering the seeds of virtue."[3]

In this battle, the church was assured support from people of letters and from such other scholars as Bruzen de La Martinière. In 1731, La Martinière issued a warning against the reading of novels:

Through them one degrades one's taste. From them one takes false ideas of virtue. In them one finds obscene images. One is insensibly inured to them and lets oneself grow soft with the seductive language of the passions.[4]

Novels—irresponsible, frivolous, licentious, mediocre, even obscene—
were accused of all the sins of civilization; from there it was only a short
step to holding them responsible for the moral decadence of the eighteenth century itself.

Around 1760, Diderot, sadly observing this critical malice, wrote: "By
the term *novel,* what we have meant so far is a tissue of chimerical and
frivolous events, the reading of which was hazardous to taste and to
morals."[5]

The situation had hardly changed by 1784, because Laclos could still
write: "Of all the genres of works produced by literature, few are less
esteemed than the genre of the novel."[6]

It is impossible to understand this situation unless we recall the hostility of the church and the moralists toward the development of the
novel as a genre, a hostility so violent in the first half of the century that
it led (or probably led—the evidence is plentiful but not completely
reliable) to an extreme measure: a secret royal decree that forbade the
publication of novels or at least barred the publication of all but edify-
ing ones.[7] Thus the problem of the novel became a matter of state, but
this was because it was first of all a matter of the institution through
which the state is reproduced, taught, learned, and internalized: the family, in which women, supposedly the family's guardians, were threatening to lose interest by demanding freedom of (public and published)
speech and freedom in amorous relationships (thereby throwing over
wifely virtue and maternal responsibilities).

And now, as an aggravating circumstance, another grievance was
added to a campaign being conducted in the name of art (the novel
was a minor genre) and virtue (the novel was dangerous): the novel was
a genre in which only women had been particulary successful. Some observers wasted no time concluding that there was no reason to look
elsewhere for explanations of why the novel was disreputable as a genre.
With the exception of Fénelon, the great novelists of the seventeenth
century were women (Mademoiselle de Scudéry, Madame de La Fayette),
and in the first half of the eighteenth the great novelists (Lesage, Prévost,
and Marivaux notwithstanding) were two women who had carved out
a true popular novelistic success: Madame de Graffigny and Madame
Riccoboni. Undoubtedly, the novel and womanhood were in league,
which is how it happens that we find detractors of the novel on the
same side as misogynists:

Voltaire: "It is women above all who bring these works into fashion, works which entertain them with the only thing in which they take any interest."[8]

Rousseau, in the first and second prefaces to *La Nouvelle Héloïse*: "No chaste girl ever read a novel"; "Big cities need spectacles; corrupted peoples, novels"; "I persist in believing that this sort of reading is very dangerous for girls."[9]

Abbé Jaquin: "The loose ways of our women contribute more than anything else to the multiplying of novels."[10]

Against this bloc of hostile critics stood Prévost, Marivaux, Crébillon, Duclos, d'Alembert, La Harpe, and Laclos, all of them authors in favor of both the novel and women. Thus La Harpe wrote:

Among all the works of the mind, novels are the one of which women are the most capable. Love, which is always the chief subject of novels, is the feeling which women know best. In passion there is a host of delicate and imperceptible nuances, which women generally apprehend better than we do, whether because love has more importance for women or because women are more interested in taking advantage of love, and so are better observers of its characteristics and effects.[11]

This, more or less, would also be Sade's thesis in his "Reflections on the Novel" (which is a preface to *Les Crimes de l'amour*), when he defended the talent of Madame de La Fayette from her detractors and expressed surprise that anyone could doubt women's superiority in the genre of the novel, "as though this sex, naturally more delicate, more given to writing novels, could not aspire in the realm of fiction to many more laurels than we."[12]

We see here how Sade, refuting Madame de La Fayette's detractors, attempts an apologia for women's novelistic talent, but with an argument that, like the arguments made by most of his contemporaries, fails to rise above the level of favorable prejudice—which is still, in a word, prejudice ("this sex, naturally more delicate"). The argument falls short on the strictly declarative plane, but the *theory* of women's privileged relationship to the novel, and to narrative discourse, seems of a wholly different caliber. Sade's texts problematize this theory in a practical way, and its logic needs to be spelled out. Doing so may impart more learning about this issue than any literary history ever could.

The irruption of women into novelistic writing can be explained on multiple levels. For example, it can be said (and it has been said) that because the novel as a genre was new and not yet subject to strict canonicity, it offered itself as territory to be conquered, as a realm without signposts, one still not marked out by generic rules and therefore able to offer greater ease of entry, without immediate subjection to judgments by the guardians of orthodoxy. Through the novel, women could launch themselves into public and cultural life without fear of encroaching on established privilege, as would have been the case in the other literary genres. And to this first explanation can be added another: the demand for equality between the sexes was a counterpoint to the demand for equality among individuals in general, a demand that was being translated into the social rise of the bourgeoisie. We know that the development of the novel was contemporaneous with the rise of the bourgeoisie and justified its values and claims. The destiny of the nobility was written in tragedy, in the great dramas of blood and the state. It was in the novel that the bourgeoisie was beginning to write its own history, the drama of the individual in search of power, money, recognition, and pleasure.

It seems clear that the eighteenth-century feminist current was tied in to the liberal progressive current embodied by the rising bourgeoisie and its thinkers. Nevertheless, it is also clear that women's remarkable entry into literature, and particularly into the novel, cannot be explained entirely on the basis of this provisional complicity. Something else entered in, something that came at the movement of history obliquely, raising an issue somewhat removed from class warfare: the battle of the sexes (it should be noted that most women novelists still belonged to the nobility). This something had to do with the contradiction brought about by the status imposed on women in the state and within the family, and with how that contradiction hinged on the form of writing that the novel made possible.

The novel's critics mocked and denounced its dealing mainly with what men, as masters of political power and father-guarantors of the law, repressed: sexual pleasure. When Voltaire, sure of his wit, cried, "It is women above all who bring these works into fashion, works which entertain them with the only thing in which they take any interest," he was only proclaiming that sexual pleasure should not speak its name, which is why Voltaire wrote tragedies. And when Rousseau — so much the moralist, the convent confessor — remarked, "I persist in believing that this sort of reading is very dangerous for girls," what he meant is that girls should know nothing of sexual pleasure.

The advent of the novel was also the advent of subjective authority, the staging of individual destiny, the demand that the subject as such *have* a history, and that this history be the adventure of his desire. This was a provocative demand, in terms of the male order (the order of the state and of its sublimating representation), an order that could be maintained only if sexual relationships, and women along with them, were cast out of the public space of the agora and thrown into the private, closed space of the home, where women were reduced to being the prop of sexual relationships, a prop legitimized through reproduction.

Thus we see the threat that was presented by the development of the novelistic form and by its striking takeover at the hands of women authors. Something that should have remained secret was passing into language. The great political-sexual-verbal divide was being challenged. The Law of the Prince and the Law of the Father were both being defied. The Abbé Jaquin had reason to be alarmed: "Novels do not merely tend to disturb the family peace; they also upset the one order that is most necessary to the preservation of society." This seizure of discourse was felt to be its usurpation and corruption. Evil was making its entrance into language just as it had made its entrance into the world: by way of Woman. Not only was she writing, but the novel was only *about* her. Whether as a novelist herself or as a character in the novel, she was returning in force as the figure of the seductress.

It is first of all within the realm of this debate, and in the thread of this history, that we should consider the narrative privilege that Sade gives women. On this basis we can weigh the paradox of a male author (perhaps one of the first to make the attempt) bringing a female narrative *I* into his writing, as if the writer, behind the mask of the storyteller, had to become a woman in order to produce narrative; as if narrative were indissolubly linked to something that concerns only women; as if women knew more about what piques men's desire. Hence the figures of those great storytellers Justine and Juliette, as well as the storytellers of Silling, not to mention the appearance in their narratives of some outstanding female characters (Clairwil, Durand, Dubois, Olympia, Charlotte, and so on). This is not to say that great male heroes are lacking (Saint-Fond, Noirceuil, Bressac, Roland, Jérôme, Minski, Brisatesta,

Blangis), but they are always discussed in the third person, or they speak for themselves (as Jérôme and Brisatesta do) within larger, "female" narratives. It is odd that not a single one of Sade's novels presents the initiation or adventures of a young male libertine. Nothing in Sade's works corresponds to such picaresque heroes as Tom Jones, Barry Lyndon, Gil Blas, or Candide. In other words, there is no male figure who in the multiplicity of his adventures and the privilege of recounting them is the equal of Juliette in particular, which is somewhat surprising because these narratives seem to be built utterly around a male control as economic and political as it is discursive.

A logical necessity is at work in this choice and in this limitation, a necessity that cannot entirely be accounted for by the eighteenth-century debate between feminism and the novel. This debate was itself shaped by something that went beyond it, something that Sade's texts stage flawlessly: the contradictory relationship between Woman's desire and the male world, her attempt to leave the realm of the family by betraying her immemorial functions as mother and spouse and seizing hold of the discourse from which she is excluded. This, then, is the question: What price must she pay for this displacement, and doesn't the male libertine still control its realization?

The Narrative Bargain

Consider the following (hypo)thesis, the implications of which have yet to be drawn: female narrative privilege in Sade's texts is quite precisely determined by the economic and political status to which Woman finds herself assigned within the form of society staged by these texts — a form of society in which the texts also, however, propose a surprising change.

At this point, what we should remember first of all is the economic stake of any narrative if we wish to understand the very particular relationship that the female position has to that stake (a relationship that precludes men). This passage by Barthes allows us to home in on the debate:

> At the origin of narrative, desire. To produce narrative, however, desire must *vary*, must enter into a system of equivalents and metonymies; or: in order to be produced, narrative must be susceptible of *change*, must subject itself to an *economic system*. . . . Narrative: legal tender, subject to contract, economic stakes, in short, *merchandise*. . . . This is the question

raised, perhaps, by every narrative: What should the narrative be exchanged for? What is the narrative "worth"? . . . [B]y a dizzying device, narrative becomes the representation of the contract upon which it is based: in these exemplary fictions, narrating is the (economic) theory of narration: one does not narrate to "amuse," to "instruct," or to satisfy a certain anthropological function of meaning; one narrates in order to obtain by exchanging; and it is this exchange that is represented in the narrative itself: narrative is both product and production, merchandise and commerce, a stake and the bearer of that stake.[13]

It may be that every narrative is both an exchange and the staging of that exchange, and that "one narrates in order to obtain by exchanging," but the question that still has to be clarified where Sade's texts are concerned (where the "dissertation versus orgy" contract underlined by Barthes is only one aspect of the deal) is the question of why Woman should hold a privileged position in this play of exchanges and contract negotiations, a position that guarantees her a sort of monopoly over narrative — in other words, a position that makes her the narrator par excellence (or, as Sade so aptly names her, the storyteller).

Male Domination and the Conspiracy of the Fathers

In *The Origin of the Family, Private Property, and the State,* Engels says (and he was certainly one of the first to make so rigorously an attempt) that the historical fact of male domination over women occurs at easily discernible points in the transformation of societies' economic conditions. His book's essential theses can be summarized as follows:

- The nature of familial and political relationships always reflects the level of technological development within a given mode of production.

- Monogamy is a recent institution, one that is exactly contemporaneous with the advent of private property and monetary exchange.

- The advent of monogamy was translated into women's enslavement by men, women's loss of maternal rights and sexual liberty, and women's relegation to the domestic sphere, which should be viewed as "the great historic defeat of the female sex. . . . Woman was degraded and put into servitude; she became a slave to man's pleasure and a simple instrument of reproduction."[14] "Historically, conjugal union is anything but a reconciliation between man and woman, and still less the supreme form of marriage. On the contrary: it appears to be the

subjection of one sex by the other, a declaration of war between the
sexes, a war unknown until then in all of previous history."[15]

But this servitude has a pedigree: it can be discerned even earlier, in the
very constitution of any society as a symbolic organization governed
by prohibitions — the constitution of any society, that is, as a cultural
reality divorced from the immediacy of nature. Thus Lévi-Strauss, when
he shows in *The Elementary Structures of Kinship* that the prohibition
of incest is the universal principle of exclusion and division, the one
around which all the syntaxes of kinship relations take shape, is led to
note, almost in passing, this rather awkward fact:

> The total relationship of exchange which constitutes marriage is not
> established between a man and a woman, . . . but between two groups of
> men, and the woman figures only as one of the objects in the exchange. . . .
> [Women] have neither the same place nor rank in human society. To be
> unmindful of this would be to overlook the basic fact that it is men who
> exchange women, and not vice versa.[16]

Taking this issue up again in *Structural Anthropology* and replying to
accusations of antifeminism, Lévi-Strauss states that the kinship system's functioning as a language does not in any way entail the idea of
superiority or inferiority on anyone's part, and that nothing, theoretically,
prevents women from being the ones who exchange men.[17] He immediately adds, however, that this has never occurred in any human society,
and certainly this fact itself, its constancy and its universality, should be
every bit as surprising as the incest taboo. Mauss clearly perceives its
importance, noting that "sex-based division is a fundamental division
that has burdened societies to an unsuspected degree, and that sociology, being only a sociology of men rather than a sociology of women
or of both sexes, is much less than what it ought to be."[18]

No matter how "admirable" the rationality introduced into human
relationships by the prohibition of incest, no matter how necessary exogamy seems as a break with the natural order and as the inauguration
of the human order as such, women are still asked to pay the price. Not
only does this prohibition bring about an unequal division between the
sexes, one that works to men's advantage, it also elevates a structural
necessity to a truth of nature, making myth responsible for transferring the acquisitions of human history to the account of human origins,
so that inequality becomes confused with the order of the world and

the decisions of the gods. Men — masters of the social order, of goods, of language — would not be masters but for the grace of the incest prohibition, which places women into their hands as objects of exchange and as signs of any exchange.

The sacred character of this prohibition, and the seriousness of the punishment meted out to whoever violates it, certainly function to preserve order in general, as well as the whole system of differences (in functions, names, and so forth). But its overriding aim is ultimately to maintain and consolidate men's power. The prohibition of incest is the guarantee, the charter, of what can be called the permanent conspiracy of men, the untouchable foundation of the male homosocial pact — the perfect means, as it were, of keeping women dependent.

This is probably why so many ethnologists have seen initiation rites less as the adolescent male's entry into the adult world in general than as a way of removing him from the circle of the women to whose care his needs were entrusted in early childhood. As Jaulin notes of the Sara, "The initiatory separation of the child affirms that this child-becoming-an-adult has his own place in the village — in his father's line of descent — and it corresponds at the same time to a separation from the mother and from the mother's kin, since it is affirmed that this child will not be a man enclosed within his mother's line of descent."[19]

The initiation of boys is first of all initiation into male privilege. Mastery over fields of knowledge and over forces is presented to them by adult males as something to which women have no access, and even as something that must remain forbidden to women. What the code of the secret and the weapon of the taboo work to preserve is not some exceptional body of knowledge in itself but rather a body of knowledge that retains its potency only through being made inaccessible to that part of society kept in a dependent state. The initiatory mysteries are nothing but a barrier of codes established as knowledge, codes whose exclusivity guarantees a kind of power. At one blow, the rite impresses upon the young male the certainty of his superiority to the female world and forces women to accept and revere, sometimes in awe or terror, their own domination. Female initiation itself, when it takes place, is completely directed to women's recognition of the status that men have imposed on them (in rites of female initiation, girls are taught about their "natural" inferiority, the need to serve men and respect the taboos that concern men, and so forth).

What do these schemata involving so-called primitive societies have in common with the workings of eighteenth-century European societies? What is the point of this digression? The answer is that it gives us a genealogical view of a situation fundamentally the same in both types of society. The inequality between the sexes is just as great and is in fact specified—sometimes even amplified—as a result of historical determinations linked to the new modes of production. The late eighteenth century combined residues of feudal law with the new relationships being introduced by mercantile and manufacturing capitalism, which amounted to conferring all the economic power in the family on men, whereas women were forced into a life of home, hearth, and total subservience to their husbands. (Engels: "The modern conjugal family is founded on the domestic enslavement, overt or concealed, of women.")[20] Moreover, only boys received the kind of training and education that could give them access to public duties and scientific knowledge. When girls were educated at all, it was solely for decorative ends, to satisfy social needs.[21] What was maintained, then, despite a few concessions, was the conspiracy of fathers and sons against mothers and daughters: the homosocial conspiracy of men for control of economic and political power.

Precisely because the power of the sons is acquired theoretically, without a struggle, and is transmitted by the fathers, the young boy does not constitute suitable narrative material. He is not problematic. Nothing can happen to him that is not already written into his status. For him, every area of his control—over power, money, discourse—is an immediate given of his sexual difference. Libertinism is the obvious correlative of that difference (added to the birthright of men's freedom under monogamy, and of the lord's absolute power under feudalism, is the banker's law and power over every kind of exchangeable good). Being a libertine is a predicate of the male subject, which is why libertines are topics for cameos rather than for narratives and why Sade wrote no great coming-of-age novel about a young man. For his story to be told, a man would have to be put in the position of a woman: the position of having nothing and being forced to conquer all. He would have to be presumed financially ruined or come down in the world. He would need to be made a thief or an adventurer, which actually is the case with the heroes of the only two "male" narratives to be found in Sade's work:

the one in *Justine* about the libertine monk Jérôme, and the one in *Juliette* about the gentleman bandit Borchamp, called Brisatesta. But even though the adventurer may be, so to speak, a good conductor of narrativity, and even if he does have access to the narrative *I* and is able to circulate the way a woman does, he himself is still not an object of exchange: he lacks the possibility of being a sign of exchange, of incarnating the monetary function. Women alone bear those marks, which is also why only a woman can carry the narrative along, with the narrative of the adventurer merely an episode embedded in her own. His narrative is still only a partial one because he only partially fulfills the conditions for narrative. It is Juliette who gives voice to Brisatesta's narrative *I* as the echo of her own. A strict corollary is that women, as soon as they stop circulating and become sedentary in turn, cease to be topics for narrative. This is what happens to Juliette: retired to her estate, transformed into a serene *rentière*, she loses her translative function and has nothing more to say. She has to disappear.

The Mothers' Counterattack, and the Daughters' Education

One of the principal effects of male domination is that women are relegated to the interior world, to the running of households and the care of families. Barred from economic power and removed from the public scene, they have no choice.

Thus the world is divided along lines that follow the opposition between the sexes. On one side, men monopolize responsibility for public affairs, work, production, and the market. On the other, women are left to run the house, prepare the meals, and educate the children (mainly girls, but also young boys until the point when their fathers take them in hand). The result, in short, is a rather odd societal structure, which can be characterized as political patriarchy coupled with domestic matriarchy — or at least with what would appear to be domestic matriarchy, for women stripped of all economic power can act only after the fact, and their daughters are all they have for countering male authority and despotism. We can say, then, that there are two lines of descent, two independent series showing the effects that accompany opposing values: the line of men, who are masters, free (and libertines), speakers, politicians, owners, producers, and merchants; and the line of women, who are submissive, dependent (and virtuous), silent, depoliticized, dispossessed, and exchanged. This, briefly, is the division found in most known human societies; it is all but impossible to name one in which women are not or have not been oppressed in relation to men.

As we know, however, every oppressed group inevitably develops compensatory structures that serve the function of revenge against the oppressor, allowing the oppressed group to nibble at its lost power, to hinder and, indeed, mystify the oppressor. This operation is always indirect and enervating, if not neurotogenic (hence hysteria as the protest of the female body deprived of discourse, and frigidity as a punishment for male power).

Barred from economic and political power, women will attempt to get all they can from the only domain still open to their control: the family and, more specifically, the education of daughters, which is left entirely up to women. Thus is fomented the conspiracy of the mothers, with the essential objective of setting the daughters against the exploiters and tyrants: men. To do this, it will suffice to make wifely virtue (intended as a barrier to the intrusion of third parties, and as a guarantee of the paternal blood's legitimacy) a tool for the denial and humiliation of men's desire.

This is precisely where Sade comes in, viewing the defiance of the mothers, who enlist their daughters in their refusal, as repressive and puritanical (and not understanding that this is the inevitable neurotic response to male domination). At the same time, however, this defiance is what determines Sade's novelistic interest in the daughters. Among Sade's works, as we have seen, there is no coming-of-age novel about a young libertine male, for this young libertine acquires everything at the outset, taken in hand as he is by his father and immediately integrated into the world of men. But the case of the daughter is completely different. Shut away inside the family with its moral and religious values, and set by her vengeful mother against the tyrannical, depraved world of men, the daughter has everything to learn, everything with which to experiment. The first order of business, then, will be to smash the conspiracy of the mothers, destroy the domestic matriarchy, and place the daughter into free circulation — but without encroaching on male privilege. To do this, it will suffice to have the daughter partake, against her mother, in male privilege. In other words, the daughter must move into the world of men. This movement is called *prostitution,* and its inaugural act is often father-daughter or brother-sister incest.

What this multiply overdetermined incest marks, first of all, is a wrenching away from the maternal sphere of influence, denial of the familial prohibition, and destruction of the closure that this prohibition brings about as the necessary order of exchanges and alliances. Through incest, the daughter mutates into a "girl" in the depraved sense: a loose, unattached woman free of duties, a vagrant pudendum—a woman who is, as Sade puts it, "vulgivagous."[22] If Sadean incest occasions pleasure through the abominable concurrence of an act ("fucking") and a familial designation ("my sister," "my daughter"), it is because the act is enough to destroy the designation. What is destroyed at the same time is the realm of the family, in a destruction that eliminates the mother's ultimate position of power, for incest frees the daughter first of all from her mother—hence not just the need for incest but also its functional limitation to fathers and daughters, and to brothers and sisters (which is why mother-son incest is left out here).

Because the issue of the daughters must be resolved, we find long dissertations in Sade on the education (or countereducation) to be imposed on daughters, whereas not a line is to be found on the education of sons, since for sons the issue is resolved from the beginning by their integration into the paternal realm. What sons are given, daughters must discover and conquer. Their being subjects of an evolution is what also makes them narrative material par excellence. In other words, male heroes are a matter for *definition*; daughters are a matter for *narrative*. What is more, for Sade they establish narrative itself, which stages the ushering out of the family, the elimination of repressive mothers, and a complicit but also *competitive* association with the men who have a stranglehold on political and economic power. The daughter, because she is nothing, can become anything; this fault is what makes her available for the trajectory by which narrative falls to her and her alone. But something else is still needed before she can express this narrative in the first person.

The Revenge of the Libertines

> Born to avenge my sex, and to control yours.
> —Madame de Merteuil to Valmont, in LACLOS,
> *Les Liaisons dangereuses*, letter LXXXI

The elimination of overpossessive mothers opens the way to resourceful daughters. The mothers' elimination is not the essential narrative element; rather, it is what enables narration, whose topic is the conquest of the male world. Entry into libertinism coincides with entry into narration. And the essential lesson of *Philosophy in the Bedroom* is that mothers have to pay the price. Eugénie's initiation, her metamorphosis from ignorant virgin into accomplished libertine, is completed through the intervention of a series of characters who have strictly allocated functions:

> *The absent but complicit father,* sign of the external male world that awaits Eugénie and in which she will have to exercise her new knowledge and carry on her new existence
>
> *Eugénie's female initiator into libertinism,* Madame de Saint-Ange, the model for what Eugénie must become, but the model as well for what a mother should be: by revealing the secrets of the depraved world of men, she also brings freed women into the conspiracy, women who mean to have their revenge on their rulers by using them as much as they allow their rulers to use them
>
> *The homosexual philosopher,* Dolmancé, through whom Eugénie will learn to prefer the anus to the vagina and, at the same time, philosophy to religion, free sexual pleasure to procreation, sexual indeterminacy to the familial realm, and libertine polyvalence to the roles of wife and mother
>
> *The incestuous brother,* to whom falls Eugénie's deflowering, as does the resulting destruction of familial designations
>
> *The outraged mother,* Madame de Mistival, who comes to take her daughter back and reintegrate her into familial space (but Eugénie, caught up in this device for tearing the family and its values apart, is ripe for the attack on the mother, the family's guardian)

Madame de Mistival is preceded by a letter from her husband, which gives the Bedroom conspirators carte blanche to punish her. Insulted by her daughter, held up to ridicule, manhandled, she is finally subjected to a torture whose stages have the purpose of denying, by gradations, the status that she claims. First she is sodomized until she bleeds, so she can be taught to acknowledge what, by definition, she impugns: the anus and its pleasures. Then she is given syphilis (by an infected valet) so she can be made to pay the price of the debauchery that she has always condemned. Finally, her vagina and anus are sewn shut, her vagina so her twin functions as mother and wife can be denied, and her anus so she can be punished for having wished to know nothing about it.

At the symbolic level, the demonstration is complete. This is why Sade opens his text with a sarcastic dedication, saying that mothers should make it required reading for their daughters. He assumes that the daughters' reading it will be the death of the monogamous family system, which is founded on male power and on women's being confined to a sexuality of simple reproduction, with modesty and fidelity as its safeguards. The system can be maintained only if daughters, as preparation for being suitable wives to future husbands, are kept dependent on their mothers. Sade wants this essential stitch dropped, and the resulting tear will cause the whole fabric to unravel. If there are no more model daughters, then there will be no more faithful spouses, no more families, no more compulsory reproduction, and no more prohibitions against sexual pleasure.

Thus it is up to the young libertine woman to get this breakdown under way. Having eliminated the mother, but without yet securing any male privileges for herself, she must acquire through her actions and her history what men possess by right and heritage (Sade does not trouble himself about the provenance of this heritage). In other words (to put the issue in Kantian terms), libertinism, which in men is an analytic predicate, in women can be only a synthetic predicate. What is over and done with for a man remains open for a woman. What can — what must — happen to her? Essentially, her discovering and seizing hold of the male world. The paradox is that the world of adventure is a male world, but only women have the possibility of discovering and moving through it, because they are unaware of it. This is why women and only women operate as narrators.

But this is the world of power and money, and conquering it means, for a woman, gaining access at the price of the only thing she owns: her body. Her strength is strictly a libidinal one, but it is a phenomenal strength because it is priceless; even in the most colossal quantities, it still comes up short against the immensity of male desire. From the moment she puts her body on the market, a woman has the power to ask men for anything because men reserve the power to own everything. Therefore, the female adventurer, and the topic of the female's narrative, is prostitution. But this is not the prostitution of poverty; it is the prostitution of libertinism, and this difference completely changes its status.

It is important that prostitution be a free choice so that it can be used to demonstrate the dissolution of the family's system of coerced, controlled exchange. Although the prostitution of poverty does exist in Sade, with its bordellos and madams, it exists only as an economic point of departure, an initiation into debauchery. The real libertine prostitute shows her true colors by cheating her madam, and she quickly departs on the arm of a rich visitor in order to gain complete independence, let herself circulate freely, and offer herself to any and all comers. Instead of pimps, she has allies and protectors. Juliette brings in nothing for Saint-Fond or Noirceuil; on the contrary, it is she who squeezes significant sums out of them. This difference is fundamental, for exploiting a prostitute and subjecting her to the institution of the bordello means shutting her up inside a subsidiary of the family—a place that compensates for the libidinal prohibitions of the family, prohibitions that men themselves have ordained—and leaving intact both the syntax of marital union and the order of the contract. But the transformation of a prostitute into an independent libertine is an attack on both the institution of the family and the economic order.

It is an attack on the institution of the family because this freedom shows that the daughter *herself* is the one who *wills* the elimination of the mother and spouse in herself. It is up to her to break the chain of marital union. Prostitution, when it is desired in this way, gains the stamp of a fact of "nature."

> Let's go awhoring, let's sell ourselves, let's get ourselves to a gutter and open grinning cunts to whole passing nations, our cunts, our mouths, our assholes, let's ope all our holes to every filthy stopper.[23]

> Woman has one innate virtue, it is whorishness; to fuck, that and that alone is what we were created for; woe unto her whom a thoughtless and stupid virtuousness ever keeps prisoner of dull prejudices.[24]

Women's libertinism is the necessary point of transition to the republican utopia of free love, the Brownian motion of desiring bodies, and this proves that the best way to destroy exchange is to make it total and indiscriminate.

The transformation of a prostitute into an independent libertine is an attack on the economic order because only women, by trading on their bodies, can carry out an operation forbidden to men: the complete perversion of capital. Although prostitution does nothing to challenge men's economic power, and even confirms it, prostitution can still pirate the effects of men's economic power and make it unrecognizable. Thus the libertine woman goes the male libertine one better: without working, through her erotic value alone, she causes the movement of capital from the male sphere to the female sphere. The point, however, is not to replicate the model of men's economic power. The libertine woman forges or breaks all her contracts, invests nothing, is wasteful, rids wealth of all productive value, and in this way libidinalizes the whole economic process, exhibiting the repressed sexual content of all political power. She grabs the machinery and puts it back together in reverse, showing that conclusion was contained in premise, and effect in cause—in other words, that the point of work is sexual pleasure, and that the point of production is waste. Because she is the one who allows the man to recognize this, however, she goes farther than he does. She is the figure of total misappropriation. The male libertine, when he lies and cheats, always does so under cover of some official function (as minister, president, financier, prelate), but the libertine woman does so only in the undisguised offering of her body to male desire. She forces the admission of this desire and disjoints its alibis.

The male libertine, forced into a static position for the sake of whatever economic or social status he has awarded himself, cannot circulate inside his own field of power. It is he who has forced himself into a sedentary function, and he offers nomadic freedom to the libertine woman. She is the mobile, indeterminate element among fixed and institutionally recognized male positions, the element that displaces and transmits desires, wealth, and messages. But the logic of the gift given and reciprocated is no longer followed because she no longer follows the imposed, limited routes of exchange, which establish families and trace the boundaries of cultural and symbolic endogeny. She *herself* exchanges herself, and with everyone. She causes wealth to circulate, but only so it can be wasted (in luxury and sexual pleasure). She makes speech circulate, but only so it can be made public and infinite (the *saying everything* of libertine philosophy). This is why she *is* narrative. She is the emblem of desire's circulation, and of its price, but she is also the figure of the ubiquitous multiplicity of *perspective*, or point of view (she goes everywhere, sees everything, covers everything). And, because she is freely exchanged and voluntarily offered, she is adventure *speaking itself*. Self-prostitution establishes the narrative *I*.

What has to be recognized, then, is that female narrative privilege is engendered in Sade only from the logical impasse at which the power of men ends up, because the power of men wishes simultaneously to maintain its traditional privileges and to abolish the familial and conjugal structures linked to them. This is a double bind to which the libertine woman provides a positive solution: without challenging men's economic and political hegemony, she can storm the maternal stronghold. Once launched into the male world, however, she has fearsome powers. She is necessary to the destroyer, but she also threatens him, which is why the signs of a ferocious confrontation (if not a war of the sexes) multiply beneath the surface of an apparent collaboration. Clairwil is the prototype of the female libertine as men's enemy (ultimately, the writer will make her pay by destroying her), and it is she who must constantly remind others of the inevitable conflict. When Juliette asks whether it is proper to deceive one's lover, Clairwil answers:

> Most certainly...; dealing with a man, we have the human nature in him to contend with, and are obliged to proceed toward him as he always proceeds in our regard; and since no man is frank, why would you have us be frank with them? Enjoy your lover's tastes where they concur with your caprices; make the most profitable use of his moral and physical faculties; heat yourself by the fire of his intelligence, be inspired by his talents; but never for one instant forget that he belongs to an enemy sex, a sex bitterly at war with your own ... that you ought never let pass an opportunity for avenging the insults women have endured at its hands, and which you yourself are every day on the eve of having to suffer; in short, he is a man, and you have got to dupe him.[25]

And when Juliette proposes the manhandling of women, it is again Clairwil who replies: "I prefer to butcher males, I've never pretended otherwise: I enjoy avenging my sex."[26]

In his own self-interest, the male libertine has ordained the advancement of women to libertine status, but as a result he has lost the self-evident character of his power. And so begins the phase of *male melancholia* as it appears in this disenchanted remark addressed by Noirceuil to Juliette, who has asked him if he still turns up at Clairwil's gatherings:

> "In the days when men were in the majority there," he replied, "I never missed a single one; but I have given up going since everything has fallen into the hands of a sex whose authority I dislike. Saint-Fond felt the same way and dropped out shortly after I did."[27]

Thus it is not surprising that the covert competition between the sexes leads each one, under the mutual threat of indifference, to develop as an erotically autarkic, closed set (the male libertine never leaves home without his buggerers, nor the female without her "cunnilinguists"). Now the homosexual pact of the men has its answer in the homosexual pact of the women. The men's pact continues as a jealous monopoly over economic and political power; the women's is a highly refined strategy for pirating and chipping away at the benefits of the men's pact. Their mutual dependence remains complete but is played out at the edge of defiance. And so begins the face-off, no holds barred, between lesbian conquerors and sodomite despots.

The Proof from Nature, or the Justine/Juliette System

If Lévi-Strauss is correct in seeing the prohibition against incest as the form assumed by the transition from nature to culture, perhaps it is because the prohibition coincides with a male reasoning—coincides, that is, with the means by which this prohibition permits women to be kept within the sphere of nature, and culture to be made a male privilege. Women, exchanged by men, are presented (among many other ways) as one more "natural" resource, for their "naturalness," institutionalized by the prohibition, is metonymically connected to a whole network of other "natural" forms. These include biological reproduction and its corollary, the life of the home, as well as physical weakness and what is seen as its corollary: unfitness for life (hunting, war, heavy work) in the outside world, and therefore unfitness for participation in public affairs. In other words, in the establishment of institutions and the shaping of the order of discourse, a fact of nature is always invoked under the sign of male control, and to the detriment of women. Thus men help themselves to the advantages of belonging to the sphere of culture, that is, the sphere of artifacts, industry, mediation, transformation, and, ultimately, power and reason. As a result, women find themselves flung back into the sphere of nature, spontaneity, immediacy, instinct, and, ultimately, dependence. Woman is Man's "primitive," the negative of his history.

Sade does not directly challenge Woman's "naturalness" as a blind spot of Man's history; on the contrary, through a remarkable reversal, he makes her "naturalness" serve his own demonstration: if indeed nature can be assumed to speak through Woman, and if a woman becomes a libertine, then here is the proof that libertinism is natural. It is in and through women that vice obtains the mark of being primordial and spontaneous. In men, by contrast, libertinism goes without saying: men, belonging to the sphere of culture, that is, the sphere of artifacts, belong from the outset to the sphere of transgression, excess, and denaturation, simply by virtue of being men. Libertinism in men is a redundancy, so to speak, if not a tautology. But it is women's prerogative to prove something more important: that nature itself is vice, cruelty, and artifact; through women, libertinism is elevated to a fact of nature.

It is precisely this proof from nature that is carried out by the Justine/Juliette system. Through Justine's and Juliette's parallel and ultimately intersecting adventures, "nature" is tested in a sort of narrative ordeal so that her truth can be told and her judgment rendered.

The first proof involves Justine, or the figure of the woman who condemns vice (pleasure, crime, and exploitation) in the name of the (Rousseauian) voice of conscience, which she takes for the voice of nature. The more firmly she stands, the more Justine is contradicted by events, forced into complicit passivity and unreasonable risks, as if her continuously denied desire precipitated her toward everything that she disavows. Justine is the continuous spectacle of nature thwarted, repressed, and unceasingly insistent as the dark side of the virtue with which nature has been identifed. This is why nature takes her revenge: Justine is felled by lightning. Nature, unable to speak through her, has spoken against her. The first verdict is in.

The second proof involves Juliette, or the figure of the woman who throws herself into sexual pleasure, crime, and prostitution, never recoiling from any horror if it will bring her satisfaction. She is successful, she grows rich, she wins friends and admirers; she is happiness and affirmation, the spontaneous motion of desire. Juliette is nature in bloom. The verdict is clear: it is in and through Juliette that nature lets us hear her authentic voice — an indisputably natural one, being a woman's.

At the same time, however, it appears that nature is not what she seems: not the ultimate referee of norms but rather their silence, not the locus of unquestionable purposes but rather the locus of all possibilities. She can no longer guarantee the old divisions at all, or she maintains them only for the sake of overturning their values. Thus the Justine/Juliette system is inscribed on bodies as the choice between vagina and anus, with this paradigm of sexual spots reflecting the paradigm of the moral opposition between virtue and vice. The vagina, like virtue, is no longer anything but the sign of a pseudonature; that is, its value is only that of a traditional prejudice under religious authority. The vagina is connected with wifely, and therefore motherly, sexuality: the legalized sexuality of reproduction, and therefore of modesty and repression. The sterile, bisexual anus completely eliminates the maternal function. It betrays a sexuality of sheer useless enjoyment. It is under the sign of the anus that Juliette renounces the family, joins the society of libertines, and freely circulates among them (whereas the vagina would have condemned her to marital stasis). At the same time, though, the vagina itself becomes an undifferentiating organ, an erotic site that is included in the series on the same basis as the others. Recourse to the concept of nature is now only the ironic guarantee of a critical, endlessly disruptive reversal, the strategic diverting of undisputed authority's referee.

But this victory of anus over vagina may be less a victory of women than one of homosexual men over women. If women cannot gain recognition and admission into the conspiracy of men unless they become libertines, this also means that they do so only by becoming male, assimilating male objectives and fantasies,[28] identifying with men as libertine masters, and pursuing the same anal mastery: violence and domination, knowledge and apathy. The libertine woman: the minor miracle of a man named Juliette.

The Storyteller and Her Pimp

Juliette's Body, Narrative's Body

Juliette's body — infinitely marketable, exchangeable, and enjoyable — is for that very reason distinguished by a mouth able to recount all the events that affect this body, and all the thoughts that run through it. Thus Juliette is the one inextinguishable narrative voice threading through the countless deeds, gestures, discourses, and arguments of those she meets. The words of others, their thoughts as well as their adventures, take up residence in her speech, but this is because her own body is always the topic of all their words and all their adventures. Her body has the same compass as her discourse: it is the verb of all her sentences but also their dictionary. It is covered with forbidden meanings, covered with other discourses, just as it is covered with other bodies. It is the body as agora, a marketplace of words, pleasures, and money: academy, bordello, and bank, and all at the same time.

It is certainly necessary to see Juliette's plurivocal status. She must recognize that, as a prostitute, she does not produce wealth; she can only
divert it, extract it from men. She must recognize that she is merely a
liquidatable body, a discursive element picked up as the predicate of a
male subject, a mobile element that is manipulable, in every respect, for
all kinds of desire's sentences (orgies, feasts, journeys, crimes). But because she is a free, libertine prostitute (and sometimes even a madam) —
in charge of her market, setting her price, and keeping all the profits
for herself — she herself attains the power of articulating the discursive
object that she is for men. In other words, she attains self-utterance, the
narrative *I*. If it is true that every narrative is the stake in an exchange,
and if narrative speech works the way money does, then we see how
Sadean narrative, by establishing Woman as "living money," definitively
and perversely reveals her as both the object and the subject of narrative: she is recounted, and she recounts herself. Therefore, Juliette both
utters and is uttered, is both active and passive, productive and produced,
both trades and is traded, is both money exchanged and an exchanger
of money. In short, she is the perfect sentence that encompasses all sub-
ordinate clauses, expresses all moods, and covers the whole dictionary.
Her body — whose mouth, uttering what the body does, produces an
absolutely performative speech — is completely coextensive with the narrative that produces this body. Her body is the encyclopedic sentence
that utters itself.

Author and Pimp

Although Juliette has the privilege of the narrative *I*, this is admittedly
a privilege that has been granted her. No matter how independent she
is as a narrated character, she remains subject, as a creature of writing,
to a master who makes it his business to remind her now and then of
his implacable authority. He is the supreme, ineluctable pimp: the author
(in his strictly textual status as writer, or scribe).

   Indeed, it should not be forgotten that Juliette's narrative takes up
where Justine's, written in the third person, leaves off. (Justine, not being a libertine, cannot attain self-narration, which would be unsustain-
able, being necessarily repressed. Sade grants Justine self-narration in
the first two versions of the novel, *Les Infortunes de la vertu* and *Justine,
ou Les Malheurs de la vertu*, but he eventually and quite logically takes it
back in *La Nouvelle Justine* so that mastery of enunciation and the privi-

lege of point of view can be restored to libertinism.) The story of Juliette is inscribed in a narrative space that is under the author's explicit control. He is there to make the introductions, and he reappears at the end ("Thus did Madame de Lorsange [Juliette] conclude the story of her adventures").[29] Juliette is also returned to the subjection of the third person, not simply brought back to her master but claimed by him as his exclusive authorial property: "Unique in her kind, that woman died without having left any record of the events which distinguished the latter part of her life, and so it is that no writer will be able to chronicle it for the public."[30] And the narrative's opening and closing are not the only places where this claim of power can be found: whenever Juliette's narration is interrupted by one of her listeners, her third-person position is reaffirmed. But the author makes his irremediable ascendancy felt even more conspicuously in the many footnotes where he interrupts his character and, from the wings, addresses the reader, his accomplice in libertinism. Discourse is in a woman's hands, but ultimately only to the extent that she is still the author's "creature," posited and sustained by his activity and his power. The writing of the pimp keeps an eye on the prostitute and contains her speech. He allows her to be as free as the logic of the roles requires, reining her in here and there to mark his silent presence, and finally taking her over completely, to conclude and have the last word.

If the advent of the storyteller is strictly determined, in Sade's writings, by the new economic and symbolic function that is the lot of the libertine woman, her advent marks this new function's stringent limits no less than its potency. What makes its appearance at the same time is the insurmountable contradiction of the Sadean utopia: the installation of a subversive countersociety in the ranks of existing society so as to infiltrate it, like a solvent in its joints. Thus the Sadean utopia attempts nothing less than a plan for the impossible: the establishment of the law of desire as the law of political power.

Writing, the Mother, and Incest

The writer, master and male, keeps his storyteller completely under his control and shows the reader his hidden, constant authority over her. To attain to writing, however, he himself had to undergo a strange mutation: he had to gain recognition from the Mother, and so he himself had to become a woman: "The novelist is the child of nature . . . she has created him to be her painter; if he does not become his mother's lover the moment she gives birth to him, let him never write, for we shall never read him."[31] Here, the mother may be nature, and the novelist her son (though the construction of the sentence is surprisingly ambiguous, and this mother could be the "real" one), but whether the relationship is metaphorical or not, the logic that it expresses remains intact: namely, that the way into writing is through mother-son incest.

It is as if the writer's path were the opposite of the storyteller's. As a libertine woman, the storyteller tears herself away from the society of the mothers and, under the sign of father-daughter or brother-sister incest, joins the society of men, thus partaking in the privileges that the sons enjoy alongside the fathers, but doing so in a specific mode: the one that belongs to the function of exchange. As for the sons, it is impossible for them to desire their mothers, for that would mean cutting themselves off from male power and betraying the conspiracy of the fathers. Nevertheless, this betrayal is one that does have to be carried out by a son: the writer. If narration is an essentially female privilege, then, in order to tell about the storyteller, the writer must turn himself into a woman, gain recognition from the female realm, which is structurally in control of the mother; to write, he must become her lover. (Note how Sade attributes the function of recognition to incest: partnership is achieved through the crime committed together, through a shared transgression, through access to the same privilege and the same secret — in other words, through entry into the circle of sameness as a conspirators' ring.)

What does the Sadean writer want? He wants to seduce the Mother, to commit incest with her so as to gain entry into narrative speech, but he also wants to remain within the Law of the Father, within the realm and potency of the symbolic, so as to lose none of the advantages of his mastery (over women). Thus he will seduce the Mother by offering her what he has received from the Father, but at the same time he makes her the Mother of law. She offers him a breast as cold as a dungeon's stones, an envious, dreadful, fascinating breast to which he runs howling. What unfurls here is the characteristically Sadean spiral of writing — incest and crime, the Mother's seduction and murder, her expulsion and veneration — engendering the dizzying collapse of instinctive into symbolic that shapes this writing's style as an outrage of, and within, language.

The paradox of the Sadean writer is a strange one: he cannot create his storyteller unless he tears her away from the Mother and lets her circulate freely among men, and yet he cannot create himself as a writer or assume narrative power unless he crosses back over into the female realm and reappropriates its privileges. A traitor and a transvestite, hatching several plots at once, the Sadean writer stands at that point of exchange and duplicity where the text, as the product of his slyness, summons us as readily to the humor of fiction as to the despair of its contradiction.

AFTERMATH II

Continuation As Exit

If we contrast life with the theater, it is because we feel that the
theater borders on death, where all liberties are granted.

—JEAN GENET

The Cruelty of Fiction: The Theater of Critical Provocation

How characteristic is it of Sade's texts to leave the reader walleyed, as it
were, as if the texts inevitably gave rise to two lines of opposed and ever
more divergent affirmations? On the one hand, despite all our methodological precautions concerning the autonomy of the text, it certainly
has to be acknowledged that the Sadean universe as such (everything in
these texts that is described as a social system with all its powers, laws,
and practices) is utterly odious, intolerable, to be rejected unconditionally. On the other hand, however, it must also be recognized that this universe, being the stuff of fiction, is never offered either as truth or as an
object for imitation. Why bother to describe it, then? What is the meaning of this remarkable provocation? What is speaking in these texts,
and how much does Sade allow this voice to be heard as his own? Is it
necessary to find the right mix, equal parts tedium and improbability,
between the delights of libertine utopia and the frenzies of cruelty? Once
again, the general question of what these paradoxical texts mean has to
be raised: What is going on in them that comes to them from somewhere
else, and that they are displaying—or disassembling—to the point, perhaps, of absurdity?

It is possible to see in Sade's texts, as Foucault does, the last stand of classical thought as the order of representation: "Sade reaches the end of classical discourse and thought. He holds sway precisely over their limit."[1] We might add that what the "saying everything" of excess reintroduced into discourse was not just the boundary of discourse but also the far edge of that boundary, and that it was through his very immoderacy that Sade filled out and completed the inventory.

But that does not explain why an enterprise of this kind was so shabbily repaid, and why so many imprecations and prohibitions were called down on Sade's texts. It may be that Sade, going beyond encyclopedic saturation, brought an end to classical thought in a more unexpected sense, in that the horror deployed by his texts, far from overstepping the bounds of reason and overrunning its margins, is actually reason's unavowable *extension,* its scandalous continuation, something that reason inevitably produces and desperately tries to present as being outside itself, its odious antithesis. Sade made himself unforgivable by forcing reason to recognize this underside as the *conclusion* of its plan and its logic.

As we know, the program of classical thought was laid out definitively by Descartes in his famous watchword of becoming lords and masters of nature. Thus Descartes innocently recognizes that the *mathesis universalis* invoked by his wishes is the key to a quite practical domination, and that the unbreakable bond between knowledge and power, henceforth joined in *technē,* is no longer even problematic. The encyclopedic enterprise—as exhaustion of both the naming and the classifying of natural facts, life, labor, and language, and carried out under the glorious sign of knowledge (against religious or barbaric obscurantism)—feels so justified in its liberal ambition that it does not scruple to hide its objective of radical, intolerant mastery: to draw everything, with nothing left over, into the trap of an irrefutable, unopposable discourse.

It was under the sign of reason that the merciless technical mastery of the world was to develop, the sign of reason as the universal rigor of knowledge, the guarantee of progress, the order of law, and the basis of contracts. The first thing to be seen in reason's self-importance is the advent of the new freedom gained over the old powers of the church and the absolute monarchy. What is not seen, because it is so self-evident, is that reason also underwrote the development of the mercantile economy and the birth of industrial capitalism, and that the nation-state, too, was founded on reason (the nation-state being the great leveler of cultural and linguistic differences, the ideal instrument with which the new bourgeoisie could assign universal value to its particular interests and, with the transcendent backing of this emblem, ship the peasant populations off to the massacre of the Napoleonic Wars).

In other words, the setting in which this deception was played out and cemented was first of all a political one. Reason, posited as the principle of equity, the principle that regulates social relationships, is supposed to have established law, posited as a just mediation between individuals, independent of their rank and power. This is precisely where we find the great bluff: because we are so used to seeing law as universal and just, so used to seeing its formal control over the many, we do not see how it favors the few. Sade analyzes this ironically in *Yet Another Effort, Frenchmen, If You Would Become Republicans*, in the article on manners: "I ask you now whether that law is truly just which orders the man who has nothing to respect another who has everything?"[2] Relationships based in law, far from taming violence, became its best mask, best because these relationships *managed*, literally, the feat of getting themselves revered by those whom they were duping. Violence was intact, but through its alliance with reason it learned to program, manage, and pluralize itself in a multitude of constraints, conditionings, and sanctions. Violence, in a word, learned *skillful* domination.

Productivist programs would now always be formulated under remorseless cover of an all-consuming rationality, and from this the pitiless exploitation of "human material" in factories would derive its unruffled legitimacy. The objection can always be raised that capital, for its own ends, diverted *technē* and falsified reason's program. If that were true, however, it would also be necessary to explain why there was nothing proposed in reason's program that could put up any resistance, and why this contradiction was not seen at the outset. The inhumanity of free enterprise was completely ignored. If this inhumanity did not arise from the domain of reason itself, and if reason was only the bride of free enterprise, then we still need to know why everyone who saw reason on the arm of free enterprise found this bride so beautiful. The marriage was hailed by all the Enlightenment philosophers except Rousseau (on this point, at least). This tenacious, invisible deception is what Sade's texts expose, through exacerbation rather than denunciation. Sade did

not insult the Enlightenment philosophers, nor did he celebrate the coming of irrationality (as has been suggested too often, and thoughtlessly);
he never denied the omnipotence of reason. He extended the Enlightenment philosophers' beam of light and became its extreme tip. He made
their enlightenment harder and harsher. He showed reason that what it
posited as its opposite, as irrational and evil, was a monster to which it
was continuously giving birth. He forced reason to recognize its illegit-
imate child, and he did this primarily in two ways: by enunciating the
crime, horror, and exploitation in reason's *form* (that is, in its language
and its discursive organization) and by enunciating the crime, horror,
and exploitation in reason's *formulas* (that is, crime, horror, and exploitation as corollaries of reason's principles, or as proofs of its hypotheses).
Sade played the card of hyperrationality to reintegrate reason with what
it preferred to know nothing about, with the thing whose sacrifice guar-
anteed reason's official innocence. He made reason acknowledge that
horror is not its opposite, but rather its most consistent result.

Sade, as I read him, is Kant's worst nightmare. As I understand him,
he is the mouthpiece of the Enlightenment philosophers, the voice of
Night at which Hegel scoffed, pointing in the night to that place of indifferentiation where "all cows are black," the place whose end Hegel
believed himself to be hailing in "the magnificent sunrise" of the French
Revolution as identified with the triumphal advent of reason. Indeed;
but Hegel did not admit that the Jacobin Terror was carried out in the
name of this very reason, and under the sign of the state in which reason is "objectified." Cows are taken out of the night only to be sent to
the slaughter. Moreover, the Terror was merely the most spectacular sign
of a practice that was to become commonplace; it was the signal that
every kind of domination, every variety of disciplinary imprinting, and
all sorts of "normalization" would be fashioned in conformity with the
most extreme logic, and under the authority of a power established by
reason.

All the way up to the dawn of the classical age, reason essentially had
been defined as wisdom capable of modulating and structuring knowledge. From now on, it would be defined as science (as *mathesis universalis*, that is, in terms of calculus or even accountancy) and as technique
(that is, in terms of domination and profitability). Sade would show reason that in its new form it was also and inevitably exploitation and destruction; and, further, he would designate this engendering as a process

of power, sexual pleasure, and death. His texts are presented as the staging of four successive phases, which, in scaled-down form, he makes legible in the figures and workings of the libertine body. To expose the body and subdivide it; to measure it by phallic standards; to program its positions and variations; to methodically extract every imaginable pleasure from it in order, at last, to take sexual pleasure in its torture and death — all of this is the rigorous development of a single logic.

Sade is showing that the body has entered upon its industrial destiny and into an era of postamorous relationships. From combinatory ordering of partners to Stakh(Cas)anovism of sexual pleasure, from standard reproduction (with a view to calibrated ejaculations) of bodies or body parts to amnesiac iterations of orgies, what is collapsing is the aura of desire and its spells, its indeterminate temporality and its ambiguous signs, its lyrical infinity; what reigns triumphant is libidinal *techne*.

Sade's excess merely concludes a demonstration that was begun at another place and time; he connects the dots, drawing out the final corollaries of theorems long since proved. What he makes obvious is the implacable continuity running from the rupture of the organic body through its ordered, quantified division and methodical profitability to its capitalist exploitation. Capital is what divides, cuts up, levies, and vampirizes, and the technology of capital is the executioner. For Sade, the libertine body is not separate from this theory of exploitation and mechanization. The erotics of accountancy and substitution implies a passion for outputs, and the abstract temporality of programming invokes the imperatives of production. Everything can figure in this manufacture of sexual pleasure, and everything can be achieved — everything but love.

The libertine body, without symptoms, sleep, dreams, secrets, or memory, is the pallid child of extremist Occidental reason, the precipitate of its deadliest light, the heart of its vertiginous yawning chasm. It is, as a whole, only a lidless eye worn out with seeing and being seen, a set of gears in a shroud of glass. Its embryo develops in the unforeseen consequences of a paranoiac science, at the outermost limit of science's calculations, accounts, techniques, and powers (the same embryo is what we also find so amusingly imagined by Mary Shelley in the monster constructed by her Dr. Frankenstein). This sleek, unfeeling body looms as the emblem of the most dreadfully abstract process, the one signaling that the era of the Earth and of gods, of works and of days, the open-ended time of space and of the gaze, of rhythm and of breath, has come to an end or been brought to one. Here begins the era of artifact and models, of program and amortization, of substitutability and credit, of the universal/undifferentiated/exchangeable:

> For the land went away, the land disappeared, trailing in its wake spinets, pink and gold harpsichords, and sandalwood violins; here was the New Age, and Sade was to be its mastermind. No more land, no more the Lubéron of fairies and sprites, no more parched hills, only parchment; Sade is master of a kingdom devoid of beings, forms, and substances, and it is prison that assumes the image of the vanished land. Space is no more, but time will be, not the eternal time of Mother Earth, but instead a pure time, a succession of bodies.[3]

Perhaps the libertine body is the body of the last man dancing on the last of the neolithic ruins. We could say that *Juliette* is this body's Gospel, in a sense, and *The 120 Days of Sodom*, its Apocalypse — only in a sense, but even so . . .

Because he articulates this limit — taking the seeds of the methodical horror invented by the joint efforts of the Enlightenment philosophers and of industrial capitalism, and quickening them to the point of enormity and intolerability — Sade is, in a way, the symptom par excellence of his century, but also its diagnosis. In Sade, the eighteenth century hears its own voice. It finds in him its precise, impassive scribe, and in him, by all accounts, it finds its accounts generously settled. The paradox of these extreme texts is probably that they did nothing more than articulate the trivial truth of an epoch and simply bring its familiar logic to a conclusion. What we discover, unless we let ourselves be deluded or deafened by all his transgressive utterances, is that Sade overturned and destroyed nothing: he reinforced what had already been established, and he intensified what was already there. Provocation, for him, meant aggravation. But surely this is also why he excites fear and why he provokes blindness and disavowals. This fear is a profound one, not confined to the compass of his books but originating outside them and detonated by them. In his books we see the trajectory, speeded up and reduced to its essentials, of the slow catastrophe that has become our ordinary reality.

This is certainly why Sade continues to affect us, and if he still disturbs, it may not be for reasons (sex, crime, obscenity) that we might think obvious. If we have become better readers of Sade, and if censorship of Sade seems to have relented, it is not because of any change in the literary tradition, nor is it the outcome of some radical reversal brought about by the refinement of critical methods. It is (and this is perhaps more serious) because Sade is no longer in front of us, but *we* are *in him*. Our century has begun to realize what his merely promised. What his texts heralded and threatened is being actualized in our history. He was, so to speak, the archivist of the future that belongs to us. We entered into the precision and actuality of the Sadean body, and from that point on, the modalities of sexual pleasure and suffering—from their ordinary to their paroxysmal forms, from the marketplace of sex to the crushing of bodies in concentration camps—have been assuming the shape of Sade's universe. In that universe, the sexual domination of bodies serves as the terminal emblem of every form of exploitation and mastery because it presupposes those forms and perfects their logic. Everywhere, in banal or dramatic ways, our hyper-Enlightenment illuminates super-Sillings.

Nevertheless, although Sade surprises us by having been so terribly right, a question about him ineluctably returns: In what respect did he wish for this mad world, and to what extent was he in league with his torturing libertines? Did he believe in their speeches, or did he hold back in a total irony that we should be able to discern in the very excessiveness of this staging, in its function as critical provocation, and in its amassing of paradoxes? Is he more responsible for the world that he organized and described than Goya is for the nightmarish scenes of *The Disasters of War*, or than Piranesi is for his *Prisons*? If we can delete the quotation marks that set all these texts off—even the name that designates them— as fiction, can we do that without falling into the most grotesque misinterpretation? This is not a frivolous question, for it determines a split in how Sade will be read, a split that is less between an admiring reading and a repulsed one than between a reading of Sade as a doctrinaire and a reading of Sade as a writer.

Sade as a doctrinaire? When we pull "philosophical" statements from *Juliette* and hold them up next to the theses (or assumptions) of Locke, Rousseau, or Kant, we draw Sade into a debate that is not and cannot be his own. A theoretical statement embedded in a work of fiction is itself a fiction, no matter how persuasive its effect. With Sade, this is true even of *Yet Another Effort, Frenchmen*. Between treatise and narrative there is a complete shift in the locus of enunciation. We recognize the treatise because it remains within the known realm of communication and responsibility. What it establishes is within the realm of the message, and it leans toward the greatest coherence and univocality; form is not its first concern. We discuss its concepts and what it intends to say. By contrast, narrative (like any other fictional production) is first of all a feat of language (and even of *the* language, when narrative is poetry). It affirms nothing. It experiments, investigates, scrambles its referents, allows contradictions to coexist, and stages codes. It serves no ethic (even if we happen to find one in it).

This is not to say that there is no Sadean thinking, but it is a thinking-of-the-text: not a thinking about its explicit statements, or even about the assumptions behind them, but rather a thinking about their logic, that is, a thinking about their staging, with its conditions, organization, emphases, workings, and slips of the tongue. It is on this level that we find the unfeeling body, the realm of the tableau, accelerated time, the economy of consumption, the hatred of the contract, the symbolic aspect of excrement, the privilege of the woman as storyteller, and the rest. This is what is essayed and investigated, or what is failed; it is what allows us to see another Sade underneath the fantastic horror and the paranoia of the speeches. Odious and atrocious though Sade's world may be (and it certainly is), that says absolutely nothing about his thinking in the texts that describe its horror. The thinking-of-the-text must be sought in the signifying structure and nowhere else, even if it should happen (and it often can, as this book has shown) that explicit statements coincide with the signifying structure. This kind of thinking, played out in fiction and sketched out in fiction's logic, offers not theses but hypotheses, not affirmations but paradoxes, not certainties but questions. (Where literature in general and Sade in particular are concerned, we have Blanchot and Barthes to thank for clarifying this difference in what is at stake.) This means, again, that even if the text gives the impression of an author in league with his characters, this impression has to be taken as another fictional effect. Until the closing quotation marks have been set down, mimesis submits everything to the law of the simulacrum and makes every position indeterminate. When we solemnly demand that mimesis give an accounting of itself, we cause ourselves to be drawn involuntarily into the realm of mimesis — we take the stage, but in the role of the buffoon, as happens sometimes at the theater when a too-literal member of the audience joins in with the actors and talks back to them. On this point, Sade has not made our work easy, and one might almost think he is asking for these misreadings, which are due first of all to the considerable space occupied by the long speeches alternating with scenes, speeches that, placed end to end, could very well constitute something of a complete treatise on libertine thinking. In fact, however, through these apparent digressions, Sade is not only unhinging narrative form but corrupting it by systematically blurring the boundary between the discursive and the narrative. Or should we say that the manifest alternation of the two, taken to the point of ultimate refinement, is what constitutes the specifically Sadean narrative form? Or, again, are we dealing here only with a variation on the form of the philosophical tale, in which narrative is reduced to the function of illustrating a thesis? Add to this all the direct addresses to the reader, in introductions or in notes (whether these are meant to supply the reader with bibliographical references on the occasion of some development or to urge that he try some erotic procedure for himself), and it certainly has to be admitted that this narrative has the look of a theoretical construct, a didactic manual calling for real-world tests, a look intensified by the highly denotative and demetaphorized nature of the writing, by its refusal to give itself the trappings of a literary work. These texts, which do not "pose," seem to focus on the form of the message, on the relationship of transitivity, on the imminence of its verification. These elements, for all their disruption of the fictional artifact, elude our vigilance over the conventions that ensure distance from it. Admittedly, there is nothing easier than taking Sade "seriously" and thus passing judgment on him in the court of the referent.

It certainly must be said, however, that the Sadean text — as a fictional endeavor, whatever its theoretical or didactic appearance may be — is still a machine for simulation, one in which it would be futile to look for laws or demand the conditions of assertive univocality. The proliferation of speeches shows only that discourse, in its demonstrative and philosophical form, is itself onstage, and that it is subject to the unpredictable work of this machine that amasses the statements of discourse, places them into contradiction, revives them, proves them, and puts them to the test in narrative scenarios.

If historic causality and the urgencies of reality are suspended in this realm of the simulacrum, it is not because of some simple irresponsibility on the part of a fiction that would have everything, even the horrific, transformed into the aesthetic. Rather, it is because, through this disconnection/distortion, everything, and especially the worst, enters into the violence of a vision. Thus fiction disturbs the peace of those codes whose slow accommodations domesticate even what is intolerable; it exaggerates their possibilities and throws them off balance. Borges said that Kafka's strength lay in the creation of intolerable situations, and surely the same could be said of Sade. In this disfiguring excess, facets of the real show their true faces—which is why the only function of the text is their methodical exposure.

This exposure strikes, to begin with, at everything on which the claim to a logic of cohesion and consistency is based, everything that can be maintained only through the causality of succession and consequences—in other words, everything administered under the guarantee of non-contradiction. Fiction's work will be to dismantle the elements of this guarantee so as to bring them into indeterminate relationships, force opposites into an impossible coexistence, and remove all hope of any idea of finality. For Sade, then, mastery absorbs the signs of nonmastery, and the discourse of power is also the discourse of power's destruction, just as freedom postulates tyrannical systems, and desire is stirred by general equivalents but yields only to unexchangeable details. This staging makes history thinkable, revealing history's antagonistic extremes but remaining itself historically unthinkable, a practical impossibility. As a creature of writing, this staging is neither odious nor seductive. It allows us to read and see what it deforms, exaggerates, and places into contradiction.

It can be said that the fictional order's right to contradiction has always been recognized, and that it is inscribed in fiction's principle of exemption, even of immunity: from Aristotle to Boileau, every *ars poetica* has reminded us that the enunciations of mimesis know no bounds. Everything can be said, on one condition: that a work of art is being made—that is, that the canons of art are being respected. But this limitlessness is itself quite limited: the aesthetic pact has the same form as the ethical pact. The speakable is always returned to the order of law. Tyranny, crime, theft, and desire can be represented on condition of being punished or redeemed. And this is where Sade the troublemaker pretends to have misunderstood. He seizes on the formal right to say everything, removes it from the pact that restrains its exercise, and, presenting crime, vice, and injustice in a favorable light and cruising the outer limits of the tolerable, attempts the unprecedented feat of seeing how far literature can go in what it says. Thus he puts literature to its greatest test, forcing it to welcome into its realm precisely what, in exchange for the reward of having its rights recognized, it prohibits itself from naming or narrating. Right here is where Sade's cruelty should be seen, in this injury to that pact; the corporal cruelty described by his texts is produced for no other reason than to signify this injury. Sade is testing not just the limits of fiction but also, and above all, the threshold of tolerance of the established order that has marked those limits out. In both cases, what he strikes at is the form of the social bond, the order of the symbolic as the unity of language and all its codes (literary, political, theoretical, and so forth). This is the only thing that Sade ever mistreated, but he went at it as an implacable, meticulous torturer.

And it is, after all, in the nature of things that the established political and literary orders avenged themselves; their fundamental collusion of interests and their similarity of structure could not be clearer, as Sade well knew. The extreme tension of his writing comes from its being a writing in a state of war: he is always writing *against*, which is also why readings of Sade are almost inevitably so polemical. But when these readings take Sade for a pioneer of sexual or anarchic liberation, or for a theoretician of fantastic acts of madness, they make the mistake of falling into the very trap set for Sade's opponents. Sade frees us from nothing if not from the limits of the speakable and from the power of codes to intimidate. He cures us (if violently) of nothing if not of this ancestral fear. And something happens, surely in and by means of this shock treatment, something that radically breaks through the enclosure of the text and the petty sexual pleasures of the signifier, for, in the same operation, the same movement, Sade tests the limits of both fiction and reason. In the case of fiction, he abuses a right, to the point of completely altering the nature of the institution that has conferred it. In the case of reason, he accelerates a logic, to the point of speeding this logic to its monstrous conclusion. Each of these two types of excess is echoed and reproduced in the other. Together they weave that ravening, inflexible knot in which the thinking-of-the-text takes shape, the extremity of both its energy and its humor. One type of excess prods literature into becoming a paroxysmal device; the other produces a panicky, stupefied acceleration of reason, to the point where reason takes shape as the psychosis of history. It is as if the knot formed by these two movements were closing over an empty space, over what subsists between the play or game of the text (its will to simulacrum) and what is at stake in the text (its will to action). Perhaps here—between these two extremities, where the Sadean text takes its stand, in this gap that is still presented— is where the rumors, which mythicize this text's themes, and the readings, which rehash its meaning, have their common point of entry. But perhaps here is also where there persists something that gives voice to rumor and reading alike: the debt, which is also to say the misunderstanding, or the intensity, of the name, the name *Sade*.

Notes

Preface

1. This is what Roger Shattuck suggests in *Forbidden Knowledge: From Prometheus to Pornography*, where he writes, in all seriousness, "We should label his writings carefully: potential poison, polluting to our moral and intellectual environment" (p. 299). Here is what the prefect of the Paris police had to say about Sade in the *Journal des Arts et de la Littérature*, on page 114 of the issue dated August 19, 1800: "Far be it from us to slander the Arts or the current state of our civilization; but can one possibly hold oneself back from reflecting at times on how greatly the Arts, to which the most virtuous souls owe the sweetest and perhaps surest pleasures, augment the power of evil men and give them the means of becoming harmful to society?"

Aftermath I

1. [The term *grand seigneur libertin* is used by Molière to describe Don Juan. — *Trans.*]
2. [The lettre de cachet was an instrument for invoking the royal power to imprison without trial. — *Trans.*]
3. ["J'ai bien lu je n'ai rien vu."]
4. [Charles Nodier (1780–1844), novelist and short-story writer, whose tales of the fantastic were precursors of Surrealism and whose gatherings at the Bibliothèque de l'Arsenal brought together a variety of Romantic writers. — *Trans.*]
5. [Johann Heinrich Füssli (also called Henry Fuseli), an eighteenth-century Swiss painter whose *The Nightmare* was seen and commented on by Thomas De Quincey. — *Trans.*]
6. Marquis de Sade, "The Author of *Les Crimes de l'amour* to Villeterque, Hack Writer," in *The 120 Days of Sodom and Other Writings* (rev. ed.), trans. Austryn Wainhouse and Richard Seaver (New York: Grove Press, 1987), pp. 127–28.

7. ["Sade souille la langue classique, il l'éclabousse des immondices de la rue et même du trottoir": the word *trottoir* (sidewalk) carries the connotation of prostitution in French, as in the idiom *faire le trottoir,* to be a prostitute. — *Trans.*]

8. [The French edition uses the English word *parties,* which in that context carries the same ironic connotation of elegance as does the French term used in this one. — *Trans.*]

9. Jorge Luis Borges, *A Universal History of Infamy,* trans. Norman Thomas di Giovanni (New York: Dutton, 1972), p. 11.

10. It is not my intention here to retrace in any detail the history of the concept of libertinism from its appearance at the beginning of the seventeenth century, when it designated a movement of intellectual resistance and dissidence with respect to imposed religious dogma, to its transformation in the first half of the eighteenth century into a materialist and sensualist philosophical current and, finally, to its having come to designate, toward the end of that century, a generalized practice of debauchery, but one that was still structured philosophically on the rejection of religious and moral principles. Sade's texts stage the third phase of libertinism, and that is what will be our topic here. Littré, in an article whose French title is "Libertinage," condensed the history of the concept of libertinism down to the following two definitions: "the license of the spirit that rejects religious beliefs" and "the state of one whose morals are dissolute." On this question in general, see Robert Mauzi, *L'Idée du bonheur au XVIIIᵉ siècle* (Paris: Armand Colin, 1960); Péter Nagy, *Libertinage et révolution* (Paris: Gallimard/Idées, 1975); and Gerhard Schneider, *Der Libertin* (Stuttgart: Metzler, 1970).

11. [The term *corps libertin,* "libertine body," can also mean "the body of libertines" or "the libertine corps"; compare remarks under the heading "Mechanical Reduction," in chapter 1. — *Trans.*]

1. The Overthrow of the Lyric Body

1. Antoine-François Prévost, *Manon Lescaut* (New York: Boni and Liveright, 1919), p. 201.

2. Jean-Jacques Rousseau, *La Nouvelle Héloïse* (Paris: La Pléiade, 1964), Part 1, letter 1.

3. Marquis de Sade, *Juliette* (rev. ed.), trans. Austryn Wainhouse (New York: Grove Press, 1988), p. 1193.

4. [Mathesis: "the science of calculable order"; see Michel Foucault, *The Order of Things: An Archaeology of the Human Sciences* (New York: Vintage Books, 1994), p. 71. — *Trans.*]

5. Alain Robbe-Grillet, "Préface," in Marquis de Sade, *La Nouvelle Justine,* ed. Jean-Jacques Pauvert.

6. Marquis de Sade, *The 120 Days of Sodom and Other Writings* (rev. ed.), trans. Austryn Wainhouse and Richard Seaver (New York: Grove Press, 1987), p. 200.

7. Sade, *Juliette,* p. 267.

8. ["une éthique du vouloir-dire": The phrase has connotations beyond "an ethic of meaning." — *Trans.*]

9. Marquis de Sade, *Œuvres complètes* 6 (Paris: Cercle du Livre Précieux, 1966–67), p. 263.

10. [Julien Offray de La Mettrie (1709–1751), French physician and materialist philosopher. — *Trans.*]

11. Marquis de Sade, *Justine*, in *Justine, Philosophy in the Bedroom, and Other Writings* (rev. ed.), trans. Richard Seaver and Austryn Wainhouse (New York: Grove Press, 1990), pp. 46–47.

12. Julien Offray de La Mettrie, *L'Homme-Machine*, p. 3. [Available in various English-language editions as *Man a Machine* or *Machine Man*; the author cites the edition published at Potsdam, 1750. — *Trans.*]

13. Sade, *120 Days*, p. 233.

14. [French *foutre*, used as a verb, means "to fuck"; used as a noun, it means "sperm" — or, given the French term's vulgarity, it means what is meant in English by the noun "come." The translators of the Grove Press editions of Sade's works rendered the noun *foutre* as "fuck," a translation that the author of the present volume has chosen to correct. Therefore, in passages quoted here from those editions, the noun "come" has been substituted for the noun "fuck" in all cases where Sade's translators used "fuck" as a synonym for "sperm." — *Trans.*]

15. Sade, *Juliette*, p. 24 [translation slightly modified].

16. Sade, *120 Days*, p. 443.

17. Sade, *Juliette*, p. 428.

18. Ibid., p. 1124.

19. [Jacques de Vaucanson (1709–82), mechanic and creator of famous automatons, among them *Joueur de flûte traversière* (The flute player) and *Canard* (The duck). — *Trans.*]

20. [Joseph-Marie Jacquard (1752–1834), mechanic and inventor of the Jacquard loom. — *Trans.*]

21. [A method for increasing production on the basis of the worker's initiative; named for its inventor, Alexei G. Stakhanov, the Russian miner who invented this method around 1935 in the mines of Donetsk. — *Trans.*]

22. [The phrase "bachelor machine" refers to a work by Marcel Duchamp, *Large Glass*, which depicts unbuildable objects. — *Trans.*]

23. ["corps-meubles": It is perhaps noteworthy that the word *meuble*, used as a noun, means in the broadest sense a movable piece of property, and, used as an adjective, describes earth or soil as loose, soft, and easily broken up. — *Trans.*]

24. Sade, *Juliette*, p. 584.

25. [Here, *le meuble* is a paradoxical play on words. As a noun, *meuble(s)* means "movables" or "furniture"; as a singular adjective, *meuble* means "loose" or "soft" (see note 23). As a plural adjective modifying the noun *biens* (goods), it can connote both "personal estate" and "personality." — *Trans.*]

26. Marquis de Sade, *Philosophy in the Bedroom* (rev. ed.), trans. Richard Seaver and Austryn Wainhouse (New York: Grove Press, 1990), p. 271.

27. Sade, *Juliette*, p. 425.

28. Ibid., p. 581.

29. Ibid., p. 897.

30. ["Une grande jouissance ce n'est pas le choc d'une séduction et d'un accord longtemps attendus, préparés et finalement consommés, c'est le nombre de 'décharges' réalisés en un lieu donné, dans un temps limité." The French text contains a play on the words *choc*, as in *choc électrique*, and *décharge*, which in English can mean a discharge or unloading of electrical energy. — *Trans.*]

31. Sade, *Juliette*, p. 488.

32. Ibid., pp. 488–89.

33. Ibid., p. 1002.

34. Ibid., p. 573.

35. Ibid., p. 1012.

36. Sade, *120 Days*, p. 672.

37. Sade, *Juliette*, pp. 8, 26.

38. Ibid., pp. 160–61; emphasis added.

39. Sade, *120 Days*, p. 254.

40. Gottfried Wilhelm Leibniz, *De Ipsa Natura*, sec. 13.

41. Ibid.

42. Gottfried Wilhelm Leibniz, *Discours de Métaphysique*, sec. 9. [Available in various English-language editions as *Discourse on Metaphysics.* — *Trans.*]

43. Gottfried Wilhelm Leibniz, *Monadologie*, sec. 12. [Available in various English-language editions as *The Monadology.* — *Trans.*]

44. Sade, *120 Days*, p. 271; emphasis added.

45. Ibid., p. 233.

46. Leibniz, *Monadologie*, secs. 1–7.

47. ["... donc gratifie les *chances* du désir (entendons-le au sens statistique des théories du jeu)." — *Trans.*]

48. Roland Barthes, *Sade, Fourier, Loyola*, trans. Richard Miller (New York: Hill and Wang), 1976.

49. [David Hilbert (1862–1943), German mathematician and logician. — *Trans.*]

50. Sade, *Juliette*, pp. 139, 413–14, 456.

51. "The addition of pleasures provides a supplementary pleasure, that of the addition itself; ... This superior pleasure, completely formal, since it is in sum only a mathematical notion, is a language pleasure: that of unfolding a criminal act into different nouns." Barthes, *Sade, Fourier, Loyola*, p. 157.

52. *Juliette*, p. 137.

53. Ibid., p. 266; emphasis in original.

54. Sade, *120 Days*, p. 334.

55. Sade, *Juliette*, p. 1175.

56. *Julienne* had already existed in this book for some time when I learned with pleasure about the arrival of her twin sister: Noëlle Chatelet's "Juline," whose story is found in the issue of *Obliques* (nos. 12–13 [1977]) devoted to Sade.

57. This hint of disrepute affecting conventionalist theories of the sign is probably what drove a number of eighteenth-century grammarians and linguists to seek, by way of a mimetic theory, a more secure foundation for the sign; hence the return to Cratylism analyzed by Gérard Genette in *Mimologics*, trans. Thaïs E. Morgan (Lincoln: University of Nebraska Press, 1995).

58. Sade, *Juliette*, p. 5; emphasis added.

59. Ibid., p. 56; emphasis added.

60. Ibid., p. 420; emphasis added.

61. Ibid., p. 428; emphasis added.

62. Ibid., pp. 482–83.

63. Ibid., p. 649.

64. ["la nécessité de remplir le programme du parcours des corps": the translation of *parcourir* leads, in English, to an ironic pun, which, if not present in the French original, is also not in conflict with the spirit of that text. — *Trans.*]

65. Barthes, *Sade, Fourier, Loyola*, p. 158.

66. There is much more to say about the critical torment that Sade inflicts on metaphor; the approach begun by Roger is instructive. See Philippe Roger, *Sade, la philosophie dans le pressoir* (Paris: Grasset, 1976), especially the chapter titled "La guerre des tropes."

2. Saying Everything, or the Encyclopedia of Excess

1. Marquis de Sade, *The 120 Days of Sodom and Other Writings* (rev. ed.), trans. Austryn Wainhouse and Richard Seaver (New York: Grove Press, 1987), p. 254 [translation slightly modified].

2. Ibid., pp. 254–55.

3. Ibid., p. 255.

4. Ibid., p. 193.

5. Ibid., p. 194.

6. Ibid., p. 197.

7. Ibid., p. 196.

8. Ibid., p. 334.

9. Ibid., pp. 350–51.

10. Ibid., p. 345.

11. Ibid., p. 372.

12. Marquis de Sade, *Juliette* (rev. ed.), trans. Austryn Wainhouse (New York: Grove Press, 1988), p. 19.

13. A "violence of proofs," as Deleuze quite rightly says; see his *Présentation de Sacher-Masoch* (Paris: Éditions de Minuit, 1967).

14. Sade, *120 Days*, p. 218.

15. G. W. F. Hegel, *L'Esthétique*, vol. 1, p. 63. [Available in various English-language editions as *Aesthetics*; the author cites the French translation by Jankélévitch. — *Trans.*]

16. Marquis de Sade, *Philosophy in the Bedroom*, in *Justine, Philosophy in the Bedroom, and Other Writings* (rev. ed.), trans. Richard Seaver and Austryn Wainhouse (New York: Grove Press, 1990), p. 199.

17. Sade, *Juliette*, p. 147.

18. Ibid., p. 54.

19. Sade, *Philosophy in the Bedroom*, p. 272 [translation slightly modified].

20. Sade, *Juliette*, p. 219.

21. Ibid., p. 312.

22. Sigmund Freud, *Totem and Taboo: Some Points of Agreement between the Mental Lives of Savages and Neurotics*, trans. James Strachey (New York: Norton, 1950).

23. See René Girard, *Violence and the Sacred*, trans. Patrick Gregory (Baltimore: Johns Hopkins University Press, 1977); Julia Kristeva, *The Revolution in Poetic Language*, trans. Margaret Waller (New York: Columbia University Press, 1984).

24. Marcel Mauss, *Œuvres complètes* 1 (Paris: Éditions de Minuit, 1968).

25. Sade, *120 Days*, pp. 253–54.

26. Sade, *Juliette*, p. 296.

27. Sigmund Freud, *Psychoanalysis and Faith: The Letters of Sigmund Freud and Oskar Pfister*, trans. Eric Mosbacher (New York: Basic Books, 1963), p. 38; emphasis added.

28. Sigmund Freud, *Jokes and Their Relation to the Unconscious,* in *Introductory Lectures on Psychoanalysis,* trans. James Strachey (New York: Norton, 1977), pp. 452–53.

29. Luce Irigaray, "Le sexe fait 'comme' signe," *Langages* 17 (1970): 42.

30. Sade, *120 Days,* p. 364.

31. Sade, *Juliette,* p. 744.

32. Sade, *120 Days,* p. 514.

33. Ibid., p. 525.

34. ["C'est le lieu du *reste* [remains], c'est-à-dire où tout le reste [all the rest, everything else] a lieu" (an untranslatable pun on the word *reste*). — *Trans.*]

35. Georges Bataille, *Death and Sensuality: A Study of Eroticism and the Taboo* (New York: Walker, 1962), p. 189.

36. ["Que *reste*-t-il à dire?": again, a pun on *reste,* which means "remains" as both noun and verb; author's emphasis. — *Trans.*]

37. Sade, *Juliette,* p. 525.

3. Libertine Apathy, or the Pleasures of Methodology

1. Marquis de Sade, *Juliette* (rev. ed.), trans. Austryn Wainhouse (New York: Grove Press, 1988), p. 309.

2. Ibid., p. 310.

3. Maurice Blanchot, *Lautréamont et Sade,* cited in Georges Bataille, *Death and Sensuality: A Study of Eroticism and the Taboo* (New York: Walker, 1962), p. 172.

4. Sade, *Juliette,* pp. 640–41 [translation slightly modified].

5. It may be useful to recall that Sade spent four years (between the ages of eleven and fifteen) as a student of the Jesuits at Louis-le-Grand and that he was probably required, like all students of his era in establishments run by the Society of Jesus, to engage in regular meditation and in the practices of Ignatian retreat.

6. Whereas Barthes treats each of these three "logothetes" (Sade, Fourier, and Loyola) separately, I thought it would be interesting to examine the intersection of the two who are thematically most unlike each other. [See Roland Barthes, *Sade, Fourier, Loyola,* trans. Richard Miller (New York: Hill and Wang, 1976). — *Trans.*]

7. Ibid., p. 51.

8. [The author, without explicitly naming his source, cites Ignatius of Loyola's *Spiritual Exercises,* available in various English-language editions. A recent one, translated with introductions and notes by Joseph A. Munitiz and Philip Endean, is *Personal Writings: Reminiscences, Spiritual Diary, Select Letters, Including the Text of the "Spiritual Exercises"* (New York: Penguin Books, 1996). — *Trans.*]

9. Sade, *Juliette,* pp. 640–41; emphasis added [translation slightly modified].

10. Blanchot, *Lautréamont et Sade,* cited in Bataille, *Death and Sensuality,* p. 172.

11. Sade, *Juliette,* p. 744.

12. Ibid., p. 509.

13. Ibid., p. 459.

14. Paul Henri, Thiry, baron d'Holbach, *Le christianisme dévoilé* p. 131. [Available in various English-language editions as *Christianity Unveiled*; the author cites the edition published by Éditions Sociales. — *Trans.*]

15. Jean-Jacques Rousseau, *Discourse on the Origin of Inequality* (New York: Simon and Schuster, 1967), pp. 202, 201.

16. Ibid., p. 203.

17. Sade, *Juliette*, p. 888.

18. Ibid., p. 702.

19. Ibid., p. 666.

20. Ibid., p. 710.

21. Marquis de Sade, *The 120 Days of Sodom and Other Writings* (rev. ed.), trans. Austryn Wainhouse and Richard Seaver (New York: Grove Press, 1987), p. 364.

22. Sade, *Juliette*, pp. 1038, 1045.

4. The Imaginable and the Space of the Tableau

1. Marquis de Sade, *Juliette* (rev. ed.), trans. Austryn Wainhouse (New York: Grove Press, 1988), pp. 160, 224.

2. [The author's play on this secondary meaning of *tableau* does not yield completely to translation. — *Trans.*]

3. Marquis de Sade, *The 120 Days of Sodom and Other Writings* (rev. ed.), trans. Austryn Wainhouse and Richard Seaver (New York: Grove Press, 1987), p. 465.

4. Sade, *Juliette*, pp. 221–22.

5. Michel Foucault, *The Order of Things: An Archaeology of the Human Sciences* (New York: Vintage Books, 1994), p. 131.

6. Ibid., pp. 132, 133.

7. Ibid., pp. 130, 157.

8. Ibid., p. 1009.

9. Ibid., p. 442.

10. The allusion here is to Bentham's Panopticon (1791), the device for surveillance and disciplinary control that was so well analyzed by Foucault in *Discipline and Punish: The Birth of the Prison*, and whose chief feature was to ensure the omnipresence of a nonreciprocal looking (seeing without being seen). Panopticism, which has a policing function for Bentham, becomes erotic for Sade simply through the elimination of a unique center of vision, and through the distribution of each body's pleasured looking over all the other bodies.

11. Sade, *Juliette*, pp. 138, 662–63.

12. Ibid., p. 7.

13. [Marc Antoine Girard de Saint-Amant (1594–1661); Jean de Sponde (1557–95); Tristan L'Hermite (1601–55); Théophile de Viau (1590–1626); Honoré d'Urfé (1567–1625). — *Trans.*]

14. Gérard Genette, *Figures* 1 (Paris: Éditions du Seuil, 1966), pp. 21–28. It should also be noted that a text by Tristan L'Hermite has the title *Le miroir enchanté.*

15. Ibid., p. 24.

16. Ibid., p. 25.

17. Roland Barthes, *Sade, Fourier, Loyola*, trans. Richard Miller (New York: Hill and Wang, 1976), pp. 128–29 [translation slightly modified].

18. Marquis de Sade, *Justine, Philosophy in the Bedroom, and Other Writings* (rev. ed.), trans. Richard Seaver and Austryn Wainhouse (New York: Grove Press, 1990), pp. 202–3.

19. Michel Tort, "L'effet Sade," *Tel Quel*, no. 28 (1967). [The term *Sade effect*, of course, reproduces the syntax of the term *Doppler effect*, but the reader will also note the serendipitous pun on the term *side effect.* — *Trans.*]

20. Sade, *120 Days,* p. 254 [translation slightly modified].

21. Barthes, *Sade, Fourier, Loyola,* p. 31 [translation slightly modified].

22. An allusion to Leibniz, of course, for whom a Characteristic would be the combinatory ordering of nonmathematical signs.

23. Hubert Damisch, "L'écriture sans mesure," *Tel Quel,* no. 28 (1967).

24. Maurice Blanchot, "La raison de Sade," in *Lautréamont et Sade* (Paris: Éditions de Minuit, 1949).

25. Gilles Deleuze, *Présentation de Sacher-Masoch* (Paris: Éditions de Minuit, 1967).

5. Time Cut to Measure

1. G. W. F. Hegel, *Encyclopédie des sciences philosophiques en abrégé* (Paris: Gallimard, 1970), sec. 257. [A recent English-language edition is *Encyclopedia of the Philosophical Sciences in Outline and Critical Writings* (German Library, vol. 24), ed. Ernst Behler (Continuum, 1991). — *Trans.*]

2. Ibid., sec. 145.

3. Immanuel Kant, *Critique de la raison pure* (Paris: Presses Universitaires de France, 1968). [Available in various English-language editions as *Critique of Pure Reason,* a work that includes *The Transcendental Aesthetic.* — *Trans.*]

4. Marquis de Sade, letters to Mademoiselle Colet, in Maurice Lever, *Sade: A Biography,* trans. Arthur Goldhammer (New York: Harcourt Brace, 1994), pp. 126–28.

5. Marquis de Sade, *Œuvres complètes* 12 (Paris: Cercle du Livre Précieux, 1966–67), p. 21; emphasis added.

6. Marquis de Sade, *Juliette* (rev. ed.), trans. Austryn Wainhouse (New York: Grove Press, 1988), p. 1014; emphasis added.

7. Ibid., p. 1011.

8. Ibid., p. 64.

9. Jean-Jacques Rousseau, *Émile* (Paris: La Pléiade), p. 447.

10. Marquis de Sade, *Philosophy in the Bedroom,* in *Justine, Philosophy in the Bedroom, and Other Writings* (rev. ed.), trans. Richard Seaver and Austryn Wainhouse (New York: Grove Press, 1990), p. 316.

11. Sade, *Juliette,* p. 63 n. 5.

12. Claude Lévi-Strauss, *The Elementary Structures of Kinship,* trans. James Harle Bell, John Richard von Strauss, and Rodney Needham (Boston: Beacon Press, 1969), p. 51.

13. Sade, *Juliette,* p. 440.

14. Sade, "Eugénie de Franval," in *Justine, Philosophy in the Bedroom and Other Writings,* p. 394.

15. Sade, *Juliette,* p. 744.

16. Ibid., pp. 974–75.

17. Marquis de Sade, *The 120 Days of Sodom and Other Writings* (rev. ed.), trans. Austryn Wainhouse and Richard Seaver (New York: Grove Press, 1987), p. 585; emphasis in original.

18. Sade, *Juliette,* p. 162.

19. Sade, *Philosophy in the Bedroom,* p. 263.

20. Sade, *Œuvres complètes* 6, p. 273.

21. Sade, *Juliette,* p. 649.

22. Ibid., p. 162.

23. Sade, *120 Days*, p. 585.

24. Karl Marx, *Capital* 1, trans. Samuel Moore and Edward Aveling (New York: International Publishers, 1967).

25. Ibid., pp. 39–40.

26. Sade, *120 Days*, p. 254.

27. Sade, *Juliette*, p. 609.

28. Ibid., p. 805.

29. [In French, of course, the second-person plural is used in polite, formal address. — *Trans.*]

6. The Libertine Mode of Nonproduction

1. Béatrice Didier, "Le château intérieur," in *Sade, une écriture du désir* (Paris: Gonthier, 1976).

2. Marquis de Sade, *The 120 Days of Sodom* (rev. ed.), trans. Austryn Wainhouse and Richard Seaver (New York: Grove Press, 1966), pp. 240–41.

3. Ibid., p. 251.

4. Karl Marx and Friedrich Engels, *L'idéologie allemande*, p. 101. [Available in English as *The German Ideology* (London: Lawrence & Wishart, 1938); the author cites the edition published by Éditions Sociales. — *Trans.*]

5. Marquis de Sade, *Œuvres complètes* 7 (Paris: Cercle du Livre Précieux, 1966–67), p. 22.

6. Soboul, "La Révolution française et la féodalité: le prélèvement féodal," in *Sur le féodalisme* (Paris: Éditions Sociales, 1974), p. 83.

7. Ibid., pp. 84–85.

8. Marquis de Sade, *Juliette* (rev. ed.), trans. Austryn Wainhouse (New York: Grove Press, 1968), p. 57.

9. Georges Bataille, *The Accursed Share: An Essay on General Economy*, vol. 1, *Consumption*, trans. Robert Hurley (New York: Zone Books, 1991), p. 108.

10. Georges Dumézil, *Jupiter, Mars, Quirinus*, vols. 1–3 (Paris: Gallimard, 1941–48); *Mythe et Épopée*, vols. 1–4 (Paris: Gallimard, 1968–73); *Mythes et dieux indo-européens*, vols. 1–4 (Paris: Flammarion, 1992); Georges Duby, *The Three Orders: Feudal Society Imagined*, trans. Arthur Goldhammer (Chicago: University of Chicago Press, 1980).

11. Roland Mousnier, *Progrès scientifique et technique au 18ᵉ siècle* (Paris: Plon, 1958); Jacques Proust, *Diderot et l'Encyclopédie* (Paris: Armand Colin, 1967); Fernand Braudel, *Civilization and Capitalism: 15th–18th Century* (New York: Harper and Row, 1982–84).

12. Gilbert Lély, *The Marquis de Sade: A Biography*, trans. Alec Brown (London: Elek Books, 1961); Maurice Lever, *Sade: A Biography*, trans. Arthur Goldhammer (New York: Farrar, Straus and Giroux, 1993).

13. "The extensive wars wherewith Louis XIV was burdened during his reign, while draining the State's treasury and exhausting the substance of the people, none the less contained the secret that led to the prosperity of a swarm of those bloodsuckers who are always on the watch for public calamities.... One must not suppose that it was exclusively the lowborn and vulgar sort which did this swindling; gentlemen of the highest note led the pack" (Sade, *120 Days*, p. 191).

306 Notes to Chapter 6

14. Ibid., p. 194.

15. Sade, *Juliette*, p. 419.

16. Karl Marx, *Capital* 1, trans. Samuel Moore and Edward Aveling (New York: International Publishers, 1967), p. 336.

17. Pierre Klossowski, in *La monnaie vivante*, stresses the importance of the exploitation that, in the last analysis, underlies libertine activity; see also Jean-François Lyotard's commentaries in *Économie libidinale*, pp. 105–7.

18. Sade, *Juliette*, p. 941.

19. Ibid., p. 952.

20. Ibid., p. 999.

21. Marx, *Capital*, p. 396.

22. Ibid., p. 397. [Marx is citing the third report, published in London in 1864, made by the Children's Employment Commission (p. 53 n. 15). — *Trans.*]

23. Ibid. p. 397.

24. Ibid., pp. 399, 395.

25. Michel Foucault, *Discipline and Punish: The Birth of the Prison*, trans. Alan Sheridan (New York: Vintage Books, 1995).

26. Ibid., p. 150.

27. Marx, *Capital*, p. 186.

28. Foucault, *Discipline and Punish*, pp. 150–51.

29. Sade, *120 Days*, p. 248.

30. Foucault, *Discipline and Punish*, pp. 139–40.

31. Sade, *120 Days*, p. 242.

32. Foucault, *Discipline and Punish*, p. 146.

33. Ibid., p. 148.

34. Marx, *Capital*, pp. 423–24.

35. Foucault, *Discipline and Punish*, pp. 141–42.

36. Sade, *120 Days*, p. 240.

37. Sade, *Justine*, in *Justine, Philosophy in the Bedroom, and Other Writings* (rev. ed.), trans. Richard Seaver and Austryn Wainhouse (New York: Grove Press, 1965), pp. 580–81.

38. Foucault, *Discipline and Punish*, p. 171.

39. Ibid., pp. 178–79.

40. Sade, *Justine*, p. 582.

41. Sade, *Œuvres complètes* 6, p. 362n.

42. Cf. F. Guerry, *Le corps productif* (Paris: Mame, 1972).

43. Marx, *Capital*, pp. 331–32.

44. Sade, *120 Days*, p. 585.

45. Roland Barthes, *Sade, Fourier, Loyola*, trans. Richard Miller (New York: Hill and Wang, 1976), p. 125.

46. Sade, *Juliette*, p. 964.

47. Ibid., pp. 974–75.

48. Marx, *Capital*, p. 345.

49. Ibid., p. 350.

50. Marx, *Capital*, p. 381.

51. Sade, *Juliette*, p. 963.

52. Ibid., p. 965.

53. Marcel Mauss, *Gift: Forms and Functions of Exchange in Archaic Societies* (New York: Norton, 1967).

54. Bataille, *The Accursed Share*, pp. 69–70.

55. Thorstein Veblen, *The Theory of the Leisure Class* (New York: New American Library, 1953), p. 40.

56. Bataille, *The Accursed Share*, pp. 72–73; emphasis in original.

57. Veblen, *The Theory of the Leisure Class*, p. 41.

58. Ibid., pp. 42, 43, 46.

59. Ibid., p. 48.

60. Sade, *Juliette*, p. 1161.

61. Voltaire (François-Marie Arouet), "Égalité," in the *Dictionnaire philosophique* (Paris: Klincksieck, 1994). [Available in English as *Voltaire's Philosophical Dictionary* (New York: Knopf, 1924).— *Trans.*]

62. Paul Henri Thiry, baron d'Holbach, *La politique naturelle*, ed. G. Olms (New York: Hildesheim, 1971), discourse 1.

63. Beausobre, *Essai sur le bonheur*, p. 25, cited, along with many other examples, by Robert Mauzi in chapter 4 ("Bonheur et condition sociale") of *L'Idée du bonheur au XVIIIᵉ siècle* (Paris: Armand Colin, 1960), p. 175.

64. Severo Sarduy, *Barroco* (Paris: Éditions du Seuil, 1974).

7. The Expenditures of the Body

1. Marquis de Sade, *Œuvres complètes* 10 (Paris: Cercle du Livre Précieux, 1966–67), p. 150.

2. Marquis de Sade, *The 120 Days of Sodom and Other Writings* (rev. ed.), trans. Austryn Wainhouse and Richard Seaver (New York: Grove Press, 1987), p. 474 [translation slightly modified].

3. Ibid., p. 330.

4. Ibid., p. 465.

5. Ibid., p. 507.

6. Ibid., pp. 361–62.

7. Marquis de Sade, *Juliette* (rev. ed.), trans. Austryn Wainhouse (New York: Grove Press, 1988), p. 761.

8. J.-J. Goux, "Calcul des jouissances," in *Les Jouissances* (Paris: Éditions du Seuil, 1978), p. 180. (I will return to other aspects of this very relevant study.)

9. Roland Barthes, *Sade, Fourier, Loyola*, trans. Richard Miller (New York: Hill and Wang, 1976), p. 124 [translation slightly modified].

10. Sade, *Juliette*, p. 8.

11. Ibid., p. 1009.

12. Ibid., p. 922 [translation slightly modified].

13. Ibid., p. 940.

14. Ibid., p. 586.

15. Gilbert Lély, *The Marquis de Sade: A Biography*, trans. Alec Brown (London: Elek Books, 1961), pp. 306–7; emphasis added.

16. Ibid., p. 307.

17. Sergio Finzi, "Le père anal," in *Psychanalyse et politique* (Paris: Éditions du Seuil, 1975).

18. Sigmund Freud, *Civilization and Its Discontents*, trans. James Strachey (New York: Norton, 1962), 47n.

19. Melanie Klein, *The Writings of Melanie Klein*, vol. 2, *The Psycho-Analysis of Children* (New York: Free Press, 1984).

20. Sigmund Freud, *Three Essays on the Theory of Sexuality*, trans. and rev. James Strachey (New York: Basic Books, 1982).

21. Sigmund Freud, "Character and Anal Erotism," in *Character and Culture*, ed. Philip Rieff, trans. R. C. McWatters (New York: Collier Books, 1963), p. 30.

22. On this whole question, see Mikhail Bakhtiu, *Rabelais and His World*, trans. Helene Iswolsky (Bloomington: Indiana University Press, 1988).

23. Jean A. Chérasse and Geneviève Guicheney, *Sade, j'écris ton nom Liberté* (Paris: Pygmalion, 1976).

24. Sade, *Juliette*, p. 1051.

25. Sade, *120 Days*, p. 433.

26. Ibid., p. 510.

27. Sade, *Juliette*, p. 218.

28. Ibid., p. 163.

29. Ibid., p. 587.

30. Sade, *120 Days*, p. 393.

31. Freud, *Three Essays*, pp. 39–72.

32. Freud, "Character and Anal Erotism," pp. 27–33.

33. Freud, *Three Essays*, p. 51.

34. Ibid., p. 53n.

35. Ibid., p. 52.

36. Freud, "Character and Anal Erotism," p. 28.

37. Ibid., p. 32.

38. Daniel Schreber, *Memoirs of My Nervous Illness* (Cambridge: Harvard University Press, 1988).

39. Finzi, "Le père anal."

40. Sade, *120 Days*, p. 372.

41. Ibid., p. 461.

42. Ibid., p. 394.

43. Ibid., pp. 471–72.

44. Georges Bataille, *Documents*, in *Œuvres complètes* 1 (Paris: Gallimard, 1970), p. 200.

45. Gilles Deleuze and Félix Guattari, *Anti-Oedipus: Capitalism and Schizophrenia*, trans. Robert Hurley, Mark Seem, and Helen R. Lane (Minneapolis: University of Minnesota Press, 1983), chapter 2.

46. Goux, "Calcul des jouissances," pp. 208, 210.

47. See chapter 1, note 22.

8. Noncontractual Exchange

1. Jean Imbert, *Le droit antique* (Paris: Presses Universitaires de France, 1961), p. 112.

2. Albert O. Hirschmann, *The Passions and the Interests: Political Arguments for Capitalism before Its Triumph* (Princeton, N.J.: Princeton University Press, 1996).

3. John Locke, *Of Civil Government, Second Treatise* (Chicago: Gateway Editions, [1689] 1971), p. 78: "Men being by nature all free, equal, and independent, no one can be put out of this estate [that is, man's natural estate], and subjected to the political power of another, without his own consent"; Jean-Jacques Rousseau, *On*

the Social Contract, book 4, chapter 2 (Indianapolis, Ind.: Hackett, [1762] 1987), p. 81: "For civil association is the most voluntary act in the world. Since every man is born free and master of himself, no one can, under any pretext whatever, place another under subjection without his consent."

4. Gilles Deleuze, in *Présentation de Sacher-Masoch* (Paris: Éditions de Minuit, 1967), quite aptly says of Sade that "his hostility toward the contract, toward any recourse to the contract, and toward any idea or theory of the contract, knows no bounds. All of Sadean derision is brought to bear on the theory of the contract." The contract, as Deleuze notes, engenders the law, only to submit to it. This is why Sade opposes the institution to the contract, for the institution defines a field of action without creating bonds between individuals: "In Sade's dual opposition to the law and to the contract there is a profound political thinking: that of the revolutionary and republican institution."

5. For an analysis of this idea, see (in addition, of course, to the first volume of Marx's *Capital*) J.-J. Goux, *Symbolic Economies: After Marx and Freud*, trans. Jennifer Curtiss Gage (Ithaca, N.Y.: Cornell University Press, 1990); Jean Baudrillard, *For a Critique of the Political Economy of the Sign*, trans. Charles Levin (New York: Telos Press, 1980).

6. Marquis de Sade, *Juliette* (rev. ed.), trans. Austryn Wainhouse (New York: Grove Press, 1988), p. 114.

7. Thorstein Veblen, *The Theory of the Leisure Class* (New York: New American Library, 1953), p. 36.

8. Marquis de Sade, *Yet Another Effort, Frenchmen, If You Would Become Republicans*, interpolated work forming part of *Philosophy in the Bedroom*, in *Justine, Philosophy in the Bedroom, and Other Writings* (rev. ed.), trans. Richard Seaver and Austryn Wainhouse (New York: Grove Press, 1990), p. 313.

9. Ibid.

10. Ibid., p. 314.

11. Sade, *Juliette*, p. 1089.

12. Ibid., p. 1015.

13. Ibid.

14. Immanuel Kant, *Grounding for the Metaphysics of Morals, with On a Supposed Right to Lie Because of Philanthropic Concerns* (3d ed.), trans. James W. Ellington (Indianapolis, Ind.: Hackett, 1993), pp. 64–65. Kant himself quotes Constant's text in full.

15. Ibid., p. 64.

16. Ibid.

17. Ibid., p. 65. Indeed, Kant imagines someone lying to a murderer, unwittingly putting the murderer onto the victim's scent, and thereby becoming not merely a liar but an accessory to the crime!

18. Sade, *Juliette*, p. 480.

19. Ibid., p. 636.

20. Sade, *Philosophy in the Bedroom*, p. 312.

21. Sade, *Juliette*, p. 597.

22. As Kant says, still writing about truthfulness in *Grounding for the Metaphysics of Morals* (p. 65), "to be truthful in all declarations is . . . a sacred and unconditionally commanding law of reason that admits of no expediency whatsoever."

23. Sade, *Juliette*, p. 275.

24. Ibid., pp. 143–44; emphasis in original.

25. Kant's text moved Hegel to remark, in *Principles of the Philosophy of Right*, that Kant had established, in all its horror, the subsuming of marriage under the concept of the contract.

26. J.-M. Benoist, *La révolution structurale* (Paris: Grasset, 1975), p. 147.

27. Ibid., p. 31.

28. Claude Lévi-Strauss, *The Elementary Structures of Kinship*, trans. James Harle Bell, John Richard von Sturmer, and Rodney Needham (Boston: Beacon Press, 1969), p. 51.

29. Ibid., pp. 61–62.

30. Ibid., p. 84.

31. Sade, *Philosophy in the Bedroom*, pp. 276, 230.

32. Ibid., p. 248.

33. René Descartes, *Méditations métaphysiques* (Paris: Vrin, 1976), p. 74; emphasis added.

34. Friedrich Nietzsche, *The Genealogy of Morals*, trans. Francis Golffing (New York: Doubleday, 1956).

35. Ibid., p. 195.

36. Ibid., pp. 196–97.

37. Sade, *Juliette*, p. 743.

38. Ibid., p. 1038.

39. Ibid., pp. 296–97.

40. Sade, *Yet Another Effort, Frenchmen*, pp. 316–17.

41. Ibid., p. 321.

42. Ibid., p. 319.

43. Sade, *Juliette*, pp. 63–64.

44. Ibid., p. 418.

45. Ibid., p. 425.

46. Ibid.

47. Ibid., p. 420.

48. Ibid., p. 418.

49. Ibid., p. 419.

50. Ibid., p. 297.

51. Ibid., p. 493.

52. Sade, *Philosophy in the Bedroom*, p. 244.

9. Woman, Prostitution, Narrative

1. For more on this debate, see Georges May's provocative book *Le dilemme du roman au XVIIIe siècle*, particularly chapter 8, "Féminisme et roman" (Paris: Presses Universitaires de France, 1963).

2. Voltaire (François-Marie Arouet), *Essai sur la poésie épique*.

3. In May, *Le dilemme du roman*, p. 9.

4. Ibid., p. 8.

5. Diderot, *Éloge de Richardson*.

6. Choderlos de Laclos, *Œuvres complètes* (Paris: La Pléiade), p. 523.

7. May, *Le dilemme du roman*, chapter 3.
8. Voltaire, *La Gazette littéraire* (Paris: La Pléiade, 1964).
9. Jean-Jacques Rousseau, *La Nouvelle Héloïse* (Paris: La Pléiade, 1964), pp. 5, 6.
10. May, *Le dilemme du roman*, p. 207.
11. Ibid., p. 220.
12. Marquis de Sade, "Reflections on the Novel," in *The 120 Days of Sodom and Other Writings* (rev. ed.), trans. Austryn Wainhouse and Richard Seaver (New York: Grove Press, 1987), p. 103.
13. Roland Barthes, *S/Z: An Essay*, trans. Richard Miller (New York: Hill and Wang, 1974), p. 89.
14. Friedrich Engels, *L'origine de la famille, de la propriété privée et de l'État*, p. 65. [Available in various English-language editions as *The Origins of the Family, Private Property, and the State*; the author cites the edition published by Éditions Sociales. — *Trans.*].
15. Ibid., p. 74.
16. Claude Lévi-Strauss, *The Elementary Structures of Kinship*, trans. James Harle Bell, John Richard von Sturmer, and Rodney Needham (Boston: Beacon Press, 1969), p. 115.
17. See Claude Lévi-Strauss, *Structural Anthropology* (New York: Basic Books, 1974), chapter 3.
18. Marcel Mauss, *Essais de sociologie*, p. 137.
19. Jaulin, *Gens du soi, gens de l'autre*, pp. 419–520; for more details, see Jaulin's *La mort Sara* (Paris: 10/18, 1971).
20. Engels, *L'origine de la famille, de la propriété et de l'État*, p. 82.
21. It should be noted that in the seventeenth and eighteenth centuries, from Fénelon to Madame de Maintenon, and from Rousseau to Madame d'Épinay, the education of girls appeared to be a new problem simply because it had not even been raised until then, or at least if the problem had been raised, it was solved expediently through the self-evident "fact" that girls did not need to learn about anything other than their wifely and motherly duties. "Moralists" still perceived girls' access to knowledge in terms of the danger of denaturation or usurpation. The misogynist Rousseau did not help matters when, in *Émile*, he wrote of Sophie's education, "Where is the need for a girl's learning at an early age to read and write? Will she so quickly have a household to run? There are very few [women] who do not abuse this fatal science more than they use it." (For lack of anything better — that is, while we wait for a methodologically valid work — much more information can be found in Rousselot's *L'Histoire de l'éducation des femmes en France*, originally published in 1883 and reissued in New York in 1971 by Burt Franklin.) [The Burt Franklin edition was also in French. — *Trans.*]
22. ["It is certain, in a state of Nature, that women are born *vulgivagous*, that is to say, are born enjoying the advantages of other female animals and belonging, like them and without exception, to all males." Marquis de Sade, *Philosophy in the Bedroom*, in *Justine, Philosophy in the Bedroom, and Other Writings* (rev. ed.), trans. Richard Seaver and Austryn Wainhouse (New York: Grove Press, 1990), p. 318. — *Trans.*]
23. Marquis de Sade, *Juliette* (rev. ed.), trans. Austryn Wainhouse (New York: Grove Press, 1988), p. 663.
24. Ibid., p. 492.

25. Ibid., pp. 526–27.
26. Ibid., p. 447.
27. Ibid., p. 298.
28. See Luce Irigaray, *This Sex Which Is Not One* (Ithaca, N.Y.: Cornell University Press, 1985).
29. Sade, *Juliette,* p. 1189.
30. Ibid., p. 1193.
31. Sade, "Reflections on the Novel," p. 110.

Aftermath II

1. Michel Foucault, *The Order of Things: An Archaeology of the Human Sciences* (New York: Vintage Books, 1994), p. 224.

2. Marquis de Sade, *Yet Another Effort, Frenchmen, If You Would Become Republicans,* interpolated work forming part of *Philosophy in the Bedroom,* in *Justine, Philosophy in the Bedroom, and Other Writings* (rev. ed.), trans. Richard Seaver and Austryn Wainhouse (New York: Grove Press, 1990), p. 313.

3. Françoise Buisson, "Les bougres ou les derniers archanthropes," *Obliques,* nos. 12–13 (1977).

Selected Bibliography

Adorno, Theodor W., and Max Horkheimer. 1979. "Juliette or Enlightenment and Morality." In *Dialectic of Enlightenment*. London: Verso.

Airaksinen, Timo. 1995. *The Philosophy of the Marquis de Sade*. London and New York: Routledge.

Allison, David, Mark Roberts, and Allen Weiss, eds. 1995. *Sade and the Narrative of Transgression*. Cambridge: Cambridge University Press.

Apollinaire, Guillaume. 1909. *L'œuvre du Marquis de Sade. Introduction, essai bibliographique et notes*. Paris: Bibliothèque des curieux.

Barthes, Roland. 1976. *Sade, Fourier, Loyola*. Trans. Richard Miller. Berkeley: University of California Press [orig. Paris: Éditions du Seuil, 1971].

Bataille, Georges. 1973. "Sade." In *Literature and Evil*. Trans. Alastair Hamilton. London: Calder and Boyars.

————. 1986. "Sade's Sovereign Man." In *Erotism: Death and Sensuality*. Trans. Mary Delwood. San Francisco: City Lights Books.

Beauvoir, Simone de. 1953. *The Marquis de Sade: An Essay, with Selections from His Writings Chosen by Paul Dinnage*. New York: Grove Press. Contains the essay "Must We Burn Sade?"

Belaval, Yvon. 1947. "Sade le tragique." *Cahiers du Sud*, vol. 26, no. 285.

Blanchot, Maurice. 1963. "La raison de Sade." In *Sade et Lautréamont*. Paris: Éditions de Minuit.

Brochier, Jean-Jacques. 1966. *Sade et la conquête de l'unique*. Paris: Le Terrain Vague.

Carpenter, Scott. 1996. *Acts of Fiction: Resistance and Resolutions from Sade to Baudelaire*. Chapter 2, "Viral Fictions: Sade and the Pox of Libertinism." Philadelphia: University of Pennsylvania Press.

Carter, Angela. 1979. *The Sadean Woman: An Exercise in Cultural History*. London: Virago.

Chanover, Pierre. 1973. *The Marquis de Sade Bibliography*. Metuchen, N.J.: Scarecrow Press.

Chatelet, Noëlle. 1972. *Système de l'agression*. Paris: Aubier-Montaigne.

Crosland, Margaret. 1991. *The Passionate Philosopher: A Marquis de Sade Reader.* London: Peter Owen.

Damisch, Hubert. 1967. "L'écriture sans mesure." *Tel Quel,* no. 28 (winter).

DeJean, Joan. 1984. *Literary Fortifications: Rousseau, Laclos, Sade.* Princeton, N.J.: Princeton University Press.

Deleuze, Gilles. 1967. *Le froid et le cruel. Présentation de Sacher-Masoch.* Paris: Éditions de Minuit.

———. 1989. *Masochism: Coldness and Cruelty.* Trans. Jean McNeil. New York: Zone Books.

Delon, Michel. 1990. Introduction to *Sade's Œuvres complètes.* Paris: La Pléiade.

Didier, Béatrice. 1973. *Sade, une écriture du désir.* Paris: Gonthier.

Fauskevaag, Sven Erik. 1982. *Sade dans le surréalisme.* Oslo: Solum Forlag.

Fink, Béatrice. 1975. "Sade and Cannibalism." *Esprit Createur,* vol. 15, no. 4 (winter).

Foucault, Michel. 1967. *Madness and Civilization: History of Insanity in the Age of Reason.* Trans. Richard Howard. London: Tavistock.

———. 1994. *The Order of Things: An Archaeology of the Human Sciences.* New York: Vintage Books.

Frappier-Mazur, Lucienne. 1996. *Writing the Orgy: Power and Parody in Sade.* Philadelphia: University of Pennsylvania Press.

Gallop, Jane. 1981. *Intersections: A Reading of Sade with Bataille, Blanchot and Klossowski.* Lincoln: University of Nebraska Press.

Gorer, Geoffrey. 1934. *The Life and Ideas of the Marquis de Sade.* London: Peter Owen.

Harari, Josue. 1973. "Sade, Exogamy and Incest: Sade's Structures of Kinship." *MLN* 88: 1212–37.

———. 1987. *Scenarios of the Imaginary.* Ithaca, N.Y.: Cornell University Press.

Hayes, Julie. 1991. *Identity and Ideology: Diderot, Sade and the Serious Genre.* Chapter 4, "Sade." Philadelphia: John Benjamin Publications.

Hayman, Ronald. 1978. *De Sade: A Critical Biography.* New York: Crowell.

Heine, Maurice. 1930. *Le Marquis de Sade.* Paris.

Hénaff, Marcel. 1995. "Mechanization of the Libertine Body and the Crisis of Reason." In *Technology, Democracy, and the Politics of Knowledge,* ed. A. Feenberg and A. Hannay. Bloomington: Indiana University Press.

———. 1997. "Oedipus, Baroque Portrait with a Woman's Face." In *The Libertine Reader,* ed. M. Feher. New York: Zone Books. 1256–75.

———. 1998. "The Naked Terror." *Substance,* no. 86 (fall).

Huet, Marie-Hélène. 1997. *Mourning Glory: The Will of the French Revolution.* Philadelphia: University of Pennsylvania Press.

Hunt, Lynn. 1992. *The Family Romance of the French Revolution.* Berkeley: University of California Press.

———, ed. 1993. *The Invention of Pornography: Obscenity and the Origins of Modernity 1500–1800.* New York: Zone Books.

Klossowski, Pierre. 1947. *Sade mon prochain.* Paris: Éditions du Seuil. Trans. *Sade, My Neighbor.* Evanston, Ill.: Northwestern University Press, 1991.

Laborde, Alice. 1990. *Les Infortunes du Marquis de Sade.* Paris: Champion.

Lacan, Jacques. 1966. "Kant avec Sade." In *Écrits.* Paris: Éditions du Seuil.

Lacombe, Roger. 1974. *Sade et ses masques.* Paris: Payot.

Laugaa-Traut, Françoise. 1973. *Lectures de Sade.* Paris. Armand Colin.

Le Brun, Annie. 1990. *Sade: A Sudden Abyss.* San Francisco: City Lights Books.

Lefort, Claude. 1992. "Le Boudoir et la Cité." In *Écrire, à l'épreuve du politique.* Paris: Calman Levy.

Lély, Gilbert. 1962. *The Marquis de Sade: A Biography.* New York: Grove Press.

Le Marquis de Sade. Actes du colloque d'Aix. 1966. Paris: Armand Colin.

Lever, Maurice. 1993. *Sade: A Biography.* Trans. Arthur Goldhammer. New York: Farrar, Straus, and Giroux.

Mengue, Philippe. 1997. *L'Ordre sadien: loi et narration dans la philosophie de Sade.* Paris: Kimé.

Michael, Colette. 1986. *The Marquis d'Sade: The Man, His Work and His Critics: An Annotated Bibliography.* New York: Garland Publishing. *Obliques,* nos. 12–13 (1977).

Miller, Nancy K. 1995. *French Dressing: Women, Men, and Ancien Regime Fiction.* New York: Routledge.

Paulhan, Jean. 1951. *Le Marquis de Sade et sa complice.* Paris: Éditions Lilac.

Pauvert, Jean-Jacques. 1986–89. *Sade vivant.* Paris: Robert Laffont.

Praz, Mario. 1933. *The Romantic Agony.* London: Oxford University Press.

Reichler, Claude. 1987. *L'Âge libertin.* Paris: Éditions de Minuit.

Roger, Philippe. 1976. *Sade, la philosophie dans le pressoir.* Paris: Grasset.

Roger, Philippe, and Michel Camus, eds. 1983. *Sade: Écrire la crise.* Paris: Belfond.

Saint-Amand, Pierre. 1994. *The Libertine Progress: Seduction in the 18th Century French novel.* Trans. Jennifer Curtiss Gage. Hanover, N.H.: University Press of New England.

———. 1996. *The Laws of Hostility: Politics, Violence and the Enlightenment.* Trans. Jennifer Curtiss Gage. Minneapolis: University of Minnesota Press.

Shattuck, Roger. 1996. *Forbidden Knowledge: From Prometheus to Pornography.* New York: St. Martin's Press.

Sichère, Bernard. 1995. *Histoires du Mal.* Paris: Grasset.

Sollers, Philippe. 1967. "Sade dans le texte." *Tel Quel,* no. 28 (winter).

———. 1996. *Sade contre l'Être Suprême.* Paris: Gallimard.

Seifert, Hans-Ulrich. 1983. *Sade: Leser und Autor.* Frankfurt am Main: Peter Lang.

Spencer, Samia I., ed. 1984. *French Women and the Age of Enlightenment.* Bloomington: Indiana University Press.

Tel Quel, no. 28 (winter 1967). *La Pensée de Sade.*

Thomas, Chantal. 1978. *Sade, l'œil de la lettre.* Paris: Payot.

———. 1994. *Sade.* Paris: Éditions du Seuil.

Thomas, Donald. 1992. *The Marquis de Sade.* London: Allison and Busby.

Tort, Michel. 1967. "L'effet Sade." *Tel Quel,* no. 28 (winter).

Yale French Studies, no. 35 (December 1965). "Sade." Articles by G. May, M. J. Temmer, J. Gicharnaud, and R. Giraud; J. Mitchell; J. H. McMahon; M. Beaujour.

Index

Created by Eileen Quam and Theresa Wolner

Violence *(continued)*, and reason, 286; and state authority, 73; in writings, 2
Voltaire, 259
Voyeurism, 2, 109
Vulgarity, 7–8, 74

Wastes. *See* Discharges
Wealth: as libertine notion, 174

Wittgenstein, Ludwig: *Tractatus Logico-philosophicus*, 82
Women: classical novelists, 258–64; education of girls, 269–71, 311n21; libertines vs., 271–77; and male domination, 265–71; as natural, 277–79
Writing: crime of, 82–83; as recording, 93–94; women novelists, 258–64

Marcel Hénaff is a philosopher and anthropologist at the University of California, San Diego. He is the author of *Claude Lévi-Strauss and the Making of Structural Anthropology* (Minnesota, 1998).

Xavier Callahan has published French and Spanish translations of poetry, fiction, and scholarly works. She lives on Vashon Island in Puget Sound.